INVENTING THE NATION

General Editor: Keith Robbins

Russia

Vera Tolz
Reader in Russian History, University of Salford

A member of the Hodder Headline Group
LONDON
Co-published in the United States of America by
Oxford University Press Inc., New York

First published in Great Britain in 2001 by
Arnold, a member of the Hodder Headline Group,
338 Euston Road, London NW1 3BH

http://www.arnoldpublishers.com

Co-published in the United States of America by
Oxford University Press Inc.,
198 Madison Avenue, New York, NY 10016

British Library Cataloguing in Publication Data
A catalogue record for this book is available from the Library

Library of Congress Cataloging-in-Publication Data
A catalog record for this book is available from the Library of Congress

ISBN 0 340 67706 6 (hb)
ISBN 0 340 67705 8 (pb)

1 2 3 4 5 6 7 8 9 10

Production Editor: Rada Radojicic
Production Controller: Iain McWilliams
Cover Design: Terry Griffiths

Typeset in 10/12 pt Sabon by Phoenix Photosetting, Chatham, Kent
Printed and bound in Great Britain by MPG Books Ltd, Bodmin, Cornwall

What do you think about this book? Or any other Arnold title?
Please send your comments to feedback.arnold@hodder.co.uk

Contents

List of illustrations

General Editor's Preface

The contemporary world is both repelled and attracted by the existence of the nation. Talk of globalisation sometimes presumes that the nation will fade away as organisations and individuals build for themselves new networks which by-pass the commonalities and loyalties expressed in the idea of the nation. Nationalism, too, whenever it is that various writers have supposed it to have 'risen', has been held to have been an unmitigated disaster, at least when it has been accompanied, as it not infrequently has been, by virulent xenophobia and intolerance. In the twentieth century there were significant attempts to restrain or circumvent the influence of nationalism by creating international or supranational structures and agencies.

On the other hand, it is apparent that the nation has not in fact faded away and, despite the surge of new nations, or at least new states, in the second half of that century, there remain across the contemporary world communities which feel themselves to be nations, or are in the process of becoming nations, and who see in the attainment of statehood a legitimate, desirable and beneficial goal. In other contexts, too, old nations reaffirm themselves as necessary carriers of individuality and distinctiveness in a world threatened by homogeneity. It is asserted that the nation remains the essential building block in the structure of the contemporary world. Nationalism need not be vicious. Nations can and do speak peace unto nations.

It becomes clear, however, reading references of 'narrow nationalism' on the one hand or 'national liberation' on the other, that how particular nations come to exist or be defined remains obscure and contentious. This series revisits these issues in the light of extensive debates about national identity which have been conducted over recent decades by historians, anthropologists, political scientists and sociologists in particular. To speak of 'Inventing the Nation' picks up one of the interpretations which has gained favour, or at least excited interest. Influential writers have seen 'invention' taking place in Europe in the 'springtime of the nations' at the dawn of 'modern' history, though their explanations have varied. Others, however, have regarded 'invention' with some suspicion and identify a medieval if not primordial 'nation'. Problems of definition and location clearly abound.

A volume on Russia, with these issues in mind, is particularly pertinent at this juncture. The demise of the Union of Soviet Socialist Republics – so often and so misleadingly shortened to 'Russia' in common Western use – has brought to the fore in contemporary politics the issue of Russian identity and the geographical definition of the new Russia. In the wake of an imperial collapse, of course, it is frequently the previously dominant ethnic element, dispersed often in some numbers beyond its population 'heartland' by the very fact of empire, which feels most disorientated. In a circumstance in which successor states reassert or re-invent themselves, Russian people ask themselves whether 'Russia' can really be only the residue of what remains of the old order once fissiparousness has run its course? To think of Russia in such a negative way, however, has been wounding for those many Russians who have felt humiliated by what has happened to a state which was in some sense 'theirs'. The Russians, they continue to feel, are a great if tragic people whose achievements have been unjustly discredited.

The contemporary relevance of these matters needs little further emphasis. The great virtue of this book is that it sets these recent anxieties and issues in an appropriate historical context. There is a long pedigree of soul-searching and spiritual agony as Russian writers and intellectuals have sought to place Russia both on a geographical map (in Europe or looking at Europe?) and on a mental map. The Soviet Union, albeit ostensibly a federation, was in territorial terms almost a continuation of a Russian Empire that in 1914 was more than twice the size of the modern United States and more than two-thirds the size of Africa. Around that date, some 45 per cent of the population spoke Russian as their first language. Was there then a 'European Russia' at its core surrounded by a non-Russian periphery? Some thought so – but was not Siberia more 'Russian' than many of the 'European' parts of the Tsar's territories? Was Moscow more 'Russian' than St. Petersburg – two cities which were themselves not connected by rail until 1852? And, to take just one more example, where did Odessa fit as a Russian city? To draw attention to such questions is at once to realize that the 'invention' of modern Russia has always somewhat had the character of a contest: and its outcome remains unclear.

Keith Robbins
Vice-Chancellor
University of Wales, Lampeter

Acknowledgements

In writing this book, I have contracted many debts. First of all, I should like to thank Christopher Wheeler at Arnold Publishers for encouraging me to think about the topic and then offering constant assistance while the book was being written. I am very grateful to Peter Gatrell, Yoram Gorlizki, Julie Hessler, John LeDonne, Teresa Rakowska-Harmstone, Keith Robbins and Julia Wishnevsky for reading drafts of the manuscript and making immensely useful comments. Some of my last conversations with my late grandfather, D.S. Likhachev, were about this book. As ever, I benefited from his vast knowledge and originality of mind. A fellowship at the Institute for Advanced Study in Princeton, financed by a grant from Gerda Henkel Stiftung, allowed me to work on the completion of the book. I am particularly grateful to Professors Jack Matlock and Heinrich von Staden for making my stay at the Institute so productive and enjoyable. I would like to acknowledge generous financial support and sabbatical leave offered by Salford University. Thanks are also due to Katya Young for her help in collecting contemporary Russian press reports on Ukraine and to Francis King for editing the manuscript. Chapter 8 incorporates portions of my article 'Forging the Nation: National Identity and Nation Building in Post-Communist Russia,' published in *Europe-Asia Studies*, vol. 50, no. 6 (1998). I am grateful to the editor and anonymous reviewer for valuable suggestions on the article and to Taylor & Francis Publishers for permission to use parts of it in the book.

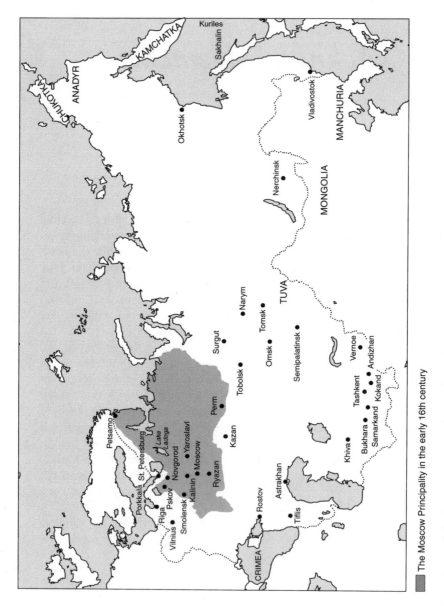

Map 1 The territory of the Moscow Principality in the early sixteenth century before the start of the imperial expansion

The Moscow Principality in the early 16th century

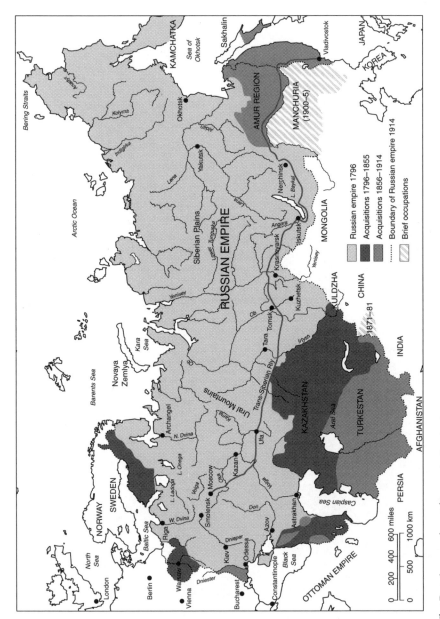

Map 2 The Russian empire at its greatest extent

KAMCHATKA

Sea of
Okhotsk

Sakhalin

Vladivostok

JAPAN

KOREA

Bering Straits

Aldan

Okhotsk

Kolyma

AMUR REGION

MANCHURIA
(1900–5)

Indigirka

Yakutsk

Lena

Aldan

Nerchinsk

L. Baykal

MONGOLIA

Arctic Ocean

Siberian Plains

RUSSIAN EMPIRE

Lower Tunguska

Angara

Irkutsk

Krasnoyarsk

Yenisey

Russian empire 1796

Acquisitions 1796–1855

Acquisitions 1856–1914

Boundary of Russian empire 1914

Brief occupations

Kara
Sea

Kuznetsk

KULDZHA

CHINA

1871–81

Novaya
Zemlya

Barents
Sea

Yenisey

Ob

Tara Tomsk

Irtysh

INDIA

Ural Mountains

Trans-Siberian Rly

KAZAKHSTAN

Archangel

N. Dvina

Kama

Ufa

Aral Sea

TURKESTAN

SWEDEN

L. Onega

L. Ladoga

Moscow

Volga

Smolensk

Kazan

Oka

AFGHANISTAN

NORWAY

W. Dvina

Riga

Don

Astrakhan

Caspian Sea

PERSIA

North
Sea

Baltic Sea

Dnieper

Kiev

Odessa

Azov

Black
Sea

London

Berlin

Warsaw

Vienna

Dniester

Bucharest

Constantinople

OTTOMAN EMPIRE

0   200   400   600 miles

0   500   1000 km

Introduction: Russian identity between empire and the West

This book studies the ways in which Russian national identity has been constructed through the efforts of intellectuals and politicians from the eighteenth century to the present day. This is done by focusing on the three main ways in which Russia and the Russians have been defined by Russian nation-builders in this period: Russia vis-à-vis the West; Russians as creators and preservers of a unique multi-ethnic community, which many intellectuals and politicians have viewed as profoundly different from European and Eastern empires; and Russians as members of a community of Eastern Slavs, the origins of which lay in Kiev Rus.

The concept of a nation as a sovereign people came to Russia from France in the late eighteenth century and it set the analytical framework for the thinking of a handful of educated Russians about their country. These Russians were a product of the policies of Peter the Great aimed at Europeanizing the country. The majority of books they read were by French, English and German authors. It is understandable that under such circumstances the imagined construction which these Russians called the West (*zapad*), became the main constituent other, against which they tried to construct a new Russian identity. The fact that Russia's political, economic and social conditions were different from Western models created an agonizing ambivalence in the intellectuals' attitude towards their chosen point of comparison. The book argues that these constant attempts to compare and contrast Russia and the West provided a powerful creative stimulus for Russian cultural figures, but proved dysfunctional as a tool of political analysis of Russia's development.

Russia differed from France, England and Germany in several ways. In addition to the persistence of autocracy, the lateness of industrialization and the delay with the emancipation of the serfs, which set Russia apart from its West European models, it was also a land-based empire, in which the political and geographical boundaries between the metropolis and the colonies were far from clear. Russia's territorial expansion into non-Russian areas began in the sixteenth century and in 1721 Peter the Great for the first time designated his state an empire. Yet it was a special kind of empire. Russia had some common characteristics with two quite different types of political unit – the West European maritime empires and large, multi-ethnic agrarian polities such as the Ottoman and the Ching empires.[1] Some members of the Westernized Russian political elite regarded the conquered peoples of the Caucasus and Central Asia in the same way as the British saw the native population of their overseas colonies. But at the same time, in the Russian land-based empire the native elites of the non-Russians, to a great extent, were integrated into the Russian ruling class. At the level of government bureaucracy, no clear distinction existed between colonial administration and internal Russian policy. On a number of occasions, institutions devised by the tsarist government to rule its newly acquired colonies were extended to the Russian core area. Under such circumstances, how could the boundaries of the Russian national homeland be defined? The Russians found it exceedingly difficult to answer this question.

Within the empire, some non-Russian areas became more closely embedded in Russian national mythology than the others. Parts of the state which geographically belonged to Asia have played an important role in helping Russians to conceptualize their position vis-à-vis Europe. The Russians' relationship with the other east Slavic peoples of the empire has also proved particularly important for Russian national consciousness. Since the mid-nineteenth century, the conflict between Russian and Ukrainian readings of east Slavic history has been a crucial element of Russian nation-building, and Russian–Ukrainian relations remain to date the most unresolved part of the Russian imperial legacy. To be sure, other ingredients have been used in the construction of Russianness, but it is these three interpretations of Russian national identity which have affected the Russian nation-building process most directly.[2]

This book seeks to account for the failure of the attempts of Russian intellectuals and politicians to construct a Russian nation, in opposition to the West, while preserving an imperial state and maintaining a particularly close union with other East Slavs. It also addresses the issue of how this historical heritage affects the current options facing Russians at a time when their imperial state is gone.

---

[1]   Dominic Lieven, 'Dilemmas of Empires 1850–1918. Power, Territory, Identity,' *Journal of Contemporary History*, vol. 34, no. 2 (1999), p. 163.
[2]   For a comprehensive account and a stimulating analysis of many of the formative elements of Russian national identity, see Elena Hellberg-Hirn, *Soil and Soul. The Symbolic World of Russianness* (Aldershot, Ashgate, 1998).

Theories of nationalism and their application to the Russian case

One can roughly distinguish three approaches to nationalism, a doctrine that holds that 'humanity is divided into nations, that loyalty to nations overrides all other loyalties, that the source of all political power lies within the collectivity of the nation, and that nations are fully realized only in sovereign states.'[3] The first is the primordial approach, which traces back the history of a nation over many centuries. The second is modernist, which dates the formation of nations to the late eighteenth century at the earliest and sees them as a product of the political, cultural and economic transformation of European societies following the French revolution. The third is post-modernist, which focuses on a deconstruction of nationalism as a particular form of narrative. Today, the perception of nationalism as a modern phenomenon prevails among academics. The primordial view is now largely the domain only of nationalist activists themselves. Yet, Anthony Smith has warned his colleagues about the danger of taking the modernist approach too far by thinking that all pre-nineteenth century phenomena, which earlier scholars often mistook for a manifestation of modern nationalism, are irrelevant for the study of the latter. He has argued that pre-modern ethnic identities were not the same, yet were often closely linked to modern national identities.[4] A number of medievalists have recently expressed a similar view.[5]

I would argue that the modernist and post-modernist approaches, as well as Smith's suggestion that pre-modern ethnic communities are relevant for the study of modern nationalism, have something to contribute to our understanding of the Russian case. At the same time, I think that none of these three approaches on its own is sufficient to provide a comprehensive analysis of Russian nation-building. The recent realization by a number of Russians that they probably still have not forged a modern nation, and that throughout most of their modern history they have lacked their own nation-state underscores the complexity of the Russian situation.

Smith's attempt to define a pre-modern ethnic community – *ethnie* – in relation to a modern nation is useful in the case of Russia. According to Smith, *ethnie* is a 'named human population with shared ancestry myths, histories and cultures, having an association with a specific territory and a sense of solidarity.'[6] In the course of the sixteenth and the seventeenth

---

3   Ronald Grigor Suny, *The Revenge of the Past. Nationalism, Revolution and the Collapse of the Soviet Union* (Stanford CA, Stanford University Press, 1993), p. 13.

4   Anthony D. Smith, *The Ethnic Origins of Nations* (Oxford, Basil Blackwell, 1986).

5   See, for instance, Adrian Hastings, *The Construction of Nationhood. Ethnicity, Religion and Nationalism* (Cambridge, Cambridge University Press, 1997).

6   Smith, *The Ethnic Origins of Nations*, p. 32.

centuries, a strong Russian *ethnie* was formed. Members of the Russian ethnic community were united by their adherence to Orthodox Christianity; their ethnic territory was limited to the areas of Moscow, Vladimir, Suzdal, Tver, Riazan, Novgorod and Pskov Principalities, which during the fifteenth and sixteenth centuries came under the rule of Moscow. Although they were racially very mixed (they included assimilated Tatars, Finns and other neighbouring peoples), the inhabitants of Muscovy spoke an east Slavic language, which was comprehensible to all. Differences between regional dialects were less pronounced than among the peoples who eventually constituted the French or German nations.

The solidarity of the Russian *ethnie* was tested in the early seventieth century, during the so-called Time of Troubles (1598–1613). In that period, Moscow fell into a state of anarchy and a series of pretenders lay claim to the Russian throne. At the same time, Poland-Lithuania and Sweden took advantage of the weakness of the Muscovite state, and sent their troops to Moscow in order to pursue their territorial and dynastic interests. In that period the concept of the Russian land (i.e. all the people of Muscovy) as a supreme force, which had the right to select a tsar, was articulated. That was a novel idea in the Russian context. In 1612, the Russians finally liberated Moscow and next year the Council of the Land (*Zemskii sobor*), which included representatives of all estates, proclaimed Mikhail Romanov as tsar. He was the first in the Romanov dynasty which was to rule Russia until 1917. A charter issued by the Council stated that Mikhail was enthroned by all the Orthodox Christians of the Moscow state. The Council did not impose any conditions to limit the powers of the tsar, and promised that the people would fully submit to the new ruler once he was elected. However, Geoffrey Hosking has remarked on this period of Russian history that 'the way in which the land recovered in the absence of a legitimate Tsar suggested that Muscovy had the potential to outgrow the dynastic patrimonial framework, that a potentially state-bearing people existed.'[7]

It is not surprising that some of the key historical myths of the Russians were forged precisely in that period. One such key myth was that of Holy Rus. This referred to the Orthodox Russian people, seen as not only separate from, but often in opposition to, a state which persecuted them. From the seventeenth century onwards, this image could often be found in popular songs. It was to become a commonplace in the classical Russian literature of the nineteenth century. Another was the image of Mother Russia represented as a peaceful and long-suffering peasant woman. First articulated in folklore, this image captured the minds of the newly emerging secular Russian poets as early as the 1720s. Finally, the myth of the historical origin of the Russians, which proclaimed Kiev Rus (the union of

[7] Geoffrey Hosking, *Russia: People and Empire, 1552-1917* (London, HarperCollins, 1997), p. 60.

east Slavic principalities in the ninth to twelfth centuries) to be the first Russian state, found resonance beyond Church circles in the seventeenth century. It was reflected in a highly popular history of the East Slavs, *Synopsis*, by the Ukrainian–German historian Innokentii Gizel. Some references to Kiev Rus were to be found in Moscow chronicles dating from before the seventeenth century. Yet on the whole, the inhabitants of Muscovy very clearly distinguished between themselves and other East Slavs. The feeling of a common past with the Ukrainians and their other Slavic neighbours was not shared by broad circles of educated Russians until the turn of the nineteenth century. Since then, however, the idea that Russian–Ukrainian unity can be traced back to Kiev Rus became a commonplace of Russian national and later Soviet historiography, with significant political implications.

The seventeenth century was also a crucial period in shaping the modern Russian terminology used to describe the process of state-building and the consolidation of the ethnic community. It is during the Time of Troubles that we find the first references to the notion of the 'betrayal of the fatherland (*otechestvo*).' In earlier periods, one can find only references to betrayal of the prince/tsar or the Orthodox faith. This notion of a separation between the state and the ruler, with its roots in the seventeenth century, began to be cultivated by Peter the Great in the next century, adding to the Russian vocabulary the word *patriot* as a person who loves his fatherland.[8] Meanwhile, during the seventeenth century the state itself acquired its modern name *Rossiia*, rather than the Moscow tsardom (*tsarstvo*) or the Moscow state (*gosudarstvo*).[9]

Scholars agree that in contrast to *ethnies*, nations are marked by economic unity and common legal rights. Membership of a community called a nation is formalized by citizenship, and most nations have or strive to have a common polity – a state. The legitimacy of the latter rests with the sovereign people, not with a royal dynasty. The subjective characteristics of a nation are particularly important – its members, without knowing each other personally, must believe that they belong to one and the same community. Benedict Anderson's definition of a nation as 'an imagined political community – and imagined as both inherently limited and sovereign'[10] captures it all. Most scholars agree that such an idea of a nation first emerged in the late eighteenth century and swept across Europe as a result of a triple revolution: socio-economic (the advent of capitalism),

---

8   The idea of the state as being separate from the ruler existed and exists even today only at the level of rhetoric, hardly reflecting Russia's reality.

9   See, *Mirovozrenie i samosoznanie russkogo obshchestva (XI–XX vv)* (Moscow, Institut Rossiiskoi Istorii, RAN, 1994), pp. 22–7.

10   Benedict Anderson, *Imagined Communities: Reflections on the Origin and Spread of Nationalism* (London, Verso, 1991), p. 6.

military-administrative (universal military conscription and bureaucracy) and cultural-educational (publishing in the vernacular and mass secular education).[11] In Western Europe fairly strong states already existed, and therefore all their inhabitants, regardless of ethnic origin, were proclaimed citizens, members of territorial or civic nations. In Eastern Europe, the different peoples were subjects of monarchs ruling land-based empires. Consequently, nation-building took a different route – a perception of a common ethnic origin became the key factor defining membership of communities newly imagined as nations. In this way, the so-called ethnic, more exclusive, nations came into existence. Many of them were granted their own states in the aftermath of World War I. Nonetheless, we should not forget Smith's point that in fact civic nations, such as France and Britain, also have a strong ethnic core. Smith does not assume a determinist link between an ethnie and a modern nation, yet he implies that the stronger an ethnic identity of a group, the more successful a nation-building process often is. This is not corroborated by the Russian case, however. There, despite the strength of the ethnic identity, nation-building has not yet been completed.

In order to explain the reasons for the peculiarity of the Russian case one needs to take on board the views of the modernists, such as Ernest Gellner, John Breuilly and others. They have stressed that nation-building can proceed only under certain political, social and economic conditions defined as modernization (the transformation of a traditional agrarian society with a dominant peasant population into an industrial, urbanized society).[12] The lateness and the peculiarity of Russia's modernization have prevented the strong Russian ethnie from becoming a fully-formed Russian nation in the course of the nineteenth and earlier part of the twentieth century. Yet the existence of a long-lasting strong Russian ethnie is not completely irrelevant. In their current attempts to finalize their process of nation-building, the Russians are still operating within the framework of ethnic myths and legends that go back to the seventeenth century. Even if the Russians succeed in forging a civic nation out of all citizens of the Russian Federation, of whom non-Russians constitute 18 per cent, such a nation would inevitably have a strong Russian ethnic core.

Up until the Soviet period, the pre-modern dynastic state, which maintained a huge divide between the imperial elite and the 'masses,' made little contribution to Russian nation-building. Although the tsars exploited Russian ethnic myths and legends, they were suspicious of any kind of nationalism within the borders of their empire. General works on nationalism tend to overestimate the significance of the tsars' Russification policy for

---

[11] Smith, *The Ethnic Origins of Nations*, p. 149.
[12] For excellent summaries of these authors' views, see their contributions to Gopal Balakrishnan, *Mapping the Nation* (London, Verso, 1996), pp. 98–174.

Russian nation-building.[13] In fact, the tsarist government sometimes enforced the Russification and conversion to Orthodoxy of its non-Russian subjects and, at other times, halted efforts in this area, depending on what seemed most likely to ensure the stability of the state. Moreover, from the time of Peter the Great the education of Russians by the state was pursued for the purely pragmatic reasons of improving the country's military, administrative and producing capacity. Educational programmes were implemented inconsistently, as the government always saw the spread of education among the population as a potential threat to autocracy. From the late eighteenth century until 1917, as the concept of a nation as a sovereign people – translated into Russian as *narod* – began to enter the lexicon of the educated Russians, it was Russian intellectuals, not politicians, who debated how to define Russia and the Russians. The post-modernist approach, aimed at deconstructing nationalist discourse, is helpful in reading the national narrative which Russian intellectuals have been producing in the past two centuries. However, to this day the Russians are still hotly debating who should be members of their national community and, more importantly, where the geographical borders of the Russian national homeland should be. Taken on its own, an attempt to deconstruct this discourse makes it no easier to pose, let alone answer, the question of why this is so. In this book, despite a strong focus on the discourse of Russian intellectuals, this question is regarded as of central importance. But before describing the ways in which the book addresses it, a few words should be said about the different perspectives on Russia which are discussed here.

Whose Russia?

Modernists and especially post-modernists emphasize that national identities (i.e. identities derived from membership of a community called a nation) are constructed by cultural and political elites, who either rely on pre-existing historical myths[14] and legends or, in the absence of suitable material, even invent national traditions. Myroslav Hroch has paid particular attention to the role of cultural elites in Eastern Europe in the production and dissemination of nationalist ideas.[15] Breuilly, however, argues that

---

13 See, for instance, Anderson, *Imagined Communities*, p. 15 describing the tsarist policies as an attempt to stretch 'the short, tight skin of the nation over the gigantic body of the empire.'

14 The word 'myth' is used here neutrally without implying that its substance is necessary false. Often contemporary scholarly assumptions constitute substantial parts of such myths.

15 Miroslav Hroch, *Social Preconditions of National Revival in Europe: A Comparative Analysis of the Social Composition of Patriotic Groups among the Smaller European Nations* (Cambridge, Cambridge University Press, 1985).

nationalism becomes a significant force only when it is used by politicians in the process of the transformation of political power.[16] In most cases it is only then that nationalist ideas can be effectively disseminated and shared by those whom nation-builders see as members of their nation. Who are the protagonists in the Russian case?

The peculiarity of the Russian case lies in the fact that politicians as conscious Russian nation-builders did not appear until relatively late. The members of the tsarist government, on the whole, were not such people. Russian nationalism had never been a state ideology of the pre-revolutionary Russian government. The fairly widely-held view that the tsars' Russification policy was applied consistently to the empire's non-Russian subjects is a myth with little substance. Yet, in the eighteenth century, Russian tsars, especially Peter and Catherine the Great, played a key role in forging the ideology of state patriotism. Some of the myths that were constructed in their propaganda campaigns were incorporated into Russian national consciousness in the nineteenth century through the efforts of intellectuals.

In its turn, the Soviet government made conscious efforts to construct a new common identity for its subjects. Therefore, if the relevant tsarist government policies are discussed fairly briefly in this book, the policies and theoretical positions of the Soviet government are allotted considerable attention. Although the proclaimed aim of the Soviet government was to create a new Soviet people out of the different subjects of the state, rather than to complete the formation of the Russian nation and to create a Russian nation-state, Russian nation-building was facilitated in the Soviet period. As most scholars now agree, the Soviet government, probably often unwittingly, created nations on the basis of culturally defined non-Russian ethnic communities. In turn, the emergence and strengthening of non-Russian nationalisms in the 1960s led in response to the construction of a new form of Russian nationalism, which was overtly anti-imperial.

Throughout the entire period considered in this book, which begins with an analysis of the eighteenth century, the main contribution to defining what Russia is and who the Russians are has been made by intellectuals – writers, poets, artists, journalists, musicians and historians. In the pre-revolutionary period, intellectuals were virtually the sole nation-builders. In the Soviet period, when the government took over the initiative in the process of identity formation, ideas that had been put forward by pre-revolutionary intellectuals continued to play a very significant role. The classical Russian literature of the nineteenth century to a very large extent shaped the views of the old Bolsheviks about their country. Throughout the Soviet period it constituted a key part of the school curriculum in the

---

[16] John Breuilly, *Nationalism and the State* (Manchester, Manchester University Press, 1985).

humanities. From the 1930s, the main concepts of nineteenth century Russian historiography were incorporated into the official interpretation of Russian history promoted by the majority of Soviet historians. It is true that some works by important thinkers, whose careers had started before the revolution and who turned against the Bolsheviks in 1917 or soon after, were banned. However, they began to be published again in the late 1980s, and today they exercise a significant influence on the way not only intellectuals but also many politicians view Russia. For this reason, the deconstruction of this extremely rich intellectual and cultural tradition is the prime focus of this book.

The perspective of the intelligentsia was not the only possible view of what Russia was or should be. In addition to the Russia imagined by the Europeanized educated elite, from the eighteenth century there was the Russia of the Old Believers (people who opposed the liturgical reform of the Church in the late seventeenth century and were therefore severely persecuted by the state) and of the Russian peasantry, some of whom adopted the Old Belief.[17] These people rejected state policies aimed at Europeanizing Russia; they proclaimed Peter the Great to be the Anti-Christ and continued to promote a view of Russia as a community of Orthodox people, in opposition to the Catholic and Protestant West.

The fact that the Russia of Old Believers is only briefly discussed in this book should not be taken as an indication that it was unimportant. Significantly, in the 1860s, one of the key periods in the intellectual debate about Russianness, one of the intellectuals came across writings by Old Believers. He was astonished to discover in these writings that their authors 'have been thinking about ... those questions of world-wide importance, which have pre-occupied the best minds of mankind.'[18] Yet, on the whole, the Old Believers' world view was purely religious and therefore premodern. It could not have served as a basis for constructing a modern national identity. Those late eighteenth century Russian intellectuals, such as Nikolai Novikov and Aleksandr Radishchev, who first tried to apply the French concept of a nation to a seemingly unsuitable Russian reality, adopted a secular world view and downplayed the significance of the religious component in Russian identity. The Westernizers of the nineteenth century did the same. It is indicative that such leading historians as Sergei Solovev and Vasilii Kliuchevskii paid little attention to Church and religion

---

[17] The existence of the two distinct discourses on Russian identity back in the eighteenth century was noted by Michael Cherniavsky, 'Russia,' in Orest Ranum, ed., *National Consciousness, History, and Political Culture in Early-Modern Europe* (Baltimore MA, Johns Hopkins University Press, 1975), pp. 118–43.

[18] 'Ispoved Kilsieva,' *Arkhiv russkoi revoliutsii*, vol. XI (Moscow, Sovremennik, 1991), p. 177 quoted in K. Kasianova, *O russkom natsionalnom kharaktere* (Moscow, Institut natsionalnoi modeli ekonomiki, 1994), p. 56.

in their analysis of Russian history.[19] Moreover, it should be remembered that these two Russias were not entirely separate, as is often assumed. Iurii Lotman has argued persuasively that the gap between the Europeanized Russian educated classes and the lower classes of society, which preserved some pre-Petrine traditions, is often exaggerated. This particularly applies to the landed gentry. Lotman reminds us that 'a noble landlord, who was born in a provincial estate and spent his childhood playing with peasant children, was in constant contact with the peasant way of life' and therefore picked up many habits of the peasantry.[20] In many ways, this image of Russia with a division between the upper and lower classes far greater than elsewhere in Europe, was at times disputed by its own constructors. Lev Tolstoi was one of the key propagandists of such an image of Russia. Yet, in *War and Peace*, when Natasha Rostova, a young woman from a wealthy aristocratic family, puts on a Russian folk-dress and starts dancing a folk-dance, her nanny, a former peasant serf, unmistakably sees in Natasha her own kith and kin.

Moreover, as is the case elsewhere, some powerful symbols originating in Russian folk culture easily migrated into the nationalist discourse of the Russian elites. The images of Holy Rus and Mother Russia have already been mentioned. In addition to these, a vision of Russia as a land without end, which first originated in folk songs, became a commonplace in intellectual discourse. The book argues that this last vision had a negative impact on nation-building, as it diminished the need to draw precise geographical boundaries for the national homeland.

Wherever possible, this book tries to assess the views of ordinary people on what it meant to be a Russian. As far as the pre-revolutionary period is concerned, it discusses how Russia and Russians are represented in folk and prison songs, short satirical poems (*chastushki*) and other genres of popular culture. With the spread of mass education in the Soviet period, the dissemination of intellectuals' and politicians' ideas concerning Russian national identity began to provoke an active response on the part of the general public. This response became a subject of Soviet scholarship in the 1960s and was to acquire particular significance in the period of Gorbachev's *perestroika*.[21] Since 1990, the popularity of the constructs of intellectuals

---

[19] Marc Raeff, 'Toward a New Paradigm?' in Thomas Sanders, ed., *Historiography of Imperial Russia. Profession and Writing of History in a Multinational State* (Armonk N.Y., M.E. Sharpe, 1999), p. 483, finds the treatment of the religious aspect of Russian history in the works of the leading liberal Russian pre-revolutionary historians 'inadequate.'

[20] Iu. M. Lotman, *Besedy o russkoi kulture: byt i traditsii russkogo dvorianstva, XVIII–nachalo XIX vv.* (St. Petersburg, Iskusstvo, 1994), pp. 110–11.

[21] See, for instance, L.M. Drobizheva, ed., *Sotsialnaia i kulturnaia distantsiia: opyt mnogonatsionalnoi Rossii* (Moscow, Izdatelstvo Instituta Sotsiologii RAN, 1998); L.M. Drobizheva and M.S. Kashuba, eds, *Traditsii v sovremennom obshchestve: issledovaniia etnokulturnykh protsessov* (Moscow, Nauka, 1990).

and politicians could be tested in elections, as politicians incorporated them in their electoral platforms. Numerous opinion polls conducted in the 1990s specifically on questions related to Russian national identity are analysed in this book, thus making ordinary Russians today another protagonist in the story.

It should be noted that the discourse on Russian identity, a key subject of this book, is largely male. As elsewhere, most intellectuals who saw them-selves as nation-builders were and still are men. This is not to say that Russian women have not contributed their own perspective on Russia. It would be an interesting task to try to identify the key texts which offer such a perspective. But the best known women intellectuals largely participated in the debate on terms laid down by men. The tone was set by Ekaterina Istomina (1747–1816), who although hailing Russia for starting to produce female poets (Russian Sapphos), nevertheless constructed the same image of Russia as her male colleagues had done before. Through Peter's reforms her Russia, which had been buried in darkness, was suddenly exposed to light (*mrachna Rossiia ozarilas*).[22]

From the 1860s, Russian women became active members in the revolu-tionary movement. This was based on a certain vision of Russia on the part of its participants and therefore was directly relevant to the question of Russian nation-building. According to Richard Stites, '[n]o other radical movement in the West showed anything remotely close to the level of women's participation as the Russian revolutionary movement.'[23] Yet, he notes that the ideas about the role women should play in this movement and in society in general were again articulated by men. Thus, in the story told in this book, the role of Russian women is the one assigned to them by men. This role is a typical one for women in other nation-building projects: they are regarded as 'the breeders' of the nation, as they socialize children into national culture. They are also perceived as the passive symbols of the nation.[24] In the Russian case, female images of Russia have been very powerful. Russian intellectuals themselves, especially Nikolai Berdiaev, argued that such images had a particularly strong impact on their percep-tion of Russia. I think they were right. It is not so much that in Russian literature we find many instances where the expression 'Mother Russia' is used or that a peasant woman is evoked as a symbol of Russianness. A more original feature of Russian discourse are instances when in a particular text Russia as a woman is addressed directly and the addresser is clearly antici-pating an answer. Among many, a famous passage from Gogol's *Dead*

---

[22] Catriona Kelly, ed., *An Anthology of Russian Women's Writers (1777-1992)* (Oxford, Oxford University Press, 1994), p. 2.

[23] Richard Stites, 'Women and the Russian Intelligentsia. Three Perspectives,' in Dorothy Atkinson, Alexander Dallin, and Gail Warshofsky Lapidus, eds., *Women in Russia* (Stanford CA, Stanford University Press, 1977), p. 50.

[24] See Sylvia Walby, 'Woman and Nation,' in Balakrishnan, *Mapping the Nation*, p. 244.

Souls can serve as a good example: 'Russia! What do you want of me? What unthinkable bond hides between us? Why do you look at me so?' This particular way of constructing a discourse on Russia probably stems from the fact that, in trying to define Russia in the absence of the objective conditions for nation-building, intellectuals were primarily concerned with the question of their own, personal, rather than national identities.[25] From such a perspective, the Russia of their imagination is easily transformed into a woman, who is seen by a male intellectual as irresistibly attractive, but at the same time unknown and therefore frightening, thus provoking a simultaneous feeling of love and hatred.

Another possible perspective on Russia stemmed from the multi-ethnic character of the Russian state. From the 1840s onwards non-Russians, who valued the distinctiveness of their own cultural and religious traditions, began to challenge the view of Russia advanced by intellectuals whose perspective was exclusively Russian. These non-Russian views of Russia deserve a separate serious study. Given the nature of this book, the views of non-Russian intellectuals are acknowledged only where they were noticed by Russian intellectuals, which happened, it seems, all too rarely.

The outline of the argument

Scholars see the 'making of nations' as a process determined by certain social, economic and political conditions, which is also 'conceived and articulated in an emerging national discourse.'[26] This process is never complete, as the national identities of members of a nation have to be constantly reaffirmed. The membership of a nation can also be redefined and the borders of a national homeland redrawn. When this happens, it is always a major dramatic political event. In twentieth century Russian history this has happened twice – in 1917 in the course of the Russian revolution and in 1991 when the USSR disintegrated. Following the revolution, the Bolshevik government was able to recreate the state almost within the same borders as those of the Russian empire. It thereby postponed any solution of the question about the actual boundaries of the Russian national homeland. In 1991, Russia's borders shrank almost to those of Muscovy at the end of the sixteenth century. As a result, over 25 million Russians found themselves living outside the borders of the new Russian state. The question of who belongs to the Russian nation and where 'the just' borders of the Russian nation-state should be is much less clear today in the case of Russia than in other European nations. Analyzing

---

[25] This idea is developed in Hans Rogger, 'Nationalism and the State: A Russian Dilemma,' *Comparative Studies in Society and History*, vol. 14 (1961–62), p. 264.

[26] Suny, *Revenge of the Past*, p. 6.

the current state of Russian nation-building, one Russian scholar has argued that the Russians 'stopped at the threshold separating ethnie from nation.'[27] A very similar feeling was also prevalent in the wake of the revolution when the tsarist empire collapsed and the non-Russian border-lands became temporarily independent from the Russian core area – that the Russians as a community which the intellectuals had imagined, had existed in their minds alone. In the writings of Russian intellectuals in 1917–1918 we find a description of Russia as a phantom, of a Russia which unexpectedly disintegrated like a house of cards. How is this incomplete-ness of the Russian nation-building project to be explained?

A number of students of Russia see the key explanation in a peculiarity of Russian state-building – the absence of the political, social and economic conditions necessary for nation-building. Back in 1962 Hans Rogger argued that whereas elsewhere in Europe, in the course of the nineteenth century, 'nationalist sentiments, ideologies and movements had helped to throw bridges across conflicts of class and religion, had created common bonds between individuals and groups and had reconciled society and its members to the state to a surprising degree,' this did not happen in Russia.[28] According to Rogger, the reason for this peculiarity was that the territorial consolidation of the Russian land-based empire 'was completed before nationalism became a major factor of Russian life, and that this consolida-tion brought with it no extension of political rights, no interpenetration of state and society, no lasting accommodation between them.' Thus, 'too often the state did not reflect in its actions the aspirations of society, and ... even when it did so it was fearful of enlisting society in a common effort born of common needs.'[29] Indeed, up until 1917 the government did not see it as its task to forge a common national identity for all its subjects. Not only it did not apply the policy of Russification of non-Russians consis-tently, it even did not launch a comprehensive programme of turning Russian peasants into citizens. The tsarist government could not organize compulsory mass education for peasants following the 1861 emancipation of serfs quickly enough to have ensured that they were better integrated into society by the start of World War I.

Other scholars, most notably Roman Szporluk and Hosking, further developed Rogger's argument. Szporluk thought that the ethnic identity of the Russians had been blurred by the fact that their empire had been created at an early period, and that the colonies were separated neither geographi-cally nor politically from the metropolis. This made it unclear where the borders of the Russian national homeland should be. Furthermore, the

[27] Georgiy I. Mirsky, *On Ruins of Empire. Ethnicity and Nationalism in the Former Soviet Union* (Westport, Greenwood Press, 1997), p. 26.

[28] Rogger, 'Nationalism and the State: A Russian Dilemma,' p. 253.

[29] Ibid, pp. 254–5.

tsarist state did not recognize the separate existence of civil society. Until the early twentieth century, its members were not admitted into governing the country. At that time, the tsarist government launched a programme of industrialization, but it was still hesitant in introducing the political liberties which elsewhere in Europe accompanied the advent of capitalism. Moreover, by the time the tsarist government embarked on economic reforms at the end of the nineteenth century, most Russian intellectuals had embraced the ideas of socialism, rather than of liberal nationalism, Szporluk argued. The socialist approach meant that the upper classes of society were excluded from membership of the Russian nation. In 1917, the victory of the Bolshevik Party led to attempts to put this concept of a national community into practice. The internationalist rather than nationalist world view of socialists helped the Bolsheviks justify the recreation of the Russian empire in the form of the USSR. Within the framework of this new state, the government's nationalities policies did not greatly assist the Russians in defining the borders of their ethnic homeland clearly. Hosking also agreed that Russian state-building had a negative effect on the Russian nation-building project. Analysing the pre-revolutionary period, he argued that the early creation of a huge land-based empire, the maintenance of which required too many economic sacrifices on the part of the Russians, resulted in the perpetuation of centralized autocratic government. Fearful of losing control over the country, the government hesitated to modernize it through political and economic reforms which would have facilitated the Russian nation-building process.[30]

However, the lack of social, political and economic conditions for nation-building did not prevent Russian intellectuals from debating what kind of a nation the Russians should constitute and where the borders of the Russian homeland should be. From the early twentieth century, some Russian intellectuals began to blame themselves rather than the government for the fact that their ideas were so clearly failing to become a unifying force in society and to bring about the reconciliation between society and the state. Not surprisingly, this criticism began after the tsarist government had allowed the election of the first Russian parliament and introduced some other liberalizing reforms. In the 1909 collection of essays *Signposts* (*Vekhi*), former socialists who had embraced the ideas of liberal nationalism attacked their fellow intellectuals for cosmopolitanism, infatuation with the West, disregard of indigenous Russian traditions and indifference or even outright hostility to the state and its policies, even when those were beneficial for the country. In the aftermath of the October Revolution, some of the contributors to the 1909 collection published a follow-up volume, *De Profundis* (*Iz glubiny*). This blamed the Bolshevik takeover partly on the ideas of the pre-revolutionary socialist, anti-national, intelligentsia and its

---

[30] Hosking, *Russia: People and Empire*.

rejection of the path of cooperation with the government. This line of argument has been supported by some Western scholars, most notably Richard Pipes.[31]

This book shares the view that Russian state-building has stood in the way of Russian nation-building. Prior to 1917 the government perpetuated a pre-modern dynastic empire, and subsequently the Bolsheviks created the USSR, which claimed to be supra-national. At the same time, I argue that the intelligentsia has to share with the government some responsibility for the Russians' failure to form a fully-fledged nation. However, the intelligentsia's failure lies not where its early twentieth century critics found it, but elsewhere. The continued criticism of government policies by intellectuals following the 1905 October manifesto was hardly a decisive reason for the Russian revolution and the subsequent failure to create a civic nation out of the empire's subjects.

This book argues that the very way in which Russian nationalist discourse was constructed by Russian intellectuals from the late eighteenth century on had a negative effect on the Russian nation-building process. The way Russia was imagined by Russian intellectuals in the pre-revolutionary period had a very profound impact on educated Russians in the nineteenth century, on the broader Russian public in the twentieth century and on the Soviet government. The Soviet government position on the nature of the Russian state from the mid-1930s onwards owed a lot to the pre-revolutionary tradition. But the Russia of the pre-revolutionary intellectual tradition proved to be an imaginary rather than an imagined community.

Two particularly important views concerning the Russian national identity, formulated by pre-revolutionary Russian intellectuals, turned out to be dysfunctional. The first was the idea that only the toiling Russian people could belong to the nation, whereas the upper classes should be excluded. Szporluk has attributed this view to Russian socialists. However, it was first formulated not by them, but by the Slavophiles of the 1840s. It then started to be shared by intellectuals and cultural figures of different political orientations. For the Slavophiles, it was only the peasantry, as the bearer of an indigenous Russian tradition, which could rightfully constitute the Russian nation. In contrast, the elites had to be excluded, because they were corrupted by Western influences. In turn, Russian socialists included either only the peasantry or the peasantry and the workers in the Russian nation. They excluded the upper classes from membership of the nation because they exploited the labour of and otherwise mistreated the lower classes. This position not only reflected the existing divide between the upper and lower classes in Russian society, but also constantly reinforced it and, in effect, stultified the process of building a modern nation in Russia.

---

[31] See, for instance, Richard Pipes, *The Russian Revolution* (New York N.Y., Knopf, 1990), the chapter 'The Intelligentsia,' pp. 121–52.

The Slavophile and Russian socialist discourse about the nation inverted the arguments of nation-builders elsewhere in Europe. German Romantics, whose ideas about the true *Volk* as a bearer of 'national spirit' inspired the Slavophiles, did not go as far as to exclude educated Germans from membership of the German nation. Moreover, in the French tradition of the second half of the nineteenth century, which had an impact on Russian Westernizers, the discourse about the nation classified the peasantry as not fully French. A comprehensive programme was launched to turn them into Frenchmen, particularly by making them learn the language and culture of Paris.[32]

Both the Slavophiles and socialists combined an idealization of the lower classes of Russian society with a highly elitist attitude towards these social groups. As the Slavophile historian Mikhail Pogodin put it, the Russian people are 'marvellous, but marvellous so far only in potential.'[33] Some Slavophiles and the majority of socialists thought that a small elite group could help the toiling people to realize their potential and act in their own best interests, of which they themselves were not yet consciously aware. This elitist view of the people, which freely co-existed in Russian intellectual thought with the egalitarian one, became a justification for dictatorship in the twentieth century.

The second idea was that the entire multi-ethnic tsarist empire was the Russian nation-state. This idea was articulated by Russian intellectuals in an attempt to apply the West European concept of a nation to Russian reality. This view of Russia reflected the personal experience of those who articulated it. Those intellectuals who first formulated it in the late eighteenth century and then developed it more fully in the nineteenth, were members of the intellectual elite residing in the two capitals, St. Petersburg and Moscow. This elite was multi-ethnic, with Ukrainians and Russified Germans playing a particularly important role. This vision of Russia was confirmed by its members' own success in integration where they were not ethnic Russians. However, it did not necessarily correspond to the experience of Russian and non-Russian peasants, who continued to identify with the places where they were born and lived. It also did not correspond to the vision of Russia of those educated non-Russians, whose loyalty to their ethnic groups was stronger than the identification with the entire state.

Indeed, in the course of the nineteenth century, this vision of the entire empire as a Russian nation-state proved to be blatantly at odds with reality. In fact, the Russians did not have their own nation-state. They probably did

---

[32] James R. Lehning, *Peasant and French. Cultural Contact in Rural France During the Nineteenth Century* (Cambridge, Cambridge University Press, 1995) and Eugen Weber, *Peasants into Frenchmen: The Modernization of Rural France, 1870-1914* (Stanford CA, Stanford University Press, 1976).

[33] Quoted in Nicholas V. Riasanovsky, *Nicholas I and Official Nationality in Russia, 1825–1855* (Berkeley CA, University of California Press, 1959), p. 99.

not have a state that they could have turned into a nation state, even if the tsarist government were to pursue consistent Russification policies. By the late nineteenth century, Great Russians constituted 44 per cent of the country's population.[34] The tsarist government had a strong fear of violent anti-imperial resistance, and this fear grew in the second half of the nineteenth century. It was manifested in the fact that the per capita expenditure on police was far higher in the non-Russian provinces than in Russian areas, and that the military assumed a large part of the responsibility for ruling Russia's borderlands.[35] The task of converting all subjects of the empire into Russian citizens, sharing Russian culture, would have been not only quantitatively but also qualitatively different from the experience of Western Europe. The ethnic diversity of the peoples that the West European nation-builders had to fuse into one nation was much lower. But most Russian intellectuals, conservatives and liberals alike, did not grasp this problem. Even when the challenge of non-Russian nationalisms from the mid-nineteenth century onwards began to show that their concept of the Russian nation-state was not viable, they stuck to it. This is because their main point of comparison remained the West, and this perspective allowed the Russians simply to ignore the arguments of non-Russian nationalists. When in 1917 it turned out that the Russian nation with a strong state did not exist, many were devastated. The behaviour of the non-Russians, especially the Ukrainians, was incomprehensible to them. Bolshevik policies served to restore that state, and this made many of their initial opponents among Russian nationalists come to terms with the new regime. Similarly, as the disintegration of the USSR loomed in 1990, many anti-Soviet Russian nationalists again struck an alliance with the Communists.

Since most Russian intellectuals and politicians up to 1990 thought the Russian empire was the only state in which Russians could exist productively as a distinct community, some scholars think that the expression 'Russian nationalism' is a misnomer.[36] The argument is that in most cases we are actually dealing with Russian imperialist rather than nationalist

---

[34] The 1897 census classified Great Russians, Ukrainians and Belorussians as Russians; in total these three peoples constituted 72.5 per cent of the country's population.

[35] S. Frederick Starr, 'Tsarist Government: The Imperial Dimension.' In Jeremy R. Azrael, *Soviet Nationality Policies and Practices* (New York N.Y., Praeger, 1978) p. 13 notes that 'while all of Siberia could, by 1869, be secured with only 18,000 troops, the Ukrainian districts of Kharkov, Odessa, and Kiev had 72,000, 61,000, and 60,000 respectively; the volatile Caucasus demanded 128,000 men; and Warsaw 126,000. St. Petersburg, seat of the tsar's own garrison, had 84,000 troops. It might be noted that in all of India the British had but 60,000 troops and 1,000 policemen.' (Of course, the troops were not deployed solely for reasons of internal security, but also against perceived threats from Germany, Austria and Turkey.)

[36] Geoffrey Hosking, 'Can Russia Become a Nation-State? *Nations and Nationalism*, vol. 4, no. 4 (1998), pp. 449–62.

ideology. In addition, at times the Russians' inability to distinguish their national homeland from the empire is branded 'archaic,' a manifestation of a pre-modern world-view.[37]

This book does not agree with that argument. It is true that many Russians themselves since the nineteenth century have attributed negative connotations to the word nationalism. They have viewed it as a purely ethnic phenomenon, which affected some non-Russian intellectuals and was threatening the unity of their state. From the late nineteenth century, such famous Russians as Lev Tolstoi and Vladimir Solovev condemned national-ism, which they thought necessarily entailed hatred of other nations. Yet they regularly used the word national (*natsionalnyi*) in a positive sense when describing their debate over the membership in the Russian nation and over the borders of their homeland. That was fully justifiable, because when they talked about the Russian empire they thought they were talking about the Russian nation-state. Therefore, the word nationalism in a neutral sense, as it is used in Western scholarly literature, is applicable to the Russian case.

The structure of the book

Since I subscribe to the view of other scholars that Russian state-building has had a profound stultifying impact on Russian nation-building, the first part of the book begins with a chapter on the policies of Peter the Great, who is justifiably regarded by most Russian and Western scholars as the founder of modern Russia. Many of his policies and the ways in which he tried to Europeanize Russia had a lasting effect on the development of the country and on the Russian nation-building project. The second chapter deals with the emergence of Europeanized Russian intellectuals in the course of the eighteenth century and their first attempts to define Russia and the Russians in modern terms. As mentioned above, they were cosmopoli-tans of the Enlightenment rather than nationalists. Nonetheless, it was they who chose the imagined West as Russia's constituent other and tried to make sense of the rapid expansion of the Russian state into non-Russian areas which was going on during their lifetime. By the end of the century, some began to speak of the peasantry as the rightful members of the Russian national community. In other words, they laid the foundation for the subsequent debate, which was truly national in a modern sense.

The Russians' view of the nature of their state has been constructed through comparisons with the West. This view has had a great impact on their ability to understand the aspirations of non-Russians. I argue that this

[37] Paul Bushkowitch, 'The Ukraine in Russian Culture 1790-1860: The Evidence of the Journals,' *Jahrbücher für Geschichte Osteuropas*, vol. 39, no. 3 (1991), p. 340.

is of central importance for Russian nation-building, and this is reflected in
the subsequent two parts of the book. Part two deals with the construction
of a Russian identity in contrast to the 'others' – the West (Europe) and the
East (Asia). The chapter on Russia and the West shows how from the
eighteenth century onwards, attempts to identify both the similarities and
the differences between Russia and different countries of Europe and the
United States of America, became the main, if not the only, perspective from
which Russian nation-builders could analyse the realities of their own
country. It discusses the problems which this perspective has presented for
Russian nation-building. The fact that, geographically, part of Russia was
in Asia has complicated Russia's relations with Europe. The chapter on
Russia and the East argues that the question of Russia's ties with Asia was
rarely of interest to Russian nation-builders *per se*, but tended to acquire
immense importance when Russia's European identity was particularly
strongly doubted by West Europeans. It shows that the situation began to
change somewhat in the 1960s and the 1970s, when an anti-imperial
Russian nationalism for the first time made some Russians perceive
Muslims from Central Asia and the Caucasus as antagonistic 'others' in
their own right.

Part three of the book discusses who the Russians think they are rather
than who they are not. Chapter five analyses the origins, and the implications for Russia's political development, of a key element of Russian
national mythology – the notion that the Russian empire was a Russian
national state, created through the peaceful and voluntary incorporation of
territories of non-Russian people. Chapters six and seven look at the
implications of this construction for Russian nation-building. Chapter six
discusses various positions taken by Russian nation-builders on the precise
membership of the Russian nation and on how to draw a line between the
Russians and non-Russian subjects of the empire/USSR. In this respect the
most difficult task from the Russian point of view was to sort out the
relationship with the Ukrainians. This issue is addressed in chapter seven,
which analyses why Russian nation-builders consistently underestimated
the strength of a separate Ukrainian identity. Parts two and three discuss
Russian nation-building in the period from the eighteenth century to the
demise of the USSR in 1991.

The last part of the book is devoted to Russia today. The final chapter
shows the relevance of ideas and concepts on what Russia is and who the
Russians are, developed during the pre-revolutionary and Soviet periods,
not only for making sense of the arguments of today's intellectuals but also
for understanding post-communist government policies. I do not want to
sound like a historical determinist. Russia's economic and political developments, and even the personalities of its future top leaders, will have a
more profound impact on the progress of Russian nation-building than the
adherence of some nation-builders to the ideas of their pre-revolutionary,

émigré and Soviet predecessors. Yet, the choice of concepts and the framework of the debate are still very much determined by the past. So far, the Russians have proved unable to escape this past. The optimistic hopes for renewal expressed in the early 1990s by the first post-communist Russian government, under Acting Prime Minister Egor Gaidar, were not borne out. In conclusion, the book surveys the problems which the Russians still face on the path of 'inventing the nation' and building a stable state.

P A R T

1

LAYING THE FOUNDATION

1

The reign of Peter the Great: the beginning of modern Russia

> The entirety of Russia is your statue, transformed by you
> through skilful craftsmanship
> > Feofan Prokopovich (*The Word ... in Memory of Peter the
> > Great*, 1726)

> [Peter the Great] tried to turn them [Russians] into Germans
> and Englishmen instead of making them Russians. He urged his
> subjects to be what they were not and so prevented them from
> becoming what they might have been
> > Jean-Jacques Rousseau (*Social Contract*, 1762)

'This monarch made our fatherland comparable with others; taught us to recognise that we too are people. In other words, whatever one looks at in Russia, everything has him as its beginning and whatever will be undertaken in future will originate in him.' So wrote Ivan Nepliuev, the Russian ambassador to Constantinople, upon receiving the news about the death of Peter the Great in 1725. Up until the 1770s, the majority of those Russians who expressed new ideas about what Russia was, concurred in Nepliuev's view of the tsar. But even afterwards, however much historians, writers and thinkers tried to challenge this view, there remained a widespread perception of Peter as the sole creator of the modern Russian state. Even if we recognize that in many ways Peter continued reforms initiated by his father Tsar Aleksei Mikhailovich and his sister Princess Sofia in the second half of the seventeenth century, it makes sense to begin the history of the formation of modern Russian national identity from the period of Peter's reign. Peter's controversial reforms laid the foundation for, and at the same time put constraints on, Russia's subsequent nation-building.

It should be said from the very outset that in the eighteenth century,

Russia was not a nation. Nevertheless, concepts about what Russia was, and especially how it compared with the 'West', first began to be elaborated in the eighteenth century. They were developed more fully in the nineteenth century, when the idea, born of the French revolution, of a nation as a sovereign people was applied by Russian intellectuals to their own country. Some of them hoped to transform Russian reality in line with their ideals. In two major ways Peter laid the basis for the subsequent emergence in Russia of people receptive to the ideas of modern nationalism. Firstly, it was under him that the consistent moves towards the secularization of the Russian state began to be made. Among other things he introduced state-sponsored secular education, the publication of secular literature and a civil Slavic script. Secondly, Peter attempted to forge a secular compound identity for his subjects, based on loyalty to, and pride in serving, the mighty state. Such state patriotism elsewhere in Europe had preceded the advent of the era of nationalism. Yet the legacy of Peter's reforms was very contradictory. His reign saw the complete consolidation of autocratic rule, firmly preventing any alternative sources of power from emerging. He further hardened and extended serfdom and accelerated the expansion of the empire. All this arguably prevented Russians from making the crucial step from loyalty to the state, embodied in the monarch, to loyalty to the nation.

The question of new legitimacy

When Peter the Great became the unchallenged ruler of Russia, the traditional Russian identity, based on the adherence to Orthodox Christianity, was crumbling. Orthodoxy had been an important force which had helped Russians to survive the Time of Troubles in the early seventeenth century. At that time, the Polish-Lithuanian Commonwealth and Sweden had tried to take advantage of Muscovy's internal weakness and impose their territorial, religious and dynastic interests by military force. Orthodoxy had been the main thing that the leaders of the Russian resistance had urged the people to defend, against the Catholicism and Protestantism of the invaders. Those Russian nation-builders from the nineteenth century onwards who wanted to emphasise the importance of Orthodoxy for Russian national identity often referred to this period to prove their point. Thus, in 1818, at the time of the first upsurge of nationalist feelings in the wake of the victory over Napoleon, the monument to 'Citizen Minin and Prince Pozharskii' (the leaders of the resistance to the Poles during the Time of Troubles) from 'grateful Russia' was erected on Red Square in front of the main Russian religious symbol, St. Basil's Cathedral.

However, the expansion of the state in the seventeenth century, especially the takeover of Ukraine in 1654, had considerably undermined the traditional Russian Orthodox identity. Although the majority of Ukrainians were also Orthodox, they were far more theologically sophisticated than their Russian counterparts, as they had to struggle against the influence of the Catholic Uniates. It was the Ukrainian clergy who confronted Muscovites with 'the Western alternative.' Starting in the 1640s, pupils of the founder of the Kiev Theological Academy, Peter Mogila, would come to Moscow to instruct Russian clergy in theological matters. It was under their influence that in the 1650s the Russian Patriarch Nikon initiated reforms aimed at bringing order and uniformity to Russian worship and revising service books according to the Greek originals, as had already been done in Ukraine. Although none of the changes actually affected the substance of theological doctrines, they provoked fierce resistance from the middle and lower level Russian clergy and laymen. In 1667, the Church Council formally approved these modifications to church worship and excommunicated all who remained faithful to the old practices (the 'Old Believers') *en bloc*. Old Belief attracted numerous followers, and its view of Russia seriously challenged the modernising state until at least the mid-nineteenth century, by attracting oppositionists of all kinds under its banners. Some historians have argued that the schism within the church divided Russia to a greater extent than Peter's policy of Westernization.[1] The Russian North, the Urals and Siberia quickly became the bastions of Old Belief. Protesting against the policies of the official Church, Old Believers began to commit acts of self-immolation. Numerous collective acts of self-immolation took place in the 1680s and 1690s. In the largest instance, which took place in 1687, more than two thousand people voluntarily burned themselves alive. According to the Russian scholar Aleksandr Panchenko, 'in the entire seven centuries of Christianity in Rus, there had never been so many martyrs for their faith … as in the first decade of the schism.'[2] Other Old Believers tried to escape persecution by resettling in the remote areas of the empire and even abroad (North Caucasus, the Crimea, the Polish-Lithuanian Commonwealth and America.) In Panchenko's words: 'Peter inherited a country with a self-destroying and fugitive population.'[3] From the nineteenth century onwards, Russian nation-builders were keenly interested in this period. Views of many Russians on the schism were shaped by Grigorii Miasoedov's and Vasilii Surikov's paintings of the 1880s, which dramatically depicted the persecution of Old Believers by the state and their heroic acts of self-immolation (Figure 1.1).

---

[1]   James H. Billington, *The Icon and the Axe* (London, Weidenfeld and Nicolson, 1966), pp. 121 and Geoffrey Hosking, 'The Russian National Myth Repudiated' in Geoffrey Hosking and George Shopflin, eds, *Myths and Nationhood* (London, Hurst and Company, 1997), pp. 205–6.

[2]   A.M. Panchenko, 'Nachalo petrovskoi reformy: ideinaia podopleka,' in *Itogi i problemy izucheniia russkoi literatury XVIII veka* (Leningrad, Nauka, 1989), p. 9.

[3]   Ibid, p. 10.

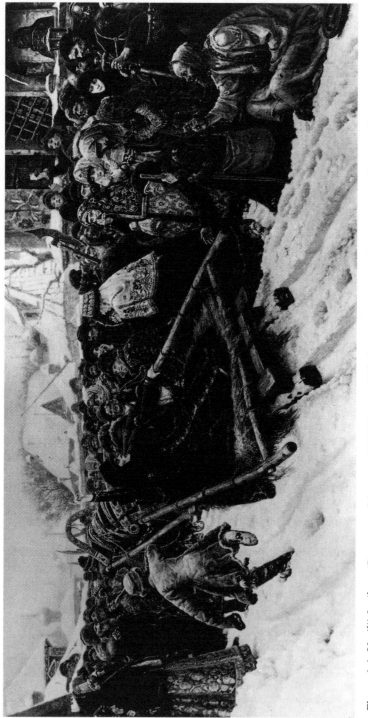

Figure 1.1 Vasilii Surikov, 'Boyarynya Morozova' (1887): an old believer on the way to be executed. (The Tretiakov Gallery, Moscow)

Yet the Old Believers' view of Russia was outdated. The persistence and strength of Old Belief and, paradoxically, even the economic success of many merchants who adhered to it in the eighteenth and especially the nineteenth centuries, seem to be largely due to government persecution. Old Believers stood against the secularization of the Russian state and in this way their identity, based on defending the old ritual, was not modern. The fierce supporter of old ritual, Archpriest Avvakum, not only was ready to die in defence of the use of two fingers in the sign of the cross, the spelling of Jesus' name as *Iisus* rather than *Isus* and other pre-reform practices, but he was also adamantly against the new realism of iconography and other signs of secularization. The message of the Old Believers was also profoundly anti-foreign. Christ was being depicted as a beer-bellied, red-faced German, Avvakum complained. Being inexperienced in dealing with mass opposition, the official Church, in turn, could do little against the spread of Old Belief other than to rely on government persecution of the schismatics.

Indeed, it was in the second half of the seventeenth century that the Russian state began its first attempts at secularization as theatre, ballet and portrait painting came to the court of the tsar Aleksei. His daughter, Princess Sofia, the regent to the young co-tsars Ivan and Peter between 1682 and 1689 became, in effect, the first woman to rule Russia. She emancipated women of the upper classes from *terem* (the special upstairs chamber to which they had hitherto been largely confined) and further opened Russia to foreign influences.[4] It had become clear that the answers to Russia's problems could no longer be offered by the Church.

Sofia was overthrown in 1689 and in 1694 Peter assumed power. He saw Russia's problems in terms of its military might. The wars of the seventeenth century demonstrated the inferiority of Russia's political and military systems to those of its European rivals. Peter's political, fiscal and economic reforms were aimed at making Russia a militarily mighty state able to expand territorially and challenge European powers. For this end he also needed not only new technologies from the West, but also a new state ideology. Orthodoxy could not have offered such an ideology. Nor could it unite all subjects of the empire, which was expanding into non-Orthodox areas.[5]

Peter's new ideology was state patriotism, a loyal service to the state rather than to him personally. His aim was to enlist all his subjects into this service. Peter's move was not unique. Elsewhere in Europe, loyalty to the ruler began to be accompanied by a sense of identification with a particular state. These rulers began to see their own role as a service for the common good (*bien public*) of the people.

---

[4]   Lower class women had never been confined to *terem*, as they could not afford to lead lives of idleness.

[5]   In 1721, Russia established control over the Baltic provinces. Following the Treaty of Versailles in 1919, these areas became the independent states of Estonia and Latvia.

Again, it was under the tsar Aleksei that the new concepts had started to
enter Russian political vocabulary. His Code of Laws (*Ulozhenie*) of 1649
defined its aim as making sure that 'all orders (*chiny*) of the Moscow state
from high to lower ones were equal before the law and punishment (*sud da
rasprava*).' The tsar himself spoke about his goals as 'improving and
strengthening the situation of all Orthodox Christians, of all estates and
ages and preventing anything that undermines the general good (*obshee
dobro*).'[6] The idea of a state separate from the persona of the ruler had also
been first suggested to the Russian tsar by Ukrainian clergy in the mid-
seventeenth century.

Although these ideas hardly reflected Russia's reality at the time, they
indicated the beginning of a new understanding of the legitimacy of tsarist
power. The transformation of Russian political discourse had begun before
Peter the Great, but it was not until his reign that these new ideas and
concepts started to dominate tsarist decrees. The decrees no longer depicted
the state as the personal domain (patrimony) of the tsar, as had been the
case in Muscovy, but as an impersonal fatherland (*otechestvo*), to which
everybody, including the tsar, owed his service. There are numerous
examples of Peter trying to instil in his subjects the idea of service to the
state. In the description of his new reorganized army, he struck out 'the
interests of His Tsarist Majesty' as the object of military devotion and substituted it with 'the interests of the state.' But nowhere was his new ideology
better revealed than in his address to the troops before the battle of Poltava
with the Swedish army in 1709: 'Let the Russian host know that hour has
come that places the fortunes of our entire Fatherland in their hands: either
to perish utterly or for Russia to be reborn in a better condition. And let
them not think that they were armed and put forward for Peter, but for the
state entrusted to Peter, for their kin, for the Russian people ...'

During that war, the Ukrainian Hetman Mazepa, who deserted Peter and
joined forces with the Swedish king, was condemned by Peter not only as a
traitor to the tsar but to the Russian fatherland.[7]

Peter himself and his supporters depicted him as a permanent servant to
the state in different capacities – not only as a tsar and a military leader, but
also as a carpenter and a ship-builder. Later this image was immortalised
for future generations by Aleksandr Pushkin: 'One moment an academician, another a [military] hero, one moment a sea-traveller, another a

---

[6]   A.S. Lappo-Danilevskii, *Organizatsiia priamogo oblozheniia v Moskovskom gosudarstve
      so vremeni Smuty do epokhi preobrazovaniia* (St. Petersburg, Tip. I.N. Skorokhodova,
      1890), p. 159.

[7]   As with many other political ideas of Peter's time, the idea of state treason first found its
      way into Russia in the seventeenth century. The story about the Time of Troubles, 'The
      New Story about the Glorious Russian Tsardom' condemned 'the traitors of our entire
      great state.'

carpenter. With his all embracing soul, he was a permanent worker on the throne.'

The tsar also expected the same attitude from his subjects, especially the nobility. During Peter's reign, an obligatory, life-long service for all groups of the existing courtly and service estates was introduced. These were now united under one category of *shliakhetstvo* (renamed *dvorianstvo* in 1762). The tsar saw the latter as a social group, defined by service to the state and merit rather than by birth. The 1722 Table of Ranks, which formalized promotion through the military and the civil service, made all officers, whatever their social origin, noblemen. Those in civilian careers, if they were non-nobles, had to reach grade eight (out of fourteen) before they became members of the nobility. Where the rank carried with it the status of a hereditary noble, an ennobled commoner passed the title to his heirs. The Table of Ranks in some respects made promotions (i.e. for service to the state) more separated from the person of the monarch and also to some extent opened the way for people of lower social origins to rise into the ruling elite of the country. Although the four highest ranks in the army (*generalitet*) and the top positions in the civil service remained in the hands of the old noble families of Muscovy, at least one third of the infantry officers during Peter's reign were of non-noble origin.[8] This social mobility, especially in the army, helped create the image of a 'popular monarchy.'

Secularization of the state

These changes in the composition of the political elite were accompanied by a changing attitude towards the individual. The word *persona*, referring to an individual, entered the Russian vocabulary. The tsar banned the Muscovite practice of killing babies born with handicaps and at the same time ordered the opening of eight pharmacies in Moscow. In 1702, the tsar outlawed 'arranged marriages.' In 1722, a ban on forced marriages was introduced. Even the substitution of the traditional household tax by the poll tax (1718–1723), although aimed at increasing revenue for the army and the state, has been seen by some historians as a factor which raised the importance of the individual in Peter's Russia.

This new attitude towards his subjects was manifested in the tsar's desire to explain his actions to the public. Many of Peter's decrees began with the word '*ponezhe*' (because), explaining the reason for his policies. In 1717, Peter edited and wrote conclusions to the treatise, *A Discourse Concerning*

---

[8]   Brenda Meehan-Waters, *Autocracy and Aristocracy. The Russian Service Elite of 1730* (New Brunswick N.J., Rutgers University Press, 1982) and John P. LeDonne, *Absolutism and Ruling Class. The Formation of the Russian Political Order 1700–1825* (Oxford, Oxford University Press, 1991), p. 12.

the Just Causes of the War Between Sweden and Russia, by the leading
diplomat Peter Shafirov, explaining to the public the reasons for Russia's
war with Sweden. This work was the first to use the word 'patriot' in the
Russian language.[9]

Women were further emancipated. From 1718 on, noble women were
expected to attend regularly public meetings or 'assemblies' together with
their fathers and husbands, where they talked, danced and dined, while
learning European manners. These assemblies provided women with some
knowledge of public life. Peter introduced some elements of education for
women, especially in foreign languages. He even suggested that a group of
young ladies should be sent to Germany to finish their education. The
proposal came to naught, however, in view of the staunch opposition from
their appalled parents. Formal education for women had to wait until the
reign of Catherine the Great. The reason behind Peter's attempts at
'emancipating women' was purely pragmatic. The argument was as follows.
A man should become a public person. But he receives his first ideas of life
from his mother, who would be unable to give him knowledge of public
duties if she was completely isolated from public life herself. Commenting
on Peter's pragmatic attitude towards noblewomen, Lindsey Hughes
observed that 'what on superficial acquaintance might be identified as
"emancipation" in fact represented a female version of service to the
state.'[10] But it should be noted that similar changes in the status of women,
with similar justifications for their introduction, were being implemented in
other modernising countries of Europe.

Peter also paved the way for future attempts to forge a modern Russian
identity in other areas. Education, especially in mathematics and engineering, was necessary for military men if they were to use new technologies.
This had been one of the areas of greatest divergence between Russia and
other European countries. The Old Rus culture was monastic. No universities or secular schools existed in Russia at the time when Peter came to
power. The two main institutions of education were theological academies
in Kiev and Moscow.

In 1701, the tsar set up a School of Mathematics and Navigation in
Moscow. This marked the beginning of state-sponsored secular education
in Russia. The school was to produce not only officers for the Russian
navy which was being created, but engineers, civil servants, teachers,
topographers, hydrographers and architects. Similar schools were soon
opened in Novgorod, Narva and Revel. These were followed by other
institutions, including the Engineering and Medical Schools in Moscow,

---

[9]   Throughout the eighteenth century, this word was used interchangeably with the expres-
      sion 'a son of the fatherland' (*syn otechestva*).
[10] Lindsey Hughes, *Russia in the Age of Peter the Great* (New Haven CU, Yale University
      Press, 1998), p. 201.

the Naval Academy in St. Petersburg and the Schools of Mines in the Urals. In 1705, the Lutheran pastor Gluck opened a gymnasium, with a curriculum which encompassed politics, philosophy, literature and foreign languages. There were also three types of primary schools in existence during Peter's reign.

Although the nobility dominated the specialist schools, their doors were opened to sons of non-nobles, including peasants (but not serfs). In 1725, indicating an interest in wider, rather than only utilitarian, knowledge, Peter signed a decree on the creation of the Imperial Academy of Sciences (on the model of the Royal Society in London and Academie des Sciences in Paris). The decree on the academy made provisions for the establishment of a university and a gymnasium. Elementary education (literacy and arithmetic) became obligatory for the nobility and government clerks (*prikaznye liudi*). Peter's decree of 1714 forbade an illiterate nobleman to marry. It was hard to implement it, however.

The publication of the first secular works in a Slavonic language began at Peter's behest in Amsterdam in 1699. Soon afterwards, the Moscow printing yard (*pechatnyi dvor*), which had hitherto published only religious literature, followed suit. The start of secular publishing was Peter's first major reform. In 1703, the first Russian 'newspaper,' the Moscow *Vedomosti* appeared. In 1708, Peter introduced a new civil script, which remained in use until 1917. He also introduced a state-maintained postal service and a new calendar, as used in the rest of Europe, which counted years from the birth of Christ rather than from the creation of the world and began the year in January instead of in September.

The growth of book publishing under Peter, compared with the previous century, was remarkable. In the last twenty five years of Peter's reign, 100 times as many books, pamphlets, maps and other types of publications were printed in Russia than during the entire seventeenth century. (Altogether fewer than 500 titles had been published in that century.) Yet, in the first quarter of the eighteenth century, books still sold badly and religious works enjoyed a wider market than secular ones. By 1728, because of bad sales and a resulting deficit, 'Peter's publishing operation was all but dismantled.'[11] After Peter's death, between 1728 and 1735, on average only 13 books a year were published. During the eighteenth century, the greatest number of books published in Russia in any one year was 366. By comparison, in eighteenth century Germany the number of printed texts published per year ranged from a low of 978 to a high of 4,012.[12]

The results of the spread of education were also modest. In 1767, 18 per cent of nobles in the Moscow *gubernia* remained illiterate. In the provinces

[11] Ibid, p. 322.
[12] Reinhard Bendix, *Kings or People. Power and the Mandate to Rule* (Berkeley CA, University of California Press, 1978), p. 504.

the situation was much worse; for instance, in Orenburg an estimated 60 per cent of nobles could not read or write.[13] During Peter's time, the introduction of secular schools notwithstanding, the Church continued to play the main role in spreading literacy.

Peter's major innovation – a regular army financed by the state and based on conscription – also made a contribution to the beginning of nation-building in Russia. The overwhelming majority of conscripts were peasants. (West European states began introducing armies based on conscription in the last decade of the eighteenth century). To promote imperial and corporate pride among soldiers, Peter ordered that all soldiers wore uniforms (something yet to come in Western Europe). Their regiments were given regional names and their banners had regional and civic emblems, so that a soldier's identification with his homeland would be maintained despite the permanent separation. Peter also began the custom of decorating soldiers after victorious battles – a practice unknown elsewhere in Europe at the time. Finally, the level of literacy was considerably higher among soldiers than among the peasants who remained in their villages. Although separation from families and harsh conditions in the army made peasants often compare conscription with a death sentence, in the words of Geoffrey Hosking 'service in the army ... was at least one sphere where serfs might begin to feel themselves citizens, members of a kind of national community, with their own pride and dignity.'[14] Popular attitudes towards the army were reflected in folk songs. From the early eighteenth century, the soldier emerged as a regular character in those songs. The songs called military service an imprisonment (*nevoliushka*). One folk song spoke about the military service in the following way:

> There is nothing more bitter in the fields than you, wormwood!
> But the military service is even more bitter than you are, wormwood,
> The military service of our white tsar, Peter the First.

Throughout the eighteenth century folk songs described the hardships of military service and never mentioned the defence of the fatherland. But from the nineteenth century onwards folk songs also began emphasising soldiers' service to the state. It is the soldiers who take enemies' fortresses during wars and they even help the tsar 'to think through his thoughts' (*dumy dumat*).

---

[13] Hughes, *Russia in the Age of Peter the Great*, p. 308.
[14] Geoffrey Hosking, *Russia. People and Empire 1532–1917* (London, HarperCollins Publishers, 1997), p. 188.

Limits of Peter's policies

Foreigners were the source of Peter's inspiration, his new knowledge and technology. They were also the first teachers of Russians in the schools the tsar had set up. On a number of occasions, the tsar went abroad himself to acquire new knowledge and skills and also sent his subjects away to do the same. From Peter's time onwards, the West became the main constituent 'other,' in comparison with which Russian identity would be forged.

In the political sphere many changes showed attempts to utilize West and North European practices. In European states, towns with municipal self-governments played a crucial role in the formation of modern national identities. Peter was conscious of the weakness of urban institutions in Russia. In early eighteenth century Russia, there were no institutions representing all town residents. Those nobles, trading peasants, and clergy who resided in towns did not share any identity with the townsfolk. They remained closer to their native villages. Moreover they competed with the townsfolk *per se* (the *posad* people) for the market without bearing the same obligations to the state as the latter. This situation prevented a bourgeois class, a leading force in forging the ideology of nationalism in Europe, from consolidating. Peter understood the connection between strong municipal government and the success of trade and industry. In 1721 he attempted to organize municipal self-government by creating the Main Magistracy in St. Petersburg to administer townsfolk throughout all Russia. In 1724, local magistracies in smaller towns were given their own instructions. Members of magistrates were elected by the first two guilds of merchants (the richest ones). Their role, however, was largely limited to ensuring that taxes were collected on time and that the townsfolk performed other services to the state. The management of the police remained in the hands of outsiders, appointed by the central state administration. Noblemen and peasants residing in towns were still tried and taxed by their own communities. In any event, the registered urban population equalled 3.5 per cent of the population in 1719, reaching only 4 per cent in 1815.[15] Thus, here, as in many other areas, the results of Peter's reforms were very limited.

The development of the bourgeoisie had been further weakened in Russia by the fact that up until 1711 most branches of trade and manufacturing had been declared royal monopolies and were licensed by the crown to either merchants or nobles. Those administering trades and enterprises had to deliver a fixed amount of money or product to the treasury, making a profit only if a surplus remained. Peter abolished most of the monopolies and strongly encouraged the development of new industries necessary for building up the Russian military. Yet, his methods of 'industrialization' still

---

15 LeDonne, *Absolutism and Ruling Class*, p. 28.

did not encourage the emergence of a coherent class of industrial entrepreneurs, capable of exercising political influence on the government and reducing the power of the autocrat. Peter's industrialization entailed setting up new branches of industry using state money. Although nobles and merchants were made to administer some factories, the state preserved its ownership over them, determined what was to be manufactured and how much was to be delivered to the state. In Western Europe, entrepreneurs had attempted to limit the power of the monarchy, protect human rights and introduce the rule of law. These had been essential elements of nation-building. Russian entrepreneurs, in contrast, were put in a situation where they were so dependent on the monarchy for their existence that they had to cooperate with it. Rather than being interested in matters of politics, Russian entrepreneurs petitioned the tsar for protection of their rights against competition from the nobility and foreigners, who began to play a significant part in Russian industry from the seventeenth century onwards.

Other policies of Peter the Great, especially those affecting the peasantry, were also to have an adverse effect upon the prospects of nation-building. In 1719, peasants constituted 93.2 per cent of the total male population of the country. By 1815, this figure had fallen only slightly, to 91.3 per cent. The system of serfdom deprived peasants of any legal rights and in the course of the eighteenth century gave the landowners virtually unlimited control over the activities and even the lives of the serfs. It was one of the main reasons why up until 1861, the year the serfs were emancipated, a concept of nation was not applicable to Russian reality. Serfs were automatically excluded from membership in a national community defined in political terms. Not all peasants were serfs, however. In 1719 66.7 per cent of the peasants were attached to a private landowner. This figure fell to 61.6 per cent in 1815. The highest concentration of serfs was in the regions of central Russia. The Kaluga *gubernia* had the highest proportion, with 85 per cent of the peasants being serfs in 1719.[16] As for those peasants who were technically free, 'peasants of the treasury' (*kazennye*), although they enjoyed property rights, pledged allegiance to a new ruler and could testify in court, they could still be transferred to any part of the country to perform different tasks on the order of the state. This was a regular practice in building up those industries in which 'peasants of the treasury' constituted the main workforce.

Under Peter, serfdom expanded. Peter's decrees on censuses (*revizii*), necessary for the introduction of the new poll tax, mixed together two different categories of serfs–peasants and *kholopy*. A member of the latter group was tied by an agreement with a landlord and had to pay him, but he had no obligations to the state. A peasant serf was under obligation to both. The new category of serf people or souls (*krepostnye liudi* or *dushi*)

---

[16]   Ibid, pp. 35 and 37.

combined both categories. This change led to an increase in the number of serfs. It also strengthened the power of the landowners over their serfs, as the landowners became responsible for the timely collection of taxes from their peasants. Peter's desire to divide the entire population into clearly defined groups for tax-raising purposes led to the eventual enserfment of certain marginal groups of free people, such as those without a clear occupation, those who did not know their social origin, those born out of wedlock, and foreign prisoners of war.

Peter's decree of 1714, which abolished the distinctions between *votchina* (a hereditary estate) and *pomestie* (an estate given to members of the nobility for their service to the state as long as they performed that service), made all estates the private, hereditary property of the nobility. This, and the subsequent decree of tsarina Anna in 1731 which confirmed the abolition of the distinction between hereditary and service estates, removed the remaining limits on the landowners' ownership of their serfs. Under Peter, the number of peasants trying to escape illegally to Siberia and other recently acquired and remote areas of the empire from their landlords or from industrial constructions increased dramatically. This was an indication of how Peter's methods undermined his own goal of forging a compound identity for his subjects through pride in serving the state. Reflecting the scale of the problem, the government issued 46 decrees against runaway peasants during Peter's reign. The fine for harbouring such a peasant was increased from 20 rubles in 1698 to 100 rubles by 1721.[17]

The division in Russian society, which had emerged during the seventeenth century Church reforms, deepened under Peter. His Westernization affected only the upper classes of the society. His controversial decrees ordering the nobles to cut their beards and replace Russian clothes with European dress did not apply to merchants and peasants. The latter could continue to wear traditional Russian clothes, if they paid a special tax. Under Peter the persecution of Old Believers continued. Initially the persecution had been relaxed, but it was intensified again during the latter part of his reign; and it was under Peter that Old Belief first became the banner of peasant opposition to the state. Old Believers claimed that Peter was the Anti-Christ and that his activities indicated that the end of the world was coming. Some claimed that the person on the throne was a pretender, a son of a foreigner by whom the real Peter had been substituted at birth. Old Belief was so widespread in Peter's time that some scholars have estimated that up to 20 per cent of the Russian population adhered to it.[18] The number of peasants' uprisings under Peter also rose compared to the previous century.

---

[17]   Iu.A.Sandulov, ed., *Istoriia Rossii: narod i vlast* (St. Petersburg, Lan Publishing House, 1997), p. 332.

[18]   M. Cherniavsky, 'The Old Believers and the New Religion,' *Slavic Review*, vol. 25, no. 1 (1966), p. 4.

The methods used by Peter to pursue his policies could hardly have made his subjects, including nobles, feel like citizens. For instance, this is how Peter went about building the new capital of St. Petersburg. The city was founded in 1703 and 40,000 peasants were transported to the construction site each year. They were taken there under guard and in chains to prevent their escape. Nevertheless the work proceeded slowly, partly because very few wanted to move there. In his letters, Peter often called St. Petersburg 'paradise,' but in reality it was a cold, damp, expensive place, threatened by devastating floods. After 1711, the tsar issued several decrees ordering the compulsory resettlement of several thousand merchants and artisans to St. Petersburg. The move was often particularly ruinous for the merchants as it broke their established ties and trade contacts. A thousand nobles were also ordered to move to the newly-built city. Although the state provided them with the work force and material, they had to finance the construction of their houses from their own pockets. The appearance of the buildings was determined by Peter and his group of invited architects. Deviation from the prescribed style was punishable by fines. In contrast to many other tsarist decrees, those concerning the resettlement of Peter's subjects in St. Petersburg did not include any explanation or justification for the tsar's policies.

Under Peter, nobles were also subjected to a kind of slavery, as the tsar constantly interfered in their private realm. He determined what clothes they could wear, the cut of their hair, the age when they began their state service and the conditions under which they served, what they were to study and even what educational qualifications they needed before they were allowed to marry. He prescribed the architectural styles of their houses and at times even their place of residence. Commenting on the contradiction between such a treatment of his subjects and the expectation of conscious performance of civic duties, the historian Vasilii Kliuchevskii observed that Peter 'hoped through strong power to provoke independent activities in the enslaved society, wanted a slave, remaining a slave, to act as a responsible free man.'[19] The contradictions in Peter's attitude towards his subjects were symbolized in his decrees prescribing the ways in which the tsar wanted the people of Russia to address him. In 1701, Peter forbade his subjects to use demeaning diminutive names when writing to him. 'Less bowing and scraping, and more ardour for service and fidelity to me and the state – that is the homage due a tsar,' Peter proclaimed.[20] Yet, just within a few months, in early 1702, the tsar issued another decree which stated that any petition to

[19]   V.O. Kliuchevskii, *Sochinenia v deviati tomakh*, vol. 4 (Moscow, Mysl, 1989), p. 203.
[20]   Quoted in Aleksandr B. Kamenskii, *The Russian Empire in the Eighteenth Century. Searching for a Place in the World* (Armonk N.Y., M.E. Sharpe, 1997), p. 74–5.

a ruler, even if written by a nobleman, was to conclude with the formula 'Your Majesty's most humble slave' (*rab*).[21]

The secularization of the state, a necessary precondition for constructing a modern society, also proceeded by draconian measures. In addition to abolishing the institution of the Patriarchate and creating the Holy Synod (a state administration under the authority of the tsar) to manage Church affairs in 1718, from 1701 onwards Peter adopted measures which under-mined the power of the monasteries – the symbols of old Muscovy. Peter ordered the registration of all monks and nuns. Nobody could take monastic vows without the tsar's permission. Moreover, monks and nuns were now bound to their own monasteries and could move to another monastery only under special circumstances and with government consent. They could not even leave monastery premises except in cases of extreme necessity, and guards were installed at monastery gates to control the movements of the inhabitants.

These methods divided society and increased opposition to reform even among members of the nobility. But even staunch supporters of Peter did not absorb his main message – namely that they were now serving the state rather than the tsar. In their public speeches and Church sermons, Peter's propaganda men, Bishop Feofan Prokopovich, Count Gavrila Golovkin and Nepliuev, continued to depict the tsar as the owner, preserver and defender of the country, as had been traditional in the sixteenth and seventeenth centuries. Peter the Great was also depicted as the sole creator of Russia *ex nihilo*. This image appeared to compare Peter to God the Father, creator of the universe, and with Jesus Christ, who resurrected the dead. (Such comparisons, which sounded blasphemous to many Orthodox Christians, reinforced the view of Peter as the Anti-Christ among Old Believers.)

At the ceremony where the new title of "emperor" was bestowed upon Peter, Golovkin declared:

> *Solely through your indefatigable labours and leadership* (emphasis added), we, Your loyal subjects, are led from the darkness of ignorance into the stage of glory in front of the whole world, and so to speak, from non-existence into existence and added to the society of political nations (*politicheskikh narodov*).[22]

Similarly, Prokopovich, the main propagandist of Peter the Great, thus described the tsar in an obituary: 'The author of our numerous successes and joys, resurrecting Russia as if from the dead and raising it to such power and glory, or rather the one who gave birth to and educated it, a real Father

---

[21] In the seventeenth century, nobles used a different word '*kholop*' (bondsman) to indicate their subordination to the tsar.

[22] Quoted in V. Mavrodin, *Petr Pervyi* (Leningrad, Izdatelstvo Akademii Nauk SSSR, 1948), p. 250.

of the Fatherland.'[23] This attributed all Russia's successes during Peter's reign to Peter's efforts alone. The concept of a state separate from the persona of the tsar, let alone the people, was absent from this analysis. If anything, the people were seen as an obstacle to Peter's reforms, as they had no understanding of the benefits of these reforms for the country. According to one of Peter's supporters, Ivan Pososhkov, the tsar pulled (Russia) uphill, while millions of his subjects pulled downward.[24]

The state symbolism of the period also portrayed this same image of the tsar. Peter's royal seal depicted him as a craftsman working on a sculpture symbolizing Russia. Similarly, according to one of the legends about the foundation of St. Petersburg, Peter was standing on Zaiachii Island in the Neva estuary, when he tore a halberd from a soldier's hand, cut out two sections of peat, laid them in a sign of the cross and proclaimed: 'The city will be here!' Then, tossing the halberd aside, Peter picked up a shovel and was the first to begin work on the construction of the city.[25] In fact, there is no reliable confirmation that Peter was at this spot where, according to legend, the city was founded on 16 May 1703. Most likely, he spent the time between 11 and 20 May visiting the shipyards at Lodeinoe Pole, and the foundation of the city was supervised by one of the tsar's closest associates, Aleksandr Menshikov.[26]

Just as little of worth had existed in Russia before Peter came to power, so St. Petersburg also rose out of empty swamps. It emerged 'on the tsar's wish' 'out of the darkness of forests and swamps and marshes,' as Pushkin said in the opening lines of *The Bronze Horseman*, thereby imprinting this image permanently on Russian minds. In fact, there were already many settlements, including the residences of Swedish officials and the fortress of Nienschants, in the area.

To further strengthen the image of Peter as the creator of Russia *ex nihilo*, the Russian past was rejected. It is true that in 1720 Peter ordered that manuscripts of medieval chronicles and other documents be collected from monasteries and preserved. But the study of Russian history made very little headway under Peter, even compared to the seventeenth century. It is notable that the overwhelming majority of 'historical' studies of the period focused solely on various events of Peter's reign. Any broader historical works begun under Peter, containing accounts of earlier periods, remained unpublished. Aleksei Mankiev's *Core of Russian History* did not appear

---

[23] Feofan Prokopovich, *Sochineniia* (Moscow, Leningrad, Nauka, 1961), pp. 126–9.
[24] Quoted in Nicholas V. Riasanovsky, *The Image of Peter the Great in Russian History and Thought* (New York, Oxford, Oxford University Press, 1985), p. 5.
[25] P.N. Petrov, *Istroiia Sankt-Peterburga s osnovaniia goroda do vvedeniia v deistvie vybornogo gorodskogo upravleniia po Uchrezhdeniiam o guberniiakh, 1703–1782* (St. Petersburg, Izdanie Glaunova, 1885), 15.
[26] Mavrodin, *Petr Pervyi*, p. 65.

until the 1770s, probably because it devoted very little space to Peter's reign.

Despite his enthusiastic rhetoric about the tsar's service to the state and the common good, Peter exercised his powers more absolutely than his predecessors. Moreover, during Peter's reign there developed an ideology of secular absolutism, which had not been present in Muscovite or Byzantine thought . It was most clearly spelled out in the 1722 work *The Right of the Monarch's Will* (*Pravda voli monarshei*) attributed to Prokopovich, which stated that the form of government in which 'all power is held in the hands of a single person is called Monarchy, that is Autocracy' (*Monarkhiia, to est Samoderzhavstvo*). Under this system, 'the people have divested themselves of their general will and have given it up to their Monarch.' Therefore 'the people must obey all the orders of the Autocrat without contradiction or murmur.'[27] This theory did not allow for the independent existence of any institution other than the monarch, including the Church. Peter's successors continued to preserve absolutism at the time when, in the wake of the French revolution, the *ancien régime* crumbled in Europe.

The concept of an absolutist monarch who articulated the popular will, while the people themselves were deprived of independent expression, contradicted Peter's ideas that the people and the tsar should equally serve the common good, that people should serve the state rather than the tsar, and that they were subordinate to the state, which was higher than the people and the tsar together. The military statute of 1716, which promoted the idea that the soldiers' service was to the state, at the same time argued: 'His Majesty is a sovereign monarch who need not account for his acts to anyone on earth, but has the power and authority to govern his Dominions and lands as a Christian Ruler, in accordance with his own will and good judgement.'[28] Not surprisingly, some of the most anti-Western Russian intellectuals of the nineteenth century, who viewed autocracy as a key element of the Russian indigenous tradition, had an immense reverence for Peter the Great. For the historian Mikhail Pogodin (1799–1875) and the literary critic Stepan Shevyrev (1806–64) Peter was not so much a symbol of Westernization, but a symbol of integral autocracy; therefore they considered his reforms to be 'eminently national.'[29]

---

[27] Quoted in James Cracraft, ' Empire Versus Nation: Russian Political Theory under Peter I' *Harvard Ukrainian Studies*, 10 (December 1986), p. 532.

[28] Quoted in Ibid, p. 529

[29] Martin Malia, *Alexander Herzen and the Birth of Russian Socialism* (New York N.Y., Grosset and Dunlap, 1965), p. 283.

Revolution in the symbolic world of Russia: how far did it go?

The image of a Peter who had created Russia *ex nihilo* was clearly inaccurate, as in many ways he continued what had begun under his father. The changes Peter introduced seemed so striking to his contemporaries partly because he launched a fierce struggle against the symbols of old Muscovy and because he used such cruel methods to achieve quick results. At times the tsar himself cut the beards and the long skirts of caftans of the disobedient nobles, or the job was performed publicly on the streets by soldiers using sheep shears. Scenes of nobles, kneeling in mud, being subjected to such humiliation, were apparently so common that they became a regular feature in eighteenth century popular prints. Merchants were forbidden to sell traditional clothes under threat of confiscation of their property, and punishment by the knout and exile.[30]

The new capital of St. Petersburg, which was given a foreign name (initially in the Dutch spelling Saint Pietersburgh) was to be built solely by foreign architects on the model of Amsterdam and Venice and to look different from traditional Russian cities, especially Moscow.[31] The old capital of Russia, with which Peter associated dark memories his childhood, symbolized for him what he disdained in old Muscovy: superstitions, traditional customs, long sleeves and beards, narrow streets and a 'chaotic' distribution of buildings. In contrast, St. Petersburg was to be constructed on a regular plan. Houses were to be built of brick not wood; if there were not enough bricks, wooden constructions were painted to imitate the brick-work. There were to be many towers with spires and roofs were to be tiled. According to the art historian Igor Grabar, the most complete fulfilment of Peter's order 'to use foreign lands as an example in every possible sphere' could be seen in the way St. Petersburg looked by the end of Peter's reign. Indeed, St. Petersburg in effect became anti-Moscow, the main symbol of a new Russia created by Peter by opening up the country to European influences.

As for royal rituals, Peter borrowed so lavishly from French, German and Swedish royal ceremonies that Richard Wortman has observed that 'By displaying themselves as foreigners, or like foreigners, Russian monarchs and their servitors affirmed the permanence and inevitability of their separation from the population they ruled.'[32] For instance, at the beginning of his reign, during a monetary reform of 1699, Peter rejected a Russian craftsman's design of a fifty kopecks coin (*poltina*) which showed the tsar in

---

[30]   Kliuchevskii, *Sochinenia v deviati tomakh*, vol. IV, p. 200.
[31]   Initially, St. Petersburg was not seen as a new capital. The court and high government moved to St. Petersburg in 1713, ten years after the foundation of the city.
[32]   Richard S. Wortman, *Scenarios of Power. Myth and Ceremony in Russian Monarchy* (Princeton N.J., Princeton University Press, 1995), p 5.

a traditional Russian dress in favour of one designed by a Dutch master which depicted Peter as a Roman emperor. Symbolism derived from the Roman empire was, according to Wortman, much more prevalent in the ceremonies of Russian rulers in the eighteenth century than in Western Europe, from where those symbols had been first borrowed.

Yet Peter's desire to use foreign examples had its limits. He was interested in winning greater popular support for his reform and for the state he was creating, and he understood that it was essential to make use of indigenous Russian traditions as well. The most important manifestation of the Russian nature of his reform was in the way Peter adopted the title of emperor. When Peter accepted this title from the Senate on 22 October 1721, Europe had only one emperor – that of the Holy Roman Empire. Many believed that Peter intended to take the title of the Eastern Roman (Byzantine) Emperor. Instead, he decided to style himself the Emperor of All Russia (*vserossiiskii*). Linking an imperial title to the name of a native land was a novelty at the time, which French, Austrian and German emperors adopted only in the nineteenth century.[33] The 'state' symbols used by Peter, although following the European tradition of heraldry, nevertheless demonstrated a strong connection with the Russian past. In the early years of Peter's reign, Russian merchant ships, as well as the Russian army in the first year of the Northern War, were decorated with the white-blue-red flag. Such a flag had first been used in 1668 by tsar Alexei on merchant ships transporting Russian goods in the Caspian sea. The flags were to indicate that the ships belonged to Russia. Their colours had specific religious symbolism in the Russian Orthodox Church.[34]

The first Russian order to honour exceptional service to the state and monarch was that of Apostle Andrew (or St. Andrew First Called), introduced in 1699. According to a legend in the *Primary Chronicle*, Apostle Andrew had passed through the lands where Kiev and Novgorod were later built. Since the Kiev Rus period, he had been regarded as the Patron Saint of Rus. In numerous laudations by his supporters Peter was often compared not only to Roman emperors and Greek and Roman gods, but also to Apostle Andrew and St. Aleksander Nevskii (the Novgorod Prince of the thirteenth century). According to one of the legends which became current during Peter's reign, Apostle Andrew had passed through the area where St. Petersburg would subsequently be founded on his way from Kiev to

[33] S.M.Solovev, *Chteniia i rasskazy po istorii Rossii* (Moscow, Izdatelstvo Pravda, 1989), p. 557.
[34] N.A. Sobolev and V.A. Artamonov, *Simvoly Rossii* (Moscow, Panorama, 1993), pp. 110–39. It is sometimes argued that this flag was introduced first by Peter the Great and was to imitate the Dutch model. (For such an interpretation see James Cracraft, *The Petrine Revolution in Russian Imagery* (Chicago IL, The University of Chicago Press, 1997), p. 266.)

Novgorod.[35] Before his death Peter also planned an order of St. Aleksander Nevskii to honour exceptional military achievements. The order bore a sign of a blue cross. Later in Peter's reign this cross became part of his military flag. The white-blue-red one gradually started to be confined only to merchant ships.

In some respects, Peter's successors relied more exclusively than Peter himself on European, especially German, heraldry. Black-yellow-white became the usual colours of tsarist dynastic banners. The concept of a national flag to replace dynastic banners emerged in Europe as a result of the French revolution. However, the tsarist government did not adopt this idea until the end of the nineteenth century. The idea of a national flag was proposed by the Russian government in 1896, in a period of promotion of Russian traditions begun under Alexandr III. Peter's white-blue-red flag was chosen as the people's (*narodnyi*) flag of Russia. After the February revolution of 1917, the Provisional government held many of its meetings under red (revolutionary) banners, but the white-blue-red flag was retained as 'a national flag of free and democratic Russia.' In 1991, President Yeltsin's government again adopted the white-blue-red flag as the national flag of the country.[36]

Conclusions

Peter the Great laid the basis upon which a Russian national identity could subsequently be constructed. The most revolutionary change was the idea, imported from Europe, that the state was separate from and superior to the personality of the tsar. The idea of service to the state and to the common good was to provide a new compound secular identity for his subjects. Peter also initiated changes in the spheres of communications, education and culture, which in Russia as elsewhere paved the way for the first attempts to construct the idea of a nation. Indeed, as the next chapter will show, by the end of the eighteenth century Peter's idea of a Russian identity separate from that of the tsar had been taken up by certain representatives of the intellectual elite. In the course of the eighteenth century they had begun to construct the first images of Russia and to define what it was to be Russian. Their ideas would be taken on board by nationalists from the nineteenth century on. Moreover, the very framework of national debate would be determined by the peculiarities of Peter's reign. The West would become the main constituent 'other', in opposition to which Russian national identity would be forged. The empire he extended would serve as another building

---

[35] Iu. Bespiatykh, ed., *Peterburg Petra I v inostrannykh opisaniakh* (Leningrad, Blitz, 1991), pp. 258–62.

[36] Sobolev and V.A. Artamonov, op. cit.

block in constructing a Russian identity. The strong presence of Ukrainians in his court and in the Church during his rule, continuing a tradition which dated from the 1640s, would leave a significant mark on Russians' view of themselves. All the most prominent Russian intellectuals have articulated their (often contradictory) views on the personality and the policies of this remarkable tsar.

Yet the way Peter implemented his reform, and the political system he created, also had a negative effect upon the subsequent process of nation-building. This led to a situation in which the majority of definitions of Russianness hotly debated by Russian intellectuals from the late eighteenth century onwards remained artificial constructs, which persistently failed to transform Russian reality. It is largely because of Peter's reforms and the way they were implemented that a society separate from the state – which despite Peter's rhetoric, the monarch continued to embody – could not consolidate. Serfdom became entrenched and extended to include new groups of people. Obligatory life-long service for all nobles made many of them, in effect, averse to performing any service to the state, including to organs of local self-government. The Church was put into a situation of dependence on the monarchy greater than ever before, and thus had even less chance of becoming a centre of power independent of the state. Peter's policies also widened the gap between different groups in society. His forced Europeanization touched only the upper classes of society, not peasants and merchants, the majority of the population. At the same time, he continued to persecute Old Believers. This group, along with those peasants who did not adhere to Old Belief but whose position was also deteriorating, formed an unprecedented opposition to Peter's Europeanizing state.

With the consolidation of the monarch's absolutist rule, nobles, merchants and townspeople were put in a situation where they strove to obtain favours and privileges from the monarch rather than to struggle for their civil rights. The development of a bourgeoisie, which elsewhere in Europe was at the forefront of nation-building, was stultified. In the words of the Russian historian Evgenii Anisimov 'Monopolies, compulsory service, duties, resettlement, artificial restrictions on commercial activity of various kinds – all these afflicted Russian merchants: historical sources testify to the utter ruination of the more substantial group of the merchantry ...'[37]

After Peter's death, Russian merchants continued to depend strongly on the monarchy. They did not turn into a bourgeoisie, with economic interests that would induce it to fight for political and civil liberties. Moreover, a large part of the merchantry, and often the most successful one, was not touched by Peter's Westernization, but continued to adhere to Old Belief, with its traditional religious identity. Consequently, as the idea of the nation

[37] Evgenii V. Anisimov, *The Reforms of Peter the Great. Progress through Coercion in Russia* (Armonk N.Y., M.E. Sharpe, 1993), p. 78.

as a sovereign people penetrated Russia after the French revolution, it was Russian intellectuals, whose analysis of Russia's situation and actions were not inspired by any particular economic or political interest but by abstract theories and concepts imported from abroad, who became Russia's main nation-builders.

|2|

Peter's legacy: the emergence of intellectual debate

The [Russian] citizen ... should use the power of his mind to help
the poor and deprived
Beseduiushchii grazhdanin (October 1789)

Soon after Peter's death, the cultural and social changes which had taken
place during his reign began to bear fruit. The first group of intellectuals
emerged, influenced by the ideas of the Enlightenment, and they were ready
to take on board some of the lessons of Peter's reign better than the tsar's
supporters had done during his lifetime. The first cohort of these intellectuals included the poet Vasilii Trediakovskii and the poet, scientist and
inventor Mikhail Lomonosov. In the 1730s–1750s, their main contribution
to the future Russian nation-building project was to take the first steps
towards the creation of a modern Russian language. It was they who in
effect laid the foundation for making the Russian language a key component of Russian national identity. Meanwhile, German scholars in the
Academy of Sciences, which had been founded by Peter the Great, began a
wide-ranging programme of studying Russian history. Then, from the
1760s onwards, the next generation of intellectuals made the first cautious
attempts to determine the matrix of the Russian national identity. Using
Catherine the Great's permission to set up private publishing houses, they
began to debate what was the best political system for Russia, whether
serfdom was to be preserved or abolished, and whether Peter's reforms had
had a positive or negative impact on Russia. This generation was the first
to articulate modern definitions of Russianness. Its nineteenth-century
successors elaborated upon these definitions, but did not invent them, as is
often assumed.

Creating the modern Russian language

Peter's policies to encourage greater social mobility were reflected in the
social origins of the first cohort of intellectuals to leave their mark on the
development of Russian culture. Trediakovskii was a son of a priest from
Astrakhan on the Caspian Sea. He was educated first in the Slavic-Greek-
Latin Academy in Moscow and then at the Sorbonne in Paris. Upon his
return, he began a career as a translator at the Academy of Sciences, receiving the title of professor in 1745. Lomonosov was the son of a peasant from
the Arkhangel *guberniia* in North Russia. He also started his education in
the Slavic-Greek-Latin Academy. He then moved to the university attached
to the Academy of Sciences in St. Petersburg and finally to Marburg and
Freiburg Universities in Germany. His subsequent career also proceeded
within the Academy of Sciences, and he made significant contributions to
chemistry and physics as well as Russian poetry, linguistics, grammar and
history. He has been hailed in Russia as 'the Peter the Great of Russian
literature.'

Education, and the intellectual careers which resulted from it, were all
these people possessed. It is not surprising that they invested so much effort
into trying to create a tool through which their achievements could be
disseminated. This tool would be the modern Russian language. The world
of St. Petersburg, where these intellectuals lived, was dominated by the
nobility. In view of their humble backgrounds, they had to look beyond
their social origins for an alternative source of pride, and found it above all
in what they believed they had created.

At the time Peter the Great assumed power, both written Church Slavonic
and spoken Russian were so inadequate for the purposes of his secularizing
state that Peter initially toyed with the idea of making Dutch the official
state language. In 1700, however, the tsar introduced the civil Russian
script. Numerous foreign words with Russian endings started to be utilized
in official discourse. This was clearly a language in transition, awaiting the
appearance of intellectuals ready to give it some shape. Trediakovskii, in
1730, was the first to suggest that the emerging Russian literature should be
written in a language closer to the vernacular Russian, rather than in
Church Slavonic. He attempted to put his theory into practice and published his own translation of a French novel in a language he thought was
close to colloquial Russian. But the language of Trediakovskii's writings
was still so rough and pedestrian that few lovers of literature among
Russians today know anything about this author but his name. Yet his idea
about the need to create a new literary language, close to the vernacular,
was revolutionary. In 1735, in his *New and Brief Method of Composing
Russian Verses*, Trediakovskii took another step towards the creation of
modern Russian. He suggested changes to the syllabic verses in use in
Russia since the mid-sixteenth century. These had been imported from

Poland, and did not correspond to the peculiarities of the Russian language. Trediakovskii's contribution has often been downplayed. Moreover, during his lifetime he was often ridiculed and put down by his educated colleagues, including Lomonosov.

Lomonosov was indeed better able to elaborate further on Trediakovskii's ideas, and was more successful in implementing them. In 1739, Lomonosov wrote *A Letter on the Rules of Russian Versification*, which introduced trochaic and iambic verses into Russian. The same year, Lomonosov published his first ode, using this new form of versification. The literary critic Vissarion Belinskii was right to claim that 1739 was the year when 'our literature began.' Whereas a contemporary Russian will find it very hard to get through Trediakovskii's poems, some of Lomonosov's writings still sound not only comprehensible but indeed beautiful. No less importantly, Lomonosov produced the first scholarly description of the Russian language, *The Russian Grammar*, published in 1757. *The Grammar*, based on Lomonosov's careful study of colloquial Russian, set out the grammatical norms of the language clearly for the first time. It also dealt with the question Trediakovskii had first posed – which Church Slavonic words should be used in Russian.

Both Trediakovskii and Lomonosov claimed that their language should be a source of pride for Russians. In fact, they had only started to create this language, which still had to await Pushkin to give it final shape. However, they had laid the foundation for making the Russian language a formative element of an ethnic Russian identity which would fully crystallize by the late nineteenth century. Both authors proclaimed the superiority of the Russian language over other European languages. Again, Trediakovskii paved the way by claiming the supremacy of 'Slavono-Russian' over the 'Teutonic language'. Lomonosov left a more eloquent glorification of the Russian language, which future 'linguistic nationalists' would repeat from the nineteenth century onwards. He argued in his *Russian Grammar* that 'Russian had the majesty of Spanish, the vivacity of French, the firmness of German, the delicacy of Italian, and the richness and concise imagery of Greek and Latin ...'

Pride in the Russian language went hand in hand with optimism about the overall intellectual potential of the Russians. Owing everything he had achieved to education, Lomonosov believed that 'The Russian land will be able to give birth to its own Platos and quick-witted Newtons' not by borrowing from the West and inviting foreign specialists, but by educating its own people.

Rivalry with foreigners and Russian identity

Lomonosov's ideas were partly shaped by his rivalry with the German scholars at the Academy of Sciences. Germans had occupied high positions in Russian politics and in the scientific establishment since the reign of Peter the Great, particularly in the period from 1730 to 1741. This whole issue of rivalry with foreigners, especially Germans, affected the future complex self-image of the Russians vis-à-vis the more advanced European nations.

It has long been argued that the strong presence of foreigners at the court and in the central bureaucracy under Empress Anna (1730–40) provoked a protest by the Russian nobility of a 'national-patriotic' nature.[1] Recently, certain American and Russian scholars have suggested, however, that this protest was unrelated to any emerging national sentiment. Instead, it amounted merely to a personal struggle between some Russian nobles and their foreign rivals for the top government positions.[2] Whatever the nature of the struggle, however, another Empress, Peter's daughter Elizabeth, did present the conflict in patriotic terms. Her claim to the throne, which she obtained in 1741 as a result of a palace coup, was shaky. The Empress Catherine I, Elizabeth's mother, indicated in her testament that her grandson, the Duke of Holstein Karl Peter Ulrich, had precedence in accession to the Russian throne. Elizabeth therefore needed some extra arguments to justify her claim. In her first accession manifesto of 25 November 1741, Elizabeth said that due to the 'external and internal troubles and disarray' during the reign of Empress Anna and her favourite, Regent Biron, 'all our loyal subjects, both civil people and the clergy, and especially the Guards, unanimously urged us ... to accept the throne,' as 'we are connected by blood to our autocratic parents' (i.e. Peter the Great and Catherine I). This reference to the wish of the people was a direct result of Peter's concept of the new role of a monarch as a servant of the state and the people. Despite the fact that Peter the Great had actually initiated a massive influx of foreigners to serve the Russian state in various capacities, under Elizabeth he began to be officially depicted as a defender of everything genuinely Russian against foreign enemies. Thereafter, an image of Peter as the defender of Russia from foreign penetration began to accompany the earlier image of the tsar as 'the creator of new Russia *ex nihilo*.'[3]

During her reign, Elizabeth was portrayed by her supporters as continuing these alleged policies of Peter, defending Russia from those foreign

---

[1] Hans Rogger, *National Consciousness in Eighteenth Century Russia* (Cambridge MA, Harvard University Press, 1960).

[2] Liah Greenfeld, *Nationalism: Five Roads to Modernity* (Cambridge MA, Harvard University Press, 1992), p. 234 and T.V. Chernikova quoted in Iu A. Sndulov, ed., *Istoriia Rossii: narod i vlast* (St. Petersburg, Lan, 1997), p. 349.

[3] In 1843 a Westernizer, Peter Chaadaev, argued that 'if not for Peter the Great, who knows, Russia might have now been a province of Sweden.' In turn, the Slavophile historian Mikhail Pogodin echoed this sentiment in 1863: 'Let Peter's critics say, whom could they juxtapose to Charles XII at the battle of Poltava. It was impossible to expect an organic development, [Russia] had to be saved by any means. Peter saved old Russia.' Quoted in A.A. Kara-Murza and L.V. Poliakov, *Reformator: Russkie o Petre I* (Ivanovo, Firma Fora Publishing House, 1994), p. 37.

enemies who had ruled it in the preceding decade. These enemies, it was claimed, had been deliberately plotting to undermine Russia. In fact, these parallels with Peter were not entirely far-fetched. For all his heavy reliance on foreign expertise, Peter had not been above thinking in xenophobic and conspiratorial terms. In his own conclusions to Shafirov's *Discourse Concerning the Just Causes of the War Between Sweden and Russia*, Peter observed that '[N]ot only the Swedes, but also other and remote peoples, always felt jealousy and hatred towards the Russian people, and attempted to keep the latter in the earlier state of ignorance, especially in the military and naval arts. This is clear from ... the histories of the past centuries ... you may conclude what was the eternal hostility of these neighbours even at the cradle of Russia's fame ...'[4]

This is not to say that anti-Western xenophobia began in Russia in the time of Peter the Great. It had been present in earlier centuries, but its nature was different. The main accusation against Europe in pre-Petrine Russia was that it was trying to subvert the Russian Orthodox faith with Catholic, Protestant or other 'heresies'. Under Peter, the idea emerged that the West was deliberately trying to conceal the light of knowledge from Russia and to exploit Russia's natural resources for its own ends.

During the reign of Elizabeth, this line of argument intensified. Russia's enemies were alleged to have found their way inside the country. Church representatives were instrumental in these propaganda efforts under Elizabeth, and both old (religion-based) and new accusations against foreigners were used. For instance, in a Church sermon on 25 March 1742, Archimandrite Dmitrii Sechenov argued that, after the death of Peter the Great and his wife and immediate successor Catherine I, enemies of Russia 'laid their hands on (*pribrali v ruki*) our entire fatherland, spit poison on loyal sons of Russia, began the persecution of the Church of Christ and the pious faith; it was their times, the times of darkness, they behaved as they pleased.' Another hierarch, Archimandrite Amvrosii, attributed the following words to Empress Elizabeth in his sermon on 18 December 1741: 'I am not so much concerned about myself, but about our precious Fatherland, which having been governed by foreign heads, has been impoverished and many innocent people have perished.'[5] This propaganda against foreigners had a fairly broad resonance. This was indicated, among other things, by the large number of mainly anti-German cartoons among popular wood-cut pictures (*lubki*).[6]

[4]   W.E. Butler, *A Discourse Concerning the Just Causes of the War between Sweden and Russia: 1700–1721* (Dobbs Ferry N.Y., Oceana Publications, 1973), p. 73.
[5]   Quoted by E.V. Anisimov, *Rossiia v seredine XVIII veka. Borba za nasledie Petra* (Moscow, Mysl, 1986), pp. 45–6. Here the analysis of Elizabeth's reign is based on Anisimov's account.
[6]   D. Rovinskii, *Russkie narodnyia kartinki*, vol. 1 (St. Petersburg, Tipografiia Imperatorskoi Akademii Nauk, 1881), pp. 448–51 (reprint Munich, Otto Sagner Verlag, 1989).

In reality Elizabeth continued to invite foreigners to work in Russia, the major change being that the German influence largely gave way to the French. Moreover, being more interested in clothes and fun than in political matters, the empress did very little to fulfil her promises to reinforce Peter's legislation and commemorate her father by deeds rather than words. Yet some important changes did take place in the cultural and educational sphere during her reign, and these contributed to the future formation of Russian national identity. Moreover, the way she conducted propaganda to justify her claims to the throne ensured that the introduction of these changes was accompanied by bitter competition with foreigners which bordered on xenophobia. It was also marked by a desperate desire to prove that Russians were not inferior to foreigners. These elements would become important ingredients in the Russian national consciousness thereafter.

The beginning of historical studies in Russia

The study of Russian history, an important step in forging a modern national identity, entered a new phase during Elizabeth's reign. It was concentrated in the Academy of Sciences, the first members of which were foreigners. Some Russians, especially Peter's strong supporter Vasilii Tatishchev, had been attempting to write histories of Russia in the 1720s and the 1730s. However, it was the German scholars at the Academy, G.-S. Bayer and G.F. Mueller, who introduced scholarly methods into the study of Russian history. Mueller began to publish the first Russian historical periodical, *Sammlung Russischer Geschichte*, in 1732. It was published in German, and for the first time it attracted the interest of foreign scholars to the history of the eastern Slavs. In a letter to his German colleagues, Mueller formulated the task of a historian in the following way: 'It is difficult to perform the tasks of a historian. He should seem to be without a fatherland, faith, ruler.'[7] Thus, Mueller regarded 'objectivity' as the main goal of a historian. As we shall see later, his Russian colleagues thought this position served to conceal anti-Russian sentiments.

First Bayer, then Mueller focused, among other things, on the origins of the East Slavic political structures. Bayer was the first to formulate the so-called Norman theory, according to which Vikings (i.e. people of Germanic origins) were the first princes of Rus. There were two underlying ideas in this theory which upset Russians, especially Lomonosov – namely that the 'Russian state' was relatively new, and that it had been founded by foreigners. A huge scandal erupted when, on the day commemorating Empress Elizabeth's name-day, 6 September 1749, Mueller delivered a speech on the

---

[7]   Quoted in M.O. Koialovich, *Istoriia russkogo samosoznaniia* (Minsk, Luchi Sofii, 1997), p. 154.

Origins of the Russian People and (Their) Name, reiterating the main points
of the Norman theory. The story about the Eastern Slavs calling on the
Varangians to come and create their state was to be found in the Kiev Rus
chronicles. *Sinopsis*, a popular history written in the seventeenth century by
the German-Ukrainian historian Innokentii Gizel, argued that the
Varangians were Slavs. Gizel's view continued to influence historical efforts
in Russia in the eighteenth century. The first 'professional' Russian
historian, Vasilii Tatishchev, advanced the same arguments in his *History of
Russia*. Ironically, Mueller had attempted, without success, to publish
Tatishchev's *History* in 1748. At that time the Academy of Sciences had
showed no interest in supporting the publication. However, when next year
Mueller rejected Tatishchev's view on the Varangians, and, following Bayer,
argued that they had been Scandinavians, the Russians in the Academy
revolted. They expressed outrage that 'In his entire speech, Mueller did not
show a single example, which could glorify Russian people, but only those
which could defame them ... At the end, one can only be surprised how
carelessly he expressed the opinion that Scandinavians with their superior
weapons easily subjugated entire Russia to its rule.'[8]

After Peter's victory over Sweden, Mueller's view on the role of
Scandinavians in Russian history seemed to sound almost blasphemous.
This is exactly the impression Mueller's opponents tried to create. In order
to introduce a parallel with recent history, Mueller's critics had to attribute
to him views he had not in fact expressed. Mueller had not claimed that the
Varangians had used arms to subjugate the East Slavs. Instead, he had
quoted medieval sources that spoke about the establishment of Varangian
rule by peaceful means.

Several months later, another discussion of Mueller's speech took place.
The attack was led by Lomonosov, who condemned Mueller for thinking
that 'the Finns gave the Russians their name and the Swedes their tsars.'
Moreover, he overtly depicted Mueller's speech as an insult to the memory
of Peter the Great. Mueller as well as Bayer had expressed doubts about the
historic validity of a passage in the *Primary Chronicle* about the visit of
Apostle Andrew to the site where Kiev was later built. As Peter had insti-
tuted the order of Apostle Andrew, the German scholars' argument was a
'political subversion.' As a result, the publication of Mueller's speech was
banned and most of the existing copies destroyed. When Mueller's student
A.L. Schloezer, who had come to work in the Imperial Academy of Sciences
in 1761, decided to publish Mueller's speech abroad he had to do it secretly.
This publication was regarded as a defamation of Russia. When, in 1764,
Schloezer intended to visit Germany, his collection of manuscripts was
confiscated, following a denunciation by Lomonosov. He thought Schloezer

8   P.P. Pekarskii, *Istoriia Imperatorskoi Akademii Nauk v Peterburge*, vol. 1 (St. Petersburg,
Tipografiia Imperatorskoi Akademii Nauk, 1870–1873), p. 405.

intended to publish material abroad which would present Russia in a bad light.[9] Lomonosov could not possibly agree with Schloezer, who had argued that 'Even if it is offensive for Russian patriots, their history ... is not as ancient as Greek and Roman, and is even younger than that of Germans and Swedes ... Wild, rude and dispersed Slavs became public people (*obshchestvennye liudi*) only with the help of the Germans, whose fate it was to spread the fruits of civilization in the North-Western and North-Eastern worlds.'[10]

Lomonosov's own history of Russia, presenting the 'Russian point of view' of events, was finished in 1763 and published three years later. It is significant that in his struggle with the German historians, Lomonosov was successful in soliciting government support. This situation would be repeated on various occasions later.[11]

The resentment towards Mueller and Schloezer in the Academy was exacerbated by the fact that Mueller had decided to choose a German (Schloezer) as his successor as the main specialist in Russian history at the Academy, rather than trying to train a Russian for this role. During the reign of Elizabeth it began to be argued that Peter the Great had invited foreigners for a limited period of time so that they could train indigenous Russian cadres. However, they had failed to do so, in order to try to perpetuate foreign domination of Russian life. This argument was put forward in 1755, when the first Russian university was founded in Moscow. The most influential favourite of Elizabeth, Ivan Shuvalov, who played a pivotal role in the spread of education at the time, argued that although Peter had invited foreigners to train Russians, they 'did not try to spread knowledge in the country, which was alien to them.'[12] Similarly, the decree of 12 January 1755 on the creation of Moscow University complained that the nobility invited French tutors for their sons, 'who (the tutors) have no skills as teachers, and do not posses any scientific knowledge.' The new university would allow these incompetent foreigners to be replaced by home-grown cadres.[13]

At the opening ceremony, explaining the need for the university, the poet and future professor of rhetoric and philosophy, Nikolai Popovskii, told the first cohort of students: 'If you are persistent and industrious, you will

---

[9] Ibid, vol. 2, pp. 829–30.
[10] Koialovich, *Istoriia russkogo samosoznaniia*, p. 145.
[11] Exactly two centuries later, in 1963, Moscow historian Aleksandr Zimin suggested that the most famous medieval Rus epic, *The Lay of the Host of Igor*, was an eighteenth century forgery. The Communist Party Central Committee demanded that this question of 'national importance' was discussed at a closed meeting of the History Department of the Soviet Academy of Sciences and ordered a ban on the publication of Zimin's work, which the History Department upheld.
[12] Quoted in Anisimov, *Rossiia v seredine XVIII veka*, p. 205.
[13] V.O. Kliuchesvkii, *Sochineniia v deviati tomakh*, vol. 5 (Moscow, Mysl 1989), p. 154.

quickly be able to demonstrate that you are as clever as the best representatives of other peoples. Show the world that Russia is late in entering the world of the enlightened people because of the belated spread of education here rather than because of its impotence.'[14]

Yet throughout the eighteenth century, professors at the university lectured in either French or Latin. Filling academic positions was initially also a daunting task. For some time the two faculties of the University had only two professors; all other chairs remained vacant for the lack of suitable candidates.

'Peter gave us life, Catherine – soul'[15]

On 28 June 1762, Peter III was deposed in a coup organized by his wife, who became known to history as Catherine the Great. She was an Anhalt-Zerbst princess, who had come to Russia in 1745 to marry the heir to the Russian throne. Catherine constantly emphasized her affinity and connection with the reign of Peter the Great, and did more than he had done to spread Western ideas and education in Russia and to shape the form of Russian intellectual thought. Initially, she had also toyed with the idea of introducing political reforms in Russia. These would have changed the nature of the Russian system and laid the basis for a nation-building process along political lines. Ultimately, however, she failed in this endeavour.

Until her accession to the throne, Catherine had spent her years in Russia in relative isolation and boredom. Her main entertainment was to read the works of French philosophers of the Enlightenment, from whom she got ideas about the equality of men before the law, the responsibility of a monarch to his people, the division of power, and about the nation as a sovereign people. Her manifesto on the accession to the throne, to which she had no 'legal' claim, was couched in national-patriotic language. Like her predecessor Empress Elizabeth, she promised to become a defender of the 'ancient Russian Orthodox faith', which she alleged was in danger of being replaced by a foreign creed through the actions of her husband. She said her motives had been love for 'our Russian fatherland' (despite the fact that she had no Russian blood and had never fully mastered the Russian language). Finally, she claimed to have assumed powers in response to 'the zealous desire of all our loyal subjects to see us on this throne, in order to be ... protected, through our efforts, from all the wrongs and coming dangers to the Russian Fatherland.' But nowhere were Catherine's 'early political ideals' expressed so well as in her *Instructions* (*Nakaz*) to the Legislative

---

[14] Quoted in Anisimov, *Rossiia v seredine XVIII veka*, p. 206.
[15] Aleksandr Sumarokov, 1768. Other poets of the time, for instance, Mikhail Kheraskov, expressed a similar idea.

Commission, which she convened in 1767 to produce a new Legal Code for the Russian Empire. Few other political documents issued by a Russian tsar bore such a glaring discrepancy with Russian reality. The failure of the commission and its dissolution in 1768 had the most profound effect on Russia's nation-building process. This failure gave the final push needed for the birth of the Russian '*intelligenty*,' concerned not only with cultural but also with political and social issues.

The nineteenth century Russian historians who studied the *Nakaz* found that most of its ideas had been taken from the works of French philosophers, especially Montesquieu's *Spirit of the Laws* and Beccaria's *Crime and Punishment*. The *Nakaz* contained proposals, which, at the time, were radical not just for Russia but for most of Europe. Had they been implemented, they might have facilitated the formation of a political Russian nation. The *Nakaz* spoke about the equality of all citizens (*grazhdane*), which would mean their equal responsibility before the law. (The word 'citizen' (*grazhdanin*), meaning a responsible member of society, had entered the Russian language in Peter's time. It became very popular in official propaganda under Catherine.) Catherine also spoke about political freedoms. These meant that citizens would not only have the right to do everything permitted by law, but also the right not to do things against their will, and to feel secure from unjust persecution. The *Nakaz* maintained that Russia needed a type of government which would ensure that people were not afraid of each other and that everybody, including the monarch, would be subject to the same laws. So radical were the views of the *Nakaz* that the French translation, published on Catherine's order, was banned in France by the king.

Yet, in contradiction to all these progressive thoughts, Catherine maintained that, given the huge size of the empire, only autocratic government was possible in Russia. On this point, Catherine was firm and she again evoked the authority of Montesquieu, who had argued thirty years earlier that the physical size of a state determined which form of government was suitable. Before she wrote her *Nakaz*, the Russian empress had rejected the idea of her aide Count Nikita Panin to set up an elected State Council, with responsibilities clearly defined by law and thereby able to limit the powers of the autocrat. Catherine had initially signed Panin's manifesto, but then decided not to publicize it. Consequently, the powers of the monarchy remained unlimited.

Serfdom was another major obstacle to nation-building. Here, Catherine's contribution was more ambiguous than it had been with autocracy. The initial draft of the *Nakaz* had included articles, aimed at limiting the arbitrariness with which serfs could be treated by their landlords. It had also included ideas on the gradual emancipation of the serfs. In her memoirs, Catherine claimed she had been in favour of emancipation, but could not act on her convictions, as the institution was staunchly supported by the nobility. On this point, Catherine was probably honest. Before her *Nakaz* had been issued, deputies of the Commission had discussed it. The main changes they suggested were to chapter XI on serfdom, from which Catherine's ideas on the limitation of the rights of landlords and possible emancipation of serfs were eliminated. Moreover, the debates in the commission demonstrated that the preservation of serfdom was the main goal of the deputies from the nobility and those other estates, especially merchants, who wanted to share the nobles' privilege of owning serfs.

More than anything else, the work of the Commission demonstrated how different Russian reality was from that of its Western models, and how little prepared even the educated strata of society were to accept the novel ideas of the Russian tsarina. The elections to the Commission proceeded with difficulty and some nobles had to be threatened by the monarch with the confiscation of their estates if they refused to participate in them. Deputies had to bring to the Commission *nakazy* from their electorate. These *nakazy* demonstrated that both the electors and most of the deputies saw the whole enterprise as their chance to lobby the monarch with requests for individual privileges and favours. The main goal of the nobility was to preserve serfdom and further expand the rights of landlords over their serfs. Even the best educated and most 'enlightened' representatives of the nobility thought along these lines. Prince Mikhail Shcherbatov, one of the best educated Russians of his time, a historian and moralist who complained in his essay *On the Corruption of the Morals of the Nobility* about the moral degeneration of the nobility since the time of Peter the Great, came up with an astonishing argument in defence of serfdom. He said that the nobility was the estate whose main task was to serve the fatherland by governing other people. They needed practice to learn to govern and they received this practice in their villages, where they could rule over serfs. Significantly, Shcherbatov, like many other deputies, called serfs 'slaves' (*raby*). Thus, in the words of Vasilii Kliuchevskii, one of the most 'enlightened' Russians of the time 'saw serfdom as a school for Russian statesmen to learn their governing skills and a serf village as an example of how the Russian state should be governed.'[16] Merchants, in turn, also argued for the preservation of serfdom and demanded the right to own serfs along with the nobility. During the work of the commission, not one of the deputies publicly challenged Catherine's view of autocracy as an ideal form of government for Russia or expressed any desire for power-sharing in central government.

Some deputies were, however, more forward looking. They wanted to strengthen local self-government, making it truly independent of the central authorities. The *nakaz* of the nobles from Dmitrovo stood out from the

---

[16] Kliuchevskii, op. cit., p. 89.

rest. It spoke clearly about the need for properly functioning local self-government. It called on the nobility to educate themselves and their children in the Russian language rather than in French, and to become responsible for spreading education among the peasantry.

The commission failed either to revise the old 1649 Code or to produce a new one, and was dissolved in 1768. However, Catherine drew some lessons from its work. Her provincial reform of 1775 gave the nobility greater control of local administration. Her 1785 Charter of the Nobility further expanded the privileges of this estate. It was already the most privileged group in Russia, having been freed from compulsory state service by Peter III's Decree on the Freedom of the Nobility of 1762. Catherine's Charter outlined all the rights of the nobility. It confirmed that they had full property and inheritance rights over their estates, including the peasants living there. Their titles could be inherited by their wives and children, and these titles could be revoked only by a court of peers for a limited number of crimes. Nobles were exempt from the poll tax (*lichnaia podat*), from recruitment into the army and from corporal punishment. Elected assemblies of the nobility received the right to petition the central administration about their corporate needs. That same year, Catherine issued the Charter of the Towns, which emancipated rich merchants. The two first guilds of the merchants were freed from the soul tax (*podushnaia podat*), which was replaced with a 1 per cent tax on their capital. Merchants could free themselves from army recruitment by paying a certain sum of money, and from corporal punishment. Towns received estates-based (*soslovnyi*) self-government and legal courts. The distinctive civic identity of local residents was to be emphasized by their town emblems. In accordance with Peter the Great's unrealized vision, several hundred such emblems were designed on Catherine's order in the period between 1775 and 1785.

Moreover, Catherine attempted to create institutions in which representatives of different estates could work together for the good of the fatherland. The main body was the Department for Public Issues (*Prikaz Obshchestvennogo Prizrenia*), an institution in charge of charity and local education, comprised of representatives of the nobility, townspeople and state (i.e. nominally free) peasants. Despite the secondary role played by the Department in local government, it was definitely a step forward in consolidating society and therefore in the nation-building process. In the 1780s, Catherine also attempted to organize a school system that could provide her government with educated officials not only for the top offices but also for the middle ranks. In 1786 there had been only 40 schools with a total of 4,400 pupils in Russia. By the end of Catherine's reign, in 1796, there were 316 schools with some 17,340 pupils.[17] In the major schools

---

[17] Patrick L. Alston, *Education and the State in Tsarist Russia* (Stanford CA, Stanford University Press, 1969), pp. 15–20.

more than half of the pupils were commoners. To the displeasure of the empress, members of the nobility still preferred to give their children private tuition at home.

Yet in two important ways, Catherine's policies stultified Russia's nation-building. Firstly, she had no intention of curbing her own powers as autocrat. Despite her stated wish to the contrary, serfdom was further expanded. More peasants became serfs during her reign, as she gave villages with nominally free peasants to her favourites. She also introduced serfdom into areas of the empire, such as Ukraine, which had not known it before.

The first Russian *intelligenty*

Catherine's contradictory policies, and the resulting unfulfilled expecta-tions, created tensions among a group of thinking people in Russia. A few nobles had expected political changes and were disappointed by the failure of the Commission. Historians of nationalism, most notably Elie Kedourie, have argued that nationalist ideas often emerged when the nobility became independent of the state but remained excluded from power sharing by the monarch. Scholars have also emphasized the role of the bourgeoisie, with its uncertain identity, in articulating and promoting nationalist ideas. These ideas, it is argued, helped the bourgeoisie find a secure identity within a broader community of equal individuals defined as a nation. In late eighteenth century Russia, there was no bourgeoisie to be affected by the ideas of nationalism. So Liah Greenfeld has applied Kedourie's theory about the role of the nobility in forging nationalist ideas to the Russian case. She has argued that the abolition in 1682 of *mestnichestvo* (the system which linked service rank to the degree of nobility of one's family) plunged the Russian nobles into a crisis of identity. The policies of Peter the Great and Catherine the Great towards the nobility only exacerbated this crisis. Consequently, Russian nobles began to articulate nationalist ideas from the second half of the eighteenth century onwards as they searched for an alternative identity.[18]

Greenfeld's conclusions create the impression that under Catherine the Great many nobles embraced nationalism. She also seems to imply that the Russian nobility did have some coherent corporate identity so long as the system of *mestnichestvo* existed. The scholarly consensus is, however, that it is precisely during the eighteenth century that the different categories of 'service people,' which had existed up to then were first amalgamated into a single estate with a corporate identity. This was the result of the adoption of Peter the Great's Table of Ranks, Peter III's Decree on the

---

[18]   Greenfeld, *Nationalism: Five Roads to Modernity*, pp. 204–22.

Freedom of the Nobility, and Catherine's Charter of the Nobility.[19] There is plenty of evidence to show that the majority of nobles enthusiastically embraced their new privileges and fought hard to secure them. Their main preoccupation was not to seek power-sharing with the monarch but to preserve serfdom, the institution which until 1861 effectively prevented the formation of a modern Russian national community. Nationalist ideas were of little interest to most people in this group who, by the late eighteenth century, spoke French not only at court but also at home, using Russian only to communicate with servants and serfs.

Yet the new liberties given to the nobility did provide some members of the estate with free time to pursue cultural and philosophical interests, if they so wished. Secular education and mastery of foreign languages, which Peter the Great first encouraged, prepared some Russian nobles, as well as a few non-nobles, for those pursuits. In the late eighteenth century some did embrace the novel idea of a nation and tried to define Russia and the Russians. One should remember, however, that these were just a few. We are not yet talking about a sizeable nationalist movement.

Back in the reign of Catherine the Great, a very significant mark on the history of Russian intellectual thought was left by those few nobles who could rise above the immediate economic interests of their class, and those few educated non-nobles who proved successful in their careers as writers, scholars and translators. Such people were the first to articulate the moral principles of a group which in the nineteenth century became known as the Russian intelligentsia. They were also first to articulate some of the definitions of Russianness which were elaborated by their successors from the 1830s onwards.

Despite the difficulty of finding a precise definition of the intelligentsia, most scholars will agree with that offered by Richard Pipes: '*Intelligent* is someone not wholly preoccupied with his personal well-being but at least as much and preferably much more concerned with that of society at large, and willing, to the best of his ability, to work on society's behalf. Under the terms of this definition, one's level of education and class status are of secondary importance.'[20]

Most scholars have dated the emergence of the intelligentsia to the 1830s at the earliest and have observed that the word 'intelligentsia' first entered the Russian language in the 1860s. In doing so, they have overlooked the fact that a similar definition was first articulated by Lomonosov back in 1755. Defining the role of a poet in Russia, Lomonosov argued in his *Comments on the Quality of a Poet*, that he should above all 'be concerned

---

[19] See, for instance, Geoffrey Hosking, *Russia. People and Empire, 1552–1917* (London, HarperCollins, 1997), p. 153.

[20] Richard Pipes, *Russia under the Old Regime* (New York N.Y., Charles Scriber's Sons, 1974), p. 253.

with the well-being of the people' (*radet o blagodenstvii obshchestva*). During Catherine's reign, the first Russian '*intelligenty*' appropriated what Lomonosov saw to be a poet's main goal as their own. Moreover, they felt that without such broad public concerns a person could not be a citizen. An example of this is provided by the periodical *Beseduiushchii grazhdanin*. Its first issue was published in 1789, and proclaimed that its aim was to instil in its readers 'a clear understanding of the main duties of a person, especially a citizen'. It defined the newly emerging type as somebody who did not necessarily have the money, but had the capacity 'to use the power of his mind to help the poor and deprived.'[21]

Initially, Catherine's policies created favourable conditions to follow intellectual pursuits. Indeed, looking for approval from her friends, French philosophers, Catherine allowed the creation of private publishing houses – something which Benedict Anderson has argued is crucial in the emergence of modern nationalism.[22] Catherine also favoured the spread of education and strongly encouraged the study of Russian history and language. In 1783, she created the Russian Academy of Letters, fully devoted to the study of Russian language and literature. She commissioned both Russians and foreigners to write histories of Russia and herself wrote *Notes Concerning Russian History* as well as dramas on various episodes from the medieval history of Slavs.

Yet, some of those who answered her patriotic call did not think that the Empress had done enough to turn her rhetoric into practice. Therefore they began to forge a Russian identity in opposition to the state and the autocrat. Following the American and French revolutions, Catherine realized the danger of her policies. However, the introduction of censorship, the closure of various publications and arrests of the critics of autocracy could not undo one of her main contributions to Russian history – giving birth to the first Russian *intelligenty*.

The 1767 Commission played a pivotal role in the emergence of a group of people concerned with the task of defining and forging a Russian identity. Some key intellectual figures who had worked in the commission frequently referred to its discussions in print, as publishing began to flourish from the late 1760s onwards. They were Mikhail Popov, Vasilii Maikov, Aleksandr Ablesimov, and most importantly Nikolai Novikov. From 1769, they became regular contributors to Novikov's journal *Truten*. Before discussing the new themes that became a key preoccupation of the newly born *intelligenty*, it is worth mentioning their publishing and educational

---

[21] *Beseduiushchii grazhdanin*, issue for the month of October (1789) p. 144.
[22] Anderson has stressed the role of 'the convergence of capitalism and print technology' in creating possibilites for nation-building. Benedict Anderson, *Imagined Communities: Reflections on the Origin and Spread of Nationalism* (London, Verso, 1991), p. 6.

activities. These are key elements in the formation of a modern nation as an 'imagined community.'

Russian intellectuals were quick to seize the opportunities offered by Catherine's permission to set up private publishing businesses. In other areas, for instance when Peter the Great began setting up new industries, the government often could not find any significant response from the population. This time, in contrast, the response was more far-reaching than the Empress had wished. Novikov was the most outstanding, but not the only example. In addition to publishing nine journals and one newspaper, he was also a key figure in book publishing. In 1779, he moved from St. Petersburg to Moscow, where he leased the Moscow University publishing house and set up two more print shops. From 1779 to 1792, when Novikov was arrested on Catherine's orders, one third of Russia's book publishing business was in his hands. Most importantly, he was concerned about the distribution of books and periodicals in the provinces. He organized book-selling centres in sixteen Russian towns. Text books were a key element of his publishing activities. Following Lomonosov, Novikov saw education as the main means of solving Russia's problems. Even more than his predecessor, he was concerned with the education of peasants and saw elementary schools, open to all, as essential for transforming Russia. By 1796–1800, the scope of publishing activities was almost 20 times greater than that of the mid-1730s. Yet this still meant that only around 250 books a year were printed. Although as many as 119 periodicals were published in Russia during the eighteenth century, with the majority of them appearing from the 1760s onwards, their average length of existence was 3.6 years.[23] (It should be borne in mind, however, that articles from periodicals and even books were often copied by hand. This was an activity in which noble women especially, among whom the level of literacy was the highest in the country, excelled.)

Russia's first Westernizers–Slavophiles debate

The main themes of the intellectual debates, on the pages of the journals, were the two key elements of the Russian political and economic systems – autocracy and serfdom. Serfdom was being abolished in those European countries which educated Russians tended to regard as models. The autocratic powers of the monarch were either already limited in England or were under attack from emerging republicanism in France. Consequently, the two most distinctive elements of the Russian system themselves posed the question of the difference between Russia and the West very acutely. This

---

[23] F.A. Brockhaus and I.A. Efron, *Entiklopedicheskii slovar*, vol. 'Russia' (St. Petersburg 1898, facsimile Lenizdat, 1991), p. 415.

inevitably meant that the dominant view of Peter the Great's reforms had to be revised. Were his attempts to borrow so much from Europe beneficial or destructive for Russia? The period was dominated by attempts to make sense of Russia's history, and this question assumed a crucial importance. Finally, the expansion of the empire, which in Catherine's time was at its peak, also meant that the attitude of the Russians to aliens (*inorodsy*) became a topical question.

These questions were to preoccupy the Russian intelligentsia for the next two centuries. From the very outset, those involved in the debate became roughly divided into two camps – conservatives and liberals or Slavophiles and Westernizers. The famous Slavophile–Westernizers debate of the 1840s in fact began in the late eighteenth century. Initially, the figures of the 1840s added relatively few new ideas.

The liberal camp was best represented by Novikov, who opened the pages of his journals to criticism of autocracy and condemnation of serfdom. But even before Novikov had begun his publishing activities, Mikhail Kheraskov's journal *Poleznoe uvesilenie* (1760–62) had already published pieces by authors who saw Britain's constitutional monarchy as an ideal form of government. French republicanism also had a strong hold. Republican ideas came from French literature. Works by French authors in the originals and in translation were to be found in the libraries of educated Russians throughout the country. One of the translators, the Ukrainian noble Vinskii, translated various French philosophical treatises while he was exiled in Orenburg in the 1770s. His translations were quickly copied and distributed, initially among his friends. In a few years, they were already on sale as far away as Siberia.[24] A prominent role in spreading the ideas of republicanism was also played by French tutors who had come to educate the sons of Russian nobles. However, their quality had been mocked during Elizabeth's reign, probably not without reason. Invitations became far more selective under Catherine.

In Catherine's time, republican ideas were also expressed in historical dramas, one of the most popular genres of Russian literature in the 1770s and 1780s. Iakov Kniazhnin's tragedy *Vadim of Novgorod* presented the Russians as a historically free people, upon whom autocracy had been imposed by force. The main hero of this tragedy was the 'Russian citizen' (*rossiiskii grazhdanin*), Vadim, a republican, who saw 'autocracy as spreading troubles everywhere' (*samoderzhavie povsiudu bed sozdatel*). Vadim opened the struggle against all-mighty prince Riurik, whom he regarded as usurper.

The peak of the eighteenth century criticism of autocracy can be found in the works of Aleksandr Radishchev, especially in his *Ode on Freedom* (1783) and *The Journey from Petersburg to Moscow* (1790). The first hailed

---

[24] Kliuchesvkii, *Sochineniia v deviati tomakh*, vol. 5, p. 159.

the American revolution and freedom as 'a source of all great deeds;' the
second explicitly condemned autocracy as 'a system most adverse to
people.' The *Journey* was published anonymously in a small private
publishing house in 650 copies. Its authorship was quickly disclosed and
Radishchev's arrest followed. The initial death sentence was commuted to a
ten-year exile in Siberia, from whence the writer was brought back in 1796
by Catherine's successor, Emperor Paul.

Criticism of autocracy went hand in hand with attacks on serfdom.
Influenced by the ideas of the Enlightenment on the equality of men, a few
liberals from the 1760s onwards called for the emancipation of the serfs
(usually without questioning the landlords' ownership of the land the
peasants worked). Novikov advised a noble who thought that through his
origin he was superior to his serfs, to 'look twice a day at the bones of landlords and peasants until he is able to see any difference' between them.
Another liberal of the time, the playwright Denis Fonvisin, dwelled in his
plays on the moral decline of the nobility under the impact of serfdom. In
developing this theme, Radishchev again left the most radical mark. In his
Journey, he unequivocally rejected the idea of such classicist writers of the
1740s and the 1750s as Aleksandr Sumarokov, that only nobles were 'sons
of the fatherland.' For Radishchev, the peasants of his time were 'prisoners
in their own fatherland,' who had the potential, however, to become true
'sons of the fatherland' to a greater extent than the nobles. The emancipation and education of peasants were key to this transformation. An army
recruit depicted in *The Journey*, who had received education, could proudly
exclaim: 'I am a person equal to everyone else.' (*Esm chelovek, vsem
drugim ravnyi*). Thus, the peasant theme, so dominant in the nineteenth
century, entered Russian literature in the eighteenth.

Meanwhile, around the time of the French revolution, Russian liberal
periodicals began to use the word '*narod*' to mean a nation as a community
of equal citizens. Such a community included not only the nobility, as the
poet Sumarokov would have it, but also other groups of Russian society,
even peasants who were expected to be educated. (It was only in the next
century that the term '*narod*' was re-conceptualized to mean the peasantry
as the embodiment of the Russian nation, as opposed to the educated
classes, termed 'the public.') Although the Russian '*narod*' as a community
of equal citizens existed only in the minds of the journals' authors and
editors, they proudly printed this word with a capital 'N'.[25]

At the opposite pole were the conservatives, the best representatives of
whom were the historian Ivan Boltin, and the writer and historian Nikolai
Karamzin in the later period of his life. Boltin's main historical study was a
rebuttal of *Histoire de la Russie,* a work by an honorary member of the

---

[25] See, for instance, *Beseduiushchii grazhdanin,* issue for the month of October (1789),
p. 145.

Russian Imperial Academy of Sciences, the French historian LeClerc. This book, published in 1774 in Paris, depicted medieval Rus in a way that Boltin viewed as a 'slander' of his country. Glorifying the deeds of the medieval East Slavic princes, Boltin spoke about the superiority of the Russians over those they conquered, especially the Tatars. He also was among the first to embark on the topic of the superiority of the Russians over Western Europeans. According to Boltin, the history of Western Europe was much more cruel than that of Russia. He argued that given the size of the Russian state, no form of government other than autocracy was possible. Moreover, autocracy was superior to a parliamentary republic, Boltin maintained. According to the historian, 'If under an incompetent and lazy tsar the government weakens, under the next one it will improve, regaining its might. If a republic weakens, it will never regain its strength, will never revive. Diseases of monarchy are short lived and light; diseases of republicanism are harsh and fatal.'[26]

As for the plight of peasants, they were better off in Russia. Boltin mocked the personal freedom of peasants who owned no land in Western Europe. He thought that the emancipation of peasants should not be on the agenda, but instead laws regulating peasants' obligations towards landlords should be properly elaborated and observed.

Karamzin's *History of the Russian State*, the first eight volumes of which were published in 1818, strongly reinforced Boltin's views on serfdom and autocracy as essentially positive features of Russia's economic and political systems. The founding father of sentimentalism in Russian literature, Karamzin did not see any contradiction in his defence of serfdom and his idealization of peasants, whom he often depicted in his literary works as morally superior to nobles. He also did not see any contradiction between his views on serfdom and his calls for education of the peasantry. Indeed his advocacy of peasant education was no less prominent than that of Novikov. According to Karamzin, elementary schools were more important 'than any academies in the world' and the work of an ordinary school teacher was far superior to that of any scholar or scientist.

The interest in Russian history inspired by the emerging nationalist sentiments meant that the role of Peter the Great and his reforms again came under scrutiny. Back in the late 1740s and the 1750s, Lomonosov had rejected the view of Western historians that life in pre-Petrine Russia was 'savage'. Yet, this rejection at the time did not necessarily lead to criticism of Peter's policies or any revision of his heritage. Even such a critic of autocracy as Radishchev did not see the strengthening of the autocratic system as the most important part of Peter's legacy. Instead, Radishchev believed that the tsar had been 'the first to give motion and direction to this

---

[26] Quoted in Koialovich, *Istoriia russkogo samosoznaniia*, p. 170.

enormous mass, which, like a primary element, had remained inactive.'[27]
With some simplification, one can say that such a view of Peter remained
the general position of the eighteenth century liberals.[28]

But Boltin and, over time, Karamzin, developed different views. For
Boltin, the heritage of Peter's reforms was unequivocally negative:

> When we began to send our youth abroad and to entrust their education to
> foreigners, our morals entirely changed... Thus we forgot the old, before
> mastering the new, and while losing our identity, did not become what we wished
> to be. All this arose out of hastiness and impatience. We wanted to accomplish in
> a few years that which required centuries and began to build the house of our
> enlightenment on sand before having laid firm foundations.[29]

Karamzin's views on Peter fluctuated. In the 1790s, when he was still close
to Novikov's camp, he described Peter in *Letters of a Russian Traveller* as
'a great man, a hero, a benefactor of mankind, as much as my own benefactor.' The first change in this attitude is to be noticed in Karamzin's
literary work *Natalia, the Daughter of a Boyar* (1792), where he described
pre-Petrine Muscovy as a true Russia: 'Who among us does not like the time
when Russians were (truly) Russian, when they wore their own dresses ...
spoke their own language and from the heart, in other words, they spoke
the way they thought? At least I love that period, I love in my imagination
... to talk with my bearded ancestors, talk to them about the adventures of
antiquity, about the character of the great Russian people.'[30]

Karamzin's position on Peter became even more revisionist in his
Memoirs on Ancient and Modern Russia of 1811. He argued that it was not
Peter whose state-building efforts had to be admired, but 'the princes of
Moscow, Ivan I, Ivan III,[31] who may be said to have built a powerful state
out of nothing, and – what is of equal importance – to have established in it
a firm power of the monarch.' As for Peter, 'by uprooting ancient customs,
by exposing them to ridicule, by making them to appear stupid, by praising
and introducing foreign elements, the sovereign of the Russians humbled

---

[27] From Radishchev's *Letter to a Friend Living in Tobolsk*.
[28] For later periods, it would be too simplistic indeed to think that Westernizers only praised
Peter, while Slavophiles criticized him. A very useful collection of comments about Peter by
Russian intellectuals, Kara-Murza and Poliakov, *Reformator: Russkie o Petre I*, op.cit,
demonstrates that we find examples of praise and criticism in both camps and often very
contradictory attitudes towards the Emperor on the part of the same authors. See also
Nicholas V. Riasanovsky, *The Image of Peter the Great in Russian History and Thought*
(Oxford, Oxford University Press, 1985).
[29] Quoted in Riasanovsky, *Image of Peter the Great*, p. 60.
[30] G.P. Makagonenko, *Russkaia literatura XVIII veka* (Leningrad, Prosveshcheniie, 1970),
p. 965.
[31] Ivan I (Kalita) became the Grand Prince of Moscow in 1325; Ivan III became the Grand
Prince of Moscow in 1462.

Russian hearts. Does humiliation predispose a man and a citizen to great deeds?' In the *Memoirs*, Karamzin also articulated the idea that Peter's reforms had split Russian society. This idea became an important tool for analysing Russian history thereafter. Karamzin argued:

> Human life is short, and the rooting of new customs takes time. Peter confined his reform to the gentry. Until his reign all Russians, from the plow to the throne, had been alike insofar as they shared certain features of external appearance and of customs. After Peter, the higher classes separated themselves from the lower ones, and the Russian peasant, burger, merchant began to treat the Russian gentry as Germans, thus weakening the spirit of brotherly national unity binding the estates of the realm.[32]

These changes in attitude towards Peter's policies were reflected in a revised view of one of his most long-lasting and glorious creations – the new capital of St. Petersburg. Rather than glorifying the miracle of the erection of a beautiful city out of 'empty swamps,' Karamzin exclaimed that 'Petersburg is founded on tears and corpses.' Thereafter, these two diametrically-opposed approaches marked the perception of Peter's city in Russian high culture. On the one hand, the city is presented as an essential part of the Russian civilization, its European part. On the other, it is perceived as foreign, alienating, indeed, hostile to the rest of the country.[33] Nikolai Gogol sarcastically called the city a German clerk, whereas Moscow, a symbol of indigenous Russian traditions, was 'a truly Russian merchant wife.'

In sum, by the turn of the nineteenth century, not only were the main themes of the intellectual debate normally associated with the 1840s already present, but some other distinctive features of Russian intellectual discourse had also appeared. I mean here the fact that the struggle between liberals and conservatives reflected the divide between cosmopolitans of the Enlightenment and (proto-) nationalists.

Although they used the word 'narod' to mean a hypothetical Russian nation as a community of citizens, intellectuals like Novikov and Radishchev did not think nationally. Novikov and other members of his circle were influenced by the ethics of Freemasonry, with its belief in a brotherhood of people regardless of class or national differences. They preached the 'universal values' represented by 'Western civilization' and expected that with time, as autocracy and serfdom disappeared and the

---

[32] The quotes from Karamzin's *Memoirs* are taken from Riasanovsky, *Image of Peter the Great*, pp. 71 and 72.

[33] In fact, in Russian folk culture, St. Petersburg was depicted as a 'foreign' enclave in Russian lands soon after the foundation of the city, but it was only at the end of the eighteenth century that such an image found a prominent place in Russian high culture.

peasantry was educated, Russia would enter the European political mainstream. The peculiarities of the Russian historical and cultural tradition, for instance the impact of Orthodoxy, were of no particular interest to them. In future most Russian liberals would remain cosmopolitans in the Enlightenment mode. In other words, in the absence of a civil society and a state able to command the respect of the population, liberal nationalism could not and did not develop in Russia.[34] Like the liberal cosmopolitans, those intellectuals who did pay attention to Russia's own traditions were from the outset unable to analyse them except in the context of a comparison with the West. In this comparison they felt the urge to argue for Russia's superiority at all costs. Consequently they were driven into the camp of political conservatives. Not in all cases, but far too often the division between liberal cosmopolitans and conservative nationalists was rigid. Representatives of both groups continued to operate within a framework of set stereotypes, determined by the comparison between Russia and 'the West,' without being able to transcend them. In some ways, this would be Russia's tragedy.

---

[34] It is only in the early twentieth century that some liberal intellectuals, associated with the 1909 *Vekhi* collection of essays, attempted to combine an interest in Russian national traditions with political liberalism.

PART

2

RUSSIAN IDENTITY AND THE 'OTHER'

|3|

Russia and the West

In the West every institution as well as every political system contains an answer to a life-important question, posed by previous centuries ... We, in contrast, have not done anything other than to follow the route shown by the West, as if we were slaves. [We have failed] to understand the one-sidedness [of this route].

> Aleksei Khomiakov (*The Impressions of Foreigners about the Russians*, 1845)

When in the conclusion of his lecture the professor addressed the audience directly and reminded it how much we owed and how strongly we should have been grateful to Europe, from which we had received free of charge the fruits of civilization and human existence, his voice was overshadowed by the outburst of applause from all corners of the auditorium.

> Pavel Annenkov about lectures by Timofei Granovskii in Moscow University in the 1840s (*A Remarkable Decade*)

This chapter deals with what is arguably the most important ingredient of modern Russian identity – the comparison with the West. Russia's relationship with the West, and especially the related question of whether Russia is part of Europe, has had the most profound impact on how the Russians have viewed themselves and the outside world, how they have interpreted their own history and how they have defined possible paths for their country's development over the past three hundred years. Ever since Peter the Great's reforms, the West has served as the main constituent other for Russians. Russian intellectuals and politicians have constructed a variety of images of the West. In their depictions of the peculiarities of the Russian national character, Russian writers have tended to compare their Russian protagonists with Europeans – with a Frenchman in Denis Fonvisin's plays, with a German in Ivan Goncharov's *Oblomov*, with an Englishman in Nikolai Leskov's *Left Handed*, etc. – rather than with the non-Russians of the empire. The question of the relationship between 'the Russian' and 'the Western' civilizations has attracted the best Russian minds and consumed their main intellectual efforts. Yet as this chapter will show, to this day the Russians have not found a solution to the tortuous contradiction in their attitude towards the West. This contradiction is between the two visions of Russia constructed for the purpose of comparison with the West. One is of a Russia as a European [imperial] power, about to catch up with the model it is emulating, the more advanced countries of Western Europe. Another is of a Russia with an identity formed along the lines of those colonial and post-colonial societies in Asia and Africa, in which nationalism derives its power by distinguishing itself sharply from the West as an anti-model.

Most of the intellectual currents in Russia which have tried to answer the questions of what Russia is and who the Russians are, have been directly influenced by ideas first articulated in Western Europe. Even the importance of such a symbol of Russianness as the peasant commune (*obshchina*) was first drawn to the attention of a wide circle of Russian intellectuals by a German scholar, Baron von Haxthausen, who had travelled in Russia to study its folk life in 1843–44.[1] At different times, various Western countries exercised a particularly important influence on Russia and therefore became the main point of comparison for the Russians. For example, in the first half of the eighteenth century Northern Europe and Germany were most important, in the later part of that century – France and England, and in the first half of the nineteenth century – France and Germany. Western thinkers had long acknowledged the existence of different Europes. From the 1830s, Europe was seen as divided into the liberal West (England and France) and the autocratic 'Northern monarchies' (Prussia, Austria and Russia). However, Russian thinkers often tended to think of the West as a single undifferentiated entity, which they regarded either as a positive model for Russia to emulate or as a negative example to be rejected. Reflecting this

---

[1]   In the early 1840s, the Slavophiles first argued that the peasant commune expressed in reality the ideal which European socialists were striving to achieve. But it was following the publication of Haxthausen's book in 1847, which offered a systematic study of this Russian phenomenon, that the *obshchina* began to attract the interest of broad circles of Russian intellectuals, including the Left. (See Martin Malia, *Alexander Herzen and the Birth of Russian Socialism* (New York N.Y., Glosset and Dunlap, 1965), pp. 395–6.) Peasant communes were created by the authorities in Muscovite Rus primarily for fiscal purposes, to ensure efficient payment of taxes by the villagers by making them collectively responsible for them. In the view of the Slavophiles, however, communes were an organic growth permeated by a peculiar Slavic and Orthodox communal spirit.

attitude, in this chapter we shall discuss this constructed category of the Russian intellectual tradition – 'the West.'

Some scholars, particularly Geoffrey Hosking, have argued that the attempts of the eighteenth century Russian tsars to Europeanize Russia actually obstructed the Russian nation-building project. According to Hosking, both the schism in the Russian Orthodox Church of the late seventeenth century, and the wide-scale borrowing of Western cultures and ethos in the eighteenth, meant a repudiation of Russian indigenous traditions. These traditions could have served as the basis for building a compound Russian national identity. The eighteenth century borrowings from the West were prompted by the requirements of Russian empire-building – the empire needed Europeanized elites to run it. In this, as in many other spheres, there was a conflict between what was needed to build the empire and what was needed to build the Russian nation.[2] Other scholars, in contrast, have argued that pre-Petrine Russian cultural traditions did not provide sufficient material for building a modern Russian nation, hence it was inevitable that modern Russia would rely excessively upon Western cultural traditions.[3] It seems, however, that the strength or weakness of Russia's pre-Petrine cultural tradition is not at issue here. The important matter is that even if we assume that the old Russian cultural tradition was strong, we have to remember that it was purely religious, with monasteries being its main cultural centres. Russia did not have a secular culture before it was opened up to European influences. Consequently, its intellectuals could only make very limited use of pre-Petrine Russian traditions for modern nation-building purposes. The very concept of a nation was a West European one. So, when Russian intellectuals began to apply it to Russian reality they had little choice but to make the West Russia's 'other.' However, the realities of the Russian empire could not be adequately described in terms of the concept of a nation. For this reason, attempts to construct a Russian national identity by means of comparison and contrast with the West often have proved futile, as this book demonstrates.

This chapter adopts a chronological approach in its analysis of Russian views of the Western world. It looks at how Russia's relations with the West have been conceptualized from the early eighteenth century up to the present – primarily by intellectuals, but also to some extent by the government, especially in the Soviet period. Wherever possible, it also assesses popular perceptions of the West as Russia's constituent other. This chapter starts by looking at how an agonizing ambivalence in the attitude towards the West took shape among Russian intellectuals in the course of the eighteenth

---

[2] Geoffrey Hosking, *Russia: People and Empire. 1552–1917* (London, HarperCollins, 1997), p. XXIV.

[3] Liah Greenfeld, *Nationalism: Five Roads to Modernity* (Cambridge, MA, Harvard University Press, 1992), p. 16.

century and how this perception of the West, in turn, created a similarly agonizing ambivalence in their attitude towards their own country. Discussing the subsequent period up to 1917, the chapter looks at the main intellectual and political groups, from the Decembrists of the early nineteenth century to the Constitutional Democrats of the early twentieth. It then analyses the Soviet period, when the Bolshevik government claimed to be fulfilling many of the hopes cherished by intellectuals in the nineteenth century.

The analysis of the Soviet period focuses on Soviet government propaganda. In the pre-revolutionary period, the government was on the margins of the debate over Europe. That Russia belonged to Europe, albeit to the Europe of the *ancien régime* (dynastic absolutism), was not doubted by the tsars and government officials. The tsars also did not regard it as a top priority to forge a compound national identity for the subjects of their empire. The Bolshevik government, in contrast, put the aim of forging such an identity at the top of their agenda, probably recognizing that the failure of the tsars to do so had facilitated the collapse of the monarchy and the state. Thus, the Soviet government launched an unprecedented propaganda campaign to shape the way in which Russian/Soviet citizens saw themselves and the world. In this campaign, the West remained Russia's main constituent other. It continues to serve the same function after the collapse of the communist regime.

The roots of the ambivalence

Before the eighteenth century the Muscovite state had not been completely sealed from Western influences. During the Time of Troubles of the early seventeenth century some educated Russians began to recognize a common identity with the West, which at that time meant Poland. But it was only as a result of the reforms of Peter the Great that the West (Sweden and the Netherlands, France and Germany, England and the United States) became an integral and the most essential ingredient of Russian identity. Peter the Great's reforms were aimed at making Russia a European state. The tsar sent his subjects to study in Europe and made them wear Western dress. Literate Russians got access to books published in Europe to a greater extent than ever before. On the surface, Peter's efforts gave quick results. The Russian elites were Westernized, if only superficially, and for the supporters of Peter's reforms Russia's European identity became axiomatic. The West, which in Peter's time meant particularly the countries of Northern Europe, became a model to be emulated. One of 'Peter's men', Andrei Matveev, described his visit to Paris in 1705 thus: 'It should be mentioned with ineffable astonishment that (I) could not find a single person either male or female of noble family, who would not be honestly educated and taught.'[4] In the first half of the eighteenth century it was clear that Russia was different, that it was not up to that standard. Nonetheless, the hope persisted that it would catch up with more advanced parts of Europe, and that it would do so fairly soon. Peter's success in making Russia accepted by major European states as a new European power after the tsar's victory over the Swedish King Charles XII gave grounds for this initial optimism. Peter made Russia 'join the community of political people' (i.e. Europeans), argued the State Chancellor, Count Gavrila Golovkin, in 1721.

The idea that Russia had been a European nation from at least the seventeenth century, and that Peter simply helped it on the path of its 'natural' development, was repeated on a number of occasions by Catherine the Great. In 1790, she emphasized that Russians were such good students in 'the school of Europe' that they had over-fulfilled all Peter's expectations.[5] This view persisted, and Aleksandr Pushkin immortalized it in the crisp statement – 'he [Peter] did not despise his country, he knew its destiny.'

But at the same time as Catherine the Great was making her optimistic boasts, many educated Russians, the only ones for whom the question of Russia's relations with Europe had any relevance, began to have doubts about Peter's legacy. His Westernization was aimed at and affected largely the upper classes of Russian society. Russian peasants and merchants continued to live in the traditional way. Moreover, among some, especially the Old Believers, there was strong opposition to Westernization; and the government persecuted its opponents. But the plight of the Westernized elite was not easy either. They began to feel alienated from their own country. This alienation was exacerbated by the fact that Peter's reforms had strengthened some of its more archaic elements, such as serfdom. The result was a feeling of rejection of Russia which, with time, acquired greater and greater passion. In 1763, Aleksandr Sumarokov wrote a poem 'A Choir to the Upside-down World,' which described an utopian overseas country. In fact, the poem reflected the author's perception of Western Europe. There 'governors are honest,' there 'they do not sell people (i.e. peasants)' or 'lose villages in card games', there 'minds are not drowned in hard drinking', 'all the noble children go to school there ... even maidens overseas must have learning,' and there 'merchants are not deceivers.'[6] But all these good things from 'Overseas' were absent in Russia, the poem made clear. This alienation from Russia made the need to identify with the West particularly strong. Yet identification with the West proved difficult, if not impossible. The problem

---

[4] A. Alferov and A. Gruzinskii, eds, *Russkaia literatura XVIII: Khrestomatia* (Moscow, Shkola, 1915), p. 37.

[5] Quoted by E. Shmurlo, *Peter Velikii v otsenke sovremennikov i potomstva* (St. Petersburg, V.S. Balashev, 1912), p. 69.

[6] A.P. Sumarokov, *Izbrannye proizvedeniia* (Moscow–Leningrad, Sovetskii pisatel, 1957), p. 40.

was that Russians did not feel fully at home in the West either. The historian Vasilii Kliuchevskii described these Russians, the product of Peter's reforms, thus: 'In Europe they were viewed as dressed up Tatars, and in the eyes of their own fellow countrymen they were Frenchmen who happened to be born in Russia.'[7] Even more importantly, for people like Sumarokov the West was an imagined ideal. And it is often not long before people turn against the object they have idealized. It is impossible to sustain for long feelings of scorn and rejection for something as close as one's own homeland.

In the 1770s, comedies began to be written making fun of Russian nobles who rejected everything Russian, while claiming they felt more French. This ridicule of those Russians who imitated foreign customs went hand in hand with the first attempts to question the view that the West provided an ideal model. The first person to articulate these new feelings was the playwright, Denis Fonvisin. He castigated the Gallomania of Russian aristocrats and simultaneously bitterly criticized France itself. In his *Letters from France*, written in the 1770s, he concluded that 'there is not much good and worth imitating here.' So 'if anybody among my young fellow countrymen, who has good brain, will begin to feel alienated from Russia, because of its corruption, there is no better way of returning him to the love of his fatherland than by sending him to France.' According to Fonvizin, 'comparing our peasant ... with theirs, I can say objectively that ours are much happier.' The French mocked others, without realizing 'how ridiculous' they were themselves: 'the corruption of mores has reached such a state that the noblest people are not ashamed to sit openly with the prostitutes in theatres.' 'A Frenchman has no reason, and to have one would have been seen as a great misfortune, as it would have forced him to think, when he could have had fun.' In sum, 'Paris has only one advantage over other places. Its appearance is grander, whereas its essence is far more revolting.'[8]

It is not surprising that Fonvizin was the first Russian intellectual to argue that the fact that Russia had been late to join Europe was an advantage. 'Because they began to live before us,' he insisted, 'we ... can give ourselves whatever form we please and avoid the shortcomings and evils, which are rooted here ... I think that the one who is just being born is happier than the one who is about to die.'[9] This idea was to dominate Russian intellectual debate in the next century. Although Fonvizin came from a Baltic German family, Pushkin clearly had good reason to call him 'the most Russian of all ultra-Russians' (*iz pererusskikh russkii*).

7   V.O. Kliuchevskii, *Sochineniia v deviati tomakh*, vol. 5 (Moscow, Mysl, 1989), p. 167.

8   D.Fonvizin, 'Pisma iz Frantsii,' in Makagonenko, ed., *Russkaia literatura XVIII veka* (Leningrad, Prosveshchenie, 1970), pp. 338–48. Fonvizin had not intended his letters to be published. They first appeared in print in the nineteenth century.

9   Quoted by E.H. Carr, '"Russia and Europe" as a Theme of Russian History' in Richard Pares and A.J.P. Taylor, eds., *Essays presented to Sir Lewis Namier* (London, Macmillan, 1956), p. 370.

As the idealized vision of the West was being destroyed, an idealized image of Russia was being constructed. Its foundations were laid by the historian and writer Nikolai Karamzin. In the late eighteenth century, Karamzin was still optimistic about Russia's ability to catch up with the West. He was, therefore, unequivocally supportive of Peter's reforms which Europeanized Russia. In his *Letters of a Russian Traveller* (1790s), Karamzin argued:

> Germans, Frenchmen, Englishmen were ahead of the Russians by at least six centuries; Peter moved us with his powerful hand, and we almost caught up with them in several years. All the pitiful complaints about the alteration of the Russian character, about the loss of Russian moral face either are nothing but a joke or derive from the lack of thorough thinking.[10]

But this was the period when Karamzin was not thinking nationally. Speaking as a typical cosmopolitan of the eighteenth century Enlightenment he exclaimed: 'Everything national is nothing in comparison with the human. The main thing is to be humans, not Slavs. What is good for humans cannot be bad for the Russians, and what Englishmen or Germans invented for the good and benefit of mankind is mine, for I am human!'

But the wave of nationalism unleashed by the French revolution swept over Europe and Russia. In the first decade of the nineteenth century, the cosmopolitan Karamzin began to feel more as a nationalist, and his attitude towards Russia and Europe changed dramatically. The first signs of change were noticeable in 1802, when he began to argue that the Russians should be more overtly proud of their own achievements and concluded: 'The one who does not respect himself, undoubtedly would not be respected by others ... I am not saying that the love for the fatherland should blind us and make us argue that we are better than everybody else in every respect; but a Russian, at least, should know how much he is worth.'[11]

By 1810, Karamzin's position had sharpened further. In his *Memoirs on Ancient and Modern Russia,* his view of Peter the Great, Russia and the West had become the opposite of what it had been two decades earlier: 'Once upon a time we used to call all other Europeans infidels, now we call them brothers. For whom was it easier to conquer Russia – for infidels or for brothers? That is, whom was she likely to resist better? ... We became citizens of the world but ceased to some extent to be citizens of Russia. Peter is at fault.'[12]

---

[10] N. Karamzin, *Pisma russkogo puteshestvennika* (Moscow, Sovetskaia Rossiia, 1983), p. 323.

[11] N.M. Karamzin, 'O liubvi k otechestvu i narodnoi gordosti,' in *Sochineniia v dvukh tomakh*, vol. 2 (Leningrad, Khudozhestvennaia literatura, 1984), p. 226.

[12] N.M. Karamzin, *Zapiska o drevnei i novoi Rossii v ee politicheskom i grazhdanskom otnoshenii* (Moscow, Prosveshchenie, 1991), pp. 32–3.

Karamzin went on to conclude that Western political institutions were unsuitable for Russia; monarchy was the ideal political system for his country and serfdom was justified, as the peasants were not ready for freedom. He rejected constitutional monarchy on the grounds that a tsar or king and constitutions were, in fact, incompatible – 'like two lions in one cage.' These were the first signs of nationalism, as Karamzin drew political conclusions from his comparison between Russia and the West.

Prologue to the Slavophiles–Westernizers debate

Not all Russian intellectuals accepted Karamzin's argument about Russia's *Sonderweg*. At the same time that nationalism in Europe was emerging during the Napoleonic wars, many Russians obtained an opportunity to see the real Europe, as the victorious Russian army marched into Germany in 1813 and into France the next year. Young Russian army officers returned to their homeland with the hope that Russia 'will be reformed, that it will have a system of government similar to those, which are found in Europe ...'[13] Indeed, the period of 1809–1812 was when tsar Aleksandr I seriously considered a series of constitutional reforms, proposed by the leading reformer in his government, Mikhail Speranskii (1772–1839). In 1809, Speranskii also facilitated the adoption of the Education Act, which stipulated that the education system was to be extended down to the village level. However, this idea, like most other provisions of the act, was not implemented. Speranskii's proposals for reforming Russia's political and educational system were based on French and English models. This was the main reason for Speranskii's dismissal and punishment by exile in 1812. His reforms encountered strong opposition from the nobility and proved to be too radical for the tsar himself.

But Speranskii's downfall did not yet signify the end of the liberal phase of Aleksander's reign. Until the end of the second decade of the century, some young Russians hoped the government might still live up to their expectations. Up to that time, the tsar continued to consider a constitutional option for Russia. In December 1815, he granted a constitution to Poland which vested legislative powers with the parliament, the Sejm. Opening the Sejm in 1818, Aleksander said that 'free institutions ... are fully compatible with public order and assure true well being of the people.' He promised to extend these 'free institutions' 'to all the lands which are under my jurisdiction.' In 1816–19, the serfs were emancipated in the Baltic region. Meanwhile, a civil society was emerging in Russia proper. In the

---

[13] P.Ia. Chaadaev, *Sochineniia i pisma pod redaktsiei M.O. Gershenzona*, vol. 2 (Moscow, Tipografiia A.I. Mamontova, 1914), p. 302.

first two decades of the nineteenth century various private groups and societies were founded to pursue cultural, philanthropic and educational goals. Describing the atmosphere of the time, the future Decembrist G.S. Batenkov observed: 'In our [country] it is not only the plight of under-ground groups to discuss political and social systems of different states; [such discussions] are an open part of life and in big cities they occur almost daily in public places among the nobility as well as merchants.'[14]

But the uprisings in Italy and Spain, and soldiers' mutinies in Russia itself put an end to the Russian government's liberal tendencies. It categorically refused to grant civil society any active role. In 1816 some Russian officers, feeling that they had returned from constitutionalist Europe to a Russia of absolutism and serfdom, set up an organization aimed at changing Russia's political institutions. Their goal was to put Russia on a par with the advanced countries of Western Europe. Up until 1820, the Union for the Salvation of Loyal and True Sons of the Fatherland existed almost openly and united up to 200 Petersburg officers. In 1821–22, the Union split into two groups, the Northern and Southern Societies, which became under-ground revolutionary organizations. The Northern Society's goal was to establish a constitutional monarchy in Russia, with a representative parlia-ment and a federal structure, similar to that of the United States. The leader of the Southern Society, Pavel Pestel, saw 'the best outcome for Russia in the creation of a republic.' Serfdom, as 'a state alien to natural laws and the Christian faith,' was to be abolished immediately. The officers attempted to force the new tsar, who was to take the oath on 14 December 1825, to accept their programme. Following the failure of this attempt, one hundred and twenty officers were tried, five of them were executed and others exiled to Siberia. This bitter experience at the very beginning of his reign probably contributed to tsar Nicholas I's concern to try to eradicate any influences of Western constitutionalism and liberalism upon Russia. Even the teaching of European philosophy was temporarily banned in Russian universities.

For many educated Russians, the failure of the Decembrist uprising, as the events of December 1825 started to be known, symbolized Russia's inability to make the transition from absolutism and serfdom to constitu-tionalism and civil liberties as France and other West European states had done. It also posed the question of Russia's relationship with Europe with unprecedented acuteness, strengthening the position of those who already doubted the similarity between the two.

Even some government officials felt the need to respond to the unresolved question of Russian identity. In 1832, the President of the Imperial

---

[14] Quoted in A.V. Semenova, 'Idei prosveshcheniia i tretie soslovie v Rossii,' *Mirovospriiatie i samosoznanie russkogo obshchestva (XI–XX vv.)* (Moscow, Rossiiskaia Akademiia Nauk, Institut Rossiiskoi Istorii, 1994), p. 134.

Academy of Sciences and the future Minister of Education, Count Sergei
Uvarov, came up with what became known as the theory of official
nationality.[15] Uvarov argued that the three main pillars of Russia's existence
were Orthodoxy (*pravoslavie*), autocracy (*samoderzhavie*) and nationality
(*narodnost*). Orthodoxy meant adherence to the teaching and rituals of the
Russian Orthodox Church, which Uvarov believed united all Russians and
also helped consolidate St. Petersburg's control over the empire's non-
Russian borderlands. The emphasis on Orthodoxy was also a reaction to
and a rejection of the religious scepticism of eighteenth-century Russian
intellectuals, whose world view had been shaped by the secular ideas of the
European Enlightenment. Autocracy, which Karamzin twenty years earlier
had reaffirmed was the most suitable form of government for Russia, signified that the constitutional experiments of the reigns of Catherine II and
Aleksandr I were at an end. Nationality, the least clear of all, seemed to
refer to the national character, the unspoiled wisdom of ordinary people
and devotion to the Russian heritage (probably pre-Petrine) which had
distinguished Russia from Western Europe. According to ideologists of
official nationality, one of the main virtues of the Russian national
character was humility (*smirenie*), best manifested in the people's voluntary
acceptance of the unlimited powers of the tsar. The use of the term
nationality to mean 'national character' was introduced by Prince Petr
Viazemsky in 1819. Neither then nor in 1832 did it mean a civic nation or
popular sovereignty in the Western electoral sense. Moreover, the inclusion
of autocracy in the triad showed that Uvarov did not think that the Russian
nation had an autonomous existence apart from the state. Indeed, the pro-
ponents of official nationality had a pessimistic view about human nature in
general, and about the qualities of the subjects of the Russian empire in
particular. They believed that people 'were feeble and perverse, they had to
be driven by a benevolent supreme authority in order to achieve desirable
social ends.'[16] As far as the Russians were concerned, one of the best known
ideologists of this state creed, the historian Mikhail Pogodin, described
them thus: 'The Russian people is marvellous, but marvellous so far only in
potential. In actuality, it is low, horrid, and beastly.'[17] This meant that
spreading secular education among such people was dangerous, as they
might misuse it to destabilize the country.

The reference to 'nationality' indicated a response by official Russia to
the ideas of nationalism, which was becoming an important ideological and
political force in Europe. Moreover, nationalism was already present in the
Russian empire itself, as reflected in the activities of the Decembrists and

---

[15] The expression was coined in the 1870s by the historian Aleksandr Pypin.
[16] Nicholas V. Riasanovsky, *Nicholas I and Official Nationality in Russia, 1825–1855*
      (Berkeley CA, University of California Press, 1959), p. 99.
[17] Ibid, p. 99.

the 1830 Polish uprising. The latter, among other things, emphasized that the Poles regarded themselves as a fully formed nation. Thus, Uvarov's 'triad' was an attempt to find an ideological justification for the preservation in Russia of the *ancien régime* of the old Europe, at a time when ideas of democratic and nationalist change had begun to penetrate the Romanov empire.

The ideologists of official nationality believed that Uvarov's triad captured the essence of Russia's social and political life. In reality, however, Uvarov's formula found little response in society at large. The idea that the state and society were one was rejected not only by many intellectuals,[18] but also by the common people. Although Russian peasants demonstrated loyalty to the tsar personally at least until the late nineteenth century, the autocratic state in general was traditionally seen as an enemy. Russian folklore contrasted the state (*Rossiia*) and the Russian (*russkie*) people. The antagonism between the two was articulated clearly in a nineteenth century peasants' song, which included the following passage:

The Mother Russian (*rossiiskaia*) land
Has spilled a lot of blood (of its people)
The land of Holy Rus (*sviatorusskaia zemlia*)
was subjected to a lot of grief[19]

Following a folk tradition which dated back at least to the seventeenth century, in this verse Russian land (*rossiiskaia zemlia*) – i.e. the state – emerged as a persecutor of the land of Holy Rus (*sviatorusskaia zemlia*) – the symbol of the suffering people.[20] Scholars have noted that attempts to implement the doctrine of official nationality only served to widen 'the gulf between the ideology of the Government and that of the people.'[21] During the reign of Nicholas I, there was a crackdown on Old Believers and other sectarians, aimed at strengthening the Russian Orthodox Church. It had the opposite effect to the one intended by the government; it led to an increase in the numbers of sectarians and made them even more hostile towards the state.

---

[18] Of the most famous Russian poets and writers only Zhukovskii and Gogol, in the later period of his life, supported the doctrine of official nationality. The interpretation of Pushkin's *The Bronze Horseman* as a reflection of the poet's sympathy with the doctrine seems questionable and is shared only by the minority of scholars.

[19] Quoted in M.M. Gromyko, *Mir russkoi derevni* (Moscow, Molodaia gvardiia, 1991), p. 229.

[20] This profoundly anti-state concept of Holy Rus, which was first articulated in Russian folk culture of the seventeenth century, became commonplace in nineteenth century literature. It was especially popular among the Slavophiles. See Michael Cherniavsky, 'Holy Russia,' *The American Historical Review*, vol. LXIII, no. 3 (April 1958), pp. 617–37.

[21] A. Kornilov, *Modern Russian History from the Age of Catherine the Great to the End of the Nineteenth Century*, vol. 1 (New York N.Y., 1943), p. 298 quoted in Riasanovsky, *Nicholas I and Official Nationality*, p. 225.

The intelligentsia was also shaken by the failure of the Decembrists. In the aftermath of the uprising, one intellectual came to such a sharp and devastating conclusion about Russia that throughout the nineteenth century most of the Russian intelligentsia felt the need to test its contentions. This one intellectual was Peter Chaadaev, a nobleman educated at Moscow University. As a cavalry officer, he had taken part in the campaign against Napoleon. He joined the Decembrist organizations, but was abroad at the time of the uprising. In 1818, i.e. well before Chaadaev had expressed his controversial ideas, Pushkin thus described him:

> By God's will, he was born
> Into the chains of tsarist service
> In Rome, he would have been Brutus,
> In Athens Pericles,
> But here he is a cavalry officer.

But Pushkin was mistaken in thinking that in a country like Russia Chaadaev was bound to waste his life. In fact, Chaadaev left a lasting impact on Russia. In 1829 he wrote (characteristically in French) *Philosophical Letters*. The first of these was published in 1836 in the liberal periodical, *Teleskop*. Described by the writer and thinker Aleksandr Herzen as 'a shot in the dark night' because of its impact on Russian intellectual thinking, the letter asserted that

> Being alone in the world we have given nothing to the world, taken nothing from the world, bestowed not even a single idea upon the fund of human ideas, we have contributed nothing to the progress of human reason, and everything we have inherited from this progress we have distorted ... we accepted only a deceiving appearance and useless luxury.[22]

Chaadaev concluded that 'we do not belong to either the West or the East, as we do not have the tradition of either.' Despite the admission that the East had its own culture, Chaadaev's world view was purely Eurocentric, as only Europe had a historic future. 'Do you think that the order of things ... which is the ultimate destiny of mankind can be achieved by an Abyssinian Christianity or Japanese culture?' he inquired. Indeed, the fact that the Russians were Christian did not make them European. For Chaadaev, Europe was Catholic and it was Catholicism that gave Europe the culture and intellectual discipline to make all its achievements. The fact that the Russians had taken Christianity from Byzantium cut them off from Europe and was the main reason for the failure of Russia's 'unique civilization.'

---

[22] Quoted in E.B. Rashkovskii and V.G. Khoros, 'Problema "Zapad-Rossiia-Vostok" v filosofskom nasledii P. Ia. Chaadaeva,' in *Vostok-Zapad* (Moscow, Nauka, 1988), p. 115.

This was the first time that a Russian intellectual had so unequivocally rejected the idea that Russia belonged to Europe.

More importantly, Chaadaev offered no solution or way to escape that dead end. Nobody in Russia could digest such a bitter pill, not even Chaadaev himself. The journal in which the letter had been published was closed down, and the chief editor sent into internal exile. Chaadaev was officially declared insane and put under medical care. It is often believed that solely under these pressures, in 1837, Chaadaev wrote the *Apology of a Madman*, which rejected some of the ideas of the *Letters* and expressed some optimism about Russia's future. The *Apology* argued that if Russia were to recognize the futility of its attempts to follow a unique path and learned from Europe instead, it might succeed. (The *Letters*, in contrast, had doubted even Russia's ability to learn, had it so wished.) Moreover, the very absence of a strong tradition might enable Russia to move faster than Europe along the same road, Chaadaev argued in his *Apology*.

There is evidence to suggest that this sharp turn in Chaadaev's thinking was not only the result of external pressures, but also of his own internal need to dispel such total pessimism. Even before the publication of the *Philosophical Letter* and his subsequent persecution, in a letter written to A.I. Turgenev in 1835, Chaadaev expressed views similar to those of the *Apology*. He repeated the verdict of the *Letters* that the Russians have not 'discovered, invented, created' anything and said that the Russians should fully acknowledge this fact. They would then be able to follow the Western path 'quicker than the others, because we entered it later, because we have got all their experience and (can make use of) their centuries-old work.'[23] This idea that Russia's backwardness was in fact a strength, because it meant that Russia's glory lay in the future, had first been articulated by Fonvisin in the previous century. From this time on, it became the essence of Russian nationalism and the main angle from which Russia's relationship with the West was assessed.

The Slavophiles

Other groups of intellectuals often drew conclusions about Russia's situation which were diametrically opposed to Chaadaev's assessment. In the words of the literary critic, Appolon Grigorev, Chaadaev's *Letter* was like a 'duel glove'. It rapidly divided the Russian intelligentsia into two camps, which became known as the Slavophiles and the Westernizers.

In response to Chaadaev's challenge, those who became known as the Slavophiles began to invent the indigenous Russian tradition, which, Chaadaev had claimed, Russia did not possess. They were influenced in this

---

[23] Ibid, p. 116.

endeavour by German Romantic nationalism, which defined nations as culturally and linguistically unique entities. Their opponents, the Westernizers, dwelled on how Russia could follow the West. Since they agreed that Russia had the advantage of being able to pick and choose the best aspects, their debates concerned which part of the Western heritage was to be taken on board.

The early Slavophiles, Aleksei Khomiakov, the brothers Ivan and Petr Kireevskii and Ivan and Konstantin Aksakov, and Iurii Samarin, all came from noble families. They had grown up on their provincial estates, where they could obtain first-hand knowledge of the life of the peasantry, i.e. their serfs. In their youth most of them, with the notable exception of Khomiakov, shared the hopes of the Decembrists and saw Russia's future development as solely European. In 1832, Ivan Kireevskii began the publication of the journal *European*, which was closed down within a year after Kireevskii's article 'The Nineteenth Century' received the following assessment from the Minister of Education, Prince Lieven:

> The author pretends to talk about literature, but has something else in mind: under the word 'enlightenment' he means freedom, under 'the activities of the mind' he means revolution, and under 'a well chosen middle path' he means nothing but a constitution.[24]

But in response to Chaadaev, the Slavophiles began their search for a unique element in Russian history and culture. They were influenced by Friedrich Schelling's argument that each nation could be defined by its own unique element which it should try to develop. Their views crystallized during 'the remarkable decade' of 1838–1848.[25] Not all the views expressed by the Slavophiles in the 1840s were novel. One can find similar ideas in the writings of intellectuals from the 1820s and earlier. Yet it is to the Slavophile writings of the 1840s that subsequent Russian nationalists would continue to refer thereafter.

First of all the Slavophiles rejected the idea that Russia needed to transplant Western institutions onto Russian soil. Instead, they favoured strengthening the indigenous Russian tradition. What was that tradition? In order to answer this question they turned to pre-Petrine, especially seventeenth century, Muscovy, and argued that its institutions were superior to those of the West. During their university years and later, Slavophiles conducted research into Russia's pre-Petrine history. They were particularly interested in medieval chronicles. However, their approach to the sources was highly biased. They looked for and indeed constructed an idealized

---

[24] N.L. Brodskii, compiler, *Rannie slavianofily* (Moscow, Tipografiia Sytina, 1910), p. XIX.

[25] The expression 'a remarkable decade' was used as the title of an essay on the Slavophiles and the Westernizers by their contemporary, literary critic Pavel Annenkov. It was then used as the title of an article by Sir Isaiah Berlin about these Russian thinkers.

image of old Russia. This image had no meaning on its own. It was essentially a comparison with the West and an answer to Chaadaev's criticism. They identified what they thought were peculiar features of the Western world, as hailed by Chaadaev, and then looked for the traditions in Russia which they thought were different and which they proclaimed to be superior. The best summary of this juxtaposition between Russia and the West can be found in Ivan Kireevskii's *On the Character of European Enlightenment and its Relation with the Enlightenment of Russia*. In this work the author identified the three main elements of Western civilization: "Roman-Catholic Church, old Roman culture and statehood which emerged out of violence' and stated that'[a]ll those were alien to Russia.'[26] Whereas Chaadaev had identified Orthodox Christianity as the main source of Russian misfortunes, the Slavophiles saw in it the main source of Russia's strength. As another Slavophile, Khomiakov, explained: 'the feeling of the true brotherhood is preserved only in Orthodoxy ... Therefore the unity between members of a community, where each member accepts the will of the brotherhood, has survived only in Orthodox countries.'[27] The Slavophiles favourably contrasted the spirit of brotherhood or collectivity (*sobornost*) with the individualism of the West. Religious identity was so important that Khomiakov even argued that 'one could not be a Slav outside the framework of Orthodoxy.' Catholic Poland rejected the idea of the Orthodox brotherhood and that rejection, according to Khomiakov, 'led to the collapse of the Polish state.'[28] About the second element of Western civilization, Kireevskii argued that 'The Roman way of thinking amounts to superficial rationality, which takes precedence over (penetration) into internal essence of things ... In famous Roman laws the brilliance of external form is logically perfected, but they surprisingly lack any internal justice.'

Russia lacked a developed legal system, and was much better for it. Thirdly, he juxtaposed 'the militaristic struggle of knights in medieval Europe' to the 'harmonious, peaceful co-existence of communes in Russia.' Khomiakov fully shared the view that Russian life was essentially peaceful: 'We inherited cruelty only from the Tatars and the Germans. But soon there will be no trace of it.'[29] According to Kireevskii, even the situation of women was better in Russia. In the West, women 'substitute happiness and worries of a nursery by noisy pleasures of a party ... There, women are brought up outside the framework of families (for instance, in cloisters)' ... This was the source of 'the moral rotting of the upper classes ... and of the infamous idea of women's emancipation.' In Russia, he claimed, in the upper classes there was no such distance from ' the people's way of life' and

---

[26] All quotes from this source are from Brodskii, *Rannie slavianofily*, pp. 1–50.
[27] Quoted in Brodskii, *Rannie slavianofily*, p. 59.
[28] Ibid, pp. 60–1.
[29] Ibid, p. 61.

therefore 'the spirit of the family has not been destroyed.' (Here, Kireevskii departed from his eighteenth century predecessor, Prince Mikhail Shcherbatov, who was convinced that Peter's Westernization had made the morals of Russian upper-class women as corrupt as those of their French counterparts.)

Rejecting the 'cold, superficial reason' of the people in the West, Russians were able to learn a greater 'inner truth.' A key part of this truth was the understanding that any form of government was essentially evil. Therefore the search for a better form of government in the West was a mistake. Other Slavophiles expressed similar views. In a *Note on Russia's Internal Situation*, written by Konstantin Aksakov to the tsar Aleksandr II in 1855, the former argued that in the West '[t]he people, who have deviated from the path of internal faith and spirit, are tempted by the idea of popular government, believe in a possibility of a perfect government, create republics and various kinds of constitutions ... and at the same time impoverish their soul and lose their faith.'[30]

In contrast, 'Russian people are not state-minded people, they do not want to share in the government of the state, they do not seek political rights for themselves.' Hence, as Karamzin had earlier asserted, autocracy was the best form of government for the Russians. 'While not seeking political freedom, they seek moral freedom, freedom of spirit, freedom of internal public life.' Here the Slavophiles struck a liberal note and encouraged the government to abolish press censorship and allow full freedom of expression of public opinion, which would help the tsar to govern according to the people's wishes. (In response to these calls, the government often banned the Slavophiles' publications.) In order to ensure the government's accountability to the people, Aksakov proposed to reinstate the Councils of the Land, which had been abolished by Peter the Great. Up until the late seventeenth century, these Councils, which represented most social groups, had debated problems facing Russia and made recommendations, which the tsar could take on board or disregard as he pleased.

The desire to create a bi-polar opposition between everything Western and Russian meant that the Slavophiles frequently contradicted themselves. Kireevskii's insistence that in Russia, women of the upper classes were closer to the peasants than in the West contradicted the main assumption of the Slavophiles about an irreconcilable gap between Russia's upper classes and ordinary people.

From the late 1860s onwards, the followers of the early Slavophiles, most notably the Pan-Slavist Nikolai Danilevskii and the writer Konstantin Leontev, sharpened the juxtaposition between Russia and the West. This was the period in which Russian public opinion became radicalized in the wake of the 1863 Polish uprising and the 1877–78 war against Turkey.

---

[30] Ibid., p. 80.

Unlike the early Slavophiles, their successors did not expect Russia to save Europe from its 'illnesses.' Instead, they felt that the liberal West European countries were the eternal enemies of Russia. In his book *Russia and Europe*, first published in 1869, Danilevskii spoke about the perennial Russophobia of the West. This stemmed from the incompatibility between the Roman-German and Slavic cultural-historical types and had little to do with the actual policies of the Russian government. Konstantin Leontev argued that Russia should not wait for the West to 'turn against it,' but that 'the destruction of the Western civilization' would strengthen Russia's 'Byzantine roots.'[31]

The Russian nation: the peasantry versus Westernized elites

The Slavophiles' emphasis on juxtaposing Russia and the West influenced their definition of the Russian nation. As mentioned in the previous chapter, in the late eighteenth century liberal journals began to use the word '*narod*' to mean all the people of the Russian state regardless of their social origin. This made it the closest Russian approximation to the word 'nation', in the inclusive sense, formulated in the course of the French Revolution. But through the efforts of the Slavophiles this definition of the 'narod' was challenged.

Under the influence of the ideas of German Romantics about the true *Volk*, close to the land and therefore a bearer of indigenous traditions, the Slavophiles began to view the Russian peasantry as the preserver of Russian 'national spirit' and uniqueness. But the Slavophiles went further than their German predecessors. The glorification of 'people close to the land' in the German tradition did not lead to the exclusion of educated Germans from the nation. In the Russian Slavophile tradition it did. The Slavophiles imagined the peasantry to be the only group of society entitled to be regarded as the *narod*, as the peasants had not been corrupted by the Westernization of Russia. Instead, Russian peasant communes already embodied in reality the ideal towards which Europe was still striving.The Westernized cultural and political elites, however, were to be excluded from the *narod*. Instead, they were termed 'the public' (*obshchestvennost*). The two groups had little in common. As Konstantin Aksakov put it: 'The public is a purely Western phenomenon ... The public speaks French, the *narod* speak Russian. The public follows Paris fashions, the people have

---

[31] Quoted in A. Ianov, 'Slavianofily i vneshniaia politika Rossiii v XIX veke,' *Polis*, no. 6 (1998), p. 160. One of the very few early Slavophiles who lived long enough to witness the upsurge of nationalism in Russia in the 1860s–1880s was Ivan Aksakov. His anti-Western views also sharpened in that period.

their Russian customs ... The public is only 150 years old; you cannot count the age of the people.'[32]

This view of the peasantry as the main symbol of a Russian nation with qualities distinctively different from Western values, and the resulting exclusion of the 'Westernized' upper classes from membership of the Russian nation had a tremendous impact on Russian public opinion. It was quickly appropriated by some of those Westernizers, who, like the writer and thinker Aleksandr Herzen, turned to socialism. Discussing how the Slavophiles and the Westernizers defined Russian national identity, Herzen observed in his autobiography, *My Past and Thoughts*:

> From a very early age, we shared one irrational, physiological, passionate feeling ... the feeling of boundless, all-embracing love for the Russian people, Russian way of life, Russian frame of mind ... All their [the Slavophiles'] love was focused [from the start] on the enslaved mother ... We [Westernizers] had been in the hands of a French governess, and only later found that she was not our mother, but that an exhausted peasant woman was.'[33]

By equating the Russian nation with the peasantry Herzen and his followers, in effect, rejected the definition of a nation articulated in the wake of the French revolution. They stood the argument of the French nation-builders of the time on its head. Indeed, in the French discourse about the nation of the second half of the nineteenth century, to be fully French was not to be a peasant, while to be a peasant was to be not fully French. The French nation-builders therefore saw it as their task to turn peasants into Frenchmen.[34] In contrast, in Russia from the mid-nineteenth century onwards, in the national discourse of intellectuals to be fully Russian was to be a peasant.

This notion of the peasantry as the symbol of the Russian nation was also popularized by numerous Russian writers, poets, artists and musicians, whether or not they agreed with other aspects of Slavophile doctrine. Starting with Aleksandr Radishchev's *Travelling from Petersburg to Moscow* (1789), the peasant became an important hero of Russian literature. We find images of peasants in Pushkin's poetry and prose. Pushkin's peasant serf nanny symbolized for the poet his own close link to his indigenous Russian roots. But it was only from the 1840s onwards that the 'little man', especially the peasant, became the main heroic type of Russian literature. James Billington has argued that the publication in 1846 of Dmitrii Grigorovich's *The Village* and the first of Ivan Turgenev's *A*

---

[32] Quoted by Carr, '"Russia and Europe"...', p. 374.

[33] A.I. Gerzen, *Byloe i dumy*, parts 4–5 (Moscow, Pravda, 1983), p. 161.

[34] James R. Lehning, *Peasant and French: Cultural Contact in Rural France During the Nineteenth Century* (Cambridge, Cambridge University Press, 1995). See also, Eugen Weber, *Peasants into Frenchmen: The Modernization of Rural France, 1870–1914* (Stanford CA, Stanford University Press, 1976).

Huntsman's Sketches signified the turning point.[35] The three most famous Russian novelists, who constructed an image of Russia for Russians and foreigners alike, Nikolai Gogol, Fedor Dostoevskii and Lev Tolstoi, painted powerful pictures of members of the *narod* wronged and persecuted by the Westernized elites. For all these writers, peasants helped members of the upper classes to find moral redemption. Moreover, the Russian peasantry symbolized not only Russia's difference from, but also superiority over the West. In Tolstoi's *War and Peace*, Pierre Bezukhov's attitude towards life was completely transformed by his meeting with a peasant, Platon Karataev. Like the peasants depicted by the Slavophiles, Karataev was an embodiment of Russia's collective spirit as 'his life, as he looked at it, held no meaning as a separate entity. It had meaning only as part of the whole of which he was at all times conscious ... He could understand neither the value nor the significance of a man's individually-taken action.'[36]

Dostoevskii put forward the idea that the Russian people were the God-bearing people (*narod-bogonosets*), as they possessed a unique consciousness of the reconciling qualities of Christianity. Dostoevskii also contrasted these ordinary people, many of whom had a well of inner goodness, to the Westernized intelligentsia, whose ideas, he feared, would bring nothing but trouble to Russia. He observed: 'Our poor, troubled land, with the exception of the upper classes, is united into a single person. All 80 million people manifest such a spiritual unity, which, of course, does not and cannot exist in Europe...'[37] Moreover, a Russian peasant was wiser and more moral than his West European counterpart, even though, on the surface, he often did not appear so. At the same time, Dostoevskii condemned the upper classes for losing all direct knowledge of Russia, and asserted that intellectuals wanted 'to study Russia as one studies a scientific subject.'[38]

The idealization of the *narod* reached its peak in populist art of the late 1860s–1890s. The most succinct image of the Russian national character, as represented by members of the lower classes of society, and its difference from the West European character was given by Nikolai Leskov in his short story *The Left-Handed*, written in 1881. Leskov agreed with the review of his story in the periodical *Novoe Vremia*, which stated that for 'the left-handed' one should read 'the Russian people'. The story depicted Russian government officials as completely uninterested in Russian affairs and

---

[35] James H. Billington, *The Icon and the Axe* (London, Weidenfeld and Nicolson: 1966), p. 374.

[36] L.N. Tolstoy, *War and Peace,* vol. 2, book 4, part 1(Harmondsworth, Penguin Books, 1972), p. 1153.

[37] F.M. Dostoevskii, 'Obiasnitelnoe slovo po povodu pechataemoi nizhe rechi o Pushkine,' in *Russkaia Ideia* (Moscow, Respublika, 1992), p. 132.

[38] Quoted in K. Kasianova, *O russkom natsionalnom kharaktere* (Moscow, Institut Nationalnoi Modeli Ekonomiki, 1994), p. 53.

mistrustful of the abilities of the Russian people. Even the tsar did not anticipate that the Russians could ever match the technological level of the English. However, the tsar was wrong and a group of craftsmen from the Russian town of Tula, traditionally known for its brilliant craftsmanship, were able to demonstrate their superiority over the English: they managed to make horse-shoes for a tiny metal flea. This metal flea was a curiosity, presented by the English to the Russian tsar to demonstrate the skills of their people. The most talented of the Tula craftsmen, who far surpassed the English, was a left-handed, one-eyed, extremely modest person. He refused the invitation of the English to stay in their country, although his life would have been much better there than in Russia. His main reason was that 'our Russian faith is the most correct one.' Upon his return to Russia, the left-handed man died from the brutal treatment he received at the hands of the Russian police. Leskov contrasted this treatment with the careful way the English authorities treated their people. Moreover, none of the Russian officials bothered to pass on to the tsar an important 'military secret,' which the left-handed man had managed to learn in England and which would have helped Russia to win the Crimean war (1853–56). As it was, Russia lost the war, and the defeat forced the government to initiate reforms. In this story, Leskov used the techniques of the popular literature of his time. Stories in which ordinary, uneducated Russians earned admiration of West Europeans by showing their talent and wit were often featured in cheap newspaper serials (the kopeck serials).[39]

Music and painting also explored the theme of the *narod* in the Slavophile sense. The main character of the first Russian national opera, Mikhail Glinka's 'A Life for the Tsar,' which was first performed in December 1836, was the peasant Ivan Susanin. According to the folk tale on which the opera was based, during the Time of Troubles in 1612 or 1613, Susanin sacrificed his own life to save the future tsar Mikhail Romanov by leading astray a group of marauding Poles who were hunting him. In Glinka's period the emerging Slavophile symbol of Russianness was the peasant loyal to the tsar. In turn, in the early 1870s, Modest Musorgskii's opera 'Boris Godunov,' devoted to the period preceding the Time of Troubles, featured a *narod* that had lost confidence in the tsar. In both cases the antagonists were the Poles, whose evil nature was particularly emphasized by Musorgskii. After the Polish lands had been incorporated into the Russian empire through the three partitions of the late eighteenth century, Poland became Russia's internal 'West'. In this capacity Poland challenged the perceptions that Russian intellectuals had concerning

---

[39] Jeffrey Brooks, *When Russia Learned to Read. Literacy and Popular Literature, 1861–1917* (Princeton N.J., Princeton University Press, 1985), p. 236. See also S.V. Obolenskaia, 'Obraz nemtsa v russkoi narodnoi kulture XVIII–XIX vv.,' *Odissei. Chelovek v istorii* (Moscow, Nauka, 1989), pp. 178, 181.

their country. In the words of the literary critic, Appolon Grigorev, 'the Polish question more than any other requires the mobilization of all our internal resources ... and development of our unique qualities,' as it 'emphasizes our difference with Europe.'[40]

In the 1820s, Aleksei Venetsianov became the first Russian painter to make scenes of peasant life the focus of his sentimental, idealized paintings. A more multi-dimensional treatment of peasants in art began in the late 1860s. At the same time, the main educational institution for artists in the country, the St. Petersburg Academy of Arts, began to award medals at graduation to those students who wanted to depict scenes from peasant life. Previously only scenes from the Bible or from ancient Greek and Roman histories would have been accepted. The art critic Vladimir Stasov thought that the first Russian painting to present a sophisticated treatment of the peasant theme rather than a 'sugary' idealization was Viacheslav Shvarts' 'The Tsar and His Court Are Going out to Pray during the time of Aleksei Mikhailovich' (1868). The painting dwelt on an already well-developed theme in Russian literature – Russia as a split nation, with an irreconcilable gap between the rich and the poor. The wealth of the members of the tsarist entourage, who dominated the front of the painting, was underscored by the poverty of the peasants, who looked like faint shadows in the background. Members of the tsarist court on horseback were depicted as if they were an army of foreign invaders. The painting could serve to illustrate the Marquis de Custine's description of the Russian ruling elite as 'captive heroes in a hostile land.'[41]

The group of painters, who called themselves the 'wanderers' because they travelled with their exhibitions around Russia, made ordinary people the main focus of their art. Probably the best ever portraits of Russian peasants were painted in the 1870s by the 'wanderer' Ivan Kramskoi (Figure 3.1). In her analysis of Kramskoi's portraits of peasants, Cathy A. Frierson has observed that they 'contain not a single trait of health or hardiness, of pleasure, or of virtue. It is very difficult to identify any positive features of humanity' in them. On the whole, she concluded that the 1861 emancipation of the serfs had destroyed the former romantic myth of the peasant. He 'had suddenly been transformed from the object of sympathy and advocacy as a young brother en route to Emancipation into an unfamiliar fellow citizen.' As a result, the peasant seemed 'further removed, more strange, more thoroughly "other" than he had been on the eve of the Emancipation.'[42] Frierson has arrived at these conclusions largely through

[40] Quoted in N.A. Rubakin, *Sredi knig*, 2nd ed., vol. 3, part 1 (Moscow, Knigoizdatelstvo Nauka, 1915), p. 155.

[41] Marquis de Custine, *Empire of the Czar. A Journey Through Eternal Russia* (New York N.Y., Anchor Books, 1989), p. 89.

[42] Cathy A. Frierson, *Peasant Icons. Representations of Rural People in Late Nineteenth Century Russia* (Oxford, Oxford University Press, 1993), pp. 24, 26 and 134.

Figure 3.1 Ivan Kramskoi, 'Mina Moiseev' (1889): portrait of a peasant. (The Russian Museum, St. Petersburg)

her painstaking analysis of the debate about the emancipated peasantry in the Russian press of the time, especially the economic journals. However, they cannot be justly applied to the Russian literature and art of the post-Emancipation period. The portraits of peasants as the embodiment of the Russian nation in the writings of Dostoevskii and Tolstoi in the post-Emancipation period had a more profound and lasting effect on the way the broader reading public viewed the *narod* than the debates in specialized journals. In particular, as far as Kramskoi's portraits of peasants are concerned, this author cannot agree with Frierson's interpretation. Despite their obvious poverty, his peasants seem to be full of dignity. There is nothing frightening in them; on the country, one can imagine that people with such faces could be easily accepted as fellow citizens by the upper classes of Russian society. In an indication of how the painter himself perceived the peasants, in his painting *Jesus Christ in the Desert* (1872), Kramskoi depicted Christ with a typical face of a Russian peasant.

Ilia Repin's painting 'Haulers on the Volga' (1870–73) (Figure 3.2) became an iconographic canon of the suffering Russian people, with a huge impact on other areas of Russian art. It is noteworthy that the initial version of the painting was completely gloomy. In the final version, Repin transformed the figure of a young hauler, who was now depicted with the high raised head, handsome face and bright eyes. (In the first version he was staring at his feet.) This completely changed the meaning of the painting: from being merely the victims of barbaric exploitation, the haulers began to symbolize the strength of the Russian people and their unwillingness to be defeated by hard labour. In developing the theme of the haulers, Repin was preceded by the poet Nikolai Nekrasov. The main theme of his poetry was the misery of the Russian people, and he condemned those responsible for it with satire. Nekrasov also made the Volga haulers a symbol of the Russian people and called a Russian peasant-woman 'the long-suffering mother of … the Russian tribe.'

It was these huge canvases by Repin that shaped the way the Russian public regarded the peasantry in the post-Emancipation era. His small sketches, like 'The Drunken Husband' (1888), on the other hand, presented the peasants less favourably. However, Dostoevskii had found a way to excuse the cruelty sometimes demonstrated by drunken peasants. The majority of the populist artists seem to have agreed with Dostoevskii's observation in his *Diary of a Writer* that a peasant's cruelty was not inherent within him, but rather was imposed from without and thus superficial.[43] On the whole, Repin's and Kramskoi's images of peasants, together with Isaak Levitan's and Valentin Serov's pictures of the Russian countryside (1890s) were perfect illustrations of the vision of Russia and its relationship with the West set out in 1855 by the poet Fedor Tiutchev:

> These poor villages, this humble landscape – native land of long-suffering, land of the Russian people!
> The foreigner's haughty glance will not understand or notice that which shines dimly and mysteriously through your humble nakedness.
> Weighed down by the burden of the cross, the King of Heaven, in the likeness of a servant, has walked up and down all of you, my native land, blessing you.[44]

[43] F.M. Dostoevskii, *Dnevnik pisatelia* (Moscow, Sovremennik, 1989), p. 365–6.
[44] Translation is taken from Dimitri Obolensky, compiler, *The Penguin Book of Russian Verse* (London, Penguin Books, 1967), p. 138.

Figure 3.2 Ilia Repin, 'The Volga haulers' (1870–73). (The Russian Museum, St. Petersburg)

The Westernizers

The source of inspiration for the early Westernizers was the same as that of their opponents, the Slavophiles – Chaadaev's letter and the German idealistic philosophers. Indeed, in the 1830s, the future Slavophiles and Westernizers were members of the same intellectual circle, set up in Moscow in the 1830s by the philosopher and historian, Nikolai Stankevich. The split into the two groups was initially merely an internal matter of the circle.

In the 1830s and the early 1840s the ranks of the Westernizers were united. However, it was inevitable that there would be splits in the Westernizers' camp, given the need to define precisely what one should admire and identify with in the varied Western heritage. The classical Westernist position was best formulated by the jurist, historian and publicist Boris Chicherin (1828–1904). Chicherin had been a student of an early Westernizer, the professor of world history Timofei Granovskii, at Moscow University. In Granovskii's lectures, Chicherin had heard the view that oppressive institutions such as serfdom and absolutism had a transitory character, and that Russia would inevitably follow the path of Western Europe. These early Westernizers did not have socialist sympathies and Chicherin followed suit. An ardent individualist and defender of private property, he regarded constitutional monarchy with a two-chamber legislature as the best form of government. Independent courts were essential for a properly functioning political system. The creation of such courts was the second most important item on his agenda for political change in Russia, following the emancipation of serfs. Chicherin did not initially believe that the conditions in Russia were ripe for a constitution and parliament, but by the end of the nineteenth century he finally concluded that they were. This classical Westernism did not identify any special path for Russia and did not argue that Russia had any important lesson to teach the world.

But the romantic idea of a nation defined through a special mission haunted Russian intellectuals, including the Westernizers. And it was one of them, Aleksandr Herzen, who was first to formulate the idea of a special Russian way. This way was not separate from the West, but was one which would allow Russia to surpass the West and teach it a lesson. Herzen's ideas had the greatest impact on Russian intellectual thinking, and arguably even on the development of Russian history itself. The force of Herzen's arguments lay in the fact that he found responses to all of Chaadaev's accusations against Russia and successfully reconciled the views of the Slavophiles and the Westernizers. In Herzen's own words, in the 1850s, after the split of the 1840s, the Westernizers and the Slavophiles again turned to each other as brothers. Both were repelled by the bureaucratic despotism of Russian absolutism: 'Like Janus or two-headed eagle, we faced different ways while our heart beat as one.' More effectively than anyone else, Herzen himself merged the two traditions together by fully articulating the ideology of 'Russian socialism'.

Socialism as a Russian nationalist ideology

In the 1840s some of the Westernizers had already come to the conclusion that in fact Western political institutions – legislatures and political parties – failed properly to represent the Western ideals of liberty, equality and fraternity. Instead, they were used by the bourgeoisie in order to deceive and manipulate the people. Contemporary Europe was a false Europe, and the true Europe was to be found elsewhere.[45] The 'true' Europe was represented by the ideals of European, especially French, socialists. Herzen was the first to think through a comprehensive theory which applied the ideas of French socialists to Russian reality. He thereby elaborated a specifically 'Russian socialism.' It can be argued that Herzen's ideas, as developed by later generations of Russian socialists, managed to transform Russia's social and political structures more than any of the other intellectual constructs of an imagined Russia. This was because, as will be shown later, they coincided with some popular perceptions and attitudes.

Herzen rejected the Europe of his time following the failure of the 1848 revolutions, which he had experienced as an émigré in Paris. This failure had dashed his hopes that the ideals of French socialists could be implemented in Europe. In post-revolutionary Europe he was appalled not only by what he regarded as the corruption and egotism of the ruling classes but also by the same trends among the proletariat. The capitalist system and private property were the root of the problem. Capitalist Europe with its deeply corrupt people ceased to be a source of hope for Herzen. He now saw the light coming from Russia, where, he began to believe, the prospects for socialism were better than in the West. He started to agree with the Slavophiles about the source of Russia's superiority. It was to be found in the peasant commune, which had a proto-socialist spirit and offered an example of the communal ownership and working of land.[46] Following the Slavophiles, Herzen began to see the commune as capturing the essence of Russian identity: 'At the very basis is a peasant commune, frozen in its waiting, slow, but confident in its development, conservative as a mother,

---

[45] B.H. Summer, 'Russia and Europe,' *Oxford Slavonic Papers*, no. 2 (1951) pp. 1–16, argued the same about Uvarov, saying that his triad did not completely reject Russia's identification with Europe, but only with the '"false" European civilization represented by the French revolution.'

[46] In fact, Bakunin had noted before Herzen that socialism in Russia could be built on the basis of peasant communes, but Herzen became the first most consistent popularizer of the idea.

carrying a baby in her womb. This feminine essence is the foundation of the construction ... which is called Russia.'[47]

Herzen's socialist ideas were particularly developed in his *Letters from France and Italy* and *From the Other Shore*, both written in 1848–49, and the *Russian People and Socialism*, written in 1851. The works were published abroad, but they found their way back to Russia. Despite the attempts of the government of Aleksandr II to introduce reforms aimed at making the Russian political system more comparable with Europe, it was not constitutional and liberal ideas, but 'Russian socialist' ideas which became the most influential among intellectuals and practical revolutionaries from the 1860s onwards. The word 'democrat' started to be used often to mean an egalitarian socialist, whereas the word 'liberal' acquired critical connotations as it seemed to denote 'English businessmen promoting the formal liberties of the middle class' alone.[48]

While Herzen developed the theory of 'Russian socialism,' his close friend Nikolai Ogarev, a landlord who had freed his own serfs and had given them his land long before 1861, was the first to put forward a comprehensive strategy of how to make the transition to socialism. This transition was to be carried out by a secret, highly centralized organization of intellectuals, led by specialists in the main branches of science and learning. This idea reflected a widespread attitude on the part of educated Russians towards the 'masses,' in which egalitarianism and elitism were closely intertwined. It was up to intellectuals to articulate the people's interests on the people's behalf – inherent interests, of which the people themselves were unaware.

Ogarev's ideas on revolutionary practice were further developed in the 1860s by a radical political thinker, Peter Tkachev. Concerned that Russia was just entering the path of capitalist development, and that this development might produce a stable government supported by the bourgeoisie, Tkachev felt that Russian revolutionaries should strike at tsarism while it was in a transition phase. In the 1870s, there was a great deal of activity by groups of practical revolutionaries, ready to put the ideas of Herzen, Ogarev, the writer Nikolai Chernyshevskii and Tkachev into effect. These were the so-called populists (*narodniki*), whose organizations, Land and Freedom and People's Will aimed to propel Russia into a socialism based on the village communes, thereby bypassing capitalism. Following Ogarev they felt that their major goal was to reveal to the people what was in their (the people's) best interests. In the wake of the assassination of Aleksandr II in 1881, the populists issued a document in which they 'gave the first place to

[47] A.I. Gerzen, 'Prolegomena' (1867), in *Russkaia ideia* (Moscow, Respublika, 1992), p. 122.
[48] Billington, *The Icon and the Axe*, p. 378. Orlando Figes and Boris Kolonitskii, *Interpreting the Russian Revolution. The Language and Symbols of 1917* (New Haven CT, Yale University Press, 1999), pp. 122–3, argue that the same definition of 'democracy' was prevalent following the February revolution in 1917.

[their] determination to reawaken the people by agitation in the name of the interest' that the people themselves felt but did not consciously appreciate.[49]

The populists developed the ideas of their predecessors somewhat. The populist economist, Vasilii Vorontsov, was the first to put forward the idea of Russia overcoming its backwardness through industrialization, conducted within the framework of a socialist rather than a capitalist system. Vorontsov thought that capitalism would not take root in Russia, as the country would not be able to develop external markets on a par with the West European overseas empires and the United States. He thought the Russian government should nationalize all the main industries and then enforce industrialization solely from above. (This indeed did happen under the Bolshevik government in the 1930s.) Commenting on Vorontsov's views, Andrzej Walicki has argued that Russian populism was 'the first ideological reflection ... of backward agrarian countries carrying out the process of modernization in conditions created by coexistence with highly industrialized nations.'[50] Indeed, the Russian socialists themselves were conscious of being an example to non-European nations and argued that the peasants of the East, including Russia, would be the driving force of a socialist revolution, rather than the proletariat of the West.

Thus, the socialism of the populists, inspired by Herzen, served the same purpose as nationalism served in Western Europe – it became an ideology of modernization. Scholars have argued that nationalist ideas are usually articulated by educated individuals, whose identities are being undermined by the social and economic changes of a modernizing society. The same can be said of the early Russian socialists. The social origin of the majority of the populists was described by the Russian word *raznochintsy*. This term referred to educated people of non-noble origin, who had come from provincial towns or villages to St. Petersburg and Moscow, where they often felt highly insecure. Such *raznochintsy* first started to make their mark in Russian culture back in the eighteenth century; Mikhail Lomonosov and Vasilii Trediakovskii fall into this category. However, it was in the 1860s that they began to constitute a critical mass among the Russian intelligentsia. Even Herzen was a person of 'threatened identity.' An illegitimate son of a wealthy Russian landlord and a German woman, from a very early age he had reflected on his special situation. In *My Past and Thoughts*, Herzen concluded that, in effect, 'he was left to his own devices' (*ostavlen na sobstvennye sily*), as he could not fully enjoy the security of a nobleman.[51]

---

[49] Quoted in Franco Venturi, *Roots of Revolution* (New York N.Y., Grosset and Dunlap, 1966), p. 719.

[50] Andrzej Walicki, *The Controversy over Capitalism: Studies in the Social Philosophy of the Russian Populists* (Oxford, Oxford University Press, 1969), p. 129.

[51] A.I. Gerzen, *Byloe i dumy*, part 1 (Moscow, Pravda, 1983), p. 51.

The assassination of Aleksandr II by a member of the People's Will party in 1881 prevented the implementation of a constitutional plan devised by the tsarist minister Mikhail Loris-Melikov. This plan had envisaged the addition of elected representatives of 'society' to the consultative organ to the tsar, the State Council. The result was that the introduction of a limited constitution and a legislature was delayed by a further twenty-four years.

The populists expected that the assassination of the tsar would lead to the replacement of the tsarist government by a revolutionary socialist dictatorship. These expectations did not materialize, however. In the 1890s, the tsarist government launched a programme of industrialization in Russia. It was no longer possible to believe that Russia could completely avoid the capitalist path of development. Thus the majority of Russian socialists accepted the inevitability of capitalism in Russia and turned to Marxism to analyse the conditions in their country. In 1898, various Marxist circles united into the Russian Social Democratic Workers' Party. Social Democrats accepted that in order to build a socialist society Russia first needed to become capitalist. They followed Marx in believing that the driving force of socialism would not be the peasantry, but the proletariat. Indeed, when in the summer of 1874 the populists had launched the campaign of 'going to the people' (*khozhdenie v narod*), when hundreds of intellectuals went to villages to preach socialist ideas to the peasants, the latter had usually handed them over to the police. However, the populist idea of Russian socialism, based on the communal way of life of the Russian peasantry, survived in the form of the Party of Socialist Revolutionaries (SRs), created at the turn of the twentieth century. Its ideologist Viktor Chernov continued to argue that in Russia, an overwhelmingly peasant country, the socialist revolution should be carried out by the peasants rather than the proletariat. For Chernov and other SRs, the difference between Russia and the West lay not only in the underdevelopment of the Russian working class. Roman law had also had no influence in Russia. This, they argued, had resulted in a peculiar attitude towards land and private property. Firstly, the land could not rightfully be owned by anyone, as it was 'God's property'; secondly, those who worked the land with their own hands had the right to use a suitable proportion of it. This 'consciousness of the right of toil' would help the Russians to introduce a new socialist law on the basis of peasant consciousness, Chernov maintained. He and other SRs argued that capitalism was alien to Russia and was making headway only because it was being artificially fostered by the tsarist government. The removal of that government would automatically pave the way for socialism.

But even among the Marxists, who began to make a significant impact on Russia's intellectual life from the 1880s onwards, some took on board ideas of 'Russian socialism' originating with Herzen. In 1903, as a result of a major split in Russian Social Democracy, those most influenced by 'Russian socialism' set up their own party – the Bolsheviks. Their opponents, the Mensheviks, believed that Russia should first copy West European capitalism and democratic institutions in order eventually to build a socialist society on their foundation. The Bolsheviks, on the other hand, thought the socialist revolution could be speeded up, and that industrialization could proceed under a socialist government along lines different from those of the capitalist world. There seems to be some logic in the fact that it was the Bolsheviks, rather than their Menshevik rivals who were much closer to classical Marxism, that came to power in Russia in 1917.

What were the reasons for the success of the ideas of Russian socialism among intellectuals, and, arguably, Russian society at large? It would seem that Herzen's attempt to blend certain elements of the Slavophile and the Westernizers' traditions of the 1830s and 1840s produced the most convincing and comprehensive answer to Chaadaev's *Philosophical Letters*, with their torturing questions about, and condemnations of, Russia. As mentioned earlier, many of the points made by Herzen were not entirely original. However, he was able to bring together the ideas of his predecessors, both the Slavophiles and the Westernizers, in the most successful way. According to this 'Russian socialism':

1. Russia's backwardness was not a handicap but an asset, as it could help Russia to implement socialist ideals more quickly than in the countries of the West where the bourgeoisie and the middle classes successfully preserved the stability of the existing political system.
2. In contrast to Chaadaev's assertions, Russia did have an indigenous tradition (peasant communes). This tradition was one that could help Russia to surpass the West quickly, and even made it superior to contemporary Western Europe.
3. Russia had not only a past, but a future, an important mission to be ahead of the West in implementing the West's own true ideals.
4. Russia could serve as a model not only for the West, but also for the East. It could teach Eastern peasants how to modernize without repeating Europe's experience of capitalism. After all, Russia could make a good use of its geography and serve as a bridge between Europe and Asia. This refuted Chaadaev's verdict that despite its geography, 'Russia does not belong to either the West or the East, does not share any tradition with either' and 'fails to bring anything to the world.'

In sum, 'Russian socialism' was the first nationalist ideology which could be therapeutic when dealing with the questions posed by Chaadaev, and which could help Russia define a comfortable place and role in the world for itself. This can account for its success among Russian intellectuals. But 'Russian socialism' was more than just an intellectual current. It turned out to have the most profound impact on Russia's twentieth century history. Why did the other intellectual constructs of an imagined Russia – Dostoevkii's Christian ideal; the Russia of the classical Westernizers, destined to copy the liberal constitutionalism of the West European democracies; and the pre-Petrine Russia of the Slavophiles – fail to have a comparable impact? It seems that Russian socialism, despite the failure of the 1874 populists' 'going to the people', most closely resembled the image of Russia held by the majority of the Russian population, the peasants. Chernov was right about the peasants' attitude towards the land. The position on land ownership described by Chernov, was reflected in the speeches of delegates to the first congress of the All-Russian Peasant Union in the summer of 1905. The Union was the first mass organization of peasantry in Russia, which by late 1905 included around 200,000 members and had branches in twelve regions. Peasants speaking at the congress demanded that private ownership of land be abolished, and that the land be transferred to those who would 'work it with their own families.' Peasants further argued that as land was created by God, 'it ought not to be bought and sold.'[52] Similar views were expressed by those peasants who were elected deputies to the first Russian parliament, the Duma, in 1906.[53] In the 1918 election to the Constituent Assembly (the first direct election with universal suffrage in Russian history) the Socialist Revolutionaries received the highest number of votes, followed by the Bolsheviks, who, for tactical purposes, had appropriated the SRs' agrarian programme. Moreover, as will be shown below, the socialist intellectuals' exclusion of 'the exploiting classes' from membership of the 'Russian nation' was not far off the mark as far as most of Russian population was concerned.

Russian nation-building and the 1917 revolution

Before analyzing the Bolsheviks' efforts to forge a compound identity of Soviet citizens, we shall assess the state of the Russian nation-building process by 1917. Following the Russian defeat in the Crimean war in 1856, the government of tsar Aleksandr II launched major political and economic reforms. These included the emancipation of the serfs, the introduction of elective local government assemblies, the expansion of primary education, the easing of political censorship and the restructuring of the legal system and the army. Most of these reforms were based on West European models. Yet, these liberalizing policies did not reconcile the radical intelligentsia to the government and did not solve the problems of the countryside. In the 1870s, radical opponents of the government began to undertake terrorist acts against members of the ruling elite. The peasants, who continued to be

---

[52] Hosking, *Russia: People and Empire*, p. 420–1.
[53] Ibid, pp. 422, 428.

segregated in their communes, were disappointed with the provisions of the new legislation concerning land distribution. During the reign of Aleksandr II some of the reforms had already been curtailed. His assassination in 1881 convinced his successor, tsar Aleksandr III, that liberalization simply endangered the internal stability of the empire.

While rejecting the Westernizing policies of Aleksandr II, the two last Russian tsars attempted to bring the elites and society together by fostering what they thought were indigenous pre-Petrine Russian traditions. In fact, a growing interest in old Russian culture and history on the part of the ruling elite had first become evident during the reign of Aleksandr II. But it was only under the last two tsars that the emphasis on the promotion of Russian traditions, in contrast to West European ones, became a key element of internal policy. In the 1880s, seventeenth century Russian architecture was taken as a model. That was the style in which the symbolically most impor- tant buildings of the period were constructed – a cathedral on the place of the assassination of Aleksandr II in St. Petersburg and the largest museum of Russian culture, the Historical Museum in Moscow. Military uniforms were changed, with the introduction of traditional Russian elements. This rejection of Westernization was particularly strongly manifested by the last tsar, Nicholas II. It is telling that in 1903, during a costume ball in the Winter Palace to mark the bicentenary of the foundation of St. Petersburg (the city of Peter the Great), participants wore costumes in the style of the period of Peter's father, the Tsar Aleksei Mikhailovich.[54] This was the tsar after whom Nicholas II named his own son and the heir to the throne. To stress further their identification with pre-Petrine Russia, the royal couple decided to spend Easters not in the 'foreign' city of St. Petersburg, but in the Kremlin in Moscow.

Finally, the two last Russian tsars applied the policies of Russifying the non-Russian subjects of the empire and converting them to Orthodoxy more consistently than their predecessors had done. However, this increased promotion of Russian culture, history, language and religion, and attempts to emphasize their uniqueness and difference from West European traditions did not mean that the two last Russian tsars had the aim of forging a Russian nation from all subjects of the empire. As will be shown later in the book, Russification policies continued to be applied inconsis- tently, and were even halted where it seemed that they might threaten the stability of the empire.[55]

In their view of the ethnic Russians, the last tsars tended to adopt the Slavophile idea that the peasantry was the only true representative of the

---

[54] Elena Hellberg-Hirn, *Soil and Soul. The Symbolic World of Russianness* (Aldershot, Ashgate, 1998), p. 73.

[55] See the chapter 'Imaginative geography: Russian empire as a Russian nation-state,' pp. 174–7.

Russian people. They also believed that this peasantry was unshakeable in its loyalty to the monarchy and its support for absolutism. Even the liberal tsar, Aleksandr II, had on several occasions rejected proposals from officials in his government to include elected representatives of society in the consultative body, the State Council, on the grounds that

> If the power, which my crown bestows me with, is limited, a hole in the halo of the nation will be created. The feeling of a deep piety with which Russian people for centuries … have been treating their tsar is impossible to eliminate. If I were to introduce into the government (elected) representatives of the nation, I would have limited, for no reason at all, the authority of the government.[56]

Only after great hesitation did Nicholas II agree, in the wake of the first Russian revolution of 1905, to remove the description of his powers as 'unlimited' (*neogranichennyi*) from official legislation. He felt he was betraying the tradition of his forefathers, undermining the state and not necessarily reflecting the aspirations of ordinary Russians. In consenting to the election of the first Russian parliament (the Duma), Nicholas II was at pains to show its difference from Western legislatures and to emphasize that the Duma would not undermine 'the union' between the tsar and his people. Announcing the creation of the Russian parliament, Nicholas II drew a parallel between the Duma and the pre-Petrine Councils of Lands, which had consisted of elected representatives of society. In fact, the Council had enjoyed only consultative powers and the tsar had had the right to ignore the opinions of their members. In contrast the Duma had legislative powers, however limited. Nicholas II nevertheless observed: 'My will, the tsar's will to summon popular electors is unswerving … Let the union between the tsar and all of Russia be established, as it was in olden times, the contact between Me and the people of the land, that will underlie the order in conformance with original Russian principles. I hope you will assist Me in this work.'[57]

At a time when the forces supporting constitutional government were stronger than ever in Russia, Nicholas II attempted to backtrack on the liberal promises of the October 1905 Manifesto whenever possible. As a result, government policies were attacked not only by the socialists, but also by the liberals, particularly members of the Russian Constitutional Democratic Party (Kadets), set up in 1905. The majority of the Kadets were university professors, whose work led them to transcend national boundaries and feel themselves to be members of the pan-European academic community. For them Russia was unquestionably part of Europe and they

---

[56] Quoted in Iu.A. Sandulov *et al.*, eds, *Istoria Rossii. Narod i vlast* (St. Petersburg, Lan, 1997), p. 413.

[57] Quoted in Tim McDaniel, *The Agony of the Russian Idea* (Princeton N.J., Princeton University Press, 1996), p. 67.

hoped that the political liberalization of the early twentieth century signified a gradual transformation of Russia's political system along West European lines. In contrast to the radical intelligentsia of the nineteenth century, the Kadets did not reject capitalism and the bourgeoisie. On the contrary, they began to believe in a close connection between capitalism and democracy. Many Kadets thought that a constitutional monarchy would have been the best form of government for Russia at that time. But the existing tsarist government did not inspire the confidence of the Kadets and, in turn, the government did not trust the Russian liberals.

The Russian revolution demonstrated how simplistically the Russian tsars had viewed their society and how wrong they had been in estimating their popular support, including the loyalty of the peasants. It is significant that from the reign of Aleksandr II onwards, those recommending the admission of elected representatives of society into the government included the police chief P.A. Shuvalov (1866) and the interior minister (1882) N.P. Ignatev. These men had little sympathy for Western liberalism, but because of the nature of their jobs, they were better aware of the public mood than anybody else in the government.[58] Indeed, the persistence of absolutism increased the alienation of the intelligentsia from the state, whilst loyalty to the tsar appeared to be less a part of identity of common people by the end of the nineteenth to the early twentieth century. The materials of the 'Programme of ethnographic study of peasants in central Russia,' undertaken in 1897–1900 by the Ethnographic Bureau under Prince V.N. Tenishev, seem to support this conclusion. In the course of this programme, the bureau sent its representatives to 23 Russian *gubernii* to collect information on how peasants spent their free time, what they read, what they knew about Russia and the outside world, their attitude towards the Russian–Turkish war, etc.[59] Additionally, as Jeffrey Brooks has pointed out, in the popular literature of the early twentieth century 'there is little reference to either the tsar or the Orthodox Church.'[60] Such references had been a common feature of popular stories from the eighteenth until the latter part of the nineteenth century. The status of the tsar, and identification with the Church fell further in World War I. During the war, popular culture (for instance, post cards, posters, etc.) hardly reflected those old identities.[61] Most evidence shows that, a few exceptions notwithstanding, in 1917 'the news of the Tsar's abdication were welcomed joyously' by the Russian peasantry.[62]

---

58   Sandulov, *Istoriia Rossii*, p. 414–5.
59   A.V. Buganov, *Russkaia istoriia v pamiati krestian XIX veka i natsionalnoe samosoznanie* (Moscow, Institut Etnologii i Antropologii RAN, 1992), pp. 59, 62–3.
60   Brooks, *When Russia Learned to Read*, p. 217.
61   Hubertus F. Jahn, *Patriotic Culture in Russia during World War I* (Ithaca N.Y., Cornell University Press, 1995).
62   Figes and Kolonitskii, *Interpreting the Russian Revolution*, p. 138.

Overall, by the time of World War I and the subsequent revolution, society and the state remained unreconciled. This was unlike the situation in the countries of Western Europe, which had become nation states in the course of the nineteenth century. In the Russian empire, there was no shared sense of belonging to a common community, either among all the subjects of the empire, or even among the ethnic Russians. The tsarist government had a utopian view about the strength of the 'union between the tsar and the people', while the intellectuals put forward conflicting definitions of Russian nationhood. Only the liberals promoted an inclusive definition of a nation comprising all citizens of Russia, which they aspired to democratize. The Slavophile and socialist views of nation reflected and perpetuated the existing divide between the upper and lower social groups.

Members of the lower social classes, meanwhile, often felt vaguely socialist, yet their world-view remained pre-national. Evidence from the period immediately following the February revolution, when Russian people enjoyed unprecedented freedom of expression, supports this conclusion. 'The cult of socialism' evident in this period was so strong that it took observers of the Russian scene by surprise. The historian Aleksandr Kizevetter spoke about 'a general aspiration of a huge mass of Russians to declare themselves, no matter what, to the amazement of foreigners, to be absolutely socialist.'[63] Despite regular references to the traditions of the French revolution in the Russian political discourse of 1917, the definition of a nation, advocated by most Russian political parties, which seemed to enjoy broad popular support, was very different from the inclusive French concept. In 1917, even before the Bolshevik takeover, the Russian nation was perceived by most politically active Russians in the terms outlined by Herzen and the populists – the bourgeoisie was excluded from membership. The folklore of the revolutionary period, which reflected the views of the broad masses of workers and peasants, was dominated by the image of a *burzhui*, who had nothing in common with, and was the main enemy of, the Russian *narod*.[64] The inclusive definition of a nation was alien to the majority of the Russian population.

In the period between the emancipation of the serfs in 1861 and the 1917 revolution, the tsarist government failed to turn Russian peasants into fully-fledged citizens to the same extent that the French government managed to turn the peasants of France into Frenchmen in the late nineteenth century. In Russia as elsewhere, the army had been an important nation-building institution. Its role in this area was further strengthened by the 1874 military reform, which introduced a six-year-long universal compulsory military service. But in the areas of education and the development commu-nications – other essential components of nation-building – Russia

---

[63] Quoted in Figes and Kolonitskii, *Interpreting the Russian Revolution*, p. 173.

[64] Ibid, pp. 171–7.

considerably lagged behind the more developed countries of Europe and the United States. At the time of the 1897 census, i.e. 36 years after the emancipation of the serfs and 33 years after the adoption of the government Resolution on Elementary People's Schools, only 31.4 per cent of men in European Russia and a mere 5.7 per cent of women were registered as literate. Rural literacy in the empire as a whole stood at 6 per cent.[65] By 1913 it had risen dramatically, but still embraced less than a quarter of the rural population.[66] At the turn of the twentieth century, Russia had only 29 communities with telephone networks – all in big cities. At the same time Italy had 51, France had 194, Britain had 213 and the United States had 1,351. The annual volume of letters and telegrams sent was considerably lower in Russia than in the above-mentioned countries.[67]

Prime Minister Peter Stolypin introduced legislation in 1906, 1910 and 1911, aimed at breaking up the communes, creating prosperous land-owning peasants and, on the whole, putting the peasantry on a more equal legal footing with other classes. It brought fairly modest results. By 1916, around 24 per cent of formerly communal households had managed to complete their legal separation from the commune.

Finally, as people's identities are, in part, shaped by their access to political institutions, it is worth looking at peasant representation in the Duma and their attitude towards the first Russian parliament. In the elections to the first and the second Dumas in March 1906 and January 1907 respectively, peasant participation was very high. In the first Duma, the faction of peasants' representatives, the *Trudoviki*, had 100 members. It was the second largest group after the Constitutional Democrats. In the second Duma, the *Trudoviki* were the largest faction, with 101 members. But the Duma proved unable to enforce a law on the expropriation of land from landlords. In June 1907 changes were introduced in the electoral law aimed at weakening the influence of left-wing groups, and peasant interest in the activities of the Duma dropped. There was much lower rural

---

[65] At the same time, it should be noted that the accuracy of the census data, particularly in relation to the question of literacy, was doubted by Russian statisticians at the time and by later scholars. The figures might have been lower than what the situation was in reality. Peasants tended to downplay their level of literacy in a hope that the claim of illiteracy would, if need be, save them from some punishment. See A.V. Buganov, *Russkaia Istoriia v pamiati krestian XIX veka*, pp. 41–2. The census also indicated that in the next generation literacy in Russia would rise dramatically. In the age group from 10 to 19 almost three-quarters of the boys and more than half of the girls were registered as literate. See, Theodore H. Von Laue, 'Imperial Russia at the Turn of the Century: The Cultural Slope and the Revolution from Without,' in Reinhard Bendix, ed., *State and Society. A Reader in Comparative Political Sociology* (Berkeley CA, University of California Press, 1968), p. 430.

[66] A.G. Rashin, 'Gramotnost i narodnoe obrazovanie v Rossii v XIX i nachale XX vekov,' *Istoricheskie zapiski*, no. 37 (1951), pp. 45–9.

[67] Von Laue, 'Imperial Russia at the Turn of the Century', p. 431.

participation in the elections to the third Duma in the autumn of 1907. As a result of this lack of interest, and of the anti-peasant bias of the new electoral legislation, the *Trudoviki* faction, with 13 members, became the second smallest, surpassing only that of the Muslims with 8 members. Meanwhile, peasants returned to unauthorized acts of expropriation of land and violence against land-owners as in the 1905 revolution.

Among numerous examples of the lack of modern national feelings among Russian peasantry of the time, the following is one of the most striking. In 1917, a Russian intellectual had the following conversation with a peasant: 'Ivan calmly and with conviction said that he did not care whether he would be a Russian or a German. If the Germans gave him more land, he would have agreed to be a German.' The intellectual concluded: 'And I have understood that it is not a cynical *'ubi bene, ibi patria.'* It is the naiveté of a person who does not think nationally. I have understood that this is how the majority of the Ivans around feel (not think). This is why there are no and cannot be any ties between the lords (*gospoda*) and the peasantry (*muzhiki*).'[68]

Russia could not withstand the combined pressure of rapid change, industrialization and World War I, unlike the West European states, where nation-building had been more successful. The February revolution of 1917 resulted in the collapse of the monarchy and the disintegration of the empire. The October revolution led to the Civil War.

The Bolshevik revolution and the perception of the West

The Bolshevik experiments of the first post-revolutionary years have sometimes been seen as an ultimate attempt at Westernizing Russia. Putting forward such an argument, E.H. Carr observed: 'No previous innovator in Russian history had drawn so frankly and unreservedly as Lenin on the experience and example of the west ... Nothing in Russian history seemed so unimpeachably and unreservedly western so free of any national taint, as the Russian Marxist movement.'[69]

However, the Bolsheviks were seen in a very different light by their opponents in Russia at the time. Not only their opponents on the right, such as the philosopher Nikolai Berdiaev and the Kadet leader Pavel Miliukov, but also the founder of Russian Marxism Georgii Plekhanov and the Mensheviks described the Bolsheviks as 'Slavophile Marxists.'[70] This

---

[68] S.V. Zavadskii, *Na velikom izlome. Arkhiv russkoi revoliutsii*, vol. XI (Moscow, Terra, 1991), p. 70–1.

[69] Carr, '"Russia and Europe"', p. 386.

[70] Iver B. Neumann, *Russia and the Idea of Europe* (London, Routledge, 1996), p. 93.

perception of the 'truly Russian' roots of the Bolshevik revolution helped some who had initially been critical to come to terms with the new regime. The leader of the Changing Landmarks (Smena Vekh) movement, Nikolai Ustrialov proclaimed:

> It is our [crisis], truly Russian, entirely embedded in our psychology, in our past, and nothing remotely similar could possibly occur in the West. And even if it is mathematically proven, as is sometimes now unsuccessfully attempted, that 90 per cent of the Russian revolutionaries are foreigners, chiefly Jews, that in no way cancels out its purely Russian nature. For better or worse, if 'alien' hands have played a role, its soul, its 'inner self' is authentically Russian intellectual, bent by the prism of the people's psyche.[71]

Indeed, it is hard to deny the close connection between Lenin's views and the position of the nineteenth century non-Marxist Russian socialists. Lenin followed the Russian populists in arguing that Russia's backwardness did not mean that the country needed to transplant Western models onto its soil. Such imitation would only lead to Russia's exploitation by the West. So Russia's national emancipation was conditioned on Russia's ability to industrialize 'without duplicating the superstructure of Western capitalist property relations.' Overall, whereas Lenin analysed domestic politics in terms of the class struggle and the exploitation of proletariat by the bourgeoisie, he looked at international relations from the standpoint of the struggle between nations, and the exploitation of backward nations by the advanced ones. In the view of both Roman Szporluk and Alfred Meyer, Lenin thus finalised the connection between Marxism and nationalism.[72]

In analysing specifically Russian conditions Lenin abandoned Marx's economic determinism for the traditional view of the nineteenth century Russian intelligentsia, that the country's path could be determined by the political actions of leaders who knew and could articulate the interests of the people. In 1902, in his pamphlet *What Is to be Done?* Lenin first argued that, left to their own devices, workers would never rise above 'spontaneous trade unionist striving.' Consequently, they would remain 'under the wing of the bourgeoisie.' It was the task of a party of professional revolutionaries to show the proletariat what was in its interests. To be sure, the masses were to be enlisted in the revolutionary movement. But only a tightly-knight organization of those 'whose profession is revolutionary work' could ensure victory against the old order. Thus, in contrast to the classical Marxists, Lenin believed that the Russian revolution could be speeded up in the

---

[71] Quoted in John Glad, *Russia Abroad. Writers, History, Politics* (Washington, DC, Hermitage and Birchbark Press, 1999), p. 125.

[72] Roman Szporluk, *Communism and Nationalism. Karl Marx versus Friedrich List* (Oxford, Oxford University Press, 1988), p. 214–15 and Alfred G. Meyer, *Leninism* (New York N.Y., Praeger, 1965), p. 262–3.

absence of a strong working class and economic wealth. He was also at least partly influenced by the traditional nineteenth century attitude towards peasantry in arguing that in a country like Russia, peasants were natural allies of the working class.

The Bolsheviks' message from the very outset was very contradictory. Yet, by 1917 the main weight seems to lie with the Russian tradition. In the wake of the 1905 Russian revolution, Lenin thought that 'The European workers will show us "how it is done," and then we together with them will tame the social revolution.'[73] However, by April 1917, Lenin started to believe, as the nineteenth century Russian socialists had done, that Russia would take the lead in the destruction of capitalism. He made his position clear in the *April Theses*. At the time, many members of Lenin's own party regarded his position as utopian, but others, including Stalin, shared it. In August 1917, Stalin observed: 'One cannot exclude that Russia will be the country, which will pave the way to socialism... We should put aside the outdated view that Europe will show us our way.'[74]

After the success of the October revolution, the Bolsheviks and those who then supported them – the Left SRs and some men of letters and artists – saw it as the final fulfilment of the hopes of most nineteenth century Russian intellectuals. Russia was going to save the West from its current state of degradation. It would teach the world a lesson and thereby carry out its historic mission. The leader of the Left SRs, Maria Spiridonova, exclaimed a week after the Bolshevik takeover: 'We are now showing the way to our brothers in Western Europe!'[75] Lenin agreed: 'We take pride in the fact that it fell to our happy lot to start the building of the Soviet state and thereby usher in a new era of history.'[76] One of the most famous Russian poets of the twentieth century, Aleksandr Blok, also interpreted the Russian revolution as Russia showing Europe the way to salvation, when in his poem *The Twelve* he compared a Bolshevik patrol with the twelve apostles of Christ.

It can be argued that the Bolsheviks' rejection of the West and what they perceived as its degradation was even sharper than that of the Slavophiles, whose most extreme representatives had compared Western Europe with a 'rotting corpse.' Indeed, upon assuming power and turning against the opposition, Lenin struck first not against the monarchists, but against the main Westernizing party, the Kadets, who were the first to be outlawed, as well as the truly Westernizing Marxists, the Mensheviks. The direct heirs of the Slavophile populists of the nineteenth century, the Left SRs, were the only non-Bolsheviks to accept Lenin's claim to power. They were therefore temporarily admitted into the Council of People's Commissars.

---

[73] Carr '"Russia and Europe"', p. 85.
[74] Quoted in M. Agurskii, *Ideologiia natsional-bolshevizma* (Paris, YMCA-Press, 1980), p. 141.
[75] Ibid., p. 17.
[76] Quoted in Greenfeld, *Nationalism*, p. 272.

Carr reminded us that even after the October Revolution, Lenin still spoke about the need to learn from the West, especially the United States, in the sphere of technological progress. Lenin also viewed the October revolution as merely the forerunner of a pan-European one. He did not believe that socialism could succeed without the help of European workers. Yet, simultaneously he put forward an idea which would dominate the Soviet government's vision up until Mikhail Gorbachev's New Thinking, that the world was divided into two irreconcilable camps – socialist Russia and the capitalist West. The latter included both Western Europe and the United States. The division between the two camps and their hostility to each other were much sharper than most of the pre-revolutionary thinkers had ever imagined.

Carr cited as further proof of the Bolsheviks' Western orientation the fact that 'the Russian past was condemned root and branch. The very name Russia disappeared from the official title of the new authority.' Yet some of those who had initially opposed the Bolsheviks, such as some former tsarist army officers and the *Smenovekhovites*, looked deeper. They had a point in thinking that the name of the new state was less important than the fact that the Bolsheviks had restored the country to similar geographical borders that it had had under the tsars. Moreover, the condemnation of old Russia, of its 'icons and cockroaches' (Leon Trotskii) notwithstanding, the Bolsheviks were clear from the very beginning that parts of the pre-revolutionary heritage were to be appropriated by the new regime. Pushkin, Tolstoi, Lermontov and Nekrasov were published in large print-runs and used as textbooks in the campaign for the spread of literacy. At no point did Lenin share the poet Vladimir Maiakovskii's view that Pushkin 'should be pushed off the board of the ship of modernity.' Similarly, the avant-garde artists whose services were extensively used by the Bolsheviks in visual propaganda in the 1920s, used old-Russian images and techniques, for instance, those of icons, more than any other post-eighteenth century Russian artists had done. This unprecedented attempt to merge the most innovative Western trends of the time with the pre-Petrine Russian tradition began among Russian writers and artists in the early twentieth century and continued into the 1920s. It was most pronounced among Russian avant-garde painters such as Kazemir Malevich and Vasilii Kandinskii.

Despite the fact that Lenin's own artistic tastes were conservative and he preferred the Russian realism of the nineteenth century to the avant-garde, the Bolshevik government solicited the services of avant-garde artists. The Commissar of Enlightenment, Anatolii Lunacharskii, called on the artists to leave their studios and go out onto the streets to spread the message of the new government. Among other things, the Bolsheviks turned porcelain objects into an effective propaganda tool. Numerous such objects with political messages and new images of Russia were sold inside the country as well as abroad in the 1920s. One of the foremost porcelain painters of the time, Shchekotikhina-Boturskaia, was from a family of Old Believers and used iconographic images extensively in her work. One common image was that of St. George slaying the Dragon. This choice had an important symbolic meaning. The dragon was to represent the old world. But more important was the fact that St. George himself had a special place in East Slavic religious mythology. He was regarded as the patron of the Grand Princes of Kiev. In the fourteenth century he became the patron of the Moscow Principality. From the sixteenth century onwards, St. George was depicted as 'the creator of the Russian land' (*ustroitel zemli russkoi*) in Russian folklore. On other propaganda porcelain plates, the new Russia was symbolized by the folklore hero (*bogatyr*) Ilia of Murom on a flying horse. Expressions from the Bible and the New Testament were also used in propaganda art as well as in the discourse of the new leaders. Thus, the expression 'If a man will not work, he shall not eat' (*Kto ne rabotaet, tot ne est*), an adaptation from St. Paul's Second Epistle to Thessalonians, became one of the Bolshevik slogans.

The way Stalin appropriated the pre-revolutionary Russian past as a tool of Soviet patriotic propaganda has often been discussed. But the foundation was laid by Lenin. It was Lenin who first provided 'a basis for a "national" interpretation' (Szporluk) of the Russian revolution, five years before the Bolshevik takeover. In an article commemorating Herzen, Lenin mentioned the Russian nobility among the successive classes in the history of the Russian revolutionary movement. 'This inclusion raised certain potentially awkward questions regarding the national, as opposed to class, character of the Russian revolutionary movement,' Szporluk concluded.[77] Moreover in Lenin's time, a greater variety of old symbols were used by those avant-garde artists who participated in the Bolsheviks' propaganda campaigns, than under Stalin. In the mid-1930s the avant-garde was condemned for its 'formalism,' and a rigid canon, prescribing what was acceptable for artists, was imposed. This canon was based on a vulgarized version of Russian realism (populist art) of the 1860s–1880s – the paintings of the wanderers, and the poetry and social criticism of such figures as Nekrasov and Vsevolod Garshin.

At the same time, Lenin's rejection of Western liberal democratic institutions was no less uncompromising than Stalin's. The vision of Russia first formulated under Lenin owed a lot to the pre-revolutionary Slavophile and populist traditions. After the revolution Russia did indeed become a unique civilization. Lenin had no doubt about its superiority to the West. He believed that the new society would eventually be free from all conflict. His successors subsequently proclaimed that this aim was being achieved. Like Karamzin and all the Slavophiles after him, Lenin and other Bolsheviks saw the West as riven by conflict. The Western legal system was also rejected by

---

[77] Szporluk, *Communism and Nationalism*, p. 229.

Lenin. Instead, 'revolutionary consciousness' was to be the main criterion in passing legal verdicts. Similarly, the Slavophiles had rejected cold, rational Western legality and counterposed to it the Russians' belief in a superior truth. Lenin accepted the myth of the *narod*, which incorporated not only workers, as Marx would have it, but also peasants. From 1918, a crossed hammer and sickle, symbolizing an unbreakable unity of workers and peasants, became a central part of the heraldry of the new state.[78] The nobility and bourgeoisie and their children were deprived of voting rights and their access to education was restricted. These violations of the rights of Russia's citizens did not bother Lenin, who rejected the idea of Western democratic freedoms as 'parliamentary cretinism.'

Although the move of the Russian capital in 1918 from Petrograd to Moscow, was motivated primarily by security considerations, it also had a symbolic character. In the symbolic world of Russian identity, St. Petersburg/Petrograd was the centre of Westernized Russian culture; Moscow, 'Russia's heart', according to an old Russian proverb, symbolized the true Russia of the Slavophiles and of eighteenth and nineteenth century peasant folklore. Some critics of the Bolsheviks asserted that with the move of the capital back to Moscow, Russia's Westernized civilization vanished. This is how the poet Joseph Brodsky saw his native city and the impact of Lenin's decision on it:

> And there was a city. The most beautiful city on the face of the earth. With an immense gray river that hung over its distant bottom like the immense gray sky over that river. Along that river there stood magnificent palaces with such beautifully elaborated facades that if the little boy [Brodsky of his childhood] was standing on the right bank, the left bank looked like the imprint of a giant mollusk called civilization. Which ceased to exist.[79]

Paradoxically, as Katerina Clarke has argued, it was Stalin who 'Westernized' Moscow. By ordering the destruction of its churches and 'straightening out' its crooked streets, he turned Moscow into a Petersburgian city.[80]

On paper at least, Stalin also introduced changes in Soviet political system, to make it less different from those of the Western liberal democracies than it had been under Lenin. In 1936, Stalin introduced a constitution

---

[78] For the first time this symbol was used in Russia on a military banner at a demonstration during the February revolution. Figes and Kolonitskii, *Interpreting the Russian Revolution*, p. 62.

[79] Joseph Brodsky, *Less Than One. Selected Essays* (New York N.Y., Farrar, Straus, Giroux, 1986), p. 32.

[80] Katerina Clarke, *Petersburg. Crucible of Cultural Revolution* (Cambridge MA, Harvard University Press, 1995), p. 300.

which, in theory, granted all citizens of the Soviet Union, regardless of their social origin, democratic freedoms, as in the Western democracies. It also created a parliament elected by universal direct suffrage.[81] Despite the fact that the scale of unlawful state persecution of citizens under Stalin exceeded that which had taken place under Lenin, from the 1930s onwards Soviet legal officials attempted to introduce a façade of order into the legal system. Nonetheless, although the Bolsheviks can be compared with the pre-revolutionary Slavophiles or populists, it should be borne in mind that after the 1917 October revolution Russia's differences with the West were emphasized with unprecedented force. Never before had the West become such a total 'other'. Never before had such a government-sponsored propaganda campaign been launched to forge a new Russian identity, based on contrasting Russia and the West, which was now dubbed 'the world of capitalism.'

Images of the West in official discourse and propaganda: from Lenin's death to World War II

Western authors have argued that the 1920s debate within the leadership of the Communist Party about the way the Soviet Union was to industrialize was also a debate about Russia's attitude towards the West. Trotskii's idea about the inevitability of Russia relying on Western technologies and expertise, the position which seemed to be close to Lenin's view, was a more 'Westernizing' position than Nikolai Bukharin's idea of 'socialism in one country,' which in 1925 Stalin appropriated as his own. This latter position owed a lot to the Slavophile belief in Russia's ability to follow its own path and in the strength and ability of the Russians to develop in isolation from the West. Indeed, Stalin's campaign against Trotskii was based on accusing him of anti-Russian sentiments and of disbelief in the abilities of the Russian people. The concept of 'socialism in one country' naturally sharpened the view, first formulated by Lenin, that the world was divided into the two irreconcilable camps. It further strengthened the belief that the 'imperialist camp' was determined to destroy the USSR. These conflicting views were reflected in the official propaganda presented to the people of the Soviet Union in the 1920s.

During that decade, Russian peasants and workers indicated a strong desire to learn more about the outside world. Village Soviets sent requests to the centre to ensure regular distribution of newspapers in the countryside,

---

[81] The fact that until 1989 this parliament had no power to challenge the decision of the Communist Party leadership is irrelevant for the purpose of this argument.

so that peasants could specifically learn about the situation abroad.[82] This interest in the outside world was partly a continuation of a trend observable from the turn of the twentieth century, when Russian popular literature became far more cosmopolitan than it had been for most of the nineteenth century. At that time, popular stories aimed at peasants and workers learning to read began to depict Western Europeans and Americans as people just like their Russian counterparts, who often deserved admiration and with whom Russian readers could identify. Early twentieth century instalment novels and detective serials featuring foreign heroes, proved to be very popular among the reading public. They represented a departure from the earlier stereotypes promoted by Russian popular culture, in which the world was bifurcated into the Orthodox Russians and the others, the alien unbelievers. This newly emerging openness of Russian popular culture was channelled by the Soviet government towards a particular interest of ordinary Russians in political events abroad. Soviet propaganda in the 1920s tried to shape a certain image of the West by using both these sets of stereotypes. The earlier stereotypes of Russian popular culture, in which foreign countries were regarded with great suspicion and hostility, was combined with the new cosmopolitan trend typical of the last years of the tsarist regime, in which Soviet workers and peasants were invited to identity with their counterparts in the capitalist world.

In order to analyse the fluctuations of this propaganda we shall look at the popular illustrated journal *Prozhektor*, which was aimed at the broadest possible audience. Throughout the entire period of the industrialization debate and the implementation of changes in industry, from 1925 until the late 1930s, virtually every issue of the journal contained information about Western Europe and the United States, and often directly compared the situation there with that in the USSR. Thus, the concept of the West as Russia's constituent other began to penetrate Russian society at large, spreading beyond intellectual circles. In 1925–1926, special attention was paid to the situation of the unemployed, workers' strikes and anti-government demonstrations. Stories about Western intellectuals sympathizing with the Soviet Union, and literary works by Western Communist writers were regularly published. These publications were aimed at creating a feeling of common identity between Soviet citizens and the American jobless, striking English coal-miners and other working class people in the West.

---

[82] Iu.S. Borisov, *et al.*, eds, *Rossiia i zapad. Formirovanie vneshnepoliticheskikh stereotipov v soznanii rossiiskogo obshchestva pervoi poloviny XX veka* (Moscow, the Institute of Russian History; Lampeter, Edwin Mellen Press, 1999), pp. 135–6. It should be noted that from the late nineteenth century on, newspapers and journals published in St. Petersburg carried more reports on political and cultural events in Western Europe than in Russia. (See, Von Laue, 'Imperial Russia at the Turn of the Century', p. 432–7.) However, due to low levels of literacy among the peasantry and the lack of regular access to the press, these reports did not have much impact on the Russian countryside.

Throughout the 1920s, certainly not all the images presented of the capitalist world were negative. The technological achievements of West European countries and especially the United States were often depicted as a model to be emulated. Such reporting at times produced unintended results. For example, in January 1927 a group of peasants from the Orel region wrote in a letter to the newspaper *Krestianskaia gazeta* (The Peasant Gazette) that although the Soviet press 'writes that [in America] the working class is oppressed, we also have read that all branches of industry there are mechanized and workers only operate machines. And the working class lives in such a luxury as our bourgeoisie' used to live.[83]

These examples notwithstanding, letters to the press and to political leaders by ordinary Russians indicate that most often 'the capitalist West' was perceived as an aggressive force, ready to launch a military attack on Soviet Russia at the first opportunity.[84] This growing hostility towards the West increased dramatically from 1927 onwards, when Britain broke off diplomatic relations with the Soviet Union, and the fear that war was inevitable grew among Soviet leaders and ordinary people. That year, *Prozhektor* regularly published articles with all-round attacks on Britain and other capitalist countries. Soviet publications focused less on the plight of the workers in those countries, and more on the exploitation by capitalist countries of their colonies in the East. The message was that if the Soviet Union did not build a strong defence system, it could face a similar plight to that of the British colonies. All in all, from 1927 until at least the mid-1930s, Britain was depicted in the Soviet press as the USSR's main enemy. In Soviet propaganda Britain was cast in a role similar to that of the United States in the post-World War II period. The promotion of international class solidarity was replaced by attempts to strengthen the national unity of Soviet citizens in view of the perceived threat from the West. After 1927 the involvement of Britain, the USA, France and Germany in the Russian Civil War on the side of the Bolsheviks' opponents became a central theme in the anti-Western campaign. This was to reinforce people's fear that another capitalist intervention in Russia was likely. In creating the image of the two irreconcilable camps, Soviet propaganda sharpened the focus on the 'peaceful nature' of the Soviet Union and the 'militaristic aspirations' of the West. From that time onwards, the overwhelming majority of cartoons in *Prozhektor* depicted 'warmongers of the capitalist world.'

From 1929, anti-Western propaganda was marked by a growing confidence in the strength of the Soviet Union compared to the West, as the economic crisis that struck the world of capitalism coincided with the advent of Soviet industrialization. The most popular image used in the media became that of Soviet Russia as a cliff in a stormy sea. The latter

---

[83] Ibid, p. 79. For other similar examples, see pp. 80, 137–8.
[84] Ibid, p. 142.

symbolized the Western world riven by economic crisis and military and political conflicts. From that time onwards, most foreign reports in the Soviet press directly compared the Soviet and capitalist economic systems, emphasizing the advantages of the former. The beginning of the industrialization drive and the launch of the first five-year plan facilitated these comparisons. The very titles of articles in *Prozhektor*, such as 'The System of Hired Slavery in Capitalist Countries Versus Socialist Organization of Labour,' invited readers to draw conclusions in favour of Soviet socialism. Reports on every major industrial construction, such as Magnitogorsk in the Southern Urals or the Hydroelectric power station on the river Dniepr (Dneproges), were compared with similar industrial projects in the United States. These reports emphasized the superiority of Soviet projects. However United States technologies were not completely denigrated even in the first half of the 1930s. On the contrary, they were sometimes praised. The main criticism was that workers were exploited during their construction.[85] That was the message of Ilia Ilf's and Evgenii Petrov's pamphlet *One-Storeyed America*, which was published in 1936 and quickly acquired great popularity.

On the whole it was in the period of industrialization that the United States joined Great Britain in Soviet propaganda as the chief rival of the Soviet Union on the international arena. In 1938, the goal of overtaking and surpassing the USA in *per capita* industrial production was officially announced. It was claimed that this would be achieved in some fifteen years. Soviet propaganda felt an almost unlimited need to compare the USSR and the West, in order to emphasize advantages of the former. Even the 1934 Soviet book *Belomor,* on the construction of the White-Sea Baltic Canal by convict labour, favourably compared Soviet labour camps to American prisons. One of the heroes of the book, a thief serving a sentence on the *Belomor* Canal, had earlier served a sentence in the USA. Whereas he was fully satisfied with his conditions in the North of Russia, he described the US prison as 'devilish,' as he had to work much harder there to be fed only with 'the soup – five spoonfuls to a person.'

By making the USA the chief constituent other, rival and enemy of the Soviet Union, Soviet propaganda departed radically from the positive image of the United States held by radical intellectuals of the late eighteenth and nineteenth centuries, and their notion that it represented a model for Russia. Radishchev, the Decembrists, Herzen and others had all thought that America did not suffer from the same social and political evils as West European countries. Herzen often compared America with Russia, arguing that only those two countries, in contrast to old Europe, could realize his

[85] See, for instance, *Rossiia i Evropa v XIX–XX vekakh* (Moscow, Institut Rossiiskoi Istorii RAN, 1996), pp. 93–4; P. Kenez, *The Birth of the Propaganda State. Soviet methods of mass mobilization. 1917–1929* (Cambridge, Cambridge University Press, 1985), p. 4.

ideals of human welfare. At the same time, Soviet propaganda further developed a less positive image of the United States that had emerged at the turn of the twentieth century. Certain well-known Russian cultural figures, such as the writers Vladimir Korolenko and Maksim Gorkii, and the poet Aleksandr Blok, had praised America's technological achievements but condemned 'the lack of spiritual values' (*bezdukhovnost*) of American society. They contrasted this negatively with Russia, which they believed held such values in great esteem.

World War II and post-war years

The beginning of World War II and the German attack on the Soviet Union seemed to confirm the fears of the Soviet leaders and added credibility to Soviet propaganda statements. The USSR's eventual victory appeared to prove the strength of the Soviet system and the correctness of Stalin's policy of industrialization. It also strengthened a common identity among citizens of the Soviet Union. Not surprisingly, the war became a key Soviet national 'myth,' for uniting the people. It has been used by subsequent communist and post-Communist Russian governments in order to rally the population around the leadership. In Gorbachev's period, even some critics of the Communist regime felt that the attempts by certain writers to destroy the 'myth of the war,' not only by attacking various policies of the CPSU but also by questioning the actions of the Soviet Army in Eastern Europe, were inappropriate and offensive to the millions of Soviet citizens who had fought and died in the war.

The military alliance between the Soviet Union, the United States, Great Britain and France notwithstanding, the war increased Russian suspicion of the intentions of the West towards Russia. This was largely due to the perception that the USSR's Western allies deliberately delayed the opening of the second front. That was Stalin's reading of the situation, and it was reflected in Soviet press reports of the time.[86] At the same time, like the war against Napoleon in the previous century, World War II allowed many citizens of the Soviet Union to see the outside world, as the victorious Soviet Army crossed the border of the Soviet Union in 1944 and marched into Europe. This exposure of Soviet citizens to foreign influences greatly alarmed the Communist Party leadership, and this shaped Soviet post-war policies and anti-Western propaganda. Rather than continuing the limited political liberalization of the war period, the Soviet leadership reversed these policies. Soviet prisoners of war were sent to labour camps upon their return to the Soviet Union. From 1946 onwards, the confrontation between the USSR and its former wartime allies began. At the same time, the Soviet

---

[86] Borisov, *et al.*, eds., *Rossiia i zapad*, pp. 286–7.

leadership began to attack those Soviet citizens who held a positive view of the West as a result of their first-hand experience during the war. Not only Party propagandists but also major cultural figures were mobilized. In January 1947, at the start of the campaign, the poet Pavel Antokolskii wrote an article in a mass-circulation journal complaining that many Soviet citizens, especially the younger ones, who had been on military or other service in Western and central Europe tended to idealize life there. They were quoted by Antokolskii as saying: 'What wonderful roads they have there! What bathrooms! bicycles! cameras! brushes!'[87] He complained that for these people the quality of 'facial make-up, cigarette lighters and stockings' were more important than spiritual superiority of Soviet culture.

The second important element shaping the post-war image of the Soviet Union and the West was the emergence of the USSR and the United States as two confrontational superpowers. (With the establishment of communist regimes in Eastern Europe, the Soviet Union was no longer the single socialist country in the world.) The trend of seeing the United States as the main 'constituent other' of the USSR, which had begun in the 1930s, was now firmly entrenched. In January 1948, the Communist Party ideologist, Mikhail Suslov, announced that 'the American imperialists are clearly seeking to take the place of Fascist Germany and Japan ...' and were hatching 'a new imperialist war ... to combat socialism and democracy.'[88] It was argued that the main preoccupation of the 'American imperialism' from 1917 onwards was the destruction of the first socialist state. The US intervention on the side of the Whites in 1919 was regularly referred to. (By contrast, when this episode was also used for propaganda purposes in 1927, the emphasis had been on British involvement in the intervention.)

The unprecedented nature of the confrontation between the USSR and the West was underscored by the isolationist image of itself that Russia/the USSR constructed at that period. The tone was set by a series of decrees issued by the CPSU Central Committee in 1946–48 on Soviet literature, theatre and music. These presented Russian/Soviet culture as entirely self-sufficient and attacked any Western influences with unprecedented sharpness as examples of Soviet artists 'kowtowing to things foreign.' Both in art and in science 'Soviet' was equated with 'Russian' and proclaimed to be unquestionably superior to everything foreign. This superiority applied not only to the Soviet period but to pre-revolutionary history as well. If, in 1931, Stalin had justified rapid industrialization by stressing the need to overcome Russia's centuries-long backwardness compared to the West, from 1946 it was denied that Russia had ever been backward. The late 1940s saw the trend that had begun in the late 1930s and strengthened

---

[87] *Znamya*, 1 January 1947.
[88] Quoted in Frederick C. Barghoorn, *The Soviet Image of the United States* (New York N.Y., Harcourt, Brace and Company, 1950), pp. 103–4.

during World War II fully consolidated – namely, to view Russian pre-revolutionary history and Soviet history as one, unbroken, single stream. A direct connection was now firmly drawn between the 'liberation from the Tatar–Mongol yoke' in the fifteenth century, the emergence of Moscow as the most powerful of all the Rus principalities, the creation of the absolutist empire under Peter the Great, the expansion of that empire, and the policies of the Bolsheviks who had continued to maintain this mighty state and had elevated it to unprecedented heights.

From the mid-1930s onwards, the Soviet regime started to claim pre-revolutionary Russian culture and history as a whole (rather than isolated elements of it) as its own. From 1936, several campaigns were waged against those scientists who maintained close ties with colleagues abroad. Various victories of Russian military leaders, and certain policies of the tsars were intensively utilized during World War II, when even traditional religious feelings and the Russian Orthodox Church itself began to be cultivated. However, the European nature of pre-revolutionary Russian culture was not yet denied. For instance, during the celebrations of the centenary of Pushkin's death in 1937 – an important country-wide event – it was argued that Pushkin was 'the heir to everything progressive and advanced in European culture.'[89]

In contrast, in the post-war years, it became far more difficult, if not completely impossible, to discuss foreign influences on Russian culture. In what became known as a campaign against 'rootless cosmopolitans', writers, artists, scholars and scientists were attacked for any sign of foreign influences on their work or for studying ties between Russian and foreign cultural figures. The attack on the 'cosmopolitans' among literary critics was launched by the writer Aleksandr Fadeev, who condemned any discussion of Pushkin within the framework of European culture. Speaking at a plenum of the Board of the USSR Writers' Union in June 1947, Fadeev singled out as an example of 'cosmopolitanism' in literary criticism the book *Pushkin and World Literature* by I.M. Nusinov, whom Fadeev accused of depicting Pushkin as a 'West European.'[90]

The anti-cosmopolitan campaign had strong anti-Semitic overtones, as many of those attacked were Jews. In 1949–1953, the press presented Jews as having traditionally conspired against Russia/the USSR, together with the forces of capitalism. There were clear parallels between the pronouncements made during the anti-cosmopolitan campaign and the early twentieth century propaganda of the extreme right wing Black Hundreds. These had exploited the idea of a 'Judeo-Masonic' plot against Russia, with 'Masonic'

[89] Quoted in Frederick C. Barghoorn, *Soviet Russian Nationalism* (New York and Oxford, Oxford University Press, 1956), p. 199.
[90] K. Azadovskii and B. Egorov, 'Kosmopolity,' *Novoe literaturnoe obozrenie*, no. 36 (2/1999), p. 90.

largely meaning the Western world. Some contemporaries actually saw the similarity. Thus, in November 1949, a journalist, D. Bulatov, wrote a letter to the Council of Ministers asking for permission to resume the publication of the periodical *The Kremlin*, which had been published at the beginning of the century by the historian Dmitrii Ilovaiskii. The author of a well-known school textbook on Russian history, Ilovaiskii was a member of the Union of the Russian People and his periodical was a rabidly xenophobic publication, which proclaimed Jews and the English to be the main enemies of the Russian people. In his letter, Bulatov emphasized that if its publication were permitted, the new *Kremlin* would continue the work of its predecessor in 'fighting against the enemy of Russia.' Without seeing any problem in his argument, Bulatov noted how it seemed to him that the official line of the late 1940s resembled the one adopted by Ilovaiskii at the beginning of the century.[91] It is unclear whether Bulatov knew that Ilovaiskii had been a staunch critic of the Bolsheviks and had been arrested following the October Revolution.

The anti-cosmopolitan campaign stopped soon after Stalin's death. Already in 1954, the Soviet press published letters from leading Soviet scientists and scholars who complained about the harmful affect on the USSR's international prestige of unsubstantiated claims about the superiority of the Russians in every possible sphere of life and of the denial that in certain areas Russia and the USSR had to learn from the West. Although the main premises of the Soviet official attitude towards the West remained intact, the tone of the attacks, although hostile, was never again as sharp as that of the late 1940s. In 1956, in his secret speech to the Twentieth Party Congress, Nikita Khrushchev re-emphasized 'peaceful co-existence' rather than confrontation with the capitalist system as the new focus of the USSR's foreign policy. In the official discourse the military term 'camp' was largely replaced by the sociological category 'system.' However, the most important novelty of the post-Stalin era was not that the language of official propaganda changed, but that genuine intellectual debate, suppressed under Stalin, revived.

Intellectual debates of the 1960s to early 1980s and during *Perestroika*

The post-Stalin liberalization led to a considerable expansion of the political public space. Whereas the official press was still severely censored, many intellectuals no longer felt intimidated enough to keep their opinions to themselves. They used alternative channels – so-called *samizdat* publishing – to revive independent discussion of what Russia was and where it was going.

---

[91] GARF, op. 47, delo 2168, ll. 5–6.

The question of the relationship between Russia and the West quickly topped the agenda. Some of those involved in the debate viewed the October revolution and the subsequent years of terror as an aberration in Russian history. It is therefore not surprising that many intellectuals felt the need to return to pre-revolutionary or émigré authors for inspiration. The two most powerful figures in this debate were the writer, Aleksander Solzhenitsyn, and the nuclear physicist, Andrei Sakharov. They represented the two traditional intellectual camps of the 'Slavophiles' and the 'Westernizers.'

The two best expressions of Solzhenitsyn's position at the time were his article 'As Breathing and Consciousness Return' for the *samizdat* collection *From under the Rubble* (*Iz pod glyb*) (1974) and his *Letter to Soviet Leaders* (1973). The titles of the article and the collection clearly indicated an attempt to return to the intellectual debate which had been interrupted in the post-revolutionary period. The title *From under the Rubble* was deliberately similar to that of the 1918 collection *From the Deep* (*Iz glubiny*), which analysed the roots of Bolshevism. (In fact, Solzhenitsyn did not share the main ideas of the 1918 collection, as its authors believed that there was a strong connection between the Bolsheviks and Russia's nineteenth century intellectual tradition.) Solzhenitsyn, in contrast, argued in 1975: 'Did not the revolution throughout its early years have some of the characteristics of a foreign invasion?'[92]

Solzhenitsyn found his main inspiration in the works of the early Slavophiles of the nineteenth century and Karamzin. Like his predecessors, he believed that Russia's path of development should be differerent from that of the West. Moreover, attempts to imitate the West had always been ruinous for Russia:

> [W]e had to be dragged along the whole of the Western bourgeois-industrial and Marxist path in order to discover, at the end of the twentieth century, and again from progressive Western scholars, what any village graybeard in the Ukraine or Russia had understood from time immemorial and could have explained to the progressive commentators ages ago.[93]

Like the Slavophiles, the writer idealized Russian peasants and elevated them to a symbol of Russia. One example is the old, religious, semi-literate peasant woman, unaffected by modern life and communist values, portrayed in one of his best short stories, *Matriona's House*.

Solzhentisyn criticized multi-party systems and the superficial and 'formalistic' legal systems of the West. He insisted that direct elections by secret ballot often failed to reflect the real wishes of society and that many political leaders in the West had forgotten Christian values. The writer

---

[92] Alexander Solzhenitsyn, et al., *From Under the Rubble* (Glasgow, Collins/Harvill, 1975), p. 126.
[93] Alexander Solzhenitsyn, *Letter to Soviet Leaders* (Glasgow, Collins/Harvill: 1974), p. 21.

believed that the state system anyway 'took second place to the very essence of people's relations. When people are honest, every system becomes tolerable; when people are bitter and selfish, then the most advanced democratic system becomes intolerable.' He also agreed with Karamzin and the Slavophiles that democracy was not suitable for Russia. He asked in *From under the Rubble*:

> If Russia for centuries was used to living under autocratic regimes and suffered total collapse under the democratic system which lasted eight months in 1917, perhaps – I am only asking, not making an assertion – perhaps we should recognize that the evolution of our country from one form of authoritarianism to another would be the most natural, the smoothest, the least painful path of development for it to follow?[94]

Solzhenitsyn's criticism of the Western democracies was strongly motivated by his conviction that the 'weak and degenerate' West was constantly retreating in the face of the Communist offensive. As Solzhenitsyn's prophecy of the imminent defeat of the West by communism was proved wrong, he temporarily softened his attacks on Western democracies. In his 1990 pamphlet *How Can We Reconstruct Russia* of 1990, the writer stated that the future Russia 'very much needs democracy.'

The question of whether Russia would be better off with democratic or authoritarian government posed by Solzhenitsyn galvanized the debate among Russian intellectuals and sharpened the divide between the neo-Slavophiles and neo-Westernizers. Some intellectuals turned away from Solzhenitsyn, although he had been hitherto held almost with universally high esteem among the critics of the Soviet regime (dissidents) for his artistic talent and for being the most powerful opponent of Bolshevik policies.

The alternative view, that Russia could solve its problems by getting closer to the West rather than through isolation as recommended by Solzhenitsyn, was promoted by those who regarded Andrei Sakharov as their main spokesman. Sakharov first became known as a political thinker in 1968, when he published abroad his *Thoughts on Progress, Coexistence and Intellectual Freedom*. In this work, he was the first in the USSR to put forward the idea of convergence between the Soviet and Western (he mainly referred to the United States) systems. He saw the USSR's hope for the future in the role played by 'leftist Leninist Communists (and leftist Westerners) in socialist countries, whose activities could eventually lead to the emergence of a multi-party system and the freedom of the press in the USSR and its satellites.' He thought this would also be highly beneficial for the West. In the capitalist world, 'the leftist reformist wing of the bourgeoisie' would move the United States to accepting socialist principles of the organization of labour. In contrast to Solzhenitsyn, he did not believe that

---

[94] Solzhenitsyn, et al., *From Under the Rubble*, p. 24.

the policies of the CPSU of his time had their intellectual basis in Marxism. He rejected as dangerous the idea that Russia had a unique path of development. Sakharov and other Westernizers also criticized what they regarded as Solzhenitsyn's and the other neo-Slavophiles' idealization of pre-revolutionary Russia. They reminded their opponents of the difficult plight of the Russian people as depicted in the great Russian literature of the nineteenth century.

Both Solzhenitsyn and Sakharov could rarely express their views in the official press and both were persecuted. However, their debate was to some extent reflected in the official media. In the late 1960s and early 1970s, literary journals such as *Molodaia gvardia* and *Nash sovremennik* published articles reflecting the Slavophile position. Some of the publications were, in fact, very radical and included not particularly well-hidden attacks on the official ideology of Marxism-Leninism. They also dwelled on the involvement of a high number of non-Russians in the activities of Lenin's secret police, the Cheka, and in Stalin's terror. Authors in these journals depicted a Russia symbolized by the peasantry, whose village world was being destroyed by the Westernized civilization of the cities. The fact that such views could be expressed in official publications indicated that the periodicals had patrons in the Party leadership. In contrast, the Westernizers' position was reflected in another literary journal, *Novyi mir*. The most notable representative of the Westernizers in the Party leadership was the head of the Central Committee Ideology Department, Aleksandr Iakovlev. In an article in *Literaturnaia gazeta* on 15 November 1972 he went so far as to suggest that the view that Russia and the West were two irreconcilable enemies had no basis in Marxism. He emphasized that there were progressive, democratic forces in the Western world. At the time, Iakovlev and his supporters proved to be in the minority in the Party leadership, and, although Iakovlev's views seemed to be consonant with the spirit of *détente*, he lost his position on the Central Committee.

In the 1960s and 1970s, most of the neo-Westernizers who criticized Soviet policies were socialists, as their late nineteenth century predecessors had been. In his *Thoughts on Progress,* Sakharov described his own views as 'profoundly socialist.' That meant that most neo-Westernizers shared a critical view of the economic relations of capitalism and did not believe such relations should necessarily be replicated in Russia. Instead, it was hoped that the majority of factories and enterprises would be collectively owned by people working there. These Westernizers regarded the Soviet economic system as state capitalist rather than socialist. At the same time, they were fully supportive of Western political institutions, and were in favour of transplanting them to the Soviet Union.[95]

---

[95] See these views expressed in Vadim Belotsirkovskii, ed., *SSSR. Demokraticheskie alternativy* (Achberg, Achberger Verlagsanstalt, 1976).

The *samizdat* debate moved to the pages of the official press in the late 1980s in the course of Mikhail Gorbachev's reforms. The framework for these reforms was set by Gorbachev's vision of the Soviet Union/Russia as part of Europe. No other Russian/Soviet leader, with the possible exception of Catherine the Great, saw his country sharing a common identity with Europe to the same extent. Gorbachev first described Europe as 'our common home' in a speech to the House of Commons in London in December 1984 (i.e. three months before becoming the General Secretary of the CPSU Central Committee). He further developed this idea upon assuming full power.[96] He argued in 1987:

> Some in the West are trying to 'exclude' the Soviet Union from Europe. Now and then, as if inadvertently, they equate 'Europe' with 'Western Europe.' Such ploys, however, cannot change the geographic and historical realities. Russia's trade, cultural and political links with other European nations and states have deep roots in history. We are Europeans. Old Russia was united with Europe by Christianity ... The history of Russia is an organic part of the great European history.[97]

At the same time, Gorbachev argued that 'We were realists, so we did not try to exclude America from the European continent.' Thus, for him Europe was synonymous with 'Western civilization' to which Russia had always belonged culturally, although politically, he admitted, it had followed a different path. Although Gorbachev's initial attention to the West was connected with the issues of military and technological competition, he soon became one of the few Russian leaders with the greatest interest in and respect for Western political systems. He was the first Russian leader to pay much attention to the idea of a law-based state. Although he did not complete the job, a far-reaching legal reform began under Gorbachev, and a parliament was elected which was to play the greatest ever role in Russian politics.

Gorbachev's reforms galvanized the debate over Russia's attitude towards the West. The clear Westernizing aim of Gorbachev's policies provoked strong opposition on the part of many Communist Party officials, who rejected Gorbachev's 'New Thinking' in favour of a Stalinist amalgam of Leninism and the glorification of pre-revolutionary Russia. At the same time, a number of neo-Slavophiles of the 1960s and 1970s decided to join forces with the communists and set up a united electoral bloc for the 1990 elections to the Russian parliament. Such formerly uncompromising

---

[96] This expression was first used by Gorbachev's predecessor Leonid Brezhnev in 1981. But it was only in Gorbachev's time that this vision of the Soviet Union completely transformed the country's foreign policy.

[97] Mikhail Gorbachev, *Perestroika: New Thinking for Our Country and the World* (London, Fontana, 1988).

anti-communists as the mathematician Igor Shafarevich no longer opposed cooperation with communists. The communists, in their turn, now accepted even such elements of the Slavophile tradition as the importance of Orthodoxy for Russian national consciousness. Both camps were united by the rejection of the West as a suitable model for Russia. They condemned *perestroika* as it 'entails the US takeover' of the USSR.[98] A dramatic image of Russia in mortal danger from the forces of the West, with whom Gorbachev and other reformist Party leaders were conspiring, was constructed in such literary periodicals as *Nash sovremennik* and *Molodaia gvardia*. From 1988 onwards, writers like Iurii Bondarev, Anatolii Salutskii, Vladimir Bondarenko and others compared the threat of Gorbachev's reforms to the Soviet Union with that of Nazi Germans during World War II. They called for 'a new battle of Stalingrad' against the reformers. For them, democracy posed the greatest danger to the cultural and spiritual development of the people, 'ever since the judges in democratic Athens sentenced Socrates to die.'[99]

The unprecedented nature of Gorbachev's reforms was sensed by his opponents, who viewed them as a complete destruction of the Russian tradition. The anti-communists in the alliance agreed it was a more significant change for Russian society even than the October revolution. The publicist Elgiz Pozdniakov thus characterized *perestroika*: 'Never before has "Westernism" taken such a barefaced aggressive form in this country, rejecting everything Russian.'[100] At the end of the existence of the USSR, Gorbachev's regime began to be called 'an occupying force,' a 'foreign invasion'. Such language was similar to the way that some of the critics of Bolshevism in the post-revolutionary years, and later Solzhenitsyn, had viewed the 1917 October revolution.[101] As far as the future was concerned, these critics were sure that 'Westernism' would be defeated. In their view, attempts to Westernize Russia could be best compared to the labours of Sisyphus: 'every attempt to roll the "European stone" up the "Russian mountain" by the gigantic effort of the whole nation ended with it rolling back downhill crushing and devastating everything in its way.'[102]

All in all, the 'Slavophiles' of the *perestroika* period added little if anything new to the pre-revolutionary or post-revolutionary émigré debate. On the whole, they reiterated the ideas of the early Slavophiles about

---

[98] N. Narochnitskaia, 'Tragediia raspada,' *Literaturnaia Rossiia*, no. 34 (1992).

[99] Quoted in Julia Wishnevsky, '*Nash sovremennik* Provides Focus for "Opposition Party"', *Report on the USSR*, vol. 1, no. 3 (20 January 1989), p. 2.

[100] *Paradigmy*, vol. 5, nos 1–2 (1991).

[101] See for instance, *Sovetskaia Rossiia* (1 August 1992), arguing that *perestroika* was masterminded by President Reagan and Pope John Paul II in 1982. See also Igor Shafarevich, 'Russofobia,' *Nash sovremennik*, no. 6 (1989), p. 171.

[102] *Paradigmy*, vol. 5, nos 1–2 (1991).

republicanism and capitalism being alien to the Russian Orthodox tradition of communes and collectivism. They also repeated the idea of the late Slavophile, Danilevskii concerning the perennial Russophobia of the West. The most extreme of Gorbachev's critics (for instance, members of the *Pamyat* organization) reiterated the paranoid ideas of a Judeo-Masonic conspiracy against everything Russian, arguing that these anti-Russian Masons either resided in or were inspired by the West.

The Westernizers of the late 1980s, in contrast, did not rely to the same extent on the ideas of their pre-revolutionary predecessors. They also departed considerably even from the Westernizers of the pre-*perestroika* period. This departure was especially apparent in two areas – their attitude towards socialism and towards the empire. This chapter will discuss only the difference in the first area – the second will be considered later in the book.[103] Not since the late eighteenth century had Russian Westernizers felt to the same extent that Russia could quickly solve its problems by simply transplanting the West European economic system and political institutions. 'The West' was depicted in the pro-Western Russian media of the late *perestroika* period as completely homogeneous, undifferentiated and almost problem-free. Gorbachev's 'Common European Home' (in which the USA had its own apartment) symbolized civilization. Russia had at least partially shared in that civilization before the October Revolution, and it had to rejoin it. As early as September 1988, the future Russian parliamentarian Vladimir Lukin wrote:

> The 'Common European House' is the home of a civilization of which we have been on the periphery for a long time. The processes that are going on today in our country and in a number of socialist countries in Eastern Europe have besides everything else a similar historical dimension – the dimension of a movement towards a return to Europe in the civilized meaning of the term.[104]

This Western civilization was based on a democratic political system and a free market economy. In the second half of the nineteenth century, many Westernizers had become disillusioned with capitalism and hoped Russia could avoid it. Similarly, many of the critics of the Soviet system in the 1960s and the 1970s had been socialists. Such a position was not the sole preserve of intellectuals in Eastern Europe. In the post-war period, their West European counterparts had also expressed a great deal of faith in a strong role for the state in managing economic matters and in the welfare system. But by the 1980s a belief in the power of the market had come back into fashion in Western Europe. By the late 1980s, market ideas had reached Russia and captured the minds of its intellectuals, filling the

---

[103] See the chapter 'Imaginative Ethnography: who are the Russians?, pp. 204–7.'
[104] *Moscow News*, 25 September 1988.

vacuum that had been left by the collapse of the ideology of Marxism-Leninism.

In 1990, the neo-Westernizers' new image of Russia had wide appeal, and candidates with Westernizing platforms won elections in many areas, defeating candidates from the 'communist-patriotic bloc.' Time would show, however, that this vote indicated a rejection of the existing order rather than conscious support for a new Russia which would break with most of its past traditions and practices.

After the demise of the USSR

Immediately following the demise of the USSR, the new Russian government of President Boris Yeltsin, including such key figures as Acting Prime Minister Egor Gaidar and Foreign Minister Andrei Kozyrev, assumed full control of Russia. It saw Russia's future in renouncing its imperial legacy and its independent path of development. It wanted Russia's speedy integration into European institutions and close cooperation with the United States. On 2 January 1992, a few days after the emergence of the independent Russian Federation, Kozyrev summed up the position of the new government:

> Our active foreign policy, our diplomacy, are necessary to guarantee entry into the world community ... and thereby to help meet the internal needs of Russia ... The developed countries of the West are Russia's natural allies.[105]

In fact, Kozyrev's position was close to Gorbachev's 'New Thinking', although this parallel was not fully acknowledged. Meanwhile, Gaidar and his team of young economists, some of whom had been educated in the West, launched an ambitious programme to transform Russia's economy along the lines suggested by Western financial institutions such as the World Bank and the International Monetary Fund. According to Gaidar, the only way forward for Russia was to enter 'the civilized world'. This could be achieved only if the country destroyed its traditional, 'pathological' forms of state and society.[106]

Support for these policies, based on a vision of a fully Westernized Russia, had crumbled by 1993. The formerly strong pro-Western feelings of ordinary people and the intellectual and political élites turned into a growing feeling of resentment towards the West. The reasons for the change were two-fold. The loss of empire turned to be too much for many Russians to swallow. Moreover, the economic reforms, widely perceived to have been

[105] *Izvestiia*, 2 January 1992.
[106] Egor Gaidar, *Gosudarstvo i evoliutsiia* (Moscow, Evraziia, 1995), p. 41.

masterminded in the West, imposed hardships on the population and failed to create a society of prosperity and abundance that had been naively anticipated.

Those critics of Gorbachev's pro-Western orientation described above further gathered strength in the post-communist period. The most significant branch of them have called themselves Eurasianists, thus identifying with the émigré intellectual movement of the early 1920s. The modern-day Eurasianists are united in their hope for the resurrection of the Russian empire. At the same time, their ideology is highly anti-Western and especially anti-Anglo-Saxon. They see the world as an arena for an eternal struggle between two global forces: maritime (Atlanticists) and continental (Eurasian). Britain and the United States represent the former, whereas Russia represents the latter. Russia's centuries-old mission is to challenge the West. The journalist Sergei Morozov argued in the leading newspaper of the neo-Eurasianists, *Den*:

> The Moscow principality, which later became Russia, was designed by its leaders to be a counterbalance to the Catholic West; [its foreign policy] was a rejection of the West. We can become European. But then Russia will lose its place as the first member of Russian civilization and will become the last member of Western civilization.[107]

A similar anti-Western position has been maintained by the Communist Party of the Russian Federation (CPRF). This was re-established in 1992 as a result of the Constitutional Court ruling that Yeltsin's ban on its primary cells in 1991 was unconstitutional. Leaders of the Communist Party view Gorbachev's reforms, the disintegration of the Soviet Union and the policies of Yeltsin's government as part of a plot aimed at destroying Russia masterminded in the West, especially in the United States. In his book, *Derzhava*, the CPRF leader Gennadii Ziuganov offered his own interpretation of Russian history, which was very close to that of Morozov. Russia had not only saved Europe from destruction by the Tatar Mongols in the thirteenth–fifteenth centuries, by Napoleon in 1812–1814 and by Nazi Germany in World War II – it had also prevented the evil influence of the West spreading to other parts of the world.

The fact that in the post-communist period, critics of Russia's Westernization continued to reject the new concept of Russia was not a surprise. What was surprising to many domestic and foreign observers of the Russian scene was how quickly many former liberals withdrew their support from Kozyrev and Gaidar. As early as March 1992, the journalist Vladimir Razuvaev wrote that

---

[107] *Den*, 21–27 June 1992.

At an extremely representative conference on problems of Russian foreign policy organized by the Foreign Ministry, I was astonished to see how many representatives of the democratic current have switched to a neo-conservative position. Evidently, some people's dreams of a rosy 'return' to 'civilization' from 'communist barbarism' have ended.[108]

Indeed, some members of the main pro-Yeltsin parliamentary bloc, Democratic Russia, as well as members of his administration, quickly rejected the Kozyrev-Gaidar concept of Russia. As early as the spring of 1992, Yeltsin's advisor on foreign policy matters, Sergei Stankevich, argued that to see Russia solely as a part of the Common European Home was a distortion. Without repeating the extremist rhetoric of the neo-Eurasianists of the *Den* mode, Stankevich put forward a position of moderate neo-Eurasianism. For him, the new Russia should become economically self-sufficient 'quickly'. In its foreign policy it needed to abandon its pro-Western course, serving instead as a bridge between the West and the East. It was mistaken for Russia's foreign policy to focus exclusively on the West, Stankevich argued, especially given that never in the past three hundred years had Russia been so separated from Europe geographically as it had become after the demise of the USSR. Russia's imperial legacy could not and should not be shaken off completely. Instead, the West should recognize Russia's special interests in the newly independent states on the territory of the defunct USSR and Russia should make the defence of the twenty five million Russians living in the non-Russian states of the Commonwealth of Independent States and the Baltics its first priority.[109] However, Stankevich did not advance the view of the Eurasianists of the *Den* variety that Russia had a historic mission to stop the spread of evil influences from the West. Instead, he only argued that, given geopolitical realities, Russia's national interests could and should at times be different from those of the West. Total identification with Western Europe and the United States, as proposed by Kozyrev, was another utopia.

By mid-1993, many of the elements of Kozyrev's pro-Western orientation had been abandoned by the Russian government and had provoked criticism from President Yeltsin. The executive branch of the government adopted a position close to the one outlined by Stankevich. At the same time, the Russian parliament, dominated by nationalists (Vladimir Zhirinovskii's Liberal Democratic Party) and communists, passed a number of resolutions, which echoed the ideas of the radical neo-Eurasianists. (These resolutions had little, if any, impact on Russia's policies, however, as the 1993 Constitution had considerably limited the role of the parliament.) Why did such a shift in the Russian attitude towards the West occur?

[108] *Nezavisimaia gazeta*, 5 March 1992, quoted in Neumann, *Russia and the Idea of Europe*, p. 181.
[109] *Rossiiskie vesti*, 27 February 1993 and 5 June 1993.

Firstly, given Russia's history, Gaidar's and Kozyrev's attempts to construct a Russian identity based on the idea of congruence between Russia and their 'imagined' West was unrealistic from the start. However, the political discourse that these efforts had created had raised the hopes of the Russian population that their lives would be radically transformed for the better in the foreseeable future. So far, these hopes have not been fulfilled. Instead, the economic reforms, which the population had closely identified with Western, especially US, influences on Russian policy, had a negative impact on many average Russians. The unpopularity of these reforms damaged the prestige of the West in the eyes of Russians. A leading Moscow sociologist, Igor Kliamkin, whose Public Opinion Foundation conducted regular opinion polls throughout Russia during the first year of reforms argued that there was a strong connection between the assessment of the reforms and the attitude towards the West. According to Kliamkin, in February–July 1992, the majority of those polled believed that the reforms would succeed. This belief was largely based on the close involvement of Western advisers in Russia's economic policies. Later on in the year, however, this optimism was replaced by 'the rejection of the West, which is provoking and supporting this bad reform.' Kliamkin further speculated that 'today's reformers' course, being Western-oriented and at the same time extremely unpopular inside the country, is once again encouraging the revival of the very anti-Western sentiment and isolationism that the authorities are trying to overcome through their sincere and quite consistent Westernism.'[110] People's dissatisfaction with the way their everyday lives had been affected by economic changes was the main reason why in parliamentary elections after 1993 many Russian voters tended to choose communist and/or extreme nationalist candidates, with political platforms based primarily on condemnation of the reforms and the West.

As far as the pro-Western liberal intellectuals are concerned, many of them have also cooled towards the West in the last few years. They do not blame Russia's economic misfortunes on Western advisers, but they feel that yet again Russia is rejected by the West, as it is not allowed to enter the European/Western political, economic and military institutions with the speed they would have wished. There is no discussion at present of the possibility that Russia could become a member of the European Union. Meanwhile, NATO is expanding, embracing the USSR's former allies from the Warsaw Pact. Expressing this feeling of frustration, the philosopher Aleksei Kara-Murza has said: 'We consider ouselves as part of Europe in a cultural sense. But Europe does not consider Russia to be European. That's the problem.'[111] In the second half of the 1990s, the liberals also began to

---

[110] *Kuranty*, 23 October 1992.

[111] Quoted in Michael Urban, 'Remythologising the Russian State,' *Europe-Asia Studies*, vol. 50, no. 6 (1998), p. 986.

agree with the conservatives that, as Russia has lost its superpower status, the United States has been trying to set the terms of world politics unilaterally. Many of the foreign policy actions of the United States began to provoke criticism from both Russian liberals and conservatives. Many Russians, liberals included, also find the US treatment of Russia humiliating. They feel that their American partners emphasize far too often that Russia lost the Cold War, rather than voluntarily ceased to pursue Cold War politics as many Russians would wish to believe.

Some scholars see a longer-term trend in this shift from an overenthusiastic embrace of Westernism on the part of ordinary people and liberal intellectuals and politicians to a much more suspicious attitude towards the West's intentions. They see it as an indication that anti-Westernism is becoming the main component of a compound new Russian national identity which is being forged after the demise of the USSR and the collapse of the Soviet identity.[112]

It seems, however, that this judgement is far too gloomy. Firstly, intellectuals and politicians who deny the European nature of Russian culture and believe in a threat posed to the existence of Russia by the West do not, at least as yet, dominate the executive branch of the Russian government, which keeps control of the decision-making. The majority of representatives of the executive branch acknowledge that Russia is much closer to Europe than to any country of the East and express a persistent desire to see Russia admitted into the political and economic institutions of the West.[113] Even the Communist Party leaders agree that various Western political and economic practices have to be introduced in Russia. They do not reject outright regular parliamentary and presidential elections and some elements of market economy. Indeed, during his presidential election campaign in 1996 Ziuganov was promising the electorate that regular elections for top public offices would continue if he became president. Moreover, while promising to alter the economic policies of Yeltsin's government completely, the Communist leader said he was not against a market economy as such. Secondly, among the Russian population, however strong its dissatisfaction with the current state of affairs may be, most people do support political liberties and do not want any return to the planned command-administrative economy of the Communist era.[114]

---

[112] Ibid, p. 986.

[113] See, for instance, President Vladimir Putin's opening statement at the EU–Russia summit in May 2000: Russia 'was, is and will be a European country by its location, its culture, and its attitude toward economic integration' (*Interfax*, 29 May, 2000).

[114] See opinion polls quoted in Richard Rose, 'Where are Postcommunist Countries Going?', *Journal of Democracy*, vol. 8, no. 3 (1997), pp. 101–2: New Russian Barometer surveys 'show that Russians are very positive about the personal freedom that the new regime gives them, and half prefer the 'window-shopping' market economy (lots of goods at high prices) to a planned economy with low prices but empty shelves.'

Finally, the anti-Western feelings expressed by most Russians, and especially criticism of the West on the part of liberals and moderates, are largely aimed at the United States rather than Western Europe. Unpopular economic reforms are mostly associated with American advice. During the NATO bombing of Serbia in the spring and the summer of 1999, which was sharply opposed by the majority of Russians, the actions were blamed almost solely on the United States. Some journalists even argued that the bombing amounted to a war waged by the United States against Europe, of which Russia was part.[115] In December 1999, the Russian political elites and mass media gave a sharp rebuff to Bill Clinton's criticism of Russian policy in Chechnia. Yeltsin even suggested that the US president 'for a minute, for half a minute' had forgotten that Russia had a full arsenal of nuclear weapons. Even fairly liberal Russian newspapers argued that the Russian president was 'right' in rebuffing his US counterpart.[116] Yet, the European Union, the foreign ministers of which condemned Russia over Chechnia in far sharper terms than Clinton had done, did not receive the same rebuke from the Russians.

Conclusions

For the past three hundred years, the views of Russian intellectuals and to some extent the government about what Russia has been, and should be, have been shaped more than anything else by a comparison with the West. In the Soviet period, the counterposition of Russia and the West became part of the identity of the Russian general public. Different thinkers have drawn different conclusions, but the one drawn by Peter Chaadaev remains especially influential. Ever since the publication of his *Philosophical Letters* in 1836, Russian intellectuals have been trying to find answers to the questions about Russia posed by Chaadaev. The 'Russian socialism' of Herzen and the later populists seemed to be the answer which dealt most comprehensively with Chaadaev's conclusions. As such, 'Russian socialism' was a form of Romantic nationalism which defined the Russians as the bearers of a specific historical mission. It fully transformed Russia's 'backwardness' compared with the West into Russia's advantage. Like nationalist intellectuals elsewhere, the early Russian socialists were people whose original identities had been challenged by education and by moving from the provinces to the two Russian capitals. In the process of dealing with their personal identity crises, they created an ideology which was nationalist in essence. Yet, paradoxically, this 'Russian socialism' hampered the development of a modern national consciousness by following the

---

[115] Viacheslav Dashichev in *Sodruzhestvo*, no. 3 (March 1999), pp. 9–10.
[116] *Nezavisimaia gazeta*, 10 December 1999, p. 1.

Slavophiles in reducing the nation only to one group in society – the exploited working people. Its popularity not only reflected but also reinforced the gap between the upper and the lower classes in society. This gap was a significant contributing factor to the Russian revolution of 1917. The Bolshevik government which came to power that year incorporated elements of 'Russian socialism' into its ideology. The idea that a small elite group could best articulate what was in the people's interests had long been inherent in Russian intellectual, and especially the Russian socialist, tradition. This became a justification for the dictatorial actions of a government that claimed to rule by popular mandate.

From the late eighteenth century, Russian intellectuals had exhibited an ambivalent, love–hate attitude towards the West. The almost exclusively negative picture of the West presented in Soviet government propaganda from the 1930s represented a break with the pre-revolutionary tradition. Previously, attitudes towards the West and the question of Russia's place in a European civilization had received a much more multi-dimensional treatment. It is not surprising that years of complete rejection of Western civilization in Soviet propaganda eventually produced the opposite reaction. They were 'balanced' by the construction of an idealized image of Western Europe and the United States in the pro-reform media in the late *perestroika* period and the first post-communist years. The extent of this idealization was comparable only to the pro-European sentiments of the supporters of Peter the Great's reforms in the early eighteenth century. Again, as happened two centuries ago, this unequivocal identification of the Russians with their 'Western ideal' could not be sustained, and once again praise has recently been replaced by bitter criticism. Yet, at the turn of the twenty-first century, the West remains the main point of comparison for Russia, just as much as it had been when Russia's 'Europeanization' first began.

4

Russia and the East

Russians 'are situated in the east of Europe ... but for all that
we were never of the East'
> Peter Chaadaev (*Apology of a Madman*, 1837)

'Yes, we are Scythians! Yes, Asians we are
With squint and lusty eyes!'
> Aleksandr Blok ('Scythians' 1917)

Russia's agonizing ambivalence over its relationship with the West has
raised inevitably the question of its relationship with the East, the 'Orient.'
As Edward Said and other scholars have shown, from the eighteenth
century onwards an 'imagined Orient' became the main constituent other
for West Europeans. Since the advent of Oriental studies in Western
Europe, the Orient has been the 'other' against which the European identity
has been constructed. This perceived 'otherness' of the East has been not a
mere recognition of difference, but an assertion of the inferiority of the
Orient compared to Europe. The main features attributed to the 'Orient'
were despotism, emotion, passivity, stagnation and indulgence in luxury for
some with poverty for the rest. In contrast, Europe was distinguished by
political freedom, reason, energy, dynamism, self-controlled moderation
and prosperity. Setting itself off against the 'Orient' in such a way,
'European culture gained in strength and identity.'[1] The world-view of a
European thus has been sharply bi-polar. Everything that was not European
was Oriental or Asian.

A number of scholars have applied Said's model to studying Russian
intellectuals' views of Asia. There is a tendency to argue that, until the early

---

[1]   Edward W. Said, *Orientalism* (London, Penguin Books, 1995), p. 3.

twentieth century, Russian intellectuals remained entirely 'European in their attitude towards Asia.'[2] But were they really? Does Said's model fully cover the entire spectrum of ideas expressed by Russian nation-builders on Russia's relationship with Asia? After all, as the previous chapter has shown, Russia's own European identity has been far from certain. In Western Europe, Russia itself has been often 'Orientalized.' Foreigners who visited pre-Petrine Muscovy saw it as a backward and profoundly non-European country. From the time of Nicholas I, Russia's political system was again regarded in the West as similar to 'Asiatic despotism.' Russian Slavophiles themselves thought that the Russian way of thinking was not based on reason in the same way that it was in Western Europe. In turn, the Russian Westernizers saw pre-Petrine Russia as an Asiatic rather than a European entity. Moreover, from the sixteenth century onwards, both geographically and culturally, 'Asia' has been part of Russia itself, not a distant overseas colony. What effect have such peculiarities had on the Russians' self-perception? This chapter argues that while Said's model can explain many aspects of the way Russians perceive Asia, it nevertheless does not cover the full range of attitudes.[3] It also aims to show that Russia's ties with Asia *per se* were rarely of interest to Russian nation-builders, but that they often acquired immense importance in the light of the debate over Russia's relations with the West. Said's model was regularly 'subverted' when Russian nation-builders attempted to strengthen the Russian identity vis-à-vis the West by appropriating certain aspects of Asian traditions as Russia's own.

The chapter starts by looking at instances when Russian nation-builders adopted an unequivocally European imperialist position towards Asia, as 'the other' which Russia, as a European power, could dominate politically and culturally. It shows that even in these instances comparisons with Europe were central to the arguments of the Russians. Many insisted that Russia's imperialist policies towards Asia were both more humane and more effective than the West European ones. The chapter then looks at various ways in which Asian cultures and traditions were appropriated as parts of Russia's own identity in the nineteenth and the early twentieth centuries. It finishes by looking at some peculiarities in the ways Russian intellectuals perceived Asia in the Soviet period.

---

[2]   See, in particular, Seymour Becker, 'Russia Between East and West: the Intelligentsia, Russian National Identity and Asian Borderlands,' *Central Asian Survey*, vol. 10, no. 4 (1991), pp. 47–64. Most forcefully, this view is put forward in Nicholas V. Riasanovsky, 'Asia through Russian Eyes,' in Wayne S. Vucinich, ed., *Russia and Asia: Essays on the Influence of Russia on the Asian People* (Stanford CA, Hoover Institute Press, 1972), p. 17.

[3]   Nathaniel Knight, 'Grigor'ev in Orenburg, 1851–1862: Russian Orientalism in the Service of Empire?' *Slavic Review*, vol. 59, no. 1 (2000), pp. 74–100 convincingly argued in favour of this position, using the work of one of Russia's ethnographers as a case study.

Russia is not of the East

Since the beginning of the modern debate on Russian identity in the eighteenth century, Asia for Russian nation-builders has been exemplified either by areas which were already part of the Russian state, by areas which Russia was in the process of conquering, or by areas which were seen as likely to be conquered in future. Although China, Egypt and the lands of the Bible also attracted the attention of some Russians, these 'Orients' hardly figured in the debates on Russian identity. Largely depending on the political realities of the period, at different times different areas were perceived as Russia's 'Orient,' against which, or by the appropriation of which, Russian identity could be constructed. In the eighteenth century, the Tatars, especially those from Kazan, constituted 'Asia' for the Russians. As the previous chapter has shown, most of the eighteenth century was a 'blissful' period for the Russian nation-builders. At that time they felt little reason to doubt that the Russian identity was fully European. Therefore the divide between Russia, a European state, and Asia was clear cut. Educated Russians felt their country had made a definitive break with pre-Petrine Rus, which used to be depicted by foreign travellers as an Asiatic despotic entity. For this reason, it is difficult to agree with the following conclusion by Roman Szporluk:

> If Russians were to learn from the experience of the West, they should have sought to forge a new common identity with the Tatars and other peoples ruled by Muscovy, just as England, Wales and Scotland had combined to produce a common British identity.[4]

In order to substantiate his argument, Szporluk refers to a book by Linda Colley on the construction of the compound British identity, which from the early eighteenth century onwards has been superimposed on the English, Welsh and Scottish identities. However, the arguments of Colley's book are hardly applicable to the Russian case.[5] In the periods under discussion by Szporluk and Colley, sharing the same religion played a crucial role in forging a common identity. The English experienced significant problems in incorporating the Catholic Irish into the British nation, as a key element of the British identity was Protestantism. It is not clear how the Russians, whose identity had been so strongly based on Orthodoxy up to, and even after, the time of Peter the Great, could have overcome the

---

[4] Roman Szporluk, 'The Fall of the Tsarist Empire and the USSR: The Russian Question and Imperial Overextension,' in Karen Dawisha and Bruce Parrott, eds., *The End of Empire? The Transformation of the USSR in Comparative Perspective* (Armonk NY, M.E. Sharpe, 1997), p. 68.

[5] Linda Colley, *Britons. Forging the Nation 1707–1837* (New Haven CT, Yale University Press, 1992).

problem that the Tatars had been Muslims since the fourteenth century. By the late eighteenth century less than 20 per cent of Kazan Tatars had been converted to Orthodoxy, according to the official statistics of the time. Moreover, many conversions existed only on paper rather than in reality. From the fifteenth century onwards, in Russian ballads (*byliny*), Tatars consistently featured as the main enemies of the Russian heroes (*bogatyri*). The very description of the invasion of the East Slavic lands by Tatar–Mongols in the thirteenth to fifteenth centuries as the 'Tatar yoke', was already in use among Muscovite Church chroniclers by the second half of the sixteenth century.[6]

A search for a secular Russian identity could have begun and did indeed begin only as a result of reforms aimed at 'Europeanizing' Russia. The move of the Russian capital to St. Petersburg in the newly acquired North European part of the empire in the early eighteenth century, and other attempts by Peter the Great to 'Europeanize' Russia, made Russia's eastern areas even more alien. In this period, when historians began to write histories of Russia, the 'Tatar yoke' started to be viewed as a central episode in medieval Russian history. They were strongly influenced by the above-mentioned writings of the Church chroniclers, which they discovered and chose to regard as objective historical accounts. According to the eighteenth century historiography and literature, Moscow was able to throw off 'the Tatar yoke' as a result of its cultural superiority. Repeating the argument of the sixteenth century chronicles, Moscow's conquest of Kazan and Astrakhan on the Volga, and of other remnants of the Golden Hordes in Siberia in the sixteenth century, were presented as retribution by the Russians for the Tatar invasion. This image was created, for instance, in Mikhail Kheraskov's poem *Rossiada* (1779) about the conquest of Kazan by Ivan the Terrible. Depicting the takeover of Kazan as the last stage in the centuries-old struggle between the Russians and the Tatars, Kheraskov exclaimed: 'I am hailing Russia freed from the barbarians.'[7]

It should be noted that the same negative view of the Tatars as enemies is to be found in eighteenth and nineteenth century folklore. Peasant songs, included in the *Kirsha Danilov Collection*, compiled in the 1740s–60s and first published in 1804, provide many examples. The song 'Tatar captivity', which was popular in villages from Arkhangel *guberniia* in the North to Ukraine in the South, included the following description by a Russian woman of her grandson, who was half-Russian and half-Tatar: 'On your mother's side, you are my native (*rodnoi*) grandson; on your father's side you are a little evil Tatar' (*zloi tatarchenok*). Other songs described the

---

[6] Donald Ostrowski, *Muscovy and the Mongols* (Cambridge, Cambridge University Press, 1998), pp. 244–5.

[7] G.P. Makogonenko, *Russkaia literatura XVIII veka* (Leningrad, Prosveshchenie, 1970), p. 18.

cruelty of the Tatar invasion and the struggle of the Slavs against them (for instance, the 1327 revolt against the Tatars in the town of Tver). The famous Battle of Kulikovo against the Tatars in 1380 was often featured in peasant songs. Popular stories about this battle were among the texts most widely read by literate peasants in the late nineteenth century.[8] Popular prints of the period also featured Russian battles against the Tatars.[9]

Since this early period, Russia's relationship with Asia has been important for the light it could shed on Russia's status vis-à-vis Europe. Two themes which would dominate Russian national discourse in the nineteenth century emerged in the eighteenth. The first was the idea that Russia's geographical position obliged it to defend Europe from invasion by Asians and cleanse it of their presence. This is how Catherine II and members of her government presented the annexation of the Crimea in 1783. In the words of the first Governor-General of the Crimea, Prince Potemkin, the annexation was 'the first step of cleansing Europe from Mohammed.'[10] Secondly, Russia was bringing the fruits of the European Enlightenment and Christianity to the barbarous, infidel, bloodthirsty East. Thus, in the words of the anonymous author of the Ode to 'The Great Tsarina Catherine on the Occasion of the Acquisition of the Crimea' (1784), the Tatar khan, the former ruler of the region, was 'enlightened by Catherine [and], hopefully, abandoned his beastly nature (*nrav zverinyi*).'[11]

As Russians were becoming less confident vis-à-vis the West in the nineteenth century, these themes were somewhat modified to emphasize more strongly Russia's 'sacrifices' in defending Europe from 'barbarians' and to claim Russia's superiority to Europe in enlightening them. These new variations on old themes were first offered in Nikolai Karamzin's *History of the Russian State*. The historian argued that on various occasions, starting with the Tatar-Mongol invasion in the thirteenth–fifteenth centuries, Russia had in effect saved Europe from being taken over by Asians. Later, it had begun to bring the fruits of civilization into Asia – and had done so much more effectively than the West Europeans. According to Karamzin, the Russians deserved particular admiration because they 'enlightened [conquered non-Christians] in the Divine Faith solely by setting them a better example, without using the violence and villainy to which other devotees of Christianity had resorted in Europe and Asia.'[12] Subsequent historians elaborated on these themes, and the historian Sergei Solovev in the mid-nineteenth century presented the struggle between Europe and Asia

8　　M.M. Gromyko, *Mir russkoi derevni* (Moscow, Molodaia gvardiia, 1991), pp. 216, 307.

9　　D. Rovinskii, *Russikie narodnyia kartinki*, vol.1 (St. Petersburg, Tipografiia Imperatorskoi Akademii Nauk, 1881), p. 150 (reprint Munich, Otto Sagner Verlag, 1989).

10　Quoted in Andrei Zorin, 'Krym v istorii russkogo samosoznaniia,' *Novoe literaturnoe obozreniie*, no. 31 (3/1998), p. 127.

11　Ibid, p. 125.

12　N.M. Karamzin, *Istoriia Gosudarstva Rossiiskogo*, vol. 1, (Moscow, Nauka, 1989), p. 15.

as the main theme of Russian history as a whole. It was a testimony to Russia's strength that, despite regular attacks from the Asians of the Steppe and the lengthy Tatar-Mongol yoke, Russians managed to preserve their Christian European identity.

Although the Tatar Mongol invasion remained a central episode in Russian history as presented in the history textbooks, in the first half of the nineteenth century another region began to attract the particular attention of Russian nation-builders and became Russia's main 'Orient.' That was the Caucasus. In the period between 1801 and 1830, Transcaucasia was annexed by Russia and from the second decade of the nineteenth century until the 1860s Russia waged a brutal war against the mountain-dwellers of the North Caucasus.

The Caucasus was 'discovered' as Russia's 'Orient' by Pushkin. In the words of the literary critic Vissarion Belinskii, 'the Russian society became acquainted with the Caucasus through the publication in 1822 of his narrative poem "The Prisoner of the Caucasus."'[13] For Belinskii, 'Caucasus was the crucible of Pushkin's poetry,' later it became 'the crucible of the poetry of Lermontov.'

The vision of the Caucasus and of its role in shaping Russia's identity held by Pushkin and Lermontov was complex. But, for all this complexity, their poetry reinforced an openly imperialistic attitude towards the area. They both hailed the military as well as the cultural superiority of Russia over this newly discovered 'Orient'. Lermontov's poem *The Dispute* counterposed the 'decrepit' (*driakhlyi*), 'speechless' (*bezglagolnyi*), 'dead' (*mertvyi*) East (*vostok*) to the young, active, militarily powerful Russia, whose 'shining' (*sverkaia*) troops were to be seen from 'the Urals to the Danube.' Pushkin's *The Fountain of Bakhchisarai* contrasted spiritual and moral power of a European (actually Polish) princess Maria to the Tatar Khan Girei. Under the influence of her love, according to Belinskii, Girei, 'does not yet become a human being, but ceases to be an animal.'

Even when Pushkin and Lermontov showed fascination with mountain tribesmen as freedom-loving people, a feeling of European superiority never seemed to disappear from their description of the peoples of North Caucasus. In Pushkin's *The Prisoner of the Caucasus*, the Russian prisoner is called a 'European', who loved 'their (tribesmen's) simple life and their quick, free (*volnye*) movement.' Yet, he urged his Circassian mistress to leave 'the dreadful place' (the Caucasus) with him.[14] Even positive comments about the mountain-dwellers were usually accompanied by strong reservations. Lermontov's *A Hero of Our Times* provides some good examples. After observing that the Ossetians were 'pitiful people ...

[13] V.G. Belinskii, *Sobranie sochinenii*, vol. 6 (Moscow, Nauka, 1981), p. 312.

[14] A.S. Pushkin, *Polnoe sobranie sochinenii*, 2nd ed. (Moscow, Izdatelstvo AN SSSR, 1957), vol. 4, pp. 114 and 127.

Extremely stupid... Cannot do anything and incapable of being educated,'
a Russian officer concluded: 'Now our Kabardianians or Chechens, even
though they are bandits and poor, at least were dare-devils ... But those
[Ossetians] do not know how to use weapons.' Explaining that he spent ten
years in Chechnia, the officer proceeded: 'We were fed up with those cut-
throats. Now, thank God, they are more peaceful ...'[15]

All in all, even if Russians were often shamefully cruel towards the tribesmen, the takeover of the Caucasus could not have been avoided. In his
poem 'Izmail-Bei', Lermontov, on the one hand, condemned the destruction
of mountain villages and called Russian troops 'beasts of prey.' But the
introductory part of the same poem called on a Circassian to 'submit
himself' to the powers of the Russian tsar, whose victory was inevitable.
Lermontov's call echoed the one in the epilogue of Pushkin's 'The Prisoner
of the Caucasus': 'Submit, Oh Caucasus! Ermolov Marches!'[16] Similarly,
the Decembrists, their occasional praise for the freedom-loving mountain-
dwellers notwithstanding, saw the takeover of the Caucasus by Russia as
historically progressive. Thus, for Mikhail Lunin, one of the main thinkers
among the Decembrists, the conquest of the Caucasus, which 'had been
under control of semi-barbarian little tribes' (*poludikie narodtsy*), made
Russia a desirable partner of Europe and put it on a par with major
European powers.[17]

In 1864, the entire Caucasus was finally fully subjugated to Russian rule,
and a new expansion into Central Asia began, with the takeover of the area
being completed by 1885 (Figure 4.1). Russian intellectuals responded to
this turn in foreign policy by focusing their attention on Central Asia as
Russia's new 'Orient.' Yet, similar themes and attitudes remained. For the
historians Dmitrii Ilovaiskii, Sergei Rozhdestvenskii and Viktor Abaza, the
Muslims of Central Asia were so treacherous that peaceful co-existence
with them was impossible.[18] Following the massacre of Turkmens by
General Mikhail Skobelev in 1881, Fedor Dostoevskii observed that in
Central Asia, Russia's civilizing mission 'will bribe our spirit and drive us
thither.' It will strengthen Russia's European identity, because 'in Asia we,
too, are Europeans.'[19] Dostoevskii and others particularly strongly insisted
on Russia's civilizing mission in the area, because this territorial extension
brought Russia in conflict with Britain. Russia's penetration into Central
Asia was perceived by the British government as a challenge to British

---

[15] M.Iu. Lermontov, *Sochineniia v shesti tomakh*, vol. 6 (Moscow-Leningrad, Izdatelstvo
     Akademii Nauk SSSR, 1957), p. 207.
[16] General Aleksei Ermolov was one of the leading figures in the conquest of the Caucasus.
[17] Quoted in Ia. Gordin, *Kavkaz: zemlia i krov* (St. Petersburg, Zvezda, 2000), pp. 15 and 19.
[18] See Seymour Becker, 'The Muslim East in Nineteenth Century Russian Popular
     Historiography,' *Central Asian Survey*, vol. 5, no. 3/4 (1986), p. 36.
[19] Quoted in Milan Hauner, *What Is Asia To Us? Russia's Asian Heartland Yesterday and
     Today* (London, Routledge, 1992), p. 1.

Figure 4.1 Vladimir Vereshchagin, 'A fatally wounded soldier' (1873): a scene from the Russian military campaign in Central Asia. (The Tretiakov Gallery, Moscow)

colonial domination of the Indian subcontinent and 'sinister Russian imperialism' was strongly attacked in the British press.

Finally, from 1885 Russian foreign policy shifted to the Far East. And for a few intellectuals this area now turned into Russia's Orient. Finance Minister Sergei Witte's policy of peaceful expansion by Russia into the Far East provoked a varied response from intellectuals. One of them was a variant of the well-known theme of Russia as a defender of Europe from Asiatic invaders, which was at the time most fully developed by the religious philosopher Vladimir Solovev. In his poem *Pan-Mongolism* (1894) and the essay *The Antichrist* (1900) he warned of a new Mongol invasion of Europe under the leadership of the Japanese. For him, Russia's strategy in the East should be cooperation with European powers in the struggle against the Yellow Peril. Later, Solovev's works were seen by his admirers as a prophetic anticipation of the Russian-Japanese war in 1904–05.

So far, the above-described examples perfectly fit Said's model of the Europeans' view of the 'Orient.' In the Russian case, these attitudes were expressed by nation-builders in an attempt to emphasize Russia's unquestionable European identity. Russia's strength vis-à-vis the West was underscored by alleging that Russians could carry out their civilizing mission in Asia more effectively than Europeans.

Russia also belongs to Asia

But, alongside these typically European attitudes towards Asia, from the early nineteenth century some Russians were willing to concede that, because of Russia's history and geography, their relationship with Asia was different to that of the Europeans. In ways, which can be regarded as 'subverting' Said's model, Russian nation-builders tried to integrate 'Asia' into Russia. As a result, the bi-polar world of a European, in which the West and the East constituted the two poles, was undermined. Instead, a new vision – a triad of Russia, the East and the West – emerged.

In 1810, Sergei Uvarov, then Russian attaché in Vienna and later to become Minister of Education under Nicholas I, put forward a proposal to create an Asiatic Academy in St. Petersburg. This was one of the first examples of a Russian contemplating that Russia's relationship with the East was somewhat different from that of Western Europe. In most respects, Uvarov's proposal reflected his typically European outlook. He was fascinated with the richness of ancient cultural, philosophical and religious traditions of the East. But he believed that these traditions were being forgotten by the Asian people themselves. The efforts of European scholars and governments had been needed to bring these traditions back to light. Russia had to join the other nations of Europe in rediscovering the intellectual treasures of Asia. However, there was one passage in the proposal which emphasized that Russia's relationship with the East was special, different from that of the Europeans, and that it was Russia's strength. Because many of Russia's own subjects were Asians, its academy of Asian studies could mediate between 'the civilization of Europe and the enlightenment of Asia.' Uvarov anticipated that there a 'European critic' could work side-by-side with 'an Asiatic lama.' In this way the Russian academy would be superior to the Oriental studies centres of France or England.[20] In other words, Uvarov believed that Russia would be able to

---

20   Riasanovsky, 'Asia through Russian Eyes,' p. 13.

give silent Asia a voice. He, and other Russians who thought that people of
the East should be allowed to speak for themselves, would have agreed with
Said's conclusion that in Western Orientalism a European always spoke for
a silent Asian. In 1833 a commentator in the journal *Teleskop* proudly
stated that some of 'our' Asians had become eminent specialists in Oriental
studies. In contrast, the British or French could not claim Indians or
Algerians among their scholars.[21] Russian specialists in Oriental studies
believed that West Europeans were often racist in their attitudes towards
the inhabitants of their colonies. In contrast, the Russians understood that,
given favourable conditions, anybody could achieve the standards currently
set by European civilization.[22] After all, had not the Russians themselves
followed precisely that route to overcome their backwardness and isolation
after Peter the Great had sent them to school in Europe?

Yet, even after Peter the Great had 'Europeanized' Russia, some Western
authors continued to Orientalize it. The French consul in Tiflis, Jacques-
Francois Gamba, argued in 1826 that Georgia had changed little after two
and a half decades of Russian rule because in Russia itself one 'habitually
finds the habits and tastes of nomads.'[23] In 1839, the Marquis de Custine
was convinced that even among educated Russians, beneath the thin veneer
of Europeanness, 'a Tatar,' 'an Oriental' was hidden. In response to these
charges, Russian nation-builders abandoned the bi-polar world-view to
which they had adhered in the eighteenth century, and created instead a
triangle, in which Russia was one separate point, in addition to the East and
the West. One of the first to create this triangle was, of course, Peter
Chaadaev, when he questioned Russia's European identity. In his *Apology
of a Madman* (1837) he suggested that 'We are quite simply a country of the
North.'[24] He attacked the early Slavophiles for allegedly claiming that
Russia was 'of the East.' In fact, the leading Slavophiles did nothing of the
sort. The East did not attract their attention. Indeed, they cherished the
traditions of pre-Petrine Rus. It was not them, but Westernizers such as
Belinskii, who saw Muscovy as a realm of Asiatic despotism.

But Chaadaev was right that from the 1820s onwards some Russian
intellectuals, influenced by the ideas of romantic nationalism, were willing
to contemplate the idea that Russia was a world of its own by virtue of its
special relationship to Asia. Thus in 1827, the periodical *Moscow Herald*
suggested that: 'Located between East and West ... our fatherland seems to
have been designed by nature to serve as a link in the chain of humanity's

---

[21] Quoted in Susan Layton, *Russian Literature and Empire. Conquest of the Caucasus from
    Pushkin to Tolstoy* (Cambridge, Cambridge University Press, 1994), p. 82.

[22] Knight, 'Grigor'ev in Orenburg, 1851–1862', p. 96.

[23] Quoted in Layton, *Russian Literature and Empire*, p. 79.

[24] See, E.B. Rashkovskii and V.G. Khoros, 'Problema "zapad-Rossiia-vostok" v filosofskom
    nasledii P.Ia. Chaadaeva, in *Vostok-zapad. Issledovaniia, perevody, publikatsii* (Moscow,
    Nauka, 1988), p. 133.

universal development, to achieve a specific conjunction of European culture and Asia's enlightenment.'[25] In his *Philosophical Letters* Chaadaev rejected this view, claiming that despite its geographical position, Russia had failed to combine the two great principles of the East and the West – imagination and reason. However, many Russian intellectuals did not agree with him and tried to find proof of Russia's uniqueness in its peculiar geography and history.

In the 1830s and the 1840s Russian poets and writers, particularly Lermontov, promoted a view of Russia as a country with something in common with both the West and the East, yet different from both. Russia's main difference was that it was a young nation, which had entered world history not even with Peter the Great, but when the Russian army defeated Napoleon. Russia's youth put it in a good position to pick and choose the best in the traditions of both the East and the West, thereby creating its own culture. Lermontov observes in *A Hero of Our Time*: 'I was fascinated by the capability of a Russian to adapt to the customs of the peoples, among whom he happens to live. I do not know whether this capacity of the mind should be praised or condemned, but it only shows its flexibility ...' In making the observation, the poet referred to Russians' relationship with the peoples of the Caucasus. Moreover, for Lermontov, Russians who were exposed to the direct influence of Asia because of their service in the newly acquired borderlands possessed qualities superior to those people who lacked such experience. Russian military-men in the Caucasus were popularly called Caucasians and in his essay, entitled *The Caucasian* (1841), Lermontov, who himself served twice in that area, thus concluded:

> A Caucasian is half-Russian, half-Asian person; oriental customs are dominant in him, but he is ashamed of that in front of strangers, i.e. those who visit the area from Russia ... A real Caucasian is an incredible man, deserving a great respect and sympathy.[26]

This perceived adaptability to foreign customs and ability to appropriate their best features on the part of the Russians thus began to be viewed as a sign of the Russians' uniqueness, as West Europeans lacked these qualities. The reason why Russians were able to develop such a quality was the multi-ethnic nature of their state and, in particular, the presence of Asians among its subjects. It is not surprising then that when Dostoevskii in his famous speech on Pushkin depicted the poet as a symbol of Russianness he attributed to him an unmatched ability to represent non-Russians authentically, because he possessed in abundance the Russian quality of

---

[25] Quoted in Layton, *Russian Literature and Empire*, p. 84.
[26] Lermontov, *Sochineniia v shesti tomakh*, vol. 6, p. 348.

'reincarnating himself wholly into an alien nationality.'[27] None of the great West European poets were capable of the same transformation. Of course, Pushkin best demonstrated this capacity when writing about Russia's 'Orient' – the Caucasus.

Among ordinary Russians this perceived ability to understand other nationalities, without being blinded by racial prejudices like the Europeans, led them often to marry aliens with whom they lived side by side. Thus, the eminent geographer and explorer, Colonel Mikhail Veniukov, observed in his *The Progress of Russia in Central Asia*:

> We are not Englishmen who in India do their utmost to avoid mingling with the natives ... Our strength, on the contrary, lies in the fact that up to the present time we have assimilated subject races, mingling affably with them.[28]

Attempts to assert Russia's affinity with Asia increased particularly whenever criticism of Russia in the West stepped up. This happened, for instance, following the Crimean war of 1854–56 and Russia's suppression of the Polish uprising in 1863. In that period, even thinkers regarded as liberals started to concede that, after all, Russia was to some extent 'of the East.' Thus, Aleksandr Herzen, who strongly condemned the Russian government's suppression of the Poles, and had thought in 1833 that the Slavs belonged to Europe, in 1867 was willing to argue:

> We are being expelled from Europe, as God expelled Adam from Eden. But why does one assume that we think Europe is Eden and that to be a European is an honourable title?... We do not blush at the thought that we come from Asia ... We do not need to join anybody. We are *part of the world between America and Europe* and this is enough for us.[29]

If Russian historians from Karamzin to Vasilii Kliuchevskii thought that the Tatar-Mongol yoke in the long run had failed to change Russia's European identity, some specialists in Oriental studies were not so sure. The geographer and explorer, Peter Semenov, interpreted the impact of history on Russian development in this way:

> Having spent its adolescence as a European hostage in captivity of Asiatic tribes, and having been cast by a will of genius (i.e. Peter the Great) into the midst of European development, she has identical similarities to both Europe and Asia, and belongs equally to both parts of the word.[30]

---

[27] F.M. Dostoevskii, *Polnoe sobranie sochinenii v tridtsati tomakh*, vol. 26 (Leningrad, Nauka, 1984), p. 146.

[28] Quoted in Hauner, *What Is Asia to Us?*, p. 43.

[29] A.I. Gerzen, 'Prolegomena' in *Russkaia ideia* (Moscow, Respublika, 1992), p. 121 [emphasis in the original].

[30] Quoted in Hauner, *What Is Asia to Us?*, p. 42. Semenov (1827–1914) was given the title Tian-Shansky by the tsar in commemoration of his exploration of the mountain range in Central Asia.

In his *Russia and Europe* (1869), Nikolai Danilevskii took another crucial step to incorporate Asia into Russia, which was to affect the thinking of Russian intellectuals in the next century. As mentioned in the previous chapter, Danilevskii denied that Russia belonged either to Europe or to Asia, and posited that it was a separate cohesive 'natural-geographical region.' But his most important contribution to the debate over whether Russia was of the East or of the West was to destroy the firm boundary between Europe and Asia, the existence of which Russians had taken for granted since the early eighteenth century. The natural boundaries between Europe and Asia were the Urals in the East and either the Caucasian range or the river Terek in the North Caucasus to the South. Danilevskii rejected the view that there was any natural barrier dividing Europe and Asia. Instead he insisted that Europe was 'simply one part of Asia, not more different from other parts of it than those parts are different from each other.'[31] Danilevskii built his view on the notion expressed earlier in the century by French and German scholars that Europe and Asia formed a single continent. But Danilevskii added an important ideological dimension to the findings of European geographers and geologists. Said has noted the signficance of drawing a geographical boundaries between 'us' and 'them' when attributing a plethora of negative qualities to foreign people. Danilevskii used his destruction of the geographical boundary between Europe and Asia to underpin his attack on the bi-polar world, in which 'the West, Europe constitutes the pole of progress, constant improvement, tireless move forward; the East, Asia – the pole of stagnation and inertness.'[32] He argued that great civilizations had been created not only by Europeans but also by Asians, using China and Egypt as the main examples. He also rejected the view that world history, including Russian history, could be interpreted as a perennial struggle between Europe and Asia.[33]

After Danilevskii's 'discovery', the search for Russia's Eastern roots gradually became fashionable. The so-called Easterners (*Vostochniki*), a group of supporters of Witte's Far Eastern expansionist policies, entered the Russian national debate in the 1880s and argued that Asia should be seen as an ally of Russia against the West. They were the first to claim that Russia was not the heir to Christian Byzantium, as most had accepted up to then, but a successor to the Mongol empire of Ghengis-Khan. For one of the leading Easterners, Prince Esper Ukhtomskii, Russians have always 'belonged to' Asia, they 'have lived its life and felt its interests.'[34] Even, Solovev, in whom Witte's Far Eastern policies provoked a different

---

[31] N.Ia. Danilevskii, *Rossiia i Evropa*, 5th ed. (St. Petersburg, Tipografiia brat. Panteleevykh, 1895), p. 73.

[32] Ibid., p. 72.

[33] Ibid., pp. 74–7.

[34] Hauner, 'What Is Asia to Us?', p. 56.

reaction, was not entirely negative about the East. Pan-Mongolism was not only a nightmare, it also 'cursed' his ear.

Cultural figures also began to question the earlier stereotypes of Asians. Educated Russians had learned about Asians from history textbooks, which throughout the nineteenth century had habitually described Asians as ferocious predators who had threatened the very existence of the Russians from time immemorial. In the medieval period, one of the main adversaries of the Russians had been the Polovtsy, a nomadic people of Turkic origin from the Pontic steppe. According to nineteenth-century history textbooks, any peace with such 'barbarians' had been impossible.[35] However, in the 1880s this image of the Polovtsy was subverted in one of the major Russian national operas, Aleksander Borodin's 'Prince Igor.' It was based on the medieval story *The Lay of the Host of Igor*. In the 1880s, when Borodin wrote the opera, *The Lay* was already perceived by Russians as an essential part of their national tradition. It is therefore remarkable that Borodin's Polovtsy were kind people with noble behaviour. Incidentally, when the Soviet historian Aleksandr Zimin questioned the authenticity of the medieval story in the 1960s, this was seen by his colleagues and the political authorities as an assault on the national pride of the Russians. Another example of rejection of the earlier stereotypes was Lev Tolstoi's semi-fictional novel *Hadji Murat*. Written between 1899 and 1902, it offered the Russian public an unprecedented condemnation of Russian imperial policies in the North Caucasus and attempted to make the Russian educated elite feel complicity and responsibility for the deeds of their forefathers.[36] Tolstoi consciously reacted against the way the Caucasus had been depicted in the Russian romantic tradition of Pushkin and Lermontov.

However, prior to World War I, the Russian attitude towards Asia was still ambiguous. It took the war, with its brutal atrocities, to make some intellectuals fully identify Russia with Asia. This identification character-ized two intellectual movements: a literary group, the Scythians of 1917–1918, and an émigré cultural and political movement, the Eurasians of the 1920s. For Aleksandr Blok in that period, Russians were 'Scythians,' 'Asians' 'with squint and lusty eyes.' They had an 'ugly Asiatic face' and played 'the barbarian lyre.' In describing Russians-Scythians as a savage, barbaric tribe, Blok followed an ancient tradition, which had started with the fourth book of Herodotus' *History* and ended with Ovid's *Tristia*. Herodotus placed the tribe of Scythians on the shores of the Black Sea, in the Crimea. They were a militant, primitive people. For Ovid they were 'scarce worthy of the name of [men],' as they were more savage and cruel than wolves.

---

[35] Becker, 'The Muslim East in the Nineteenth-Century Russian Popular Historiography,' p. 33.

[36] Toltsoi's contemporaries did not have a chance to read *Hadji Murat* in full, because the first uncensored edition was published only in 1950.

Figure 4.2 Pavel Kuznetsov, 'A woman sleeping in a *koshar* (Kirghiz tent)' (1911). (The Tretiakov Gallery, Moscow)

But from the eighteenth century onwards, a very different image of the Scythians had been constructed in Russia. Since that time Russian historiography has presented the Scythians as ancestors of the Slavs. So when in 1787 Catherine the Great published her 'Notes Concerning Russian History,' the portrait of the Scythians that she offered to her readers was entirely different from that of the ancient Greek and Roman traditions. Catherine's Scythians 'honoured friendship and virtue, loved those who were brave, were indifferent to wealth... Bravery and feel for justice of the Scythians were commended by their neighbours.'[37] Thus, while Borodin had subverted earlier stereotypes by presenting the traditional Asian enemies of Russia, the Polovtsy, in a positive light, Blok restored the image of Russia's perceived ancestors as savage Asiatics, but did so with pride not shame.

---

[37] Quoted in Zorin, 'Krym v istorii russkogo samosoznaniia,' p. 133.

The Eurasians, in turn, completed the dissociation of Russia from Europe and its affinity with Asia. The Mongolian element among the inhabitants of Russia–Eurasia was their main focus of attention. Central Asia, which for Danilevskii had still been a colonial domain clearly separated from 'Russia proper,' became an integral part of the indivisible Russia–Eurasia of the Eurasians. One of the Eurasians, Nikolai Trubetskoi, firmly rejected the notion that the word 'yoke' was applicable to Russian–Tatar relations in the thirteenth to fifteenth centuries. He followed the Easterners by repeating, without acknowledging them as his source, that Russia was the successor to the 'legacy of Ghengis Khan.'[38]

The Scythians and Eurasians saw the Russian revolution as Russia's struggle against Western, Roman–Germanic civilization, in which the toilers of the East were Russia's main allies. In the words of Trubetskoi, 'the orientation towards Asia has become the only possible [outlook] for a Russian nationalist.'[39] From 1905 till the early 1920s, Lenin also saw the importance of Russian–Asian solidarity in the promotion of the world revolution.[40]

Notes on the Soviet period

The Soviet period added few new ideas concerning the impact of Asia on Russian national identity. When in the 1960s–1980s, Russia's relationship with Asia again attracted the particular attention of Russian nation-builders, Russian intellectuals rediscovered their pre-revolutionary heritage and émigré thought and tried to apply them to new conditions. Some imagined Russia as a European state, historically threatened by Asia. Others followed the ideas of the Eurasians and regarded Russia as a unique civilisation with many Asiatic characteristics, threatened by the nations of the West to a much greater extent than by the peoples of the East. As in the pre-revolutionary period, for most intellectuals the question of Russia's relations with the West, Europe, was the main reason which made it necessary to consider their country's ties with Asia. However, in a few instances, new political and social realities necessarily brought about some modification of the pre-revolutionary arguments. For a few, Russia's relations with Asia became important *per se*, regardless of Russia's position vis-à-vis Europe. We shall start by considering this latter group.

---

[38] N.S. Trubetskoi, *The Legacy of Genghis Khan and Other Essays on Russia's Identity*, ed. by Anatoly Liberman (Ann Arbor MI, Michigan Slavic Publications, 1991), pp. 244–67.

[39] Quoted in Mikhail Agurskii, *Ideologiia natsional-bolshevizma* (Paris, YMCA-Press, 1980), p. 99.

[40] See *Pravda*, 4 March 1923, quoting Lenin as saying that 'the Soviet Union and the peoples of the East,' who constituted the majority of mankind, collectively opposed Western capitalism.

In the late 1960s and 1970s, for the first time in Russian history, some Russian nation-builders began to see the empire as a threat to the survival of the Russians as a nation. This development will be discussed in more detail later in the book.[41] Here it will be discussed in the context of the problem of Russia's relationship with Asia. One of the key ways in which the empire began to be seen as a threat to the Russians was in the sphere of demography. In the post-Stalin period, demographic trends seemed to indicate that the Russians and indeed the Slavs as a whole might become a minority in the USSR, in view of the high birth rate in Central Asia and the Caucasus. It began to be argued that non-Slavs, particularly the Muslims of the Soviet Union, were endangering the very survival of Russians as a distinct ethnic community. These arguments were advanced mainly by *samizdat* authors, but also by some contributors to certain Soviet periodicals. These fears for the first time made some Russians see the Muslims rather than the West as the main constituent 'other' against which the Russian national identity could be constructed. In the early 1970s, the journal *Priroda* published several articles proposing racial segregation and the prohibition of marriages between Slavs and 'Turkic-Muslim' people.[42] The picture 'Moscow in 50 years' by the dissident writer and painter Aleksandr Zinovev, depicting Moscow with minarets and Soviet leaders in Central Asian clothes on Lenin's Mausoleum reflected this fear that Russia would be taken over by Asians. (In fact, according to the 1989 census, almost 90 per cent of Moscow residents were still Slavs.) Refuting the myth that Russians did not have racial prejudices, among the broader public resentment towards the presence of people from Central Asia and the Caucasus in Russian cities also became very visible in that period.

By most of those who did not share such extreme views, Asia nevertheless continued to be regarded as inferior. Therefore, the impact of the traditions and cultures of Asia on Russian culture was a highly sensitive and politicised issue. Only if we bear this in mind can we understand the reaction in Moscow in 1975 to the publication in Kazakhstan of the book *Az i Ia* by the well-known Kazakh poet Olzhas Suleimenov. The book argued that *The Lay of the Host of Igor*, as originally written in the twelfth century, had been heavily influenced by Turkic culture. In the sixteenth and eighteenth centuries the text had been edited to eliminate Turkisms. In the nineteenth and twentieth centuries, Russian nationalist scholars had refused to acknowledge any significant influence of Turkic culture on medieval Rus, because they wanted to maintain the myth of Russia's superiority over Asia.

---

[41] See, the chapter 'Imaginative ethnography: who are the Russians?,' pp. 204–6.
[42] G. Fetisov, 'Rossiia i Asiia,' *Veche* (Munich), no. 4 (1984), pp. 195–201. For the survey of such views in the Soviet press, see V.I. Kozlov, 'O biologogeograficheskoi kontseptsii etnicheskoi istorii,' *Voprosy istorii,* no. 12 (1974), pp. 73–85.

As Suleimenov's scholarly credentials were more than shaky, his book was an easy target for criticism. However, the fury which it provoked in the Russian scholarly community, and the close involvement of the Party leadership in the controversy could only be explained by the fact that the book had touched upon the question of Russian national identity. As public debate in the post-Stalin period became less restricted, this question once again attracted the attention of intellectuals and even some politicians.[43] The book was criticised at a series of meetings in the USSR Academy of Sciences, which were closely supervised by the Departments of Culture and Science of the CPSU Central Committee. The book was condemned as anti-Russian by the scholars, and was banned. Existing copies were pulled out of libraries and book stores.

Further discussion of Russia's relations with Asia took place in 1980–82, during the two-year celebrations of the 600th anniversary of the Battle of Kulikovo. In the course of these discussions, a range of different opinions on the influence of Asia on Russian national identity was expressed. It was evident that pre-revolutionary and émigré ideas had had a strong impact upon the positions of the participants. And, as in earlier periods, the discussion of Russia's relations with Asia was closely intertwined with the contributors' views on Russia's position vis-à-vis the West. Indeed, some participants managed to devote their entire contributions to the historical discussion to mounting various accusations against the West, alleging that the West Europeans had supported the Tatars in order to weaken Russia.[44] Others, such as the liberal medievalists Dmitrii Likhachev and Gelian Prokhorov, viewed the Tatar–Mongol invasion and Battle of Kulikovo in the same way that Solovev and Kliuchevskii had done. They regarded Russia as a European nation, and saw the Russian victory on the battlefield at the Kulikovo as an indication of the superiority of Christianity and Russian (European) culture over Asia.[45]

A third group saw the impact of the Tatar–Mongol invasion on Russian identity through the eyes of the Eurasianists of the 1920s. Pride of place in the revival of Eurasianism belongs to the geographer and ethnographer, Lev Gumilev, the son of the two famous Russian poets Anna Akhmatova and Nikolai Gumilev. During his imprisonment in Mordovian labour camps in the 1950s, Lev Gumilev had met a leading Eurasianist, Petr Savistskii. In his 1970 book *Searching for the Imaginary Kingdom*, dedicated to 'the fraternal Mongolian people,' and in popular articles of 1980, Gumilev

---

[43] For the discussion of Suleimenov's book, see *Molodaia gvardiia*, no. 12 (1975), pp. 270–80; *Russkaia literatura*, no. 1 (1976), pp. 251–8; *Zvezda*, no. 6 (1976), pp. 203–10; *Moskva*, no. 3 (1976), pp. 202–8.

[44] See, for instance, the discussion of the Kulikovo battle in *Nash sovremennik*, no. 9 (1980).

[45] Dmitrii Likhachev, 'Russkaia kultura i srazhenie na Kulikovom pole za Donom,' *Zvezda*, no. 9 (1980), pp. 1–8; Gelian Prokhorov, 'Kulturnoe svoeobrazie epokhi Kulikovskoi bitvy,' *TODRL*, vol. 34 (1979), pp. 3–17.

argued that the Russian nation should trace its origins to the Russian–Great Steppe civilisation, which emerged during the period of the Tatar–Mongol invasion of Rus.[46] In Gumilev's view, the pagan and Nestorian Christian Mongols, who invaded Rus in the thirteenth century, had not been hostile to the Christian culture of Rus. It was their symbiotic relationship that gave rise to the Russian nation that was born within the borders of the Moscow Principality. In 1312 one of the Mongol Khans converted to Islam and joined the Muslim civilisation of the East, which was hostile to Russia. However, other Mongols refused to convert and fled to Muscovy, thereby continuing to enrich the newly emerging Russian civilisation. Like the Eurasians, Gumilev regarded the Russian–Steppe civilisation as a unique world of its own, to which both the European civilisation of the West and the Islamic civilisation of the East have been hostile. Similar views were expressed in 1981 by the literary critic Vadim Kozhinov, who argued, following Trubetskoi, that the perception of the Tatar–Mongol invasion and the Battle of Kulikovo as a struggle between Europe and Asia was an invention of eighteenth and nineteenth century Russian historians.[47] For Kozhinov, Russia's origins were in Asia, whereas Europe was its eternal enemy.

In the 1970s and 1980 neither Gumilev nor Kozhinov openly acknowledged the source of their ideas. But they were able to do so in the *perestroika* period. In the late 1980s and the early 1990s they were joined by other authors, and in 1990 they set up their own newspaper, *Den*. At that time, the supporters of the idea that Russia was a unique civilisation, which was, however, closer to Asia than Europe, began to call themselves neo-Eurasianist and to refer openly to their predecessors of the 1920s. In contrast, some others continued the line of the late 1960s and the 1970s and defined the Russian nation in direct opposition to Muslims of Central Asia and the Caucasus. A leading representative of this trend was Nikolai Lysenko's National Republican Party. Its members rejected the views of another extremist organization of the *perestroika* period, Pamiat, which constructed a Russian identity in opposition to the Jews. Lysenko's NRP argued that the Muslims of the USSR rather than the Jews endangered the very survival of the Russians. It urged the creation of a purely ethnic Russian state, smaller than the Russian Federation.[48]

---

[46] L.N. Gumilev, *V poiskakh vymyshlennogo tsarstva* (Moscow, Nauka, 1970); *Ogonek*, no. 36 (1980) and *Dekorativnoe iskusstvo*, no. 12 (1980).

[47] *Nash sovremennik*, no. 11 (1981).

[48] Vladimir Pribylovsky, 'A Survey of Radical Right-Wing Groups in Russia,' *RFE/RL Research Report*, 22 April (1994), pp. 28–37.

Conclusions

The range of views on the impact of Asia on the Russian national identity among Russian nation-builders has been as broad as the range of positions on Russia's relationship with Europe. In most cases, any particular individual's perception of Russia's relationship with Asia was determined by his perspective on Europe. In the period between the eighteenth century and 1917, the views of Russian nation-builders on Asia underwent a dramatic transformation. In the eighteenth century they had regarded Russia as a European nation, and looked at Asia from a position of unquestionable cultural and political superiority. By the early twentieth century and particularly in the wake of World War I, many Russian intellectuals felt more comfortable asserting Russia's closer affinity with Asia and dissociating it from Europe. This transformation was gradually prepared in the course of the nineteenth century, when some intellectuals began to see Russia as a world of its own, which incorporated the features of both the West and the East.

The Soviet period added few new ideas to the debate. Russian liberals, who saw Russia as a European nation and supported a pro-Western Russian foreign policy, failed to rethink many of the anti-Asian prejudices which their pre-revolutionary predecessors had shared with other Europeans. Among the broader public, anti-Asian attitudes have been on the increase since the 1960s and extremist groups calling for discriminatory measures against people from Central Asia and the Caucasus were set up in the *perestroika* period. Meanwhile, as in the pre-revolutionary period, pro-Asian sentiments and an affirmation of Russia's Asian roots were closely associated with anti-Westernism and political conservatism. In the Soviet period, and particularly during *perestroika*, representatives of these different trends had little time for their opponents' views, thus making a dialogue on this crucial aspect of Russian identity virtually impossible. This configuration of the intellectual landscape created problems for the post-communist period. The new Russia is still partly in Europe and partly in Asia. The question of its identity is important not only in determining the orientation of its foreign policy, but also for its internal situation. This is particularly true for Moscow's policies towards one of Russia's main 'Orients' – the North Caucasus. Overall, in contrast to West Europeans, whose identity was strengthened through comparison with the 'Orient,' proximity to 'Asia' did not clarify Russia's view of itself. On the contrary, by the 1990s it had only added to the confusion of Russian identity.

DEFINING RUSSIAN IDENTITY

|5|

Imaginative geography: Russian empire as a Russian nation-state

'But where are its limits, where are its boundaries set?'
Fedor Tiutchev ('Russian Geography', 1849)

'Russia has never had colonial domains ...'
Nikolai Danilevskii (*Russia and Europe*, 1869)

Comparisons with others help people to define who they are by gaining an understanding of who they are not. Whereas the previous part of the book dealt with the question of 'who Russians are not,' this part will focus on how Russians identified the positive substance of their identity. This chapter analyses the framework within which the question was considered: who are the Russians? It argues that this framework was determined by a vision of the Russian empire as a Russian nation-state. The origins of this vision can be easily traced. Because Russian territorial expansion had begun in the pre-national era, it is not surprising that, in the sixteenth and seventeenth centuries, neither the rulers nor the Russian people viewed their state in the way we now regard modern empires.[1] But even after Peter the Great had officially designated the country an empire, and attempts had been made by some historians and geographers to distinguish clearly between 'Russia proper' and its colonial domains, most Russian intellectuals and many politicians still insisted that the Russian state should not be regarded as an empire. This continued right up to the demise of the USSR in 1991. The

---

[1] In E.J. Hobsbawm's words an empire is a political structure in which 'some outlying region or regions are ruled from a more or less remote center which is not believed to represent the interests of their inhabitants or local rulers.' (E.J. Hobsbawm, 'The End of Empires,' in Karen Barkey and Mark von Hagen, eds, *After Empire. Multiethnic Societies and Nation-Building* (Boulder CO, Westview Press, 1997), p. 12.

leaders of the empire's non-Russian nationalities had been challenging the Russians' vision of their own state since at least the 1840s. Why did most Russians consistently neglect their views?

The often-repeated argument that the perceptions of the Russians were formed in the pre-nationalist period seems unable adequately to explain Russian attitudes in the era of modern nationalism. As we shall see, Russian intellectuals were well aware of the views of nationalist ideologists in Europe. Their claim that the Russian empire was the Russian nation-state stemmed precisely from their attempts to apply the modern nationalist view of the role and the sources of legitimacy of a state to Russian reality. The chapter looks at the origins of this vision of the Russian empire as the Russian nation state. It examines its promotion by eighteenth century politicians, nineteenth-century intellectuals and to some extent the Soviet government in the twentieth century, and assesses its impact on the way the broader Russian public perceived their own country.

The origins of the idea

A number of scholars have observed that both the government's and the people's perception of the Russian state were affected by the timing of the creation, the patterns of expansion and the geography of the Russian empire.[2] The formation of the empire began in the sixteenth century, before the awareness of national distinctions had emerged. There was an understanding of differences in religion and way of life, but not nationality. The first stage of the empire's creation – the conquest of the non-Slavic and non-Christian Kazan and Astrakhan Khanates by Ivan the Terrible in the 1550s – immediately followed the takeover by Muscovy of the other east Slavic principalities, described in the medieval chronicles as 'the gathering of the indigenous Russian lands.' Not necessarily reflecting the views of the tsar Ivan the Terrible, the Moscow chronicles also justified his conquest of Kazan as the 'return' to Moscow of the original lands of the east Slavic princes. Thus from the very beginning the line was blurred between the absorption into the Muscovite state of what are now undisputed parts of 'Russia proper' – Novgorod, Pskov, Riazan, Tver, etc. – and of the territories of people who were culturally and religiously very different from the Russians. The distinctions were further blurred by the geographical dimension – Moscow was moving into neighbouring areas, some of which were sparsely populated by nomadic peoples. In this pre-national era the concept

2   Hans Rogger, 'Nationalism and the State: a Russian Dilemma,' *Comparative Studies in Society and History*, vol. 4 (1961–62), pp. 254–5; Roman Szporluk, *Communism and Nationalism: Karl Marx versus Friedrich List* (Oxford, Oxford University Press, 1988), pp. 205–24; Geoffrey Hosking, *Russia: People and Empire: 1552–1917* (London, HarperCollins, 1997).

of fixed state boundaries did not exist. Moscow had open frontiers and no state borders. Indeed, at times, peasants searching for new agricultural lands were the first Russians to move into new territories, with the government following later. In other instances peasant penetration and government military initiatives occurred simultaneously. These patterns of territorial expansion could be observed in the areas between the Volga and Kama rivers, in Siberia and in the south. By the seventeenth century, the Volga river was featuring in folk songs as an important symbol of Russianness, even though the lower parts of the river were populated by non-Russians and non-Slavs. In the words of Marc Raeff, the overall result of the timing and the patterns of Moscow's territorial expansion in earlier periods was that 'Russian society remained unaware of the state's having become a multinational empire.'[3]

Indeed, it was only in 1721, 169 years after Moscow's conquest of Kazan that the Russian state was first designated an empire rather than a tsardom, and its tsar became an emperor. The new name was supposed to emphasise Russia's similarity with Europe. The foremost historian of the time, Vasilii Tatishchev, constructed a new geographical image of the Russian state. In his *Russia or as it is now called Rossia*, Tatishchev divided the country into the Russian metropolis west of the Ural mountains, which belonged to Europe, and the Asiatic colony of Siberia, taken over in the late sixteenth and seventeenth centuries. The Urals created a 'natural' boundary between the metropolis and the colony in Russia in the same way as the sea separated England, the Netherlands, Spain and Portugal from their respective colonies.[4]

This new image of Russia, neatly divided into a European metropolis and an Asiatic colony, was disseminated during the eighteenth century in the geography textbooks and maps that began to appear in ever greater numbers from the middle of that century. Between 1739 and 1765, the Geography Department of the Imperial Academy of Sciences published some 250 maps. Commenting on the development of Russian and European cartography in the eighteenth century, James Cracraft has observed:

> [The Senate's senior secretary I.K.] Kirilov's general map of Russia (1737) and especially the academy's of 1745 ... soon appeared in atlases published in such European cartographical centers as Amsterdam, Berlin, London, and Paris ... The Urals were herewith proposed, and would rapidly gain acceptance, as the continental boundary between Europe and Asia, with the Russian Empire clearly divided into a European heartland and colonial or semicolonial Asian provinces.

---

3   Marc Raeff, 'Patterns of Russian Imperial Policy Toward the Nationalities,' in Edward Allworth, ed., *Soviet Nationality Problems* (New York N.Y., Columbia University Press, 1971), p. 30.

4   Mark Bassin, 'Russia between Europe and Asia: The Ideological Construction of Geographical Space,' *Slavic Review*, vol. 50, no. 1, Spring (1991), pp. 3–6.

A critical question of Russian national identity, and of Europe's as a whole, was being visibly resolved.[5]

The fact that the state had a multi-ethnic rather than purely Great Russian character was to be reflected in its name: *Rossiiskaia [imperiia]*. Unlike the word *russkaia*, which denoted the ethnic Russians, *rossiiskaia* had a political connotation.[6] But the new terminology was not applied consistently and the distinction between Russia proper and the whole empire proved to be difficult to sustain. The words *rossiiskii* and *russkii* were used interchangeably, particularly in the eighteenth century but also later. Moreover, the acknowledgement that the Russian state was an empire did not change the rulers' ultimate goal of assimilating the empire's non-Russian subjects by achieving social and administrative, if not necessarily full linguistic and religious, uniformity within its borders.

Thus Tatishchev's vision of Russia, divided between the European metropolis and the Asiatic colony by the clear boundary of the Urals, would seem to have been short-lived. The notion of Russia as a centralized, unitary state inspired some 'Peter's men' to launch a propaganda campaign that challenged this vision. Appropriating the tradition of pre-Petrine literature and folklore of 'an almost obsessive interest in the extent of Rus, its inviting spaciousness,'[7] this campaign hailed the vastness of the Russian state without distinguishing between its Russian and non-Russian areas. The campaign was aimed at instilling state patriotism in the tsar's subjects, based on a pride in living in a country of huge size and of great ethnic and cultural variety. In 1709, in a 'Laudatory Speech on the Glorious Victory over Swedish Forces,' Feofan Prokopovich fully articulated the idea of Russia's size as the main source of pride for its people and one of the greatest achievements of Peter's policies:

> Were someone to travel or rather fly in one's mind over (this territory), starting from our River Dnieper to the shores of the Black Sea... from there to the East to the Caspian Sea, or even to the borders of the Persian kingdom and from there to the remotest limits of the Chinese kingdom of which we have hardly heard, and from there... to the New Land (*Novaia Zemlia*) and the shores of the Arctic Ocean, and from there to the West to the Baltic Sea ... and (back) to the Dnieper: those are the limits of our monarch.[8]

---

[5]   James Cracraft, *The Petrine Revolution in Russian Imagery* (Chicago IL, The University of Chicago Press, 1997), p. 280–1.

[6]   The word '*rosskiiskii*' was imported into Russia from scholarly Polish, itself influenced by Greco-Latin conventions. The word *rossiiskii* (or *rosiiskii*) and its derivatives, such as *rossiianin* (*rosiianin*) as a subject of the Russian tsar, first started to be used in the seventeenth century.

[7]   Robin Milner-Gulland, *The Russians* (Oxford, Blackwell, 1999), p. 209.

[8]   Quoted by Liah Greenfeld, *Nationalism: Five Roads to Modernity* (Cambirdge, MA, Harvard University Press, 1992), p. 226.

Prokopovich made one of the first attempts to articulate the view that nature itself assigned the seas – the Baltic, Black and Caspian – as well as the Arctic Ocean as boundaries of the Russian state. In the nineteenth century, this view would be promoted by historians from Nikolai Karamzin to Sergei Solovev and Vasilii Kliuchevskii, in their 'national' histories of Russia. The creation of a unitary state within these natural boundaries would be seen as Russia's 'manifest destiny.'

In the eighteenth century, panegyrics to the tsars routinely mentioned the vastness of the Russian land as the country's most distinctive feature. The size of the country was such that its borders could not be clearly defined. Thus in one of his *Odes* to the Empress Elizabeth, Aleksandr Sumarokov said that her laws governed the areas which stretched so far that they were difficult to identify (*do kraia oblastei bezvestnykh*).[9] Commemorating the anniversary of Peter's death, Mikhail Lomonosov proclaimed: 'The far-flung Russian state, like a whole world, is surrounded by great seas on almost every side. On all of them we see the Russian flag flying ...'[10] Maps of the Russian empire, apart from serving other more practical purposes, underscored the vastness of Russia, both to the empire's own subjects, and to foreigners.

The emphasis on the vastness of the country and its ethnic and cultural variety became especially strong towards the end of the eighteenth century, when Russian imperialism was at its height under Catherine the Great. Above all, she referred to the vastness of the country in order to justify the absolutist power of the tsar. In her *Nakaz* to the Legislative Commission in 1767, Catherine stated that 'the Sovereign is absolute,' for no other government 'can act with a vigour proportionate to the extent of such a vast dominion.'

During Catherine's reign, the Academy of Sciences conducted a series of expeditions to collect information on the customs and cultures of various ethnic groups, especially in Siberia. A twelve-volume collection of prints was published, based on drawings of folk costumes of non-Russians produced by the expeditions' participants. In the 1780s, the empress personally commissioned the French sculptor J.O.D. Rachette to create a series of china statues of 'Peoples of Russia.'[11] But this emergence of ethnographical studies by no means indicated that Russia's rulers had abandoned the goal of achieving administrative and social uniformity in the empire through the assimilation of non-Russians. Moreover, in the eighteenth century this goal

---

[9] G.P. Makogoneko, compl., *Russkaia literatura XVIII veka* (Leningrad, Prosveshchenie, 1970), p. 107.

[10] Quoted in Marc Raeff, *Russian Intellectual History. An Anthology* (New York N.Y., Brace and World, 1966), p. 32.

[11] T.V. Kudriavtseva, 'Dekorativno-prikladnoe iskusstvo ekateriniskoi epokhi,' in *Ekaterina Velikaia. Russkaia kultura vtoroi poloviny XVIII veka* (St. Petersburg, AO Slaviia-Interbuk, 1993), p. 34.

was underpinned by the belief of the Enlightenment era in a universal pattern of cultural progress, in which the benchmark was set by European cultural tradition. The Russians believed they were setting superior European standards for the peoples of the eastern and southern parts of the empire. Ethnographic studies reflected such attitudes. Thus, one of the most famous works of the period, I.G. Georgi's *The description of people inhabiting the Russian state*, published first in German and subsequently in Russian in St. Petersburg in 1776–80, expressed the hope that through Christianization and the spread of education Russians would succeed in the task of 'leading our rude peoples (non-Russians and non-Christians) by giant steps toward the common goal of general enlightenment in Russia, of a wonderful fusion of all into a single body and soul, and of creating, as it were, an unshakable Giant that will stand for hundreds of centuries.'[12]

The identification of the entire empire as the Russian homeland was considerably reinforced by the view that its creation was a process of 'the gathering of indigenous Russian lands.' It was in the time of Peter the Great that politicians first adopted such arguments as a justification of their policies. The leading diplomat Peter Shafirov explained the takeover of the Baltic provinces in such terms. In the 1717 *Discourse on the Just Reasons of the War between Sweden and Russia*, Shafirov justified the conquest not only by the right of victory in war but because the Baltic territories 'did of ancient times belong to the Russian empire' (*iz drevle ko vserossiiskomu imperiiu prinadlezhali*).[13] (The political importance of *The Discourse* was emphasized by the fact that Peter the Great personally wrote its conclusions.) This claim that the territories had at some point in time been recognized as under the jurisdiction of the Russian ruler could be substantiated only in respect of Ingria, a small part of the conquered land. Moreover, the Baltic provinces were the first area which Russia acquired using modern imperial techniques – through military conquest ratified by international treaty.

Thus the two great Russian tsars of the eighteenth century, Peter the Great and Catherine the Great, waged propaganda campaigns with long historical roots and clear political aims. The hailing of the vastness of Russia, the state where the boundaries between Russian and non-Russian areas were blurred, and the idea that the creation of the state to a large extent amounted to the gathering of the indigenous Russian lands were part of these campaigns. By the end of the eighteenth century, through the efforts of Russian intellectuals, the tsars' vision of Russia proved to be stronger

---

[12] Quoted in Yuri Slezkine, 'Naturalists versus Nations: Eighteenth Century Russian Scholars Confront Ethnic Diversity,' in Daniel R. Brower and Edward J. Lazzerini, eds, *Russia's Orient. Imperial Borderlands and Peoples, 1700–1917* (Bloomington IN, Indiana University Press, 1997), p. 39.

[13] James Cracraft, 'Empire versus Nation: Russian Political Theory under Peter I,' *Harvard Ukrainian Studies*, vol. 10, December (1986), p. 536–7.

than the image of an empire with a clear divide between the metropolis and colonial domains.

Intellectuals take over

In the era of nationalism, from the beginning of the nineteenth century, it was, paradoxically, Russian intellectuals – including those opposed to the state – that reinforced and further elaborated the tsars' imperial vision of Russia. From that time on, the word 'empire' was not commonly used in the intellectuals' discourse about Russia. They preferred to refer to it as 'the Russian state' (*russkoe* (sic!) *gosudarstvo*). Many intellectuals also upheld the view that Russian empire-building was largely the gathering of the indigenous Russian lands. They forged the myth that the process had been peaceful and voluntary. This became one of the main myths of Russian national historiography and intellectual thought, and it enjoyed a broad popular resonance. Why did such a perception of Russia find support among the intellectuals? Why did the 'revolution of national consciousness' (Raeff) in Europe at the turn of the nineteenth century fail to change the intellectuals' view of the Russian state, a view which had been formed in the pre-national era?

In the wake of the French revolution, Russian intellectuals were exposed to the ideas of nationalism, and particularly to the idea that only the nation-state could be legitimate. It would appear that the most effective way of applying these new Western ideas to Russia's realities was to deny that the Russian state was an empire.

As chapter three argues, from the eighteenth century, comparison between Russia and the West has been a constant feature in the construction of a Russian identity. Such comparisons have given rise to tensions in the minds of Russian nation-builders. Since the late eighteenth century, a standard way to resolve these tensions has been to insist that the Russians in fact possess many of the same features as West Europeans. Any differences that cannot be denied altogether are proclaimed to be a sign of Russian superiority. The argument about the Russian empire as the Russian nation-state fits this pattern precisely. The Russians could not acknowledge that they did not have a nation-state, as that would amount to an admission that the Russians were not a historical nation like the British and the French. Any parallel between Russia and other empires such the Roman, Ottoman or Habsburg had to be rejected. Moreover, the obvious difference between multi-ethnic Russia and the much more ethnically homogeneous West European nation-states could be presented as a sign of Russia's uniqueness and advantage.

Building on Shafirov's line of argument, the historian Ivan Boltin, who worked during the time of Catherine the Great, became the first modern

Russian historian to create an image of Russia expanding into neighbouring, sparsely-populated lands almost peacefully. Boltin contrasted that
image with the creation of West European states and empires by military
force. Whereas West European history was marked by cruelty and annihi-
lations of large groups of people, Russia knew only one cruel tyrant – Ivan
the Terrible. According to Boltin, the subjection of the Ukrainians and
Belorussians to Moscow rule took place at the request of these two
branches of the Russian people, which longed to become part of Russia
again. In effect, Boltin laid the foundation for regarding the Russian empire
as the Russian nation-state.

The idea that the Russian state, unlike West European states and empires,
was created through the peaceful colonization of the previously dispersed
Russian lands was echoed in Karamzin's *History of the Russian State*. It
was fully developed by the early Slavophiles in the mid-nineteenth century.
Konstantin Aksakov (1817–60) argued in his *On the Foundations of
Russian History* that

> All European states are based on conquest. Struggle is their essence. There,
> political power is forced upon the subjugated peoples by a military enemy ... The
> Russian state, on the contrary, has been created through a voluntary invitation of
> political leaders. There not a struggle, but peace and harmony are the essence.[14]

Another Slavophile, Orest Miller, maintained that special positive qualities
of the Russian people attracted non-Russians 'into their orbit.'[15]

As the early Slavophiles were trying to offer historical and philosophical
arguments to prove that the Romanov empire was in fact the Russian
nation-state, Russian cultural figures disseminated the same message by
artistic means. From the early nineteenth century, classical Russian literature and art portrayed images which downplayed the role of military force
in the creation of the Russian state and blurred the boundaries between
'Russia proper' and its colonial domains. These images shaped the view of
the educated public and then, with the spread of mass education in the
Soviet period, of virtually all Russians about their homeland.

From the 1820s onwards, certain authors further developed the earlier
images of a Russia without end. They emphasized its constantly moving
borders and huge size as formative elements in the Russian national
character and as a major source of national pride. The works of these

---

[14] K.S. Aksakov, *Polnoe sobranie sochinenii*, vol. 1 (Moscow, Universitetskaia tipografiia,
1861), p. 20. The view of the creation of West European states through military conquests
was developed in the works by French historians Guizot and Thierry, which influenced
Aksakov.

[15] O. Miller, *Slavianstvo i Evropa. Stati i rechi 1865–77 gg.* (St. Petersburg, 1877) quoted in
N.A. Rubakin, *Sredi knig*, 2nd ed., vol. 3, part 1 (Moscow, Knigoizdatelstvo Nauka, 1915),
p. 130.

authors were used as the basis of the school literature curriculum. The difficulty of identifying Russia's borders began to be seen as a sign of Russia's national uniqueness. The evasiveness of Russia's borders, due to the constant expansion of the state, was well depicted in Aleksandr Pushkin's *Journey to Erzerum* (Arzrum). He wrote this story on the basis of travel notes made while visiting the Russian troops at war with Turkey in 1829. Arzrum was the Armenian fortress in North-East Turkey, taken by the Russians that year. Pushkin observed:

> 'Here is Arpachai,' a Cossack told me. Arpachai, our border! ... I galloped towards the river with indescribable feelings. I have never yet seen foreign lands. A border had a mystic meaning for me; from the very childhood travelling was my favourite dream. Later in life, I was a nomad for a while, traveled extensively in the south and in the north, but I have never before escaped from Russia's vast lands. I happily rode into the cherished river and my good horse got me onto the Turkish shore. But this shore had already been taken over. I was still in Russia.[16]

One of the most famous passages in Nikolai Gogol's *Dead Souls*, memorized by pupils in tsarist and Soviet schools, also created an image of Russia without clear boundaries: 'Thought grows numb confronted with your vast expanse. What do those immense, wide, far-flung open spaces hold in store? Is it not here, is it not in you that some boundless thought will be born, since you are yourself without end?'[17]

Meanwhile, those areas of the country, which in the eighteenth century had been proudly perceived as Russia's colonial domains, in the nineteenth began to be incorporated into 'Russia proper' by writers, artists and other intellectuals. The rejection of the eighteenth-century image of Siberia as an Asiatic colony provides the best example. At the time when Tatishchev depicted Siberia as a colony, Russians already constituted up to 67 per cent of the region's population.[18] But the majority of these Russians were either peasants or government bureaucrats, who did not think in national terms. The recasting of Siberia as part of Russia proper and as a model to be emulated by the European part of the country had to await the appearance in this region of a group of nationalist intellectuals in the late 1820s. These were the Decembrists, who served their sentences in that eastern part of the empire. They emphasized that because Siberia did not know the institution of serfdom it was much freer than European Russia, and therefore could offer the Russians a place of escape and salvation. The Decembrists' glorification of the progressive qualities of Siberia was further developed by Aleksandr Herzen. During his exile in London from the late 1840s onwards, Herzen turned from a belief in the need to Europeanize Russia to

---

[16]   A.S. Pushkin, *Dramaturgiia, prosa* (Moscow, Pravda, 1981), p. 574.

[17]   Nikolai Gogol, *Dead Souls* (London, Penguin Books, 1961), p. 232.

[18]   V. Kabuzan, *Russkie v mire* (St. Petersburg, Blits, 1996), p. 44.

a search for 'indigenous roots' in the hope of achieving Russia's political transformation. Whereas European Russia symbolized the autocratic oppression of Nicholas I, Siberia became the genuine Russia of the unspoiled people. Like the Decembrists, Herzen thought that Siberian traditions could be applied to Russia west of the Urals to save it from autocracy.[19]

This idealization of Siberia was connected with the fact that some Russians detected in Siberian life elements of an indigenous pre-Petrine Russian tradition. This was precisely the way in which Siberia was seen by the painter Vasilii Surikov, the author of the famous *The Conquest of Siberia by Ermak* (1890s) (Figure 5.1). To the contemporary viewer, Surikov's work looks like an unashamed glorification of imperialist policies, but that was hardly the message the artist intended to convey. Surikov, who was born in Krasnoiarsk and whose ancestor had come to Siberia in the sixteenth century with the forces of the Don Cossack Ermak, recalled that during his childhood 'people were strong, with a powerful spirit ... [Figure 5.2] The life in Siberia was tough. A real seventeenth century.'[20] These perceptions helped to deconstruct the image of Siberia as an Asian colony and incorporate it into Russia proper.

This deliberate confusion of Russia's national and state boundaries was reflected in powerful images constructed by nineteenth-century Russian cultural figures. It ran against the trend in Western Europe of seeing clearly marked state borders as strictly defining the limits of national communities. To be sure, the vastness of some European empires, particularly the British empire, was also glorified. But on the whole, the borders of European national homelands and the boundaries of their (overseas) empires were fairly clearly distinguished and separated. In contrast, the limits of the Russian national community could not be defined with certainty due to the country's vastness and its continuing expansion. And, as Gogol best emphasized, that was precisely the source of the powerful Russian spirit.

In addition to creating an image of Russia without boundaries, where non-Russian areas were freely incorporated into 'Russia proper,' Russian classical literature also helped construct a vision of a Russia with little in common with European states and empires created through military conquest. The peaceful nature of the Russian state was regularly underscored by writers and poets, who rejected the view of a sinister Russian imperialism that emerged in Western Europe during the nineteenth century. In Russian literature, feminine images of 'Mother Russia', or, more precisely, of Russia as a peasant woman, were often viewed as more representative of

[19] See Mark Bassin, 'Inventing Siberia: Visions of the Russian East in the Early Nineteenth Century,' *The American Historical Review*, vol. 96 (1991), pp. 763–94.
[20] Quoted in D.V. Sarabianov, *Istoriia russkogo iskusstva vtoroi poloviny XIX v.* (Moscow, Izdatelstvo MGU, 1989), p. 221.

Figure 5.1 Vasilii Surikov, 'The conquest of Siberia by Ermak' (1895). (The Russian Museum, St. Petersburg)

Figure 5.2 Vasilii Surikov, 'The capture of a snow town' (1890). This shows a folk game in Siberia observed by Surikov during his childhood. (The Russian Museum, St. Petersburg)

the true Russia, in contrast to imperial images. Peter the Great had consistently tried to deploy masculine images of the Russian state, for instance, by regularly using in his decrees the word 'fatherland' (*otechstvo*) rather than the feminine motherland (*rodina*) (more common in the seventeenth century) and by utilising imperial military symbolism in state rituals. However, this failed to put down deep roots as far as the Russian cultural tradition was concerned. Instead, starting with Vasilii Trediakovskii's *Poems of Laudation for Russia* (1728), the pre-Petrine Russian folklore image of 'Mother Russia' firmly entered Russia's high culture.

From Peter's reign onwards, hundreds of buildings and monuments related to military events and imperial conquests were erected in St. Petersburg. Yet numerous Russian poets and writers did not dwell on this particular aspect in their descriptions of the new Russian capital. To be sure, references to Russia's military power are to be found in the works of the greatest nineteenth century Russian poets and writers. In popular culture, the iconography of military heroes can be traced back to the sixteenth century *lubok*. Yet, most songs invented and sung by ordinary soldiers were about the defence of Russia from the Tatars, Turks, French, Germans, etc. Hardly any glorified the empire-building – Russia's territorial expansion in non-Russian areas.[21] A similar trend can be seen in high culture. Militarised imperial images of Russia similar to the figure of Britannia with a trident, ruling the waves, were to be found more often in military hymns and marches than in poetry. The most famous example was the Russian victory march, composed in 1791 during the second war with Turkey (1787–91) by the foremost poet of the time, Gavriil Derzhavin, and the musician, Osip Kozlovskii, *Made a Thunder of Victory Ring Loud!* The words displayed the unashamed imperial pride typical of the eighteenth century but seriously challenged in the nineteenth:

> Quick waters of Danube
> Are already in our hands
> Recognizing the bravery of Russians
> Tavr and the Caucasus are under our rule (*pod nami*).[22]

This hymn was performed at military parades and battles as well as at the opening of ballets and receptions in royal palaces. Yet this was not the image of Russia that the most famous Russian writers and poets portrayed from the nineteenth century onwards. Even such a poet as Mikhail Lermontov, who wrote poems full of pride at Russia's colonial conquest of

---

[21] *Istoricheskaia pesnia XIX veka* (Leningrad, Nauka, 1973), pp. 6, 11, 14–5, 170.

[22] Tavr is the Crimea. At the time, Russia was conducting operations to impose its control over the mountaineers of the North Caucasus. In 1783 it signed a treaty in Georgia, by which the Georgian king Erekle renounced his allegiance to Persia and gave up the right to conduct foreign policy without Russia's consent.

the Caucasus, depicted peasant Russia as the main symbol of his country and the object of his love. In his poem *The Motherland* (*Rodina*) he said that he loved his country not for 'the glory purchased with blood' (i.e. imperial conquests), but 'with a pleasure unknown to many I see a well-stocked barn, a cottage covered with thatch, a window with carved shutters.' One of the most powerful feminine images of Russia, rejecting the glory derived from building the empire, was created by the poet Maksimilian Voloshin in his poem *Holy Rus* at the time of the October Revolution. Voloshin's Russia is a peasant girl who could have become a princess, but she lent her ear 'to the evil counsel,' 'went out humiliated and a beggar, and the slave of the meanest slave,' she is 'homeless, wanton, drunken Russia – fool in Christ!' And this is despite the fact that 'Suzdal and Moscow gathered the land' for her (i.e. created the empire).[23]

At the turn of the twentieth century, the philosopher Vladimir Solovev made a general observation about the Russians' mental image of their own country. To the question 'how do they [Russians] praise Russia?' he responded: 'Do they call it beautiful or old, do they speak of Russian [military] glory ...? They speak only of Holy Rus.' Holy Rus was a symbol close to Mother Russia. Originating in seventeenth century Russian folk culture, it referred to the Orthodox Russian peasantry, persecuted by its own government. In the words of the poet Vasilii Zhukovskii, Holy Rus was 'the particular hereditary property of the Russian people, confirmed to it by God. It was always in opposition to Russia (*Rossiia*),' the European empire.'[24]

The rejection of the challenge from non-Russian nationalism

When Boltin was first advancing his idea about the nature of the Russian state, his vision of it as basically a Russian nation-state was not completely utopian. That was the time when the Caucasus and Central Asia, the areas most culturally different from Russia, had not yet been incorporated into the Russian empire. From Poland, Boltin claimed as 'Russian' only the lands acquired through the first partition of 1772, which were populated by Belorussian and Ukrainian peasants. In the late eighteenth century most educated Ukrainians were busy inventing a common pan-Russian identity rather than forging a separate Little Russian identity. However, between the time of Boltin was writing and the mid-nineteenth century, the Russian

---

[23] Translations from Lermontov and Voloshin are taken from Dimitri Obolensky, *Russian Verse* (Harmondsworth, Penguin Books, 1967), pp. 168–9 and 257–8.

[24] See Michael Cherniavsky, 'Holy Russia,' *The American Historical Review*, vol. LXIII, no. 3, April (1958), pp. 617–37.

nation-building project did not make any significant headway. Russian government policies were aimed not at nation-building but at maintaining a pre-modern dynastic empire. This empire could not find a way to incorporate a modern and more European nation – the Poles – and it continued to advance into areas where the people's cultural traditions and way of life were distinctly different from the Russian. Russia had some success in assimilating the elites of the conquered peoples, who became members of a cosmopolitan ruling class, loyal to the imperial state rather than to the Russian nation. The poor retained their own cultural traditions and way of life. When, from the 1840s onwards, leaders emerged among these people, they began to articulate nationalist ideas based on local peasant traditions. The government's unpreparedness for this development will be discussed later. Here we will look at the intellectuals' response.

Only a few Russians took any notice of the arguments of their non-Russian counterparts that the Russian empire was, in fact, not the Russian nation-state and from the mid-nineteenth century onwards tried to distinguish between 'Russia proper' and the empire's colonial domains. These were Russian socialists. Mikhail Bakunin, for instance, argued:

> We want Poland, Lithuania, Ukraine, Finns and Latvians in the Baltics, as well as the Caucasian region, to receive full freedom and the right to govern themselves according to their own desires, without any direct or indirect interference on our [Russian] part.[25]

These socialists hoped that a voluntary federation could emerge on the empire's territory. They felt that if the integrity of Russia was to be preserved, not Western Europe but the United States of America should be taken as a model. But federalism was not an option favoured either by the government, or by the majority of Russian intellectuals. Both the government and the broader public tended to deny that the nationalism of non-Russians presented any serious problem for the state. According to Raeff, federalism 'was anathema for historical as well as political reasons ... because the specter of a return to the appanage divisions seems to have been an ever-haunting theme.'[26] In turn, Roman Szporluk thinks that the fact that the empire had been formed before a modern Russian national identity had been consolidated prevented Russians from understanding the arguments of nationalism. Neither explanation seems adequate. Although some intellectuals, arguing against federalism, referred to the appanage divisions that in the eleventh and the twelfth centuries had weakened Kiev Rus and thus made it an easy target for the Tatar Mongol invasion, this argument

---

[25]   M. Bakunin, *Federalizm, sotsializm i antiteologizm* (St. Petersburg, Mysl, 1907), quoted in Rubakin, *Sredi knig,* pp. 113 and 155.

[26]   Raeff, 'Patterns of Russian Imperial Policy' p. 32.

was peripheral. Indeed, what had happened in the early medieval period could not seriously account for the policies of the mid-nineteenth century. Moreover, even though Russian empire-building had started in the pre-national era, this does not mean that European ideas of modern nationalism were unknown to the Russians in the nineteenth century. As we have seen, the intelligentsia attempted to define the Russians in national terms. The problem was that the challenge of non-Russian nationalism within the empire failed to alter the main perspective of Russian intellectuals. They continued to construct Russian national identity and analyse Russian state-building by comparing and contrasting Russia and the West. This peculiar framework, in which comparison with the West was the intellectuals' main concern, prevented them from taking the arguments of non-Russian nationalists seriously. Moreover, with the emergence of non-Russian nationalism, the Russian intellectual debate over the nature of the Russian state became even more of a debate with and against Western Europe than it had been in the time of early Slavophiles. At the same time as non-Russian nationalists began to question the assumptions of the Russians, criticism of Russian imperial policies in the West also stepped up. It was this Western criticism that shaped Russian intellectual discourse about their state from the second half of the nineteenth century onwards. Many intellectuals responded to Western European criticism of Russia's treatment of its non-Russian subjects, particularly the Poles, and of its policies in the North Caucasus, by sharpening the argument that the Romanov empire was in fact the Russian nation-state. They insisted that the treatment of its subjects was a purely internal Russian matter.

That was particularly true after the 1863 Polish uprising, the brutal suppression of which provoked the condemnation of Russia in Europe. The Pan-Slavist Nikolai Danilevskii set the tone for rebutting the arguments of non-Russian nationalists and West European critics of Russian imperialism. His argument in *Russia and Europe* stemmed from the premise of modern nationalism that 'a nationality ... creates the basis of a state, is the reason for its existence; its [the state's] main *raison d'être* is to preserve the nationality.' He further concluded that

> It is clear from this definition of the state that states, which do not have national foundations, ... do not have any reasons to exist. If, indeed, a state consists of a mixture of different nationalities, what national dignity, what national liberty could it maintain and protect, when their dignities and liberties (in most cases...) are in conflict with each other?[27]

Danilevskii's entire book is aimed at showing that Russia is not a multi-national empire, but a nation-state with a high degree of unity among the

---

[27]   N.Ia. Danilevskii, *Rossiia i Evropa*, 5th edition (St. Peterburg, Tipografiia bratev Panteleevykh, 1895), p. 237.

people. In order to prove his point, he took his predecessors' argument about the peaceful nature of the creation of the Russian state to extremes. He also had to claim the existence of a common cultural tradition and way of life among all subjects of the state by greatly exaggerating the extent to which non-Russian peoples had become assimilated into Russian culture, and to which the customs of the non-Russian people had become incorporated into Russian traditions. For Danilevskii, the way the Russians treated the empire's non-Russian subjects could not in any way be compared to how Austria–Hungary and the Ottomans 'suppress and insult' the dignity and liberty of their people. Moreover, 'Russia had never had colonial domains as did Rome and does England. From the time of the first Moscow princes, the Russian state is Russia itself, gradually and constantly expanding in all directions, inhabiting neighbouring unpopulated areas and moulding in its own image those aliens whom it incorporates into its borders.'[28]

Russian policies in the North Caucasus should be compared not with the way that the British treated the population of their colonies but with how the English, in creating Britain as a nation-state, had treated the inhabitants of the Scottish highlands.[29] The early Slavophiles had tended to speak about the peaceful nature of the creation of the Russian state through the gathering of indigenous Russian lands only in connection with the earlier stages of Russian expansion. Danilevskii presented all Russia's colonial conquests in those terms.

Danilevskii condemned those authors who 'cannot look at things from the Russian point of view and use the European perspective instead.'[30] In fact, the same criticism could be levelled against his own vision of Russia, which was entirely based on drawing parallels between the Russian and West European experiences of state-building.

Danilevskii was not alone in equating the patterns of Russia's earlier territorial expansion with its imperial policies of the nineteenth century. For instance, the historian Adolf Berzhe objected to the use of the word conquest in relation to the Caucasus, arguing that its annexation had unfolded over the centuries in a virtually involuntary manner, as had been the case with Siberia.[31] Prince Aleksandr Gorchakov explained Russia's conquest of Central Asia by the need to defend settled communities of Russian peasants from nomads.[32]

The main response of the extreme Russian nationalists to the challenge of nationalism on the part of the empire's non-Russian subjects was to step up

---

[28] Ibid, p. 531.

[29] Ibid, p. 37.

[30] Ibid, p. 531.

[31] Susan Layton, *Russian Literature and Empire. Conquest of the Caucasus from Pushkin to Tolstoi* (Cambridge, Cambridge University Press, 1994), p. 3.

[32] Raeff, 'Patterns of Russian Imperial Policy,' p. 25.

forced Russification and conversion to Orthodoxy. This was the message of
Moskovskie vedomosti, edited in the 1860s by the journalist Mikhail
Katkov, which he proclaimed to be the organ of 'a party which may be called
Russian, ultra-Russian, exclusively Russian.' In 1906, groups of extreme
nationalists, popularly known as the Black Hundreds, described
Russification as 'a blessing, recognized as such by alien tribes, who are
quickly merging with the core nation in a single family – Russian, Orthodox,
with one father, autocratically leading it to glory and prosperity.'[33]

Not only the conservatives, but also the majority of Russian liberals in
effect downplayed the imperial nature of the Russian state. Although the
two main liberal nineteenth century historians, Solovev and Kliuchevskii,
did not altogether deny the imperial nature of Russia's policies in the
Cacausus and refrained from analyzing the expansion into Central Asia,
they almost completely ignored the non-Slavic subjects of the empire in
their histories of Russia. They shared the view that large parts of Russia's
western borderlands were in fact indigenous Russian lands, dispersed in the
thirteenth and fourteenth centuries as a result of the Tatar–Mongol yoke
and annexation by the Polish–Lithuanian Commonwealth. In discussing
Russia's territorial expansion east- and southwards, their histories presented an image of Russian penetration into virtually uninhabited areas. In
his magisterial *History of Russia*, Solovev described Russia as a state which
had emerged organically, through the gradual colonization by the Russians
of a geographical area they had been predestined to occupy by nature. For
Solovev, the East European plain was a 'virgin country, which awaited
population.' A Russian settler was confronted with 'open space all round,
waiting to receive him.' 'Because of this,' Solovev concluded, 'the history of
early Russia is the history of a country which is colonizing itself.'[34] Solovev
also passionately argued that the Russian state, which had emerged organically and largely peacefully, could not be compared with such land-based
ancient empires as Assyria, Persia or Rome. Kliuchevskii later reiterated the
same view in his *Course of Russian History* and also mentioned, in passing,
that the 'swallowing of the peoples' whom the Russians encountered in the
course of their territorial expansion was a natural process.[35] In sum, the two
main Russian liberal historians of the nineteenth century upheld the view
that the Russian empire was a Russian nation-state. In doing so they
employed one of the most common myths of imperial European historians
– the myth of an organic territorial expansion and of the original emptiness
of a colonized area.

All pre-revolutionary school (gymnasia) textbooks of Russian history
presented the same view of the formation of the Russian state, thereby

[33] *Groza*, 4 July 1910.
[34] S. Solovev, *Istoriia Rossii s drevneishikh vremen*, (Moscow, Nauka, 1959), vol. 2, p. 648.
[35] V.O. Kliuchevskii, *Sochineniia v deviati tomakh*, vol. 1 (Moscow, Mysl, 1987), pp. 50–1.

promoting among the educated public the perception that the Russian empire was the Russian nation-state.[36]

The early twentieth century Russian liberals, members of the Constitutional Democratic Party (the Kadets), were very concerned with the preservation of the empire. They regarded it as synonymous with the Russian state, and were not particularly sympathetic to the right of non-Russians to self-determination. The most vocal spokesman on the nationalities question among the Kadets was Peter Struve. In 1911, Struve summed up his position on the question in the periodical *Russkaia mysl*, which he edited. Rejecting calls from non-Russian intellectuals for the cultural emancipation of non-Russians, Struve justified Russian hegemony in view of what he regarded as the undisputed superiority of Russian high culture. He made exceptions only for the Poles and the Finns. He argued that 'One can partake in local cultural life in Warsaw and Helsingfors without the knowledge of the Russian language, but without the mastery of Russian one cannot partake [in the cultural life] of Kiev, Mogilev, Tbilisi or Tashkent.'[37] For Struve, Russia was different from the land-based Habsburg empire. Its development towards the Habsburg model was thoroughly undesirable. Instead, Russia had to consolidate further as the Russian nation-state, along the lines of Germany.[38] Another leading Kadet, the historian Pavel Miliukov also saw the Russian empire as the Russian national state, whose territorial expansion he explained as 'in part an elemental need for self-defense and self-preservation, and in part a conscious policy of territorial seizures guided by the idea of national unification.'[39]

The views of the Kadets shaped the policies of the liberal Provisional Government in 1917. Although it recognized the right of non-Russians in the empire to self-determination, the government postponed the resolution of the national question until the convocation of the Constituent Assembly, and even admonished the Finns for trying to speed up recognition of the full independence of Finland. In June 1917, a leading member of the Kadet Party, Baron Nolde, put forward the party's programme on the nationalities question. He suggested that extra-territorial cultural autonomy would be the best solution for non-Russians in the Russian state. His language makes it clear that he saw the Russian empire, which he called *russkoe gosudarstvo*, as basically a Russian nation-state. In his programme, cultural

---

[36] For the survey of nineteenth-century school textbooks of Russian history, see Seymour Becker, 'The Muslim East in Nineteenth-Century Russian Popular Historiography,' *Central Asian Survey*, vol. 5, no. 3–4 (1986), pp. 25–47.

[37] P.B. Struve, 'Chto takoe Rossiia,' *Russkaia mysl*, no. 1, January (1911), pp. 175–8.

[38] Ibid, pp. 184–7.

[39] P.N. Miliukov, *Ocherki po istorii russkoi kultury* quoted in Terence Emmons, 'On the Problem of Russia's "Separate Path" in Late Imperial Historiography,' in Thomas Sanders, ed., *Historiography of Imperial Russia. The Profession and Writing of History in a Multinational State* (Armonk N.Y., M.E. Sharpe, 1999), p. 165.

autonomy for the Armenians and the Georgians was presented as a way of solving the Russian (*russkii*) national question.[40] Finally, Struve and other liberals who joined the White Movement helped to put the idea of a 'one and indivisible Russia' at the top of the movement's agenda. They thereby prevented the movement from forging an alliance with anti-Bolshevik forces among the non-Russians of the empire, and ultimately contributed to the defeat of the Whites.[41]

The ability of the Bolsheviks to put the empire back together did impress some of the former Kadets and helped them to come to terms with the new regime. Thus, in the late 1920s, a former leading Kadet, Academician Vladimir Vernadskii, himself of Ukrainian origin and sympathetic to the Ukrainian national cause, nevertheless observed: 'Most of all I feared the disintegration of the Russian state.... I think that Russian people will survive the test [of communist rule], so long as the state is preserved.'[42] By 'the Russian state' Vernadskii meant the entire multiethnic empire.[43]

The nature of the state and the policies of the tsars

The tsarist government envisaged Russia as a centralized unitary state, and from the early days of Moscow's territorial expansion into non-Slavic and non-Christian areas the goal was to achieve administrative and social uniformity within its borders. The tsars attempted, with varying degrees of success, to impose the laws and regulations governing Russian provinces onto non-Russian areas. They tried to make non-Russians, particularly the nomadic peoples, change their way of life and adopt what the rulers regarded as superior Russian customs. If any special status and privileges had been granted to newly conquered areas, the government tended to revoke them as soon as it felt secure enough.

But the creation of homogeneity and uniformity within the empire's borders always remained only an ideal. Policies of Russification and conversion to Orthodoxy were never pursued consistently. The greatest success was achieved in integrating the elites of the conquered peoples into the Russian ruling class. The poor were usually left out of the project of

---

[40] Boris Nolde, 'Natsionalnyi vopros v Rossii (doklad, chitannyi na IX delegatskom sezde partii Narodnoi Svobody, 24-go iiulia 1917g)' reprinted in *Druzhba narodov*, no. 8 (1992), pp. 169–72.

[41] This argument is forcefully put forward by Anna Procyk, *Russian Nationalism and Ukraine. The Nationality Policy of the Volunteer Army during the Civil War* (Toronto, Canadian Institute of Ukrainian Studies Press, 1995).

[42] *Nezavisimaia gazeta*, 9 June 1992.

[43] Vernadskii described his own identity in the following way: 'I am a Russian according to my culture and way of life, but a Russian whose entire life has been connected with Ukraine and its struggle for liberation.' (*Rodina*, no. 1 (1990), p. 1).

achieving social uniformity. The tsars, who claimed that their legitimacy had divine roots, had never understood the forces of nationalism. Their goal was to maintain the integrity and stability of the empire rather than to turn it into a Russian nation-state. Therefore Russification and conversion to Orthodoxy were used pragmatically. They were applied when they could facilitate integration but halted when they seemed to threaten internal stability.

Such pragmatism was particularly visible in the reign of Nicholas I. In the 1840s the Ministry of Education, under the author of the doctrine of Official Nationality, Count Sergei Uvarov, decided to launch a wide-ranging programme to spread knowledge of Russian among the non-Russian subjects of the empire. Various historians and journalists that advocated the doctrine of official nationality demanded that the tsar take consistent measures to Russify his subjects.[44] But the tsar stepped in when he thought the goal of uniformity was threatening the survival of the *ancien regime*. Thus, in 1848, the tsar personally intervened to halt measures, adopted under pressure from Russian nationalists, to revoke some of the privileges of the Baltic Germans. In the aftermath of the revolutions in Europe, the Russian emperor did not want to jeopardize his relationship with a group which had proved to be among the most loyal to the crown.[45] Moreover, the transformation of the empire into a Russian nation-state was also undermined by Nicholas's fear of the rise of national sentiments among the Russian subjects themselves. Thus, in 1851, because of his general suspicion of any projects to advance enlightenment in Russia, the tsar turned down the historian Mikhail Pogodin's offer to set up the first all-Russian public (*vserossiiskii, narodnyi*) museum in Moscow. The tsar did not share the historian's view that such a museum, based on Pogodin's rich collection of Kiev Rus and Muscovite icons and objects of applied art, 'would constitute a separate page' in the history of Nicholas' reign.[46]

A more consistent Russificiation policy began in the 1860s. Even then, this did not mean that the goal of the tsarist government was to turn the Russian empire into a Russian nation-state. Analyzing the situation in the western provinces at the turn of the twentieth century, Theodore Weeks has convincingly argued that aggressive actions to suppress minority cultures did not signify that the tsars had accepted Russian nationalism. Instead, it

---

[44] Nicholas V. Riasanovsky, *Nicholas I and Official Nationality in Russia, 1825–1855* (Berkeley CA, University of California Press, 1959), p. 229.

[45] On the focus of Nicholas I on the preservation of autocracy, often at the expense of the two other parts of Sergei Uvarov's triad (Orthodoxy and Nationality) and the emperor's general distrust of any forms of nationalism, see Riasanovsky, op. cit.

[46] G.I. Vzdornov, *Istoriia otkrytiia i izucheniia russkoi strednevekovoi zhivopisi, XIX v.* (Moscow, Iskustvo, 1986), p. 81.

indicated that they were trying to curb centrifugal tendencies in order to preserve the integrity of the state.[47]

After the emancipation of the serfs in 1861, Russian tsars attempted to integrate both Russian and non-Russian members of the lower social classes into the empire by promoting the concept of citizenship (*grazhdanstven-nost*), as an extension of comparable responsibilities and status to all subjects of the tsar. After the military reform of 1874, which introduced a six-year-long universal military service, the army started to be viewed as a key tool of schooling in citizenship. Yet, by the time World War I broke out, the government was still unable to compel men from the North Caucasus mountains to serve in the army. Often local elites, feeling that attempts to turn non-Russians into citizens of the empire undermined their privileged positions in local societies, opposed the efforts of Russian officials.[48] The government was also hesitant about integrating non-Russians into the state through participation in political institutions, particularly the Russian parliament, the State Duma. The changes in the electoral law, introduced in June 1907 in order to reduce the number of left-wing deputies, meant that the number of deputies from the non-Russian borderlands in the third Duma dropped by 63 per cent when compared to the first Duma and by 68 per cent when compared to the second. The representation of the Muslim population of the country fell particularly steeply, by 74 per cent. This was largely because the June 1907 electoral law completely deprived the people of Central Asia of the right to send representatives to the Duma.[49]

The spread of the Russian language and Orthodoxy among non-Russians, especially among the Muslim population of the empire, also proceeded with great difficulty. Moreover, influential representatives of the imperial government were, at times, opposed to such efforts. For instance, at the turn of the twentieth century, officials at the Ministry of Interior rejected a programme of opening secular schools with classes in Russian language and culture among Volga Tatars. The ministry even struck an alliance against such schools with the conservative wing of the Muslim clergy, which was in general opposed to any Russian influence in Muslim education. The reasoning of the ministry officials was that the stability of the empire was best served by keeping Muslims, who were perceived as inherently hostile to Christianity, away from secular education altogether. Otherwise, they would develop a nationalist consciousness and, equipped

---

[47] Theodore R. Weeks, *Nation and State in Late Imperial Russia. Nationalism and Russification on the Western Frontier, 1863–1914* (DeKalb IL, Northern Illinois University Press, 1996).

[48] Dov Yaroshevski, 'Empire and Citizenship' and Austin Lee Jersild, 'From Savagery to Citizenship: Caucasian Mountaineers and Muslims in the Russian Empire,' in Brower and Lazzerini, eds., *Russia's Orient*, pp. 58–79 and 101–14 respectively.

[49] Alfred Levin, *The Second Duma* (New Haven CT, Yale University Press, 1940) and his *The Third Duma: Election and Profile* (Hamden, Archon Books, 1973), pp. 3–6.

with elements of European culture, would be in a better position 'to undermine the Christian world.'[50] But even if the policy of Russification had been applied consistently, it would seem that the project of integration would have been unfeasible, given the ethnic and demographic composition of the state. The non-Russians were simply too numerous; by the late nineteenth century they constituted 56 per cent of the population.[51] Finally, as the 1917 revolution showed, the government's failure to launch a comprehensive educational programme for Russian peasants following the emancipation of the serfs, had hindered their integration into Russian society. As we shall see, Russian peasants identified the entire Russian state as their national homeland only to a limited extent by the time World War I broke out – a war which severely tested the integrity and unity of all the European states.

Popular perceptions of the Russian national homeland before the revolution

Scholars agree that up until the late nineteenth century, the concept of a nation as people with shared loyalties had little, if any, effect on the lower classes of Russian society, particularly the peasants. People identified with their villages and families. They did not regard any wider geographical areas of the Russian empire, let alone the entire country with its non-Russian colonial domains, as their national homeland. The Slavophile Ivan Aksakov made some interesting observations about peasants' identities and their perception of the state while travelling through the Tambov *guberniia* in central European Russia in 1844. Aksakov was particularly interested in the attitude among the peasantry towards those who temporarily left their villages and travelled long distances to different parts of the empire in search of seasonal jobs. The latter were called *otkhodniki* 'those who leave temporarily'. The practice had begun among the peasantry in the last quarter of the eighteenth century. *Otkhodniki* had a much broader knowledge of their country than the average peasant and, according to Aksakov, they often spoke very favourably about the regions that they had visited. However, peasants who remained in their villages looked at *otkhodniki* with great suspicion. As one of the peasants explained to Aksakov, because an *otkhodnik* had spent time in a different area which had its 'own language, songs and proverbs (*svoi iazyk, svoi pesni i pribautki*), the family ceased to be important for him' (*semeistvo dlia takogo ischezaet*).[52] Thus, in the eyes of these peasants, *otkhodniki* lost their main identity for which there was no substitute.

---

[50]   Robert Geraci, 'Russian Orientalism at an Impasse: Tsarist Education Policy and the 1910 Conference on Islam,' in Brower and Lazzerini, eds., *Russia's Orient*, pp. 138–62.

[51]   This figure includes Ukrainians and Belorussians.

[52]   I.S. Aksakov, *Pisma k rodnym. 1844–1849* (Moscow, Mysl, 1988), pp. 6 and 14.

Similar conclusions have been reached by Jeffrey Brooks, who has studied the context of the *lubok* stories and newspaper serials which reflected and shaped the views of peasants learning to read. He has shown that until the late nineteenth century, the non-Russian areas of the empire, especially those populated by Muslims, were represented in popular culture as hostile and completely alien. Some *lubok* stories, depicting Russians being captured by Tatars or nomadic people of the steppe, were full of fear about the possibility of a Russian being converted to the captors' faith, thereby losing what for the peasantry was the main element of the Russian identity – Orthodox Christianity. The borders between the Russian and non-Russian areas of the empire were clearly drawn in *lubok* stories. These were natural boundaries, such as rivers, lakes and forest. For instance, 'the rapid and terrible river Terek' clearly separated Russia from the lands of North Caucasian mountain-dwellers. Popular stories depicted the landscape of the Russian side as friendly and 'civilized,' whereas the territory of the tribesmen was wild.[53]

In the late nineteenth century, as Russia began to industrialize, Russians became more mobile and better-educated. The introduction of general male conscription in 1874 also broadened peasants' knowledge of their country; as elsewhere in Europe, it facilitated the penetration of a modern national consciousness into the lower classes of Russian society. Brooks observed a major change in the way the empire was represented in some genres of popular literature in this period. At the turn of the twentieth century, in particular, serials in cheap newspapers began to hail the cultural variety of the empire and its huge size as Russia's strength, thereby developing the theme that had been firmly present in tsarist propaganda and Russian high culture since the eighteenth century. Rather than being threatening and alien, non-Russian areas of the empire such as the North Caucasus began to be presented as contributing to Russia's richness and beauty. The serials gave readers plenty of information about all parts of the empire, including such non-Russian areas as Bessarabia, the Caucasus, the oilfields of Baku and the recently acquired Far East. As Catherine the Great's propaganda had done in the eighteenth century, these newspaper serials tried to instil in the readers a pride in belonging to such a diverse and enormous country. Brooks has argued that this territorial nationalism, cultivated by popular literature from the turn of the twentieth century, shaped a new sense of nationality among the Russians 'that could survive the collapse of the autocracy and motivate Great Russians to fight to maintain the empire during the chaos of revolution and civil war.'[54]

Yet there is reason to doubt that this broader identification with the

[53] Jeffrey Brooks, *When Russia Learned to Read. Literacy and Popular Literature, 1861–1917* (Princeton N.J., Princeton University Press, 1985), pp. 216–45.

[54] Ibid, p. 245.

entire empire as a Russian state had really supplanted local and family identities among the Russian peasantry by the time of the revolution. It would seem that newspaper serials did try to shape new perceptions, but to what extent did they reflect the views of the lower classes of Russian society? Brooks has not examined other types of popular culture, such as the prison songs and *chastushki* (humorous short poems), created by peasants and workers themselves and known to virtually all of them without exception. These show that up until the collapse of the tsarist regime, any identification on the part of lower-class Russians of the entire state as their national homeland was counterbalanced by a persistent tendency to see certain areas as alien and hostile and to equate 'homeland' solely with one's place of birth.

This trend was reinforced by Russia's size and by the fact that the government was able to use certain areas of the country as places of internal exile. Despite the fact that Russia's size was hailed in government propaganda and by cultural figures as a sign of its strength, in fact, for Russian nation-building it turned out to be more of a handicap. A proper communications system, so necessary for nation-building, proved to be exceedingly difficult to set up. Moreover, Russia's size made it difficult to establish the idea that the nation's constituent parts were at least theoretically equal. The very concept of internal exile, established in Muscovy in the sixteenth century, dramatically symbolized the inequality of Russia's different areas. Remote areas of the empire, for instance Siberia, acquired the status of a prison, and it became a punishment to send people charged with various offences to live there. To be sure, exile to colonies was a form of criminal punishment used by other European states. But Siberia continued to be a place of exile long after the Russian nation-builders had imagined it to be a part of Russia proper. Up to the end of the tsarist regime the main symbolic function of Siberia in popular culture was that of an alien land, where a person could be sent to exile, thus losing contact with his homeland (*rodina*). The majority of Russian prison songs of the late nineteenth-early twentieth century described Siberia and other places of exile as an 'alien region' (*chuzhoi krai*) and contrasted them to the 'native land' (*strana rodnaia*) – the place where a prisoner was born and where his family continued to live. In these songs exile is represented as an act of severing all ties with the homeland and as the gloomy prospect of being buried in the 'alien soil' (*zaryt v zemle chuzhoi*). Siberia's wild forests, big rivers and lakes (particularly Lake Baikal) are depicted as boundaries, separating alien from native lands. It is these boundaries that the protagonists of many songs have to cross as they escape from prison. On the other side of the border a successful prison-breaker is met by his mother or wife.[55] Prison songs were

A.M. Novikova, 'Narodnye tiuremnye pesni vtoroi poloviny XIX-nachala XX vv.,' *Russkii folklor*, vol. XV (Leningrad, Nauka, 1975), p. 186.

not confined to those sentenced to various forms of detention. They were
extremely popular among broader strata of Russian society, especially the
peasantry and the urban lower classes, and both shaped and reflected their
perception of the Russian state and empire. In turn, members of families
who had lived in Siberia for many generations strongly felt the difference
between themselves and their fellow countrymen from west of the Urals.
They also had a sense of the separateness of their region from Russia. It is
indicative that they used to call those people who moved to Siberia from the
European part of Russia in the wake of the industrialisation of the 1890s
rossiiane (which could mean either Russian citizens or simply Russians),[56]
whereas they described themselves as Siberians (*sibiriaki*).

Even the most geographically mobile Russian peasants, the *otkhodniki*,
developed the language to distinguish clearly between the villages of their
origin and the places where they travelled to earn money. Their places of
birth and residence of their families were 'inner Russia' (*vnutreniaia Rasseia*
or *vnutri Rassei*), whereas the destinations of their journeys were outside.[57]
The expression 'inner Russia' was still widely used at the turn of the
twentieth century.

In European states, World War I tested how far the concept of a nation
as a people with shared loyalties had penetrated broader segments of
society. The ability of wars either to bring people together in defence of a
nation-state or to tear them apart was well understood by Russian intellectuals and politicians. In 1914, Struve pointed out that national ideas hold
communities together during wars and argued that Russia was a 'nation
state-empire.'[58] However, his view was not corroborated by the behaviour
of the peasants. The war was unpopular with the peasantry, who constituted the main bulk of the army, and it was marked by a high number of
desertions. Peasants were reported as saying that because they came from
Riazan or Tambov (*riazanskie, tambovskie*) – areas far from the borders of
the huge country – it was unlikely that Germans would ever reach them.[59]
Thus, for these peasants there was no reason to fight. *Chastushki* of the war
period reflected not only the unpopularity of the war, but also included
explicit statements to the effect that if the Germans wanted to annex non-
Russian parts of the empire, Russian people would not mind:

[56] V. Kabuzan, *Russkie v mire* (St. Petersburg, Blitz), p. 21.
[57] Gromyko, *Mir russkoi derevni*, p. 257.
[58] Quoted in Dominic Lieven, 'Dilemmas of Empire 1850–1918. Power, Territory, Identity,'
       Journal of Contemporary History, vol. 34, no. 2 (1999), p. 179.
[59] Such attitude was still present in the 1920s. See Francine Hirsch, 'The Soviet Union as a
       Work-in-Progress: Ethnographers and the Category of *Nationality* in the 1926, 1937, and
       1939 Censuses,' *Slavic Review*, vol. 56, no. 2 (1997), p. 259.

You German, You German ...
Take Riga and Warsaw
We would not be upset (*my ne budem unyvat*).[60]

In sum, by the time of the 1917 revolution, 'territorial nationalism' had had only a limited effect on the lower classes of Russian society. It hardly constituted a unifying force that could keep the Russians together as a nation. It was only in the Soviet period that the spread of mass education, the drastic increase in mobility of Russians in the course of industrialization and other government policies established a sense among the broader Russian public that the entire empire was the Russian nation state.

The impact of the Soviet period

When the Bolsheviks came to power in October 1917, their initial vision of the state was very different from that of the majority of Russian intellectuals described above. It was informed by the socialist position, whose advocates attempted to draw a clear distinction between Russia and its colonial domains and argued that the Russian empire had been created by brute force. In the official post-revolutionary discourse, the Russians, an oppressor nation, were counterposed to the collectively-defined non-Russians. Under the influence of this view, and in an attempt to accommodate the nationalist and separatist aspirations of non-Russians, the Bolshevik government, particularly in the 1920s, pursued policies that helped to strengthen the ethnic identities of the non-Russians. They were encouraged to view the Union republics and the other administrative units the government had created for the country's nationalities, as their national homelands.

But it was not the ultimate goal of the Soviet government to encourage the formation of embryonic national states and promote the indigenous cultures and traditions of the non-Russians. The Bolsheviks paradoxically believed that by promoting the elements of national identity, which they perceived as being not threatening to the centralized socialist state, they would de-politicize nationalist aspirations and thereby encourage eventual disappearance of national distinctions. Thus their initial concessions to nationalities would lead to the eventual unity of all members of a new multi-ethnic socialist community, created on a voluntary basis on the territory of the defunct Russian empire. Lenin argued that the greater the freedom enjoyed by the peoples in building their own statehood, the stronger would be their desire for a voluntary union. While understanding the need to accommodate ethnic and national aspirations of the non-Russians in the short-term, Lenin

---

[60] V.F. Bakhtin (compl.), *Chastushka* (Moscow–Leningrad: Sovetskii pisatel, 1966), p. 249.

never disputed the Marxist view that in a socialist society boundaries
between nations – the phenomenon of the capitalist stage of development –
would eventually disappear. In his 'Critical Remarks on the National
Question' (1913), the Bolshevik leader observed that

> The development of nationality in general is the principle of bourgeois
> nationalism ... The proletariat, however, far from undertaking to uphold the
> national development of every nation, on the contrary, warns the masses against
> such illusions, stands for the fullest freedom of capitalist intercourse and
> welcomes every kind of assimilation of nations, except that which is founded on
> force or privilege ... it supports everything that helps to obliterate national
> distinctions and remove national barriers; it supports everything that makes the
> ties between nationalities closer and closer, or tends to merge nations.[61]

In the Stalin period, Marx and Engels's belief in the disappearance of
national distinction under the impact of socialism was merged with, and
underpinned by, the traditional pre-revolutionary view of the empire as a
Russian nation-state, in which all ethnic groups could live peacefully and
harmoniously.

Thus the concept of the single Soviet people (*edinyi sovetskii narod*),
whose creation was proclaimed to be the government's eventual goal, was
born. Although it was constantly undermined by policies which encouraged
ethnic particularism in the USSR, the goal of creating a single Soviet people
nevertheless persisted on the level of rhetoric. In 1971, Leonid Brezhnev
proclaimed that this people had at last been fully formed. The single Soviet
people was supposed to be the first example in the world of 'a socialist
community of nations and nationalities which rests on their common economic, political, ideological and cultural interests ... The socialist economy,
policy and ideology merge the lives of all Soviet nations and nationalities
into a single whole.'[62] Although each nation and nationality of the USSR of
a significant size had its own administrative territory, all members of the
single Soviet people were expected to identify with the common territory of
the entire USSR. One of the leading propagandists of the idea of the single
Soviet people observed in this connection:

> National territorial borders in the USSR do not in the least influence migratory
> processes, or the movement of people of all nationalities, which has become free
> and unrestricted. There are borders in the USSR, but no border problems. This
> notable fact manifests the decisive significance, the pre-eminence that is common
> to the entire Soviet Union, to all its nations and nationalities over the national
> and the specific.[63]

---

[61] V.I. Lenin, *Collective Works*, vol. 20, pp. 34–5.
[62] Maxim Kim, *The Soviet People – A New Historical Community* (Moscow, Progress, 1974),
     p. 35.
[63] Ibid, p. 38–9.

In other words, in the eyes of Soviet leaders the single Soviet people was supposed to comprise a political community. The distinction between such a community and an empire was stressed:

> Socialist inter-nation communities are absolutely new, formerly unknown communities, wholly unlike the 'commonwealths of nations' which were forcibly created by the imperialist colonial powers under their own aegis and which easily disintegrated at the first opportunity.[64]

In the 1960s and the 1970s, when the concept of the single Soviet people was promoted most intensively, there were clear signs that much of this rhetoric was, in fact, wishful thinking. State policies, which both encouraged and repressed the ethnic and national aspirations of non-Russians, served to increase local particularism and undermine integration. But the situation of the Russians was different. Among them the idea of the single Soviet people had more appeal. They were supposed to be the core of the new socialist community. Their language was to be the USSR's *lingua franca* and their culture, albeit in the Sovietised version, was to be taken as a model by other nationalities. Russians and Russified representatives of non-Russian nationalities constituted the main bulk of economic migrants to all parts of the USSR. Russians had migrated into the newly colonized areas from the earliest days of empire's creation and this migration had been an integral part of the process. It intensified with the construction of the railways and the first attempt at industrialization at the turn of the twentieth century. But it reached its highest momentum only during the industrialization drive in the Soviet period. The settlement of millions of Russians in the non-Russian areas of the empire from the 1930s onwards encouraged their identification with the entire state, particularly because the government granted the settlers educational and career privileges in their new homes.

The Russians' identification with the entire USSR was also promoted by the fact that the Russian Soviet Federated Socialist Republic (RSFSR) was not envisaged by the Soviet government as an embryonic national homeland for the Russians in the same way in which the non-Russian Union republics were created as national homelands for the non-Russians. The RSFSR was created from those territories which remained after the borders of the non-Russian republics had been drawn. Its institutions overlapped with those of the Union centre. Until 1990, the RSFSR did not have its own Communist Party or Academy of Sciences. Instead, the all-Union institutions were de facto the Russian institutions. This situation reflected both Lenin's aversion to Russian nationalism and Stalin's realization of its danger if it were to become anti-imperialist and separatist. Terry Martin shows that as early as

---

[64] Ibid, p. 19.

the 1920s Stalin was conscious of the fact that if powerful political institutions separate from all-Union ones were to exist in this huge and economically wealthy republic, its leader might use them to challenge the powers of the all-Union centre. In other words, in the early period of Soviet rule, Stalin could foresee the threat to the very existence of the USSR posed by a power struggle between a Soviet leader and a leader of the RSFSR, similar to the one that eventually did take place between Mikhail Gorbachev and Boris Yeltsin.[65]

In the 1920s, and from the 1960s onwards, some politicians at the RSFSR level and some Russian intellectuals did complain about discrimination against their republic. However, at least from the 1930s onwards, non-Russians began to see the RSFSR's separate status as a sign of the privileged position of the Russians in the USSR. Indeed, they had a point. While Russians had privileged education and employment opportunities when they moved to the non-Russian republics, non-Russians lost such privileges when they moved outside the borders of their own Union republics. Russians constituted a majority within the ruling organs of the all-Union Communist Party. The Soviet Academy of Sciences was also largely the Russian Academy, so the absence of an Academy and a Communist Party organization at the RSFSR level hardly indicated discrimination against Russians. This overlap between the RSFSR and the centre facilitated Russians' identification with the entire country.

As in the pre-revolutionary period, historians and cultural figures helped encourage Russians to equate their national homeland with the empire. From the mid-1930s, as the consolidation of the Soviet state became Stalin's main priority, the arguments of Mikhail Pokrovskii and his school concerning the brutality of Russian imperialism and the need to study the histories of non-Russian nationalities separately from Russian history were gradually abandoned. Instead, in Soviet textbooks the histories of all the peoples of the USSR started to be presented as organic parts of Russian history. Historians began to claim that virtually all the non-Russians had come under Moscow/St. Petersburg control voluntarily. In other words, with the help of Kliuchevskii's former students such as Sergei Bakhrushin and Vladimir Picheta, a benign view of Russian imperialism was gradually rehabilitated. Initially the argument was advanced that Russian imperialism constituted a lesser evil for the non-Russians than rule by other powers, for instance Britain, would have been. By the late 1940s the official line was further modified. It began to be maintained that the subjugation of non-Russians to Russian rule was an unquestionably positive development. Incorporation into the Russian state enabled non-Russians to join Russian workers in achieving victory in the revolution and thereby propelled many

---

[65] Terry Martin, 'The Russification of the RSFSR,' *Cahiers du Monde russe*, vol. 39, nos 1–2 (1998), pp. 99–118.

non-Russian peoples straight to the higher, socialist stage of development, by-passing capitalism.

The annexation of all the non-Russian territories by Russia again started to be described as a largely voluntary phenomenon. Whereas the first, 1939–1940, edition of *The History of the USSR*, edited by Academician Boris Grekov, stated that Peter the Great founded the Russian empire, the second edition of 1948 did not use the word 'empire' to describe the tsarist state. On the whole, Stalinist historiography painted the crudest picture of the creation of the Russian state. It was similar to that advanced by those pre-revolutionary nationalist thinkers who had even applied the idea that Russian territorial expansion had been peaceful to the takeover of the Caucasus and Central Asia. In other words, Stalin's historians went much further than Kliuchevskii in claiming that the imposition of Russian control over the non-Russians had been voluntary and peaceable. After Stalin's death some of the crudest presentations of the creation of the Russian state were dropped. Yet the same basic outline continued to dominate Soviet historiography and textbooks on Russian history, creating an image of the entire country as a nation-state of the Russians. Thus the 1973 school textbook *History of the USSR* argued that 'everywhere [in Transcaucasus] the actions of the Russian army were actively supported by local people ... All the peoples of Transcaucasus in effect joined Russia voluntarily.' 'The success of the Russian Army in Central Asia was largely due to the fact that ordinary people did not want to support their exploiters – khans and emirs.' Even in the North Caucasus, it was only local 'feudal lords who tried to set their people against the Russians.'[66]

While the Soviet school curriculum included the works by the classical Russian writers and poets mentioned above, which presented a blurred image of the Russian imperial set-up, Soviet culture, both official and dissident, promoted the same line with even greater intensity. Russian/Soviet culture of the communist period constructed new and powerful images which emphasized the lack of distinction between the Russian and non-Russian areas of the state. As a well-known Soviet song of the 1970s went: 'My address does not have a house number or a street name, my address is the Soviet Union.' The writer Mikhail Zoshchenko began one of his stories by saying that the events were taking place 'either in the steppes of Turkestan or at the foothills of the Urals, in other words in Saratov.' This passage meant to show that the Soviet government erased the differences between various parts of the state – Central Asia, the Urals, traditionally seen as a natural boundaries between Europe and Asia, and a city in the European part of Russia proper. Similarly, the dissident poet Iulii Kim could not precisely provide the address of one of the heroes of his songs: the

---

[66] I.A. Fedoseev, ed., *Istoriia SSSR* (Moscow, Prosveshchenie, 1973), pp. 57–8, 83 and 149.

guy could have been either from Kustanai (Kazakhstan) or from Odessa (Ukraine), 'most likely from Serebriannyi Bor' near Moscow.

In the 1960s, an anti-imperial Russian nationalism began to emerge. Its advocates tried to draw clear boundaries between 'Russia proper' and the non-Russian areas and even urged their independence. Nonetheless, the idea that the multi-ethnic Soviet Union was the only state able to preserve the Russians as a distinct community continued to have many defenders among the Russians.[67] On the whole, many more Russians began to identify the entire USSR as their national homeland as than had been the case vis-à-vis the tsarist empire. Increased migration into the non-Russian areas, and the spread of a mass education which denied the USSR was an empire, shaped the way most Russians perceived their homeland. They were proud of its huge size and the majority believed it had been formed peacefully.

During the *perestroika* period, when different ideas about the future of the Russian nation and state could be debated freely, the question of whether Russia was something different from its empire or whether the tsarist state/the USSR and Russia were one and the same became important in shaping the Russian political landscape. On the eve and in the wake of the demise of the USSR this question tore pro-democracy movements apart. It also brought together former staunch opponents such as Communists and anti-Soviet Russian nationalists.

Among the reformers, the most consistent defender of the Union was the Soviet President Mikhail Gorbachev, who hoped to be able to preserve the USSR as a true, democratic federation. Gorbachev fully subscribed to the view that the USSR could not be seen as an empire and emphasized that 'Russia proper' could not be separated from the entire state . He observed in 1990:

> The profound truth of the matter is that Russia can be and is unique and great only by being surrounded and permeated by the life-giving force of [other] cultures and languages, by being tied to them and by enriching them and, conversely, being enriched by them. Tear apart this accretively rooted system and you will no longer have Russia at all ...[68]

Some liberal intellectuals who supported democratic reforms also subscribed to the same view of 'Russia''s relationship with the USSR/tsarist empire. The philosopher Aleksandr Tsipko argued that same year that the declaration of sovereignty of the Russian Federation, adopted by the Russian parliament through the efforts of Yeltsin and the Democratic Russia movement, was nonsensical. Yeltsin's attempts clearly to distinguish

---

[67] The emergence of anti-imperial Russian nationalism in the 1960s is discussed in more detail in chapter 6.

[68] Quoted in Roman Solchanyk, 'Ukraine, The (Former) Center, Russia and "Russia",' *Studies in Comparative Communism*, no. 1, March (1992), p. 36.

'Russia' from the USSR, in fact, amounted to a call for 'Russia to leave Russia,' as the USSR and the pre-revolutionary empire were in fact the Russian national state.[69] In his writings, Tsipko consistently used the word 'empire' sarcastically, putting it in quotation marks. It was not long before some members of the Democratic Russia movement agreed with Tsipko. When, after the abortive coup of August 1991, the complete disintegration of the USSR became a quickly approaching reality, these DR members took fright at the prospect. As a result, the movement split over the issue of the USSR's disintegration and several of its subgroups joined the pro-Union opposition to Yeltsin.

The staunchest, most consistent and numerous supporters of the preservation of the USSR were the members of the so-called Communist-patriotic opposition to Gorbachev's reforms. In the wake of the 1990 Russian parliamentary elections, communists and anti-communist national-ists set up a joint electoral bloc, the main aim of which was to prevent the demise of the Union. The importance of this goal was such that members of the bloc cast aside differences on other issues, particularly the impact of the October revolution on Russia. Nationalists, such as the mathematician Igor Shafarevich, regarded the revolution as the worst tragedy which had ever befallen Russia. Yet, he and other nationalists were willing to put their names to an electoral platform which, rather than calling for the abolition of the Communist Party, urged the Party to toughen its stand against 'left radicals.' Both nationalists and communists concurred in their praise of Stalin for having strengthened the Russian state and having appropriated some old Russian traditions (for instance, reinstating the Patriarch as the head of the Russian Orthodox Church).

This seemingly puzzling alliance between former ideological opponents was easy to explain. What united them was that they equated Russia with the empire. Russian nationalists softened their attitude towards the CPSU and the system created during the seventy years of Soviet rule. They accepted that only the Soviet regime, founded as it was on the Party's monopoly of power and the might of the Soviet Army, could have preserved the Russian empire intact. A leading ideologist of the bloc, the military writer Aleksandr Prokhanov, summed up this position well by arguing that it was only the CPSU that was able 'to pervade with its nerve tissue the country's whole giant muscular system, resolving all the ethnic, class, professional, and ideological conflicts.' Prokhanov depicted an apocalyptic picture of Russia if the Soviet Union were to disintegrate:

> Strikes at nuclear power plants and munitions factories threatened us with Chernobyls of unprecedented force. Fire on the horizons of the city, refugees from the exploded nuclear boilers, involuntary launches of ballistic missiles, the

---

[69]   *Sovetskaia kultura*, 26 May 1990.

biosphere destroyed over huge expanses ... a civil war with all the mercilessness of the previous war (World War II) plus nightmarish new components introduced by military and technological civilization. The world will stare in terror at our blood-soaked expanses, belching nuclear and chemical miasma into the atmosphere.[70]

The 1990 communist–nationalist alliance replicated very closely a similar alliance of the early 1920s. The 1990 bloc largely reiterated ideas which had been expressed in the 1920s by Nikolai Ustrialov and other ideologists of the *Smena vekh* movement. They accepted Bolshevik rule once they saw that the Red Army had the power to preserve the empire. According to Ustrialov, the main thing was for Russia to 'remain powerful, great and horrifying to its enemies,' and then 'everything else would come by itself.'

In the 1990 parliamentary elections, candidates of the communist–nationalist alliance lost, in many constituencies, to Democratic Russia candidates. These promoted a vision of Russia separate from the USSR, which they regarded as an empire. It would seem that Democratic Russia's promotion of this image contributed to the fact that the Soviet Union's disintegration in December 1991 was peaceful. But the intellectual debates and opinion polls of the post-communist period indicate that the vision of the tsarist empire/USSR as a Russian nation-state is not dead.

Conclusion

The image of a Russia embracing all areas of the empire, including the non-Russian ones, had a very powerful impact on the way Russia's educated elites saw themselves from the late eighteenth century onwards, and this view extended to the broader public in the twentieth. Its origins lay in the fact that the Russian empire had begun to be created well before the 'revolution of national consciousness' in Europe, and that the early patterns of Moscow's territorial expansion differed from modern forms of imperial military conquests. In modern times, the image was reinforced in the propaganda campaigns of the two great tsars of the eighteenth century – Peter I and Catherine II. They emphasized the vastness of the country and its ethnic and cultural variety in order to instil state patriotism into their subjects and legitimize their autocratic rule. In subsequent periods, especially in the Soviet era, the government continued with great success to encourage such identification of the Russians with the entire state.

From the mid-nineteenth century non-Russian intellectuals in the empire began to force their Russian counterparts to define the boundaries of the Russian nation more precisely. Yet there was no serious response to this

---

[70] *Literaturnaia Rossiia,* 5 January 1990

challenge until an anti-imperial Russian nationalism began to emerge in the 1960s. In 1990–1991, it contributed to the peaceful disintegration of the USSR. However, even in that period the imperial and national conscious-ness of the Russians had not been fully separated. Many Russians still did not understand the point of view of non-Russian nationalists. Even some liberals continued to argue that the Russians could lead a fulfilling existence only within the framework of a multi-ethnic community. Such a perception prevented Gorbachev from properly assessing the strength of non-Russian nationalism. Here a strong parallel could be drawn with the period of 1917–1919, when the main Russian liberal party, the Constitutional Democrats, supported the slogan of 'one and indivisible Russia' and rejected a federal option for Russia. This lost them the support of non-Russians and thereby contributed to the defeat of the anti-Bolshevik opposition.

The attempts by some scholars to explain the persistence of the position that the empire was the same as the Russian nation-state, by arguing that in the era of modern nationalism Russians continued to think in pre-national terms and by referring to their alleged fear of reliving the troubles of the medieval period, are adequate. Medieval experience was occasionally evoked, but few Russians seriously regarded it as a guide for action. It is also wrong to think that Russians failed to use the ideas of nationalism in their analysis of the situation in their country. On the contrary, attempts to apply to Russia the concept of modern nationalism that only a nation-state can claim real legitimacy and therefore survive in the long-term led Russian intellectuals to insist that the Russian empire was the Russian nation-state. From the eighteenth century onwards, Russia's comparison with the West led intellectuals to underscore the similarities as well as the differences between their country and its main 'other.' On the question of the nature of the Russian state, it was claimed that Russia was a nation-state comparable to Britain or France. But the difference was also impossible to deny. West European states were far more ethnically homogeneous than Russia. Therefore, Russia's multi-ethnic nature was proclaimed to be a sign of Russia's uniqueness and superiority.

This artificial construction was born out of the dialogue which the Russians constantly conducted with the West. This framework had no place for a serious analysis of the aspirations of the empire's non-Russian subjects. Only a few scholars and socialist intellectuals were inclined to narrow the boundaries of the Russian nation in response to the challenge from non-Russian intellectuals. The majority of intellectuals continued to define the Russians in terms of their mission of preserving a unique multi-ethnic state, profoundly different from the West European empires. Even Bakunin and other socialists, who supported the idea of self-determination for non-Russians, made too much of a comparison between the United States, a country whose multi-ethnic nature was largely the result of voluntary emigration, and the Russian empire, which was based on various forms of conquest of the territories of non-Russian peoples.

At the turn of the twentieth century, the tsarist government was pursuing an inflexible policy of suppressing minority cultures in order to preserve the unity of the empire. In such circumstances, the ideas of Russian intellectuals about Russia as a unique and voluntary multi-ethnic civilization, both similar to, and different from, West European nations, could not convince non-Russian intellectuals. The latter had already begun constructing separate language-based national identities for their own nationalities. By the time of the revolution, Russian peasants and workers also identified with the entire multi-ethnic state only to a very limited extent. The Bolsheviks combined the idea of a unique multi-ethnic community led by the Russians with highly contradictory nationalities policies. These policies unintentionally only served to strengthen the ethnic affiliations of non-Russians which, in turn, forced an increasing number of Russians to begin to see the preservation of the USSR as a burden. Therefore in 1991, as in 1917, the state disintegrated, as no single nation had been created within its borders out of the empire's various nationalities.

6

Imaginative ethnography: who are the Russians?

The Russians possess 'the assimilating power (*upodobitelnaia sila*)..., which converts the aliens, with whom it comes into contact, into the Russian flesh and blood.'
Nikolai Danilevskii (*Russia and Europe*, 1868)

'Everything which did not accord with their [Russian] nationality was subjected to their disdain and considered heretical. They haughtily looked down on everyone.'
Mykola Kostomarov (*Two Russian Nationalities*, 1860–61)

'The Russians cannot exist without the [multi-ethnic] state ... As a separate Great Russian ethnos they will soon die out.'
Iurii Borodai (*Ethnos, Nation, State*, 1989)

Given the persistence of the idea that the entire empire was the Russian nation-state, the question arises of how the Russians distinguished themselves among all the inhabitants of the empire. How was the membership of the Russian nation defined? In what circumstances could non-Russians become members of the Russian nation? In her book on nationalism, Liah Greenfeld has argued that by the end of the eighteenth century: 'The "Russian nation" was ... formed by ethnic, primordial factors such as blood and soil.'[1] Therefore all non-Russians, including Ukrainians, were automatically excluded from the Russian nation. According to Greenfeld, there was a consensus on this issue which was rarely challenged. This

---

[1]   Liah Greenfeld, *Nationalism: Five Roads to Modernity* (Cambridge MA, Harvard University Press, 1995), pp. 258 and 261.

presentation oversimplifies the situation to a great extent. Had they adopted such an exclusive definition of Russianness, the Russians could have hardly maintained a multi-ethnic land-based empire for another two centuries. Indeed, among Russian nation- and state-builders, many were not Russians by ethnic origin and this fact affected their perception of Russian nationality. At the same time, the modern European notion of a national community proved to be difficult to apply to the realities of a multi-ethnic empire. Therefore, from the turn of the nineteenth century, there was a constant and unresolved debate among educated Russians about who, precisely, could be regarded as belonging to the Russian nation. This chapter looks at the first attempts in the eighteenth century, when traditional religious identity began to crumble, to tackle the question of the status of Russians within the multi-ethnic state. It then discusses how the challenge of non-Russian, particularly Ukrainian, nationalism forced some Russian nation-builders to contract the boundaries of the Russian nation, while others rejected the arguments of the non-Russians and insisted instead that a single Russian nation was being created out of all the different nationalities and ethnic groups of the empire. Finally, the chapter analyses the survival as well as the transformation of these pre-revolutionary ideas in the Soviet period.

Posing the question

In Muscovite Rus the main distinction between people was religion. To convert to Orthodoxy was to become a Russian, and this lifted the restrictions imposed upon the non-Orthodox subjects of the empire. In the early eighteenth century, although the reforms of Peter the Great diminished the role of the Russian Orthodox Church, the first Russian poets to hail the birth of a 'new Russia' as a result of the tsar's bold policies still defined the Russians as 'Orthodox.'[2] But such a simple definition began to be challenged from the 1730s onwards, when, with support and encouragement from the government, scholars from the Imperial Academy of Sciences in St. Petersburg began to organize expeditions to study the non-Russian subjects of the empire, particularly in Siberia. These scholars, most of whom had come to Russia from Germany, gradually developed ways of classifying the different peoples of the empire. In addition to religion, the other criteria of language, customs and habits (*nravy i obyknoveniia*) began to be used as the main means of distinguishing people from one another. In these classifications, the Russians became just one of the peoples of the empire, to be

---

[2]   See, for instance, Vasilii Trediakovskii, 'Stikhi pokhvalnye Rossii' (1728), which said that 'all your [Russia's] people are Orthodox.' (G.P. Makogonenko, compl., *Russkaia literatura XVIII veka* (Leningrad, Prosveshchenie, 1970), p. 80.

described according to the same parameters as the Chukchi, Tatars or Tungus.[3] By the end of the eighteenth century, the scholars gradually began to regard language as the main classification criterion for distinguishing between the different subjects of the empire. Not only was language 'the most reliable sign of kinship between peoples,' but also 'the similarity of languages' seemed to prove 'the common origins of peoples.'[4] In the reign of Catherine the Great, the first dictionaries of both Russian and the non-Russian languages of the empire began to be compiled.

This does not mean that the criterion of religion lost all significance. Up to the end of monarchy Orthodoxy remained a key element of identity for many Russian subjects of the empire. The Slavophile Ivan Aksakov argued in the 1870s that 'a Jew, a Catholic or a Muslim can be a Russian subject, but cannot be a Russian. In contrast, in the eyes of ethnic Russians, anyone who has converted to Orthodoxy can be a Russian.'[5] The best known reflection of this position in classical Russian literature can be found in Anton Chekhov's story 'Lady with Lapdog,' which was written in 1899. In it, a Russian woman whose surname is von Diederitz is asked whether her husband is a German. Her reply is: 'No, his grandfather, I believe, was German, but he himself is Orthodox.'

The government continued to view religion as a key element of identity. As late as in 1904 one government document stated that 'persons of Russian descent will be considered exclusively those of the Orthodox faith, including *edinovertsy*[6] and Old Believers.'[7] Yet the interest of scholars in people's 'ethnic origin', based on language and customs, began to influence government policies as well. In the eighteenth century, the so-called *revizii* (attempts by the government to count the male population of the empire) usually mentioned the 'ethnic origins' of the people registered.[8] The superior and dominant position of the Russians over the non-Russian subjects of the empire was not in doubt, however, and both scholars and rulers shared the hope that the non-Russian subjects of the tsar would gradually accept the religion, language and the way of life of the Russians.

---

[3] Yuri Slezkine, 'Naturalists versus Nations: Eighteenth-Century Russian Scholars Confront Ethnic Diversity', in Daniel R. Brower and Edward J. Lazzerini, eds, *Russia's Orient. Imperial Borderlands and Peoples, 1700–1917* (Bloomington IN, Indiana University Press, 1997), pp. 27–57.

[4] Quoted in ibid, p. 47.

[5] Quoted in N.A. Rubakin, *Sredi knig*, 2nd ed., vol. 3, part 1 (Moscow, Knigoizdatelstvo Nauka, 1915), p. 119.

[6] *Edinoverie* was a union between Old Believers and the official Russian Orthodox Church, according to which the former were allowed to follow pre-reform rituals and use old prayer books, but in return agreed to accept the jurisdiction of the official Church.

[7] Theodore R. Weeks, *Nation and State in Late Imperial Russia. Nationalism and Russification on the Western Frontier, 1863–1914* (DeKalb IL, Northern Illinois University Press, 1996), p. 8.

[8] V. Kabuzan, *Russkie v mire* (St. Petersburg, Blits, 1996), p. 10.

Since the eighteenth century, scholars had been debating not only the contemporary ethnic make up of the empire, but also the historical origins of the dominant nationality, the Russians. Its origins were traced back to Kiev Rus – a union of principalities, which between the ninth and the twelfth centuries recognized the supreme authority of the Grand Prince of Kiev. The view that the Moscow principality and therefore Russia is the direct and only heir of the Kiev Rus heritage is still dominant among Russians today. In fact, Moscow was mentioned in the medieval chronicles for the first time only in the middle of the twelfth century. The rise of its political significance dates back to the fourteenth century. Thus the formation of the Moscow principality occurred mainly in the post-Kiev period, during the time of the Tatar Mongol invasion. How and when did the idea that the Russians originated in Kiev Rus come about?

In the thirteenth century, some principalities of Kiev Rus were invaded by the Tatar Mongols. After the fall of Kiev, the Kievan Metropolitan See moved to the north eastern principality of Vladimir, and in 1326 to Moscow. That was the main reason for the hierarchs of the Orthodox Church in Moscow to stake their claim to the Kiev heritage. But in the same century, the Western principality of Kiev Rus, Galicia, also established a Metropolitan See as a successor to the one in Kiev. Thereafter Galicia and Moscow struggled over the Kievan ecclesiastical heritage. When, in the fifteenth century, the Muscovite rulers began to expand their principality, gradually taking over the territories that had once been part of Kiev Rus, some Moscow churchmen saw the princes' policies as the process of the 'gathering of the Russian lands.' Historians disagree over whether either the princes or the lay-people of Muscovy had much awareness of a shared historical heritage among all East Slavs and drew any connection between Moscow and Kiev. [9] Whatever the case, by the time of the Pereiaslav treaty of 1654, which marked the beginning of Moscow's rule over parts of today's Ukraine, the difference in political culture and the way of life between the people of Muscovy and those which became known as Little Russians (Ukrainians) was very pronounced. However, in 1674 Innokentii Gizel, the Archimandrite of the Kiev Cave Monastry, published a history of the East Slavs, the *Synopsis*. This work, which was much more widely read than any of its predecessors, promoted the idea that Moscow was a legitimate heir of Kiev Rus. According to *Sinopsis*, all East Slavs were one people, a *slaviano-rossiiskii narod*. Thus the basis was laid for regarding the Russians (Great Russians), Ukrainians and Belorussians as one *narod* in

[9]   Edward L. Keenan, 'Muscovite Perceptions of Other East Slavs before 1654 – An Agenda for Historians,' in Peter J. Potichnyj, Marc Raeff, Jaroslaw Pelenski and Gleb N. Zekulin, eds., *Ukraine and Russia in Their Historical Encounter* (Edmonton, Canadian Institute of Ukrainian Studies Press, 1992), p. 22. The majority of Western and, of course, Russian scholars disagree with Keenan. See, for instance, Robin Milner-Gullnar, *The Russians* (Oxford, Blackwell, 1999), p. 212.

modern times. When in 1749 a bitter controversy broke out in the Imperial Academy of Sciences between the German scholars and their Russian counterpart Mikhail Lomonosov on 'the origins of the people and the very name of *Rossiia*,' neither side disputed that the origins of the Russians were to be found in Kiev Rus.[10]

The first signs of Russian nationalism

Eighteenth century historians, most notably Vasilii Tatishchev and Ivan Boltin, adhered to Gizel's view. But even among the literate subjects of the empire, very few, other than scholars, were interested in the question of the historic origins of the Russians. It was Nikolai Karamzin's *History of the Russian State* (1818–29) that changed the situation. In the words of Pushkin, 'Old Rus seemed to have been discovered by Karamzin, as America was discovered by Columbus.' The print-run of 3000 copies, substantial for the time, was sold out in the first 25 days. The historian set out in detail his view of how and when the Russians had come into being. According to Karamzin, by the twelfth century the Slavic, Finnish and Norse people who populated the principalities of Kiev Rus were bound by language, religion, civic codes and customs into a single Russian nationality. This nationality united three main subgroups, the Great Russians (former Muscovites), Little Russians (Ukrainians) and Belorussians. But the divisions between these subgroups were of little importance. Little Russians and Belorussians did not have their own languages, instead their peasants spoke farmyard dialects of Russian. In sum, Ukrainians and Belorussians were Russians.

The non-Slavic population of the Russian empire is hardly mentioned in Karamzin's history. Nor were the first Russian intellectuals, affected by the ideas of romantic nationalism, interested in the non-Slavs. Instead, the early Slavophiles dreamed of creating a state, led by the Russian tsar, which would embrace all the Slavs, not only the Eastern Slavs of Russia, but also the Slavs of the Habsburg and Ottoman empires. The Slavophiles were not particularly interested in Russifying the non-Slavic subjects of the Russian empire or converting them to Orthodoxy. It was another group of early nineteenth century intellectuals, affected by the ideas of nationalism, that put the question of Russifying all the imperial subjects at the top of their agenda. These were the members of the Southern Society, one of the sections of the Decembrists. In his political programme, *The Russian Code of Laws* (*Russkaia pravda*), the leader of the society, Pavel Pestel, articulated his vision of a Russian nation uniting all the people of the empire

---

[10] For the details of this controversy see chapter 2, 'Peter's legacy: the emergence of intellectual debate', pp. 50–2.

regardless of their ethnic origin. He viewed the Russian empire as the Russian nation-state and tried to apply to Russia the concept of a political nation of equal citizens, united by loyalty to a constitution and to other political institutions. With time, this nation was to become a culturally homogenous entity.[11] The second chapter of Pestel's programme discussed methods of creating 'only one people' (*tolko odin narod*) out of the different nationalities of the Russian empire. Pestel acknowledged the right of nationalities (*pravo narodnostei*) to self-determination only in theory. In practice, as far as the smaller peoples were concerned, this right was an illusion, as state independence could not be maintained. Pestel predicted that the Russian state would eventually take over the Far East, the 'Kirghiz lands' and the Black Sea shores of the Caucasus, at a time when these areas had not yet become part of the empire. Meanwhile, it was inevitable and progressive that all the ethnic groups, including non-Slavs, should eventually merge into a single united Russian people (*edinyi russkii narod*) and lose their separate identities. Some non-Russians could be Russified gradually and peacefully. For the others the use of force was inevitable. Pestel proposed particularly brutal measures towards the 'wild and ungovernable' (*buinye*) mountain-dwellers of the North Caucasus.[12]

The challenge of the non-Russians: the first response

The Decembrists and the early Slavophiles operated in an environment in which their views on the boundaries of the Russian nation were not seriously challenged by any non-Russian subjects of the empire. Until the mid-1840s, only the Poles had been influenced by the ideas of nationalism. But the Poles were recognized as a separate nation by many Russian intellectuals at an early stage. The Decembrists, for instance, thought that the independence of Poland should be restored. The early Slavophiles, particularly Konstantin Aksakov, realized that Catholicism was so strong among the Poles that attempts to convert them to Orthodoxy would be futile. For this reason Poland was excluded from the pan-Slavic state envisaged by the early Slavophiles.[13] The challenge of Polish nationalism was political and did not pose too great a problem for Russian intellectuals in their attempts to set the boundaries of the Russian nation. The first serious challenge to the Russian intellectuals' definition of their nation came eventually from the Ukrainians.

---

[11] Another group of the Decembrists, the Northern society, advocated greater cultural autonomy for non-Russians and imagined an ideal Russia as a federal state.

[12] Quoted in Iakov Gordin, *Kavkaz: Zemlia i krov* (St. Petersburg, Zhurnal 'Zvezda', 2000), p. 7–9.

[13] Rubakin, *Sredi knig*, pp. 154–8.

In 1845–46, members of the Ukrainian pan-Slavic group, the Brotherhood of Sts Cyril and Methodius, began to dispute the position of their Russian counterparts that most Slavs should eventually belong to one state, join the Russian Orthodox Church and become subjects of the Russian tsar. In contrast, Ukrainian pan-Slavists argued for the equality of different Slavic cultures and languages. They favoured the creation of a federal rather than a unitary state of the Slavs. It is within the framework of this broader approach that the historian Mykola Kostomarov (1817–1885), half Ukrainian and half Russian by origin, began to argue that the Ukrainians or Little Russians (*malorossy*) and the Great Russians (*velikorossy*) were in fact two different nationalities. Kostomarov was the first consistently to use the term Great Russians (*velikorossy*) as opposed to Little Russians or South Russians (*malorossy* or *iuzhnorossy*) to describe the two different East Slavic peoples. The word Great Russia (*Velikorossiia*) started to be used under tsar Aleksei Mikhailovich in the seventeenth century, after 'Little Russia' had been subjugated to the rule of Moscow. But it was Kostomarov who applied the words Great Russians and Little Russians to describe and distinguish not the territories but the peoples. The majority of Little Russians at the time were peasants, while the Ukrainian elites were either Russified or Polonised. However, Kostomarov argued, this did not mean that the peasants who spoke the Little Russian language could not constitute a nation. The scholar insisted that his Great Russian contemporaries were the descendents of the inhabitants of the Moscow Principality, whose way of life had been strongly influenced by the Tatar Mongol yoke in the thirteenth to fifteenth centuries. Ethnically these people were Slavs, but with strong Finnish and Tatar elements. They had been geographically and historically (through the Tatar Mongol yoke) separated from the other East Slavs, particularly from the Little Russians. Kostomarov dwelled on the differences in religious attitudes (Little Russians had not been affected by the seventeenth century Church schism), folklore, everyday life and language between the Great and Little Russians. In the 1840s and 1850s, Kostomarov further argued that the inhabitants of Novgorod in North East Russia, who had not been affected by the Tatar Mongol invasion, were more similar to the Little Russians than to the Great Russians. Kostomarov supported his proposal for a federal Slavic state by trying to find elements of ethnically-based federalism in Kiev Rus. In his work 'The Federal Structure of Kiev Rus,' he argued that there were ethnic similarities between the inhabitants of Novgorod and Kiev. How did the Russians respond to this challenge?

In 1847, the tsarist government arrested members of the Brotherhood. The views of its members on the equality of Slavic cultures, and their advocacy of religious tolerance and federalism challenged the official view of Russian nationality. This official conception, formulated by Count Uvarov in 1833, declared Autocracy and Orthodoxy to be integral parts of the Russian nationality. But the government's administrative measures did not remove the challenge of Kostomarov's views. He continued to develop his ideas. In the period of liberalization in 1859–62, Kostomarov even held the chair in Russian history at St. Petersburg University. His most articulate expression of the view that Ukrainians and Great Russians constituted two different nationalities came in an article entitled 'Two Russian Nationalities'. He wrote it in 1860–61, and it was published the next year in the journal of Ukrainian intellectuals, *Osnova*, which was openly printed in St. Petersburg in 1862–63. Although they argued against his views, leading Russian historians of the time recognized Kostomarov as one of the best experts in east Slavic history.

Kostomarov's attempt to argue that there was a national distinction between the Great Russians and the other East Slavs, particularly the Ukrainians, and to trace back their significant differences to the early medieval period, was rejected by Mikhail Pogodin, Sergei Solovev, Vasilii Kliuchevskii and other eminent Russian historians. They continued to develop the line articulated by Karamzin and contended that the national unity of all Eastern Slavs could be traced back to the tenth to twelfth centuries. These Russian historians particularly disputed the view of Kostomarov and of some Polish historians that the influence of the Tatars during the Tatar–Mongol invasion had been so great that the Slavic element was weak among the Great Russians. In response, the Russian historians argued that a Turkic element was in fact stronger among Ukrainian Cossacks, because they had assimilated Turkic peoples from the southern steppes. This accounted for the dark hair of the majority of Little Russians.

Although most Russian scholars continued to accept Karamzin's view of the origins and composition of the Russian nation, some Russians did not altogether deny some difference between what they termed the tribes of the Russian nationality (*plemena Russkoi narodnosti*). Solovev's *History of Russia from Earliest Times*, the first volume of which was published in 1851, was particularly eloquent in describing how the Great Russian sub-group had been developing from the thirteenth century onwards in isolation from 'Western Russia.' Whereas the latter was open to European influences, the Great Russians lived in 'the wilderness (*pustynia*) of the North-East' and this situation had an adverse affect on their cultural and political develop-ment. Some Russian liberals, such as the historian Konstantin Kavelin, agreed with Kostomarov that Little Russians were more freedom loving than the Great Russians. Kostomarov contrasted the domination of a father figure (*bolshak*), collective use of property and restrictions on rights of individual members which characterized the Russian family, with the position of Little Russians who thought 'that a strong control of parents over grown-up children was a manifestation of despotism.' Kavelin sug-gested that the role of the tsar in the Russian state and the attitude of the Great Russians towards him closely replicated the position of the *bolshak* in

Russian families.'[14] Later in the nineteenth and early twentieth centuries, some other historians, particularly Aleksandr Pypin, Aleksandr Presniakov and Matvei Liubavskii, also looked carefully at the differences between Eastern Slavs. Pypin's *History of Slavic Literatures*, first published in 1865 and reprinted with significant amendments in 1879-81, discussed works written in Little Russia, Galicia and Belorussia separately from Great Russian literature. Pypin made no reference to the unity of the peoples and their cultures. Early socialist intellectuals, such as Aleksandr Herzen and Mikhail Bakunin, accepted the narrow definition of the Russian nation which included only those who spoke the Great Russian dialect. They were the first to recognize in the late 1850s that Ukrainians had their own language and therefore were a separate nationality.

A further challenge to the view that a homogenous Russian nationality subsumed all Eastern Slavs was made by ethnographers and members of the Imperial Geographical Society in St. Petersburg. The first *Ethnographical Map of European Russia*, compiled by the statistician P.I. Keppen and published in St. Petersburg in 1851, had marked the areas inhabited by members of the 'Russian nationality,' without dividing them into Great Russians, Ukrainians and Belorussians. But a new ethnographical map of European Russia, compiled by A.F. Rittikh on the basis of police reports in 1867, marked the borders between Great Russian, Ukrainian and Belorussian settlements. In the 1870s, the Geographical Society organized expeditions in the 'West Russian regions' which produced *The Description of Belorussia from the Point of View of Ethnography* and a volume on Little Russia. Both of these works highlighted the differences in culture and customs of the Belorussians and Ukrainians from those of the Great Russians. Finally, the popular twelve-volume *Russia in Illustrations* (*Zhivopisnaia Rossiia*), which began to be published in 1874, emphasized the ethnic, cultural, linguistic and religious differences of the subjects of the empire. It thereby implicitly challenged the view of the Russian empire as a Russian nation-state in the eyes of the broader reading public. The majority of volumes in the series were devoted to describing the non-Russian borderlands of the empire. Written with a large input from ethnographers, they provided rich material on the histories, cultures and traditions of the non-Russians. Volume three, 'Western and Southern Russia' (on Lithuania and Belorussia) presented a particular challenge to the concept of a homogeneous Russian nationality uniting all Eastern Slavs. The volume undermined the idea that these parts of the empire were indigenous Russian

---

[14] F.A. Brockhaus and I.A. Efron, *Entsiklopedicheskii slovar*, vol. XVIIIa (St. Petersburg, Tipo-Litografiia I.A. Efrona, 1896), p. 485.

lands, particularly by stressing the importance of Polish influences. It was therefore attacked in the press by Russian nationalists.[15]

As in the 1840s, so in the 1860s and 1870s, the government responded to attempts to promote a separate Ukrainian nationality with repression. A decree, issued in 1863 by the Minister of the Interior P.A. Valuev, banned the publication of books in Ukrainian, other than *belles-lettres* and folklore. The so-called Ems decree of 1876 argued that 'permitting the creation of a special literature for the common people in the Ukrainian dialect would signify collaborating in the alienation of Ukraine from the rest of Russia.'[16] In the late 1870s, the government closed down the south-western section of the Imperial Geographical Society, which was accused of pro-Ukrainian sentiments. Supporters of a separate Ukrainian identity lost jobs in Kiev University. These measures against the Ukrainians were uniquely harsh. No other ethnic group in the Russian empire had to contend with attempts to suppress completely the development of a literary language and culture. David Saunders has argued that for demographic reasons, it was of paramount importance for the government to assimilate the Ukrainians, the second largest people in the empire, fully into the Russian nation. Without Ukrainians and Belorussians, the Great Russians would have constituted less than half of the empire's population.[17] But if the Russian nationality was defined as including all the East Slavs of the empire, then its proportion in the total population of the empire would rise to 72.5 per cent, as the 1897 census proudly stated. It was not until 1905 that the government accepted the verdict of the Russian Academy of Sciences that Ukrainian was not a dialect of Russian but a separate language. (As the 1897 census indicated, the government took language to be the main criterion of identity.) Therefore the government's definition of a Russian was modified. The ethnographer Lev Shternberg thus described the government position in 1910:

> The term *inorodtsy* (aliens) is understood by the government and in the nationalist press in a double sense – a political one and a technical-juridical one. In the political and most important meaning of this word, the basic characteristic of *inorodstvo* is language. Only the population which speaks the Great Russian dialect has a privilege to be called the Russian people (*russkii narod*).[18]

---

[15] See, M.I. Koialovich, *Istoriia russkogo samosoznaniia* (Minsk, Luchi Sofii, 1997), pp. 480–8. Although he was of Belorussian origin, Koialovich fully accepted the Russian nationalist definition of the Russian nationality.

[16] David Saunders, 'Russia's Ukrainian Policy (1847–1905): a Demographic Approach,' *European History Quarterly*, vol. 25 (1995), p. 187.

[17] Ibid, pp. 181–208.

[18] L. Shternberg, 'Inorodtsy. Obshchii obzor,' in A.I. Kastelianskii (ed.), *Formy natsionalnogo dvizheniia v sovremennykh gosudarstvakh. Avstro-Vengriia, Rossiia, Germaniia* (St. Petersburg, Obshchestvennaia polza, 1910), pp. 529–74.

Shternberg further maintained that neither race nor political loyalty played an essential role in the way the tsars viewed their subjects. To the very end, the tsarist government tried to disregard the significance of ethnicity and nationalism in its domains. No strict legal definition of either 'Russian' or of any other nationality was ever introduced.

The challenge of the non-Russians: the second response

Despite the challenges of non-Russian nationalism, the most widespread view among Russian intellectuals remained that Russian national identity was inseparable from the imperial one. Moreover, the challenge of non-Russian nationalism caused many Russian intellectuals to defend the view that the Russian empire was the Russian nation-state with greater vigour. Similarly, it made them further exaggerate the success of Russification and adopt an ever more inclusive definition of Russianness. Again, these inclusive definitions were promoted by both conservatives and liberals. Thus, in his *Russia and Europe*, Nikolai Danilevskii hailed 'the assimilating power (*upodobitelnaia sila*) of the Russian people, which converts the aliens, with whom it comes into contact, into the Russian flesh and blood.'[19] By pulling non-Russians into their orbit the Russians not only 'enlightened' the non-Russians, but also enriched their own culture. This perceived openness to other cultures and traditions was elevated by Fedor Dostoevskii into one of the key elements of the Russian national character, which he defined as the ability to be open to all nations (*vsemirnaia otzyvchivost*), to perform peace-keeping functions (*vseprimirenie*) and to take on (*perevoploshchatsia*) the qualities of other nations.[20]

The liberals further developed the idea of 'Russian culture', both as the main unifying force among all the nationalities of the state, and as a combined product of those nationalities. The historians Kliuchevskii and Pavel Miliukov presented the intermixing, merging and assimilation of various tribes (*plemena*) into the Russian nation and culture as one of the main themes of Russian history. Peter Struve was probably the most eloquent in promoting the idea of a pan-Russian nationality. In one of his articles in *Russkaia mysl*, he stated that the Russians as a nation could not be limited to the Great Russian tribe. Instead, they were 'a living cultural force, great and developing, the ever growing national substance, the nation in the making (*tvorimaia natsia*),' embracing all the peoples of the empire.

[19] N.Ia. Danilevskii, *Rossiia i Evropa*, 5th ed. (St. Petersburg, Tipografiia brat. Panteleevykh, 1895), p. 532.

[20] F.M. Dostoevskii, 'Obiasnitelnoe slovo po povodu pechataemoi nizhe rechi o Pushkine,' in *Russkaia ideia* (Moscow, Respublika, 1992), p. 132.

The unity of this nation was achieved by the force of Russian culture, based on language. This was 'the language of ... Pushkin, Gogol, Turgenev and Lev Tolstoi, which in a purely linguistic sense is the Great Russian language, but in its cultural and historical sense is the pan-Russian language, the common language of all the nationalities, which are part of the Russian empire.'[21] Philosopher Ivan Ilin similarly argued that the Russians could

> either disappear or colonise the open Eurasian plain, to come to terms with its harsh climate and ... to create spiritual, cultural and legal fatherland for all these multi-language human mass; pacify everybody, allow everybody to pray the way they wished and to select the best for the purpose of state-building and cultural development... And so, the Russians took over and carried the burden of all [Russia's] different nationalities (*narodnosti*) – this is the only such phenomenon in the world.[22]

This view of the Russian nation was taken to its logical conclusion in the theories of the Eurasianists in the 1920s. If Miliukov and Struve thought that the process of creating the Russian nation out of all the empire's nationalities was far from complete, the Eurasianist, Petr Savitskii, thought that a single nation had already been fully created on the territory of the former Russian empire. In the process not only cultural assimilation, but genetic mutation (*geneticheskaia mutatsiia*) had occurred.[23]

The challenge of the non-Russians: the third response

The final, racial, definition of Russianness by blood, was articulated in response to the challenge of non-Russian nationalism. It existed on the margins of the Russian national debate and at the turn of the twentieth century was advanced by members of such extreme right-wing groups as the Russian Assembly, the Union of the Russian People and the Union of Archangel Michael. They claimed that the influence of non-Russians, especially Jews, on the Russians was harmful. The newspaper *Russkoe znamia* argued on 4 December 1905: 'We, the Russians, do not repress aliens (*inorodtsy*), but aliens repress us, the Russians.' The main element in defining a Russian was blood. The periodical *Veche* proclaimed on 31 October 1906: 'We should accept only such a government (*uprava*), whose

---

[21] P.B. Struve, 'Obshcherusskaia kultura i ukrainskii partikularism,' in *Russkaia mysl*, no. 1 (1912), p. 66.

[22] I.Ilin, 'O Rossii' (Sofia 1934) quoted in *Russkii vestnik. Izdanie Leningradskogo otdeleniia Vserossiiskogo Fonda Kultury* (Leningrad, Molodaia gvardiia, 1990), pp. 48–9.

[23] Quoted in Milan Hauner, *What Is Asia to Us?* (London, Routledge, 1992), p. 61.

members have pure Russian blood in their veins, in whose chests Russian hearts beat and whose leaders have unquestionably Russian names.'

How the purity of Russian blood was to be established they did not elaborate. Indeed, the purist search for a true Russian in racial terms would immediately stumble at the example of the unchallenged symbol of Russianness – Pushkin, whose grandfather was an Abyssinian. Despite the great publicity that these organizations received in the press, they did not enjoy mass public support in pre-revolutionary Russia. Only in Volynia (Belorussia) did they manage to create a mass organization among the peasantry. Extreme nationalists had temporary successes among workers in various parts of the empire. On the whole, however, they could not compete with the much more effective socialist propaganda among workers and peasants. During World War I, the activities of these organizations virtually came to an end in Russia itself, although they continued to exist in emigration.

Overall, by the time of the revolution there was no unanimity among the Russians on how to define their nation. Whereas at the turn of the century an ethnic definition of the Russians by language and religion had supporters among intellectuals and government officials, only numerically small extreme nationalist groups saw 'blood' as the main element defining nationality. At the same time, the view that the productive existence of the Russians required the preservation of a multi-ethnic state prevailed among liberals and conservatives alike, as the Russian nation was in the process of assimilating and incorporating all the nationalities of the empire.

The impact of the Soviet period

As the previous chapter has shown, the nationalities policies of the Soviet government were highly contradictory. These policies both challenged and encouraged two different definitions of the Russian nation. One limited it to ethnically-defined Great Russians, while the other promoted the idea of a new type of community (the single Soviet people) on the territory of the USSR, among whose members Russian language and culture, albeit in a Sovietised version, were a binding force.

The successful development of one community united by Russian culture on the territory of the USSR was particularly strongly advocated by the Soviet leadership in the 1960s and the 1970s. In 1961, at the Twenty-Second Party Congress, Nikita Khrushchev spoke about the fusion of different nationalities of the Union. The new Party programme adopted at the congress stated that over the next two decades, 'the nations (of the USSR) will draw still closer together and their complete unity will be achieved.' In 1971, at the Twenty-Fourth Party Congress, Leonid Brezhnev announced that 'A new historical community of people, the Soviet people,

took shape in our country during the years of socialist construction.'
However, in reality, the 1960s and the 1970s were precisely the period
when clear signs emerged that the creation of the USSR as a state with
ethnically-based administrative units, along with the policies of industrialization, urbanization and the expansion of education, had provided fertile
soil for the articulation and spread of ethnic nationalist ideas, particularly
among the bigger non-Russian nationalities. Even Soviet sociological
surveys of the 1960s had to admit the effect of the ideas of ethnic nationalism on highly educated, professional people in the cities.[24] The indices of the
extent to which non-Russians were becoming fully assimilated into Russian
culture were also not very encouraging. Communist Party leaders hailed the
fact that, according to the 1970 census, 76 per cent of the population of the
USSR could communicate in Russian. Yet, a closer look at the census data
revealed a more complex picture. In 13 out of 15 Union republics, over 90
per cent of the titular nationality regarded the local language as their native
tongue. Inter-ethnic marriages were fairly common only between East Slavs
and between Russians and Jews, otherwise they happened rarely.[25] The
1979 census indicated that with the exception of Russians, Ukrainians,
Belorussians and Armenians, over 90 per cent of the titular population of all
other union republics still lived in the traditional ethnic territories
encompassed by these republics.[26] Most importantly, in the 1960s and the
1970s Party and government leaders in the non-Russian republics
increasingly began to seek new sources of legitimacy, both in the histories
and traditions of the republics' titular nationalities, and in representing
these nationalities' interests at all-Union fora. These interests were not
necessarily identical to those of the USSR as a whole and were, at times,
antagonistic to the interests of those Russians who lived in the non-Russian
republics.

As in the late nineteenth century, in the Soviet period the growing ethnic
nationalism of non-Russians started to compel Russians to consider
whether they had a national identity separate from the imperial one. There
were differences and similarities with the pre-revolutionary period. On the
one hand, the intellectual responses to the rising nationalism of non-
Russians were roughly the same as in the pre-revolutionary period. Some
insisted that in fact the Russians were successfully assimilating non-
Russians into their own culture, thereby creating a new type of a national
community. Others promoted a narrower definition of the Russians, limited
to those who regarded the Russian language as their native tongue. Finally,

---

[24] Teresa Rakowska-Harmstone, 'The Dialectics of Nationalism in the USSR,' *Problems of
    Communism*, vol. 23, no. 3 (1974), p. 10.

[25] Ibid, p. 8.

[26] Teresa Rakowska-Harmstone, 'Chickens Coming Home to Roost: A Perspective on Soviet
    Ethnic Relations,' *Journal of International Affairs*, vol. 45, no. 2 (1992), p. 540.

there was the racial definition of Russianness 'by blood.' But, on the other hand, there was also a significant difference from the pre-revolutionary period. Industrialization and mass education allowed nationalist views to influence a broader public than had ever been the case in the pre-revolutionary period. In particular, from the 1960s, an anti- or non-imperial definition of Russianness became more popular among the elites and the public than had ever been the case before.

It seems that the policies of Party and government officials in the non-Russian republics were the main reason for the increase in the ethnic definition of Russianness by language, emphatically excluding all those who did not regard the Russian language as their native tongue. From the 1960s these local officials began to undermine the traditionally privileged access to jobs and education of the Russians and Russian-speakers who lived there. Russian-speakers who had settled in the non-Russian borderlands without learning the local languages began to complain about discrimination in the late 1960s and early 1970s. These Russian-speakers were not necessarily ethnic Russians. Some of them were Russified representatives of non-Russian nationalities, particularly Ukrainians and Belorussians. But in the late 1960s they all began to be regarded by Russian intellectuals and some politicians in the RSFSR as belonging to the ethnic Russian nation defined by language and culture, and, it was argued, this nation was suffering from not having its own nation-state. Such views were articulated not only in *samizdat* by such authors as Aleksandr Solzhenitsyn, but were also reflected in official publications, in particular the journals *Nash sovremennik* and *Molodaia gvardia*.

The feeling that Russians and Russian speakers outside the borders of the Russian Federation were suffering discrimination was fuelled by the view that the preservation of the Soviet Union was forcing the Russians to take on an excessive economic burden. From the Russian point of view, the benefits of maintaining the empire started to be seriously doubted. Some Russians began to argue that despite the promotion of the Russian language and culture by the Soviet authorities, in reality Russian culture was suffering from Sovietization no less than the cultures of the non-Russian ethnic groups, as some of its crucial components, such as religion, were denied validity. Moreover, demographic trends (a high growth rate in Central Asia and the Caucasus) threatened to make the Russians, and even the Slavs, a minority in the USSR. This was the final straw for some authors who began to argue in favour of a racial definition of the Russian nation as a biological category. A parallel with the early twentieth century was clear. In the late 1960s, as in the early twentieth century, racial definitions of the Russian nation appeared in response to the challenge of the ethnic nationalism of non-Russians. For the first time in the official Soviet press of the 1960s, a racial definition of a nation was advanced by such scholars as Lev Gumilev and Iurii Borodai, among others. According to Gumilev, an ethnos, out of which a nation emerged, was a 'phenomenon of nature' rather than a social one.[27] Gumilev and Borodai argued that for ethnoses and nations to survive, endogamy should be encouraged. Borodai advocated this policy especially in relation to Russians.[28]

These 'new' ideas notwithstanding, the view that the Russians and the Soviet people were one and the same, and that the Russian identity could be fully realized only within the framework of the Union, remained strong. Sociological studies conducted in the USSR in the 1970s showed that most Russians saw the increased unity of the USSR's different nationalities as highly desirable. Only between 2 and 8 per cent of those polled manifested negative attitudes towards inter-ethnic family or business contacts.[29] Many intellectuals, both publishing in the official press as well as in *samizdat* or abroad, continued to express a belief in the creation of a culturally homogenous national community in the USSR. Ethnographers, publishing in official journals, maintained that 'the Russians have virtually died out as a separate ethnic group,' owing to the emergence on the territory of the former tsarist empire of a new community, which is 'a fully-fledged, mature nation.'[30] In turn, a dissident writer, the mathematician Igor Shafarevich, argued that 'a common history has welded the nations of our land together.' For another samizdat author the Soviet Union 'was not a mechanical conglomerate of disparate nations but a mystical organism ... , a small mankind with the Russian people at its head.'[31]

All these positions started to be vigorously debated in the official media in the *perestroika* period. One significant trend was an increase in the number of Russians willing to separate the Russian identity from the imperial one. This approach was closely intertwined with attempts to separate the Russian identity from the Soviet one, in view of the negative assessment of the October revolution and Communist Party policies in the most influential media organs in the *glasnost* period.

Most importantly, this separation was manifested in the policies of the Russian parliament under the leadership of Boris Yeltsin, which in June 1990 adopted the RSFSR declaration of sovereignty. This declaration was informed by the view that the USSR was an empire, and by the belief that in

[27] L.N. Gumilev, 'O termine etnos,' *Doklady geograficheskogo obshchestva SSSR*, vol. 3 (Leningrad, Nauka, 1967), pp. 14–15.
[28] Quoted in V. Torukalo, *Natsiia: istoriia i sovremennost* (Moscow, Institut Etnografii i Antropologii, 1996), p. 73.
[29] Leokadia Drobizheva, '*Perestroika* and the ethnic consciousness of Russians,' in Gail W. Lapidus and Victor Zaslavsky, eds, *From Union to Commonwealth: Nationalism and Separatism in the Soviet Republics* (Cambridge, Cambridge University Press, 1992), p. 110.
[30] Ibid, pp. 108–9.
[31] Both authors are quoted in Victor Swoboda, 'Prospects for Soviet Slavs in Conditions Favorable to the Establishment of National Freedom,' in Alexander Shtromas and Morton A. Kaplan, *The Soviet Union and the Challenge of the Future*, vol. 3 (New York NY, Paragon House, 1989), pp. 400 and 402.

order to preserve and develop their identity, Russians needed to have their own, clearly-defined nation-state. The images of the empire as an economic burden for the Russians, and of the Soviet regime as a destroyer of Russian culture and traditions, first articulated in the late 1960s, were evoked by Yeltsin and his followers. The position of the new Russian leadership had very important consequences. It contributed to the peaceful way in which the USSR disintegrated. However, the proclamation of sovereignty by the RSFSR did not in itself fully solve the question of how to define a Russian. Like the USSR, the RSFSR was multi-ethnic, although the ratio of ethnic Russians was much higher in the former. Moreover, millions of Russians lived outside the borders of the Russian Federation.

In response to these challenging issues one truly new approach to defining what constituted the Russian nation was articulated during the last years of the USSR's existence. That was the concept of a civic or political Russian (*rossiiskaia*) nation, which could crystallize within the borders of the Russian Federation. This nation would include all citizens of the Federation regardless of their ethnicity, and would be united by loyalty to the new (democratic) political institutions. Although some critics of the idea thought that in effect the Russian Federation was the Soviet Union on a smaller scale, its supporters rejected the comparison. They emphasized that in contrast to the USSR where the Russians made up around half of the population, Russians in the RF constituted over 80 per cent. Moreover, the non-Russians in the RF were far more Russified than those who had had their own Union republics. Therefore the non-Russians in the RF would agree to be part of the civic, democratic Russian (*rossiiskaia*) nation, where Russian would be the state language and Russian culture would be a unifying one. The problem with such nationalities within the Russian Federation as the Tatars and Chechens was not foreseen at the time. The main advocate of this concept was the director of the Institute of Ethnology and Anthropology in Moscow, Valerii Tishkov. He argued that his main goal was to 'dismantle,' from academic and official language, the term nation as an ethnic category.[32] Tishkov also kept reminding his readers that nations were modern phenomena, constructed through the efforts of intellectual and political elites. This view was already widely accepted by Western scholars, but less so by their Soviet colleagues and non-Russian ethnic elites, who insisted on the primordial, organic qualities of nations.[33]

---

[32] See, V.A. Tishkov, 'Ob idee natsii,' *Obshchestvennye nauki*, no. 4 (1990); and 'Natsionalizm i natsionalnaia identichnost,' *Novoe vremia*, no. 7 (1991).

[33] Terry Martin, 'Modernization or Neo-Traditionalism. Ascribed Nationality and Soviet Primordialism,' in Sheila Fitzpatrick, ed., *Stalinism. New Directions* (London, Routledge, 2000), pp. 348–67 explains why in the mid-1930s the Bolsheviks abandonened the Marxist view of nations as fundamentally modern constructs in favour of a primordial approach to nationalism.

At the time the USSR was disintegrating, Tishkov's civic *rossiiskaia* nation did not yet exist in reality. First, many Russians continued strongly to identify with the Union. An opinion poll conducted in Moscow in November 1990 indicated that only 25 per cent unequivocally supported the separation of the RSFSR from the Soviet Union; 44 per cent were still in favour of the preservation of the Union and the rest were undecided.[34] The possibility of a civic nation emerging on the territory of the RSFSR was further undermined by growing ethnic prejudices on the part of the Russians. According to polls conducted in the late 1980s, the proportion of Russians who opposed inter-ethnic marriages and professional contacts had almost doubled as compared with the 1970s.[35]

All in all, the Soviet period did not solve the problem of what it meant to be a Russian. Many Russians retained the view that all the citizens of the USSR/former tsarist empire constituted a single nation in the making. At the same time, from the 1960s onwards, an anti-imperial Russian nationalism attracted more support than at any time in the pre-revolutionary period. However, questioning the benefits of the empire from the Russian point of view did not necessarily point to a single set of conclusions about how to define the Russians outside of the imperial framework. Were they the citizens of the Russian Federation regardless of their ethnicity? Was the Russian nation limited to those classified as ethnic Russians in their internal passports? Should the Russian nation include all the citizens of the USSR who regarded Russian as their native language? On top of that, as the next chapter will show, the daunting question of Russian versus Ukrainian identity remained unresolved. All these questions had to be addressed again after the disintegration of the Soviet Union.

---

[34] Drobizheva, '*Perestroika* and the Ethnic Consciousness of Russians,' p. 110.
[35] Ibid, p. 110.

|7|

*Ukraine in the Russian national consciousness** *

'[A nation is] a group of persons united by a common error
about their ancestry'
      Karl W. Deutsch (*Nationalism and Its Alternatives*, 1969)

'I am deeply convinced that, alongside all-Russian culture and
the all-Russian language, Little Russian, or Ukrainian, culture is
a local or regional culture. This position of the Little Russian
culture ... has been determined by the entire course of Russian
history and can be changed only by the total demolition not
only of the historically developed structure of Russian statehood
but of Russian society as well.'
      Petr Struve ('Pan-Russian Culture
      and Ukrainian Particularism' 1912)

The Russians' relationship with the Ukrainians was the most complex of all
their relationships with other subjects of the empire. The rejection by many
Ukrainians of a compound pan-Russian identity, which showed itself
particularly strongly in 1991, dramatically highlighted the failure of the
Russians' vision of the Russian empire/USSR as their nation-state. From the
mid-nineteenth century onwards, the Russians had taken a paradoxical
attitude towards Ukraine. For most of the time, it was taken for granted
that Ukrainian history and culture constituted an integral part of the
broader Russian tradition. In general, most Russians have not regarded
Russian–Ukrainian relations as a special problem. However, starting in the
1840s, the tsarist government suppressed manifestations of Ukrainian

---

* Some material from this chapter will be published in Taras Kuzio and Paul D'Anieri, eds,
  Nationalism, Nation-Building and Identity in Ukraine (forthcoming).

nationalism and, from the 1930s, the Soviet authorities did likewise. Both
governments thereby implicitly acknowledged its importance, yet both
tended to argue that the phenomenon was limited to a few disgruntled
intellectuals. In contrast, at times of major crisis in Russian history – the
Russian revolution of 1917 and the disintegration of the USSR in 1991 –
'the Ukrainian question' – i.e. Ukrainian separatism – would suddenly be
seen as a key issue for the very existence of the Russians as a national community. The Russian philosopher, Georgii Fedotov, argued in the aftermath
of the October revolution that 'the Ukrainian problem has an infinitely
more profound meaning for Russia than all other national problems ...
[Ukrainian separatism] is the question not only of the political structure of
Russia and of its boundaries, but of its spiritual existence.'[1] Similarly,
following the demise of the USSR, Aleksandr Solzhnitsyn said that he could
not 'without deeply penetrating pain speak about the *artificial* (emphasis
added) break-up of eastern Slavdom.'[2]

The paradox is to be explained, at least partially, by the way in which
Russians perceive their own history. As the previous chapter has shown,
Russians view Ukrainian history and culture as an integral part of the
Russian national identity, because they regard Kiev Rus as the first Russian
state and Kiev as the first Russian capital.[3] Yet the Russians' view of their
own historical origins cannot be the only reason why Russian and
Ukrainian nation-builders have not managed to conduct a dialogue leading
to a mutual understanding. From at least the 1840s, Ukrainian nationalists
have been consistently challenging the Russian perception of Ukraine as an
integral part of Russia. Several works by Ukrainian nationalists advocating
a separate Ukrainian identity have been published in Russian. They began
to appear in the nineteenth century, and were produced in greater number
in the early twentieth century and subsequently in the period of Mikhail
Gorbachev's *glasnost*. Why did Russian nation-builders not take these
writings seriously? In order to answer this question, the chapter first looks
at the encounter between Russia and Ukraine in the seventeenth and
eighteenth centuries. It then discusses the impact of the intellectual debates
of the 1840s on the ways both Russians and Ukrainians began to view
themselves and each other. Finally, it analyses Russian-Ukrainian relations
in the Soviet period.

[1] G.P. Fedotov, *Polnoe sobranie statei v shesti tomakh*, vol. 4 (Paris, YMCA-Press, 1998),
    p. 207.
[2] A. Solzhenitsyn, *Rossiia v obvale* (Moscow, Russkii put, 1998), p. 75.
[3] In the eighteenth century, Ukraine (Little Russia) for the Russians included Chernigov,
    Poltava and Kiev regions, but, in the course of the nineteenth century, Podoliia and Volynia
    also began to be recognized as parts of Ukraine.

The origins of the Russian 'Ukrainian myth'

There is no place here to discuss how far a perception of Moscow as a direct heir of Kiev Rus and an awareness of a shared East Slavic heritage spread beyond the clergy of Muscovy in the fourteenth to sixteenth centuries. But one should recognize that the differences in the way of life, culture and political traditions of Moscow and the Cossack Hetmanate were very significant in 1654, when an alliance was established between the two polities. When establishing the alliance, the tsar Aleksei Mikhailovich was far more influenced by the realities of contemporary politics, particularly Moscow's relationship with Poland, than by the idea of the earlier Moscow chronicles that it was the goal of Moscow princes and tsars to gather back together the dispersed 'Russian lands' of Kiev Rus.[4] It may sound implausible to many Russians today, but in the seventeenth and early eighteenth centuries, the ideas of East Slavic historical unity and that the Russian state originated in Kiev Rus were most eloquently expressed by Ukrainian Orthodox clergymen and representatives of the Cossack elite, who had joined Russian imperial establishment following the Pereiaslav treaty. In the seventeenth and early eighteenth centuries Ukrainians were better educated than their Great Russian counterparts. They were therefore extensively used by Russian rulers in Church and civil administration. The prominence of Ukrainians, particularly in the affairs of the Russian Orthodox Church, was resented by the Russian clergy. It was largely in order to overcome this resentment that the Ukrainians emphasized the common East Slavic roots of Russians and Ukrainians, dating back to the Kiev Rus period.

In the 1760s, the influence of Ukrainians in Church matters and politics declined. In the late eighteenth century, an interest in the separate, traditional ways of Ukraine emerged, as the Ukrainian nobility tried to preserve its corporate rights against the policies of Catherine the Great to abolish the nobility's privileges in the peripheral regions of the empire. However, that was not a manifestation of modern nationalism, but rather a struggle for regional autonomy.[5] Meanwhile, many Ukrainians continued to settle in St. Petersburg or Moscow and play a significant role in the cultural life of the two capitals. From the 1770s until the early nineteenth century, publishing activities in Moscow and St. Petersburg were dominated by immigrants from Ukraine. Previously Ukrainians had been transmitters of European culture, but at the turn of the nineteenth century they became the chief

---

4   Hans-Joachim Torke, 'The Unloved Alliance: Political Relations between Muscovy and Ukraine in the Seventeenth Century,' in Peter J. Potichnyj, Marc Raeff, Jaroslaw Pelenski and Gleb N. Zekulin, eds, *Ukraine and Russia in Their Historical Encounter* (Edmonton, Canadian Institute of Ukrainian Studies Press, 1992), pp. 40–52.

5   Marc Raeff, 'Ukraine and Imperial Russia: Intellectual and Political Encounters from the Seventeenth to the Nineteenth Century,' in Potichnyj *et al.*, eds, *Ukraine and Russia in Their Historical Encounter*, p. 78.

advocates of indigenous East Slavic traditions. According to David Saunders, many of these immigrants felt insecure in the new Russian capital of St. Petersburg, where the nobility imitated European fashions and spoke French. They therefore tried to prove that they were 'more Russian than the Russians.' Starting with the editor of the periodical *Zerkalo sveta* (1786–87), Fedor Tumansky, it was these Little Russians who began tell the Great Russians that the East Slavic cultural heritage they shared with Ukrainians, was different from, but no weaker than, Western European cultures. These Little Russians believed Great Russian intellectuals were wrong to regard Western Europe as the only model to be emulated.[6] It was these Ukrainians who kept reminding Great Russians of the role of Kiev in their history. In a detailed topographical description of Kiev published in 1810, a Ukrainian, M. Antanovsky, described the city as 'this Russian capital more ancient even than Novgorod.'[7] Until the 1840s, Russians responded positively to these suggestions. This was a time when the ideas of Romantic nationalism, based on cultural and linguistic definitions of a nation (Ukrainian was seen as just a dialect of Russian) were sweeping across Europe in the wake of the Napoleonic wars.

Both liberal and conservative cultural figures and periodicals picked up the idea that Ukrainian traditions, if accepted as a part of the Russian cultural heritage, would help to strengthen a unique Russian identity. Thus, the liberal periodical *Vestnik Evropy* argued in 1819 that 'If, for example, our notorious Karamzin had previously known the songs of southern Russia (i.e. Ukraine) … then probably he would not … have increased for no reason the activity of aliens in our land.'[8]

Interest in and sympathy towards Ukraine reached their peak in the 1830s, in the wake of the Polish uprising against the Russian state. Then both Russian intellectuals and the government saw the Ukrainians as allies in containing the Poles.[9] It was in this period that Nikolai Gogol made his debut in Russian literature with his *Evenings on a Farm near Dikanka*, through which the Russian reading public became acquainted with the life and traditions of Ukraine. Discussion of Gogol's stories in Russian literary journals became an important cultural event in the early 1830s. Russian

---

[6]   David Saunders, *The Ukrainian Impact on Russian Culture, 1750–1859* (Edmonton, Canadian Institute of Ukrainian Studies, University of Alberta, 1985), pp. 131–5.

[7]   Ibid, p. 138.

[8]   Ibid, p. 195.

[9]   For instance, in 1843 the government set up a Provisional Commission for the Study of Ancient Documents, one of the tasks of which was to prove that the territories on the Right Bank of Dnieper were Russian and not Polish. A number of leading Ukrainian historians worked in the commission. In effect, its creation inadvertently encouraged the development of Ukrainian national historiography. See Zenon E. Kohut, 'The Development of a Ukrainian National Historiography in Imperial Russia,' in Thomas Sanders, ed., *Historiography of Imperial Russia. The Profession and Writing of History in a Multinational State* (Armonk N.Y., M.E. Sharpe, 1999), pp. 465–7.

literary critics observed that Gogol's works pointed to 'the contributions Ukrainians could make toward the definition of a Russian national character.' At the time it was freely acknowledged that Gogol was both a Russian and a Ukrainian writer. (In fact, this is how Gogol viewed himself.)

In sum, between the late seventeenth century and the 1830s, those Ukrainians who came to live and work in the two Russian capitals were inclined to emphasize the common East Slavic roots of both Russians and Ukrainians. At the turn of the nineteenth century they were the first advocates of a unique pan-Russian culture, the East Slavic historical roots of which made it equal to cultures and traditions of Western Europe. In the early nineteenth century, Russian intellectuals strongly sympathized with this idea. What happened then to cause the Russian and Ukrainian paths to diverge so much?

Rethinking the role of Russia, rethinking the role of Ukraine

The divergence occurred in the 1840s, although several scholars have tended to downplay the significance of this period. Saunders has observed that the interest in Ukraine on the part of Russian intellectuals declined in the 1840s, when the two main groups of Russian intellectuals (the Slavophiles and the Westernizers) got locked into the debate about what Russian national identity meant vis-à-vis the West. Paul Bushkovitch, who has analysed the treatment of Ukraine by Russian intellectuals in the nineteenth century, rejects the idea that the 1840s constituted a landmark in Russia's attitude towards Ukraine. According to Bushkovitch, Russians began to change their positive attitude towards Ukraine and its contribution to Russian national identity only in the 1850s. This change became more pronounced in the 1860s, when another Polish uprising and the growth of Ukrainian separatism provoked a number of Russian intellectuals to adopt a highly critical attitude towards Ukraine. As for the 1840s, Bushkovitch maintains that the influential Russian Westernizer Vissarion Belinskii was an exception in his criticism of Taras Shevchenko's poetry in the Ukrainian language.[10]

In contrast, I would argue that the 1840s were of paramount importance in shaping the way both Russians and Ukrainians came to view themselves and each other for generations. The Russian debate between Slavophiles and Westernizers in effect was a rejection of the position of those Ukrainians who had argued that the East Slavic heritage was sufficiently strong for Russians to understand themselves on their own terms without

---

[10]   Paul Bushkovitch, 'The Ukraine in Russian Culture 1790–1860: the Evidence of the Journals,' *Jahrbücher für Geschichte Osteuropas*, vol. 39, no. 3 (1991), pp. 359–61.

getting involved in constant competition and comparison with the West. Instead, for both the Westernizers and the Slavophiles of the 1840s, Russian culture and history could only be understood if measured according to the West European yardstick, though the two groups read their measurements differently. As Ukrainian traditions and customs were a central element of the East Slavic heritage, many Westernizers began to reject them as non-European, parochial and inferior to the Europeanized Russian culture of the post-Petrine period. For the Slavophiles, pre-Petrine East Slavic history and culture were an essential aspect of their claim that Russia was superior to the West. Therefore, the existence of any separate Ukrainian traditions had to be denied and Ukrainian culture appropriated as part of Russian culture more unquestionably than before.

In turn, for the emerging Ukrainian nationalist movement of the 1840s Russia became the 'constituent other' against which Ukrainian identity was to be constructed. Mykola Kostomarov's *The Book of the Genesis of the Ukrainian People* (1846) offered a comparison between Russia and Ukraine, in which on every point Russia turned out to be inferior. Kostomarov's approach was very similar in tone and style to the attacks on the West by those Russian authors who argued for Russia's superiority. Thus, in the 1840s, Russian and Ukrainian national identities began to be constructed separately from and even in hostility towards each other. With nationalist discourses being constructed in such a way, it became particularly difficult to reach an understanding between Russian and Ukrainian nation-builders.

Belinskii's comments on the writings of the first Ukrainian nationalists should be understood within the framework outlined above. Disregarding the seventeenth and the early eighteenth centuries, when Russians had been learning about European ideas and culture through the Ukrainians, Belinskii described Ukrainians as 'some sort of strange commune in the Asiatic manner.' He thought 'Ukraine could never have developed ... while it lay beyond the pale of Western European culture. It could get access to that culture only by subordinating itself to Russia,' which began to Europeanize thanks to Peter the Great.[11] For Belinskii, 'the history of Little Russia is no more than an episode from the reign of Aleksei Mikhailovich ... the history of Little Russia is a tributary flowing into the great river of Russian history.' At the same time, a leading representative of the Slavophiles, Konstantin Aksakov, argued in the same vein, if not so offensively: 'Little Russia is a living part of Russia, which has been formed by the mighty Great Russian spirit. Under the aegis of that spirit, Little Russia can display its character and become a living element of the general life of Rus ... Of course, unity stemmed from the Great Russian element.' From that

---

[11] V.G. Belinskii, *Polnoe sobranie sochinenii* (Moscow, Izdatelstvo Akademii Nauk SSSR, 1953–9), vol. 7, pp. 60–5.

time onwards, works by Ukrainian writers in Russian have been viewed by Russians as belonging solely to Russian culture. Aksakov thus observed about Gogol in the late 1840s: 'Gogol is Russian, wholly Russian.'[12]

While denying Ukrainians their own history and culture, Belinskii furiously condemned the attempts of early Ukrainian nationalists, particularly Shevchenko, to write literary works in the Ukrainian language. Belinskii's position on the issue was informed by his general views on nationalism and his definition of a nation. With his usual ferocity he rejected the view of the Russian Slavophiles that a true nationality manifested itself in customs and habits of the peasantry. Instead, in his review of Pushkin's *Eugene Onegin*, he argued 'it is time to recognize that a Russian poet can show himself as truly national, if he depicts in his work the life of the educated class.'[13] For Belinskii, it was the educated people, not the peasantry, who represented the best features of a nation, because the former had absorbed the fruits of European civilization. Shevchenko and other Ukrainian nationalists committed a double crime from Belinskii's point of view. First, they tried to elevate the Little Russian peasantry to the status of a nation and to write literary works in what 'furious Vissarion' regarded as a regional peasant dialect. Second, by their actions, Ukrainian nationalists unnecessarily annoyed the government and provoked it to tighten censorship against liberal Russian journals, preventing them from publishing translations of works by French authors. For this reason, in 1847 Belinskii had little sympathy indeed for the arrested members of the Brotherhood of Sts Cyril and Methodius.[14]

Because of his brilliant analysis of contemporary Russian literature, Belinskii had a tremendous impact on Russian public opinion, which stretched far beyond his lifetime. And thus his view of Ukraine helped form the Russian attitude towards Ukrainians from the 1840s onwards. This view – sceptical, offensive and filled with a sense of Russian superiority, denying Ukrainians any history of their own and downplaying their cultural impact on the Russians – still persists today. This scepticism towards Ukraine, and an inability to take seriously any manifestation of a separate Ukrainian identity, were reinforced in Russian literature by such prominent writers as Ivan Turgenev and Mikhail Saltykov-Shchedrin in the nineteenth century and Mikhail Bulgakov in the twentieth. At the same time, from the second half of the nineteenth century onwards, Russian literature paid relatively little attention to Ukraine. At the time of the revolution, Fedotov complained that: 'It is incredible, but it is a fact that modern Russian literature has passed Kiev by.' On these grounds, Fedotov accused the Russians of 'voluntarily surrendering Kiev ... to *samostiiniki* [supporters of

---

[12]   Saunders, p. 241.
[13]   Belinskii, *Polnoe sobranie sochinenii*, vol. 7, p. 439.
[14]   Belinskii, *Polnoe Sobranie sochinenii,* vol. 12, p. 441.

Ukrainian independence].'[15] The Westernizer, Aleksandr Herzen, who unequivocally recognized Ukrainians as a separate nation with a right to independence, and who saw the Cossack 'republic' of pre-Petrine Ukraine as a model for Russia to emulate, stands out as a rare exception among Russian cultural figures.[16]

Meanwhile, from the 1840s onwards, the Russian government unwittingly encouraged the formation of a separate Ukrainian identity by persecuting Ukrainian intellectuals. A new wave of government repression against Ukrainian language and culture began in the 1860s and 1870s. As in the 1840s, Russians expressed little concern over these government policies and the Russian intellectuals' view of Ukrainian nationalism became even more negative. Only a few Russians, most notably the literary critic and writer Nikolai Chernyshevskii, criticized the anti-Ukrainian policies of Aleksandr II. The majority of Russians saw Ukrainian nationalism as a result of intrigues either by the Poles or the Austrians. Those Russian authors at the turn of the twentieth century who held official positions in Ukraine were particularly hostile. They justified the government restrictions against the Ukrainian language on the grounds that its development would 'destroy the unity and solidarity of the Russian people, as an autocratic unit in Europe.' According to these authors, the native language of the Little Russians should be 'the Russian language of Gogol, not the ugly Ukrainian dialect, which is a distortion of the Polish language.'[17]

The liberals and populists of the 1860s to 1880s, although not anti-Ukrainian, also found it difficult to accept the existence of a separate Ukrainian identity. Bushkovitch spoke about the sympathy of the populists for Ukrainians, citing the populist painter, Ilia Repin, as an example.[18] Indeed, Repin was particularly interested in the history of the stronghold of the Cossacks on the Dnieper, Zaporozhian Sich, and was inspired by the 'freedom-loving spirit of the Cossacks.' During his work on one of his most famous pictures 'The Zaporozhians Are Writing a Letter to the Turkish Sultan' (1880–1891), Repin wrote to the art critic Vladimir Stasov about

---

[15] G.P. Fedotov, *Litso Rossii* (Paris: YMCA Press, 1988), p. 65.

[16] Herzen posed the question in his London-based journal *Kolokol*, on 15 January 1859 'And what if after all our talk, Ukraine, which remembers all the persecution from the Muscovites ... and also remembering how it was to be with Rzeczpospolita won't want to be either Polish or Russian? I think, the question could be solved very easily – in this case Ukraine should be recognized as a free and independent country.'Quoted in N.A. Rubakin, *Sredi knig*, (2nd edition), vol. 3, part 1 (Moscow, Knigoizdatelstvo Nauka, 1915), p. 142. On Herzen's praise of the Cossack 'republic', see Martin Malia, *Alexander Herzen and the Birth of Russian Socialism* (New York N.Y., Glosset and Dunlap, 1965), pp. 399–400, 402.

[17] S. Shchegolev, *Ukrainskoe dvizhenie kak sovremennyi etap iuzhno-russkogo separatizma* (Kiev, 1912), quoted in Rubakin, *Sredi knig*, p. 143.

[18] Bushkovitch, 'The Ukraine in Russian Culture', p. 360.

his visit to Zaporozhe: 'Never before have I sensed the spirit of liberty, equality and brotherhood so deeply.' Yet, in another letter to Stasov he described his work as 'a picture of an episode from Russian history.' During his work on the 'Zaporozhians' Repin consulted about historical events with Kostomarov, who suggested that the painter should create a portrait of Mazepa, the Cossack Hetman who had sided with the Swedish King against Peter the Great in the battle of Poltava in 1709. Repin rejected the idea, saying that 'Mazepa was a typical old fox (*proidokha*), a Pole, who is ready to do anything to enrich himself and satisfy his Polish arrogance ... No, the majority (of Little Russians) were right in thinking that it was safer to remain with Moscow.'[19]

The greatest sympathy for the Ukrainian nation-building project at the turn of the twentieth century was to be found among members of left-wing groups – Social Democrats and Socialist Revolutionaries. However, even socialist leaders spoke about the all-Russian (*vserossiiskii*) revolutionary movement. This annoyed the leaders of nationally-minded ethnic minorities, who saw in this language an attempt by Great Russians to usurp the right to speak in the name of all the nationalities of the empire. Russian revolutionary songs from the 1860s onwards also appropriated the Ukrainian Cossack heritage as part of the Russian heritage. One of the songs, for instance, called on the Russians (*russkie*) (sic!) to get together 'from the ice-cold White Sea, from the Black Sea steppe, across vast Mother Rus, from the Cossack land of Ukraine' to topple the tsar.

Among the liberals who set up the Constitutional Democratic Party (Kadets) in 1905, some were more sympathetic to Ukrainian aspirations than the others. On one side of the spectrum was the historian Pavel Miliukov, who in 1914 called on the government to recognize the existence of the Ukrainian movement, which could be neither suppressed nor ignored. The least sympathetic was Petr Struve. In an article in the January 1911 issue of the periodical *Russkaia mysl*, he lambasted Ukrainian intellectuals for trying to preserve and reinforce Ukrainian particularism 'for selfish and sentimental reasons.' Struve was sure that the Ukrainian masses would never join the Ukrainian nationalist movement, because industrialization, urbanization and the existing system of education drew them into the realm of Russian culture. Struve's views eventually grew to dominate the thinking of Russian liberals towards Ukraine. The Provisional Government in 1917 never defined its position concerning Russia's national minorities, promising only to recognize for all nationalities the right of self-determination on principles to be determined by the Constituent Assembly.

When the Civil War broke out, even Miliukov, who acted as a political adviser in the Volunteer Army, opposed the idea of dealing with the

---

[19] Quoted in O.A. Liaskovskaia, *Ilia Efimovich Repin* (Moscow, Iskustvo, 1982), pp. 305 and 314.

political leaders of the independent Ukrainian People's Republic in 1918–1919 as long as they insisted on a federal arrangement with Russia. The VA spoke in favour of a unitary Russian state and proclaimed its task to be the 'gathering of the Russian lands.'[20] At the same time, other representatives of pre-revolutionary Russia, a group of tsarist Army generals, decided to join the Reds as they believed the Bolsheviks stood a better chance of recreating the Russian state (i.e. the disintegrated empire). They called on their officers to 'work ... for the benefit, freedom and glory of our motherland – mother Russia,' so that the 'single Russian-Ukrainian people (*Russkii i ukrainskii narod*) can organize its life as it wishes.'[21]

The proclamation of Ukraine's independence in early 1918 shocked Russian intellectuals and politicians, despite the fact that the majority of Ukrainian leaders at the time would have agreed to join in a federal state with Russia. Even some liberals began to see Ukrainian separatism solely as a result of intrigues of foreign powers aimed at dismembering Russia. (In fact, as in the last years of the existence of the USSR, the opposite was true. Ukrainian politicians were put under considerable pressure by the Entente to seek a federal union with Russia.) A profound analysis of the confusion among the Russians which Ukraine's independence provoked was offered by Fedotov, who noted that 'the awakening of Ukraine ... amazed the Russian intelligentsia, and, to the end, remained incomprehensible.'[22] He criticized the Russians for paying little attention to the growing Ukrainian nationalist aspirations in the early twentieth century and for knowing shamefully little about Ukrainian history and culture.

It is hard to say whether Ukraine would have been 'lost' for Russia in 1917 and then again in 1991, if from the 1840s onwards those intellectuals and politicians at the forefront of the Russian nation-building project had been sympathetic to the idea of a Slav federation as proposed by the Ukrainians. There was no shortage of information in the Russian language representing the Ukrainian nationalist point of view. However, Russians often disregarded this information owing to the attitude towards Ukraine that Belinskii and other Russian intellectuals had helped to shape in the 1840s. They therefore found it difficult, if not impossible, to understand developments in Ukraine. As early as the 1820s, the anti-Russian *History of the Russes*, written from the Ukrainian point of view, was circulated as a manuscript in St. Petersburg and Moscow. It was reviewed in 1836 in Pushkin's *Sovremennik* and was even published in 1846. The journal of Ukrainian nationalists, *Osnova*, was published in St. Petersburg in the early

---

[20] Anna Procyk, *Russian Nationalism and Ukraine* (Edmonton, Canadian Institute of Ukrainian Studies Press, 1995), p. 77.

[21] Quoted in M. Agursky, *Ideologiia natsional-bolshevizma* (Paris, YMCA-Press, 1980), p. 56.

[22] G.P. Fedotov, *Rossiia i svoboda* (Paris, YMCA Press, 1981), p. 213.

1860s. Some works by the foremost Ukrainian historian, Mykhailo Hrushevsky, were also available in Russian. These included excerpts from *History of Ukraine-Rus*, the first volume of which was written in 1898.[23] Hrushevsky's *History* fully articulated the Ukrainian nationalist view. It presented Ukraine as the sole legitimate heir of Kiev Rus. It thereby fully separated Russian and Ukrainian histories, something which Kostomarov had only cautiously begun to do.

A few Ukrainians with an interest in and sympathy towards Ukrainian national aspirations were fully-fledged members of the Russian intellectual movement on the eve of the 1917 revolution. One of them was the scientist and member of the Imperial Academy of Sciences, Vladimir Vernadskii. Another was the legal writer Bohdan Kistiakovskii. (The latter had contributed to the famous collection of essays, *Landmarks* (1909), in which a group of Russian intellectuals discussed Russian national identity, Russian history and Russia's future.) It was Kistiakovskii who in 1911 and 1912 had polemicised with Struve about Ukrainian national identity in *Russkaia mysl*. Writing under the pen-name 'a Ukrainian,' Kistiakovskii attacked Struve for not saying a word 'in favour of even some of the cultural aspirations of the Ukrainian people' and not objecting 'to the violence committed against them.' He questioned Struve's view that 'the hegemony of Russian culture ... is the result of the entire historical development of our country and is a completely natural fact.' In fact, Kistiakovskii maintained, this 'natural' state of affairs was a result of the forced Russification of Little Russia for the past hundred and fifty years. In response to Struve's indignation that the efforts of Ukrainian and Belorussian intellectuals meant 'that "the Little Russian" and the "Belorussian" cultures will be consciously created,' Kistiakovskii offered an observation to which the majority of modern scholars of nationalism would now subscribe: 'Allow me ... to note that in our age of machine manufacturing not only material culture but every kind of spiritual culture is "consciously created". "Russian" culture too is "consciously created" especially under the strong influence of the Russian autocratic and bureaucratic government.' Elsewhere in the article he argued in the same vein: 'The "Russian nation and Russian culture" exist nowhere but among the Russian intelligentsia and in its consciousness.'[24] The revolution and the Civil War made a number of Russian intellectuals

---

[23] See, for instance, M. Grushevskii, *Ocherki istorii ukrainskogo naroda* (St. Petersburg, 1901); *Edinstvo ili raspadenie Rossii?* (St. Petersburg, 1907); *Osvobozhdenie Rossii i ukrainskii vopros* (St. Petersburg, 1907); *Ukrainstvo v Rossii, ego zaprosy i nuzhdy* (St. Petersburg, 1906); *Istroiia ukrainskogo kazachestva do soedinenia s moskovskim gosudarstvom*, tom 1, (Izvlecheniia iz t. VII Istorii Ukraini–Rusi (St. Petersburg and Kiev, 1913)); *Illiustrirovannia istoriia ukrainskogo naroda* (St. Petersburg, 1912).

[24] Exceprts from Kistiakovskii's essay are published in Ralph Lindheim and George S.N. Luckyj, eds., *Towards an Intellectual History of Ukraine* (Toronto, Toronto University Press, 1996), pp. 216–26.

come round to Kistiakovskii's view on Russia. These Russian intellectuals, liberals and conservatives alike, expressed shock at how quickly their Russia had disintegrated. They speculated that the Russian nation, even if defined as consisting solely of Great Russians, probably did not exist in reality, so wide was the gap between the educated classes and the peasantry.[25] Yet, Kistiakovskii's arguments about Ukraine failed to make an impact on the Russian public.

Russia and Ukraine in the Soviet period and during the demise of the USSR

The Bolsheviks recreated a state, the borders of which largely coincided with those of the Russian empire. Nevertheless, they had to recognize the aspirations for autonomy or outright independence of the non-Russian nationalities of the empire. Ukrainians were allotted their own Union republic, in recognition of their separate identity from the Great Russians. Although from the very outset the Union republics had virtually no real political power, in the 1920s they had a fair amount of independence in cultural and educational matters. In this period, nationally-minded Ukrainian leaders emphasized the existence of a separate Ukrainian identity and a lot was done to strengthen education in the Ukrainian language. Meanwhile, in 'Russia proper,' the Marxist historian Mikhail Pokrovskii and his followers were accusing pre-revolutionary Russian historians of Great Russian chauvinism. They argued that these historians had upheld the tsarist government's Russification policies by downplaying the brutal nature of Russian imperialism and by presenting the evolution of the Russian state as a product of the combined efforts of Great Russians, Ukrainians and Belorussians. Therefore, they maintained, in pre-revolutionary historiography Ukrainians and Belorussians had been denied distinct national identities.

However, the favourable attitude in Moscow towards a distinct Ukrainian identity began to change as early as in 1926. That year Stalin for the first time condemned the rapid pace of Ukrainization. He claimed that at times it assumed the form of a struggle against 'Moscow in general, against Russians in general, against Russian culture and its highest achievement, Leninism.'[26] Thus the first signs of a merger of Bolshevism and Russian nationalism were already visible in Stalin's pronouncements in the mid-1920s. It is no coincidence that these pronouncements concerned Ukraine. From that time onwards, as in pre-revolutionary Russia,

---

[25] See, for instance, Vasilii Rozanov's letter to Pavel Florensky of 3 March 1917 (*Novyi mir*, no. 7 (1999), p. 146.)

[26] I.V. Stalin, *Sochineniia*, vol. 8 (Moscow, Politizdat, 1954), p. 152.

Ukrainian nationalism would be viewed by the political leadership as more dangerous than other minority nationalisms.

In 1928, the First All-Union Conference of the Society of Marxist Historians launched an attack on Russian historians with a pre-revolutionary background. These historians were criticized for including in their overviews of 'Russian history' the non-Russian regions from the moment they became part of the Russian empire. But at the very same time, a leading official of the society, P. Gorin, published an article attacking Ukrainian historians for exaggerating the differences between Ukraine and Russia and overemphasizing the West European influences on Ukraine at the expense of the Russian influence. A history of Ukraine separated from Russian history by a 'Chinese wall' was a mockery of the past, Gorin concluded.[27] Meanwhile, nationally-minded politicians in Ukraine began to be persecuted. From the mid-1930s onwards, official historiography again began to be dominated by the conception of a Russian and Ukrainian ethnic, cultural and historical unity, dating back to the Kiev Rus period. This official view made any talk of Ukrainian uniqueness more subversive than was the case with the other, non-Slavic nationalities.

After 1937 Soviet history textbooks promoted the idea of a single ancient Russian people in Kiev Rus and downplayed the difference between the Moscow principality and Kiev Rus. The expansion of the Moscow Principality into the territories of other eastern Slavs continued to be called the 'gathering of the Russian lands', fulfilling their desire for reunification. The three-hundredth anniversary of the Pereiaslav treaty was lavishly celebrated in 1954. An important policy document, *Theses on the Three-Hundredth Anniversary of the Reunion of Ukraine with Russia*, produced on this occasion, defined the treaty as marking 'the reunion of Ukraine with Russia.' 'In this historic act,' the document said 'culminated the long struggle of the freedom-loving Ukrainian people against alien (i.e. Polish) enslavers for reunion with the Russian people in a single Russian State.'[28] Soviet historians also spoke in condemnatory terms about the Ukrainian nationalist movement of the pre-revolutionary period. They denied that tsarist government policies towards Ukraine could be viewed as imperialist, said little about the crackdown on Ukrainian political institutions in the eighteenth century and on the Ukrainian language and culture in the nineteenth century, and mentioned only in passing the independent Ukrainian People's Republic of 1918–1919. From 1954 on, there was a tendency to downplay the role of Ukrainians in developing Russia's

---

[27] Quoted in Stephen Velychenko, *Shaping Identity in Eastern Europe and Russia. Soviet-Russian and Polish Accounts of Ukrainian History, 1914–1991* (New York N.Y., St. Martin's Press, 1993), p. 51.

[28] Lindheim and Luckyj, eds, *Towards an Intellectual History of Ukraine*, p. 303.

political and religious institutions and culture between the seventeenth and the early nineteenth centuries.[29]

In one area, official Soviet historiography somewhat modified the traditional pre-revolutionary position on Kiev Rus. As the government acknowledged that Ukrainians and Belorussians were separate nationalities, rather than part of a larger Russian nation, Soviet historians, at least in theory, began allotting equal rights to the claims of Russians, Ukrainians and Belorussians to be the heirs of ancient Kiev. But the usage of the adjective Russian (*ruski/russkii*) to describe the people and lands of Kiev Rus in pre-revolutionary Russian and Soviet historiography reinforced a special link between contemporary Russians and Kiev Rus. (The adjective *ruski*, derived from the word Rus, is be found in medieval chronicles.) Its usage without the explanation of its origins implied that the Moscow state was the sole legitimate heir of Kiev. Thus, in referring to the population of Kiev and other parts of today's Ukraine in medieval times, Soviet history textbooks often called these people Russians (*russkie*) or the Russian people (*russkie liudi*). (The latter expression was not in use in the Kiev Rus period.) Describing the 1240 destruction of Kiev by the Tatar–Mongol Khan Baty, the 1972 school textbook, *The History of the USSR*, observed: 'Contemporary archeologists have found the remains of many warriors who perished in those days – both Russians and Mongols.'[30] The territory of Western Ukraine, Galicia, which was annexed by the USSR in 1939–1944 and which had never before been part of the Russian state was referred to in this textbook as 'South Russian lands' and its population in medieval times was often referred to as Russian. The annexation of Western Ukraine was thus justified by the Soviet government and in Soviet history textbooks as the continuation of the process of the 'gathering of indigenous Russian lands'. These lands had been taken over by 'Polish and Lithuanian feudal lords' in the fourteenth century, when 'the Old Russian nationality was exhausted by the struggle against the Tatar–Mongol invasion.'[31] Such an interpretation was supported even by people whose knowledge of and sympathy towards Ukrainian traditions was well above average. Thus, Academician Vernadskii observed in October 1939 that 'the actions of Stalin-Molotov seem to be correct, as it is the Russian statist policy.'[32]

[29] Velychenko, *Shaping Identity in Eastern Europe and Russia*, pp. 139, 140, 147–8. One of the few exceptions was D.S. Likhachev's speech on 'The Greatness of Kiev' on 3 December, 1981, which paid considerable attention to the impact of Ukrainians on Russian culture. For its English translation see, D.S. Likhachev *Reflections on Russia* (Boulder CO, Westview Press, 1991), pp. 74–7.

[30] M.V. Nechkina and P.S. Leibengrub, eds, *Istoriia SSSR* (Moscow, Prosveshchenie, 1972), p. 76.

[31] ibid, p. 84.

[32] Quoted in Iu.S. Borisov, *et al.*, eds, *Rossiia i zapad* (Moscow, Institut Rossiiskoi Istorii RAN; Lampeter, The Edwin Mellen Press, 1999), p. 162.

Alternative views of Ukrainian history were not available to the overwhelming majority of Russians. The works of Kostomarov and Hrushevsky were banned in the 1930s. A volume of Kostomarov's historical writing, with an introduction summarizing his pro-Ukrainian position, was published in Moscow only in 1991, whereas Hrushevsky's main writings have not yet been re-published in Russia. The most widely respected Soviet/Russian historians, as well as most Western historians of Russia, did not question the schema of Russian history outlined in the works of the major pre-revolutionary Russian historians.

It is not surprising then that Ukrainian-Russian unity was taken for granted even by the majority of Russian dissidents. The liberal dissidents of the 1960s–1980s such as Andrei Sakharov and members of the Moscow Helsinki group, who wanted the establishment of a Western-style democracy in Russia, acknowledged the right of Union republics to independence. On the whole, however, they did not see the situation of Ukraine as a special problem. In contrast, those Russian dissidents who were particularly concerned with the national question, tended to uphold the pre-revolutionary view that all East Slavs constituted one all-Russian nation. The All-Russian Social Christian Union for the Liberation of the People (1964–1967) was adamantly against the break-up of the East Slavic Union; Vladimir Osipov's Russian nationalist journal *Veche* considered Ukrainians and Belorussians as simply Russians.

At the same time, from the 1960s onwards an anti-imperial ethnic Russian nationalism emerged. As mentioned in the previous chapter, it was developed by Russian intellectuals in response to the growing nationalism of non-Russians. Most of those Russian intellectuals who began to doubt the benefits of the empire for the Russians, still favoured preserving the union between the Russians and the other East Slavs. Nonetheless, a few authors did tolerate the idea of Ukrainian independence. A good example is the writer Aleksandr Solzhenitsyn, who showed a fair amount of sympathy towards Ukrainian separatism, even though he hoped that an East Slavic Union could be preserved. In *The Gulag Archipelago*, he acknowledged that, if Ukrainians were to decide for themselves, it would be difficult to preserve unity, because the two peoples 'have not succeeded over the centuries in living harmoniously.' Solzhenitsyn then asked:

> Why are we so exasperated by Ukrainian nationalism, by the desire of our brothers to speak, educate their children, and write their stop signs in their own language? ... Given that we have not succeeded in fusing completely; that we are still different in some respect (and it is sufficient that *they*, the smaller nation, feel the difference); that however sad it may be, we have missed chance after chance ... why does their desire to secede annoy us so much?[33]

---

[33] Aleksandr Solzhenitsyn, *The Gulag Archipelago*, vol. 3 (New York N.Y., Harper & Row, 1976), p. 45–6.

The writer concluded that 'We must leave the decision to the Ukrainians themselves.' The two dissident authors Andrei Amalrik and V. Gorsky went further than Solzhenitsyn. Back in 1969 they predicted the demise of the USSR and thus Ukrainian independence. They, like Solzhenitsyn, were known to a very limited number of readers, the majority of whom hardly took the prediction seriously.

Just as at the turn of the twentieth century manifestations of Ukrainian nationalism took the overwhelming majority of Russian intellectuals and politicians by surprise, their successors were caught unawares in the late 1980s and 1990s. Various Soviet government policies had unwittingly created fertile soil for the development of nationalist aspirations among the non-Russian nationalities. With the relaxation of political control under Gorbachev, nationalism became the main political discourse in the non-Russian Union republics. By 1989, nationalist movements demanding either complete independence or at least significant political, cultural and economic autonomy from Moscow, had become vocal in all the non-Russian republics, including Ukraine. It was in fact in the Soviet period that the different territories populated by Ukrainians were brought together into one administrative unit. This included the incorporation in 1939–44 into the Ukrainian Soviet Socialist Republic of Western Ukraine, with its strong nationalist tradition. Commenting on this development, the Ukrainian poet Lina Kostenko observed that 'by combining in one entity what the Poles called "Little Poland" with what the Russians called "Little Russia", Stalin made a "Greater Ukraine."' Moreover, a number of Ukrainian nationalist leaders of the *perestroika* period came precisely from the area annexed by the USSR in 1939 – a development Stalin and his successors had not anticipated.[34] Overall, in the Soviet period, there was great progress in nation-building among the non-Russians, including the Ukrainians. However, the same did not happen with the Russians. Instead, Soviet government policies reinforced many of the pre-revolutionary stereotypes concerning how Russians viewed their relations with non-Russians, particularly Ukrainians.

As a result, in 1989 and in 1990 many Moscow-based reformers still continued to think largely in all-Union terms and to emphasize the special nature of Russian-Ukrainian relations. Thus Gorbachev argued in 1990 that 'these Slavic states, Russia and Ukraine, were the axis along which, for centuries, events turned and a huge multinational state developed.'[35] Although the main alternative democratic group in the Russian Federation, Democratic Russia, in 1990, pushed a declaration of sovereignty through the Russian parliament, its leaders did not seriously contemplate that

---

[34] Roman Szporluk, 'After Empire: What?' *Daedalus*, vol. 123, no. 3 (1994), pp. 33–4.
[35] Quoted in Roman Solchanyk, 'Ukraine, The (Former) Center, Russia, and "Russia",' *Studies in Comparative Communism*, no. 1, March (1992), pp. 36–7.

Russia and Ukraine would separate. A consistently positive treatment of the Ukrainian People's Front Rukh in the pro-reform Russian press stemmed from the fact that Rukh was seen as an ally in the struggle against communism.

One of the very few reform-minded Russian intellectuals to think at the time about what the demise of the USSR and Ukrainian independence would mean for the Russians' perception of themselves was the philosopher Aleksandr Tsipko. He criticized Russian parliamentarians for failing to think through the consequences of their declaration of Russian sovereignty and argued that most Russians could make sense of their identity only within the framework of a multi-national state. He felt that Democratic Russia had not taken this peculiarity into account in its policies. At the same time, Tsipko, like Gorbachev, singled out the special nature of Russian–Ukrainian relations and defined them from the traditional Russian point of view. He wrote in *Izvestia* in 1990: 'Many Russians have forgotten not only that they are Russians, but also that they are Slavs, that they are bound by one common fate to the Ukrainians and Belorussians, that they carry the main responsibility for the Slavs of Kievan Rus.'[36]

Tsipko was right in suspecting that even those Russians, who, in theory, had supported Ukrainian separatism might start behaving differently once Ukrainian independence became more real. Indeed, those Russians who in the late 1960s and the 1970s had expressed some understanding of Ukrainian pro-independence sentiments, became much less tolerant after 1990. The change in attitude was similar to the one that occurred in 1917–1918, when Kadets such as Miliukov became far more hostile towards Ukrainian separatism than they had been at the very beginning of the twentieth century. To support the Ukrainians' right for independence, in theory, was one thing. To come to terms with an independent Ukraine, which was or was about to become a reality, was another. Solzhenitsyn was among the first to change his attitude towards Ukraine's independence. In his 1990 essay *How Are We to Organize Russia?* the writer's position towards Ukrainian separatism was more negative than it had been in the 1970s. He expressed the hope that the three Slavic republics would form a new state structure to be called the 'Russian Union.' The essay included a subsection 'A Word to Ukrainians and Belorussians,' which Solzhenitsyn began by saying that he was addressing Ukrainians and Belorussians 'not from outside, but as one of you.'[37] The writer's view of the history of Ukrainian-Russian relations had also moved more into line with the traditional approach of Russian and Soviet historiography. In the *Gulag Archipelago* he had called the 1654 Pereiaslav treaty 'the so-called "reunion,"' which 'was a very awkward though perhaps in some minds a

---

[36] *Izvestiia*, 26 May 1990.
[37] *Komsomolskaia pravda*, 18 September 1990.

sincere attempt to restore our former brotherhood'.[38] In 1990, the same event was described as 'the return of these lands to Russia,' which 'was acknowledged by everyone then as *reunification*' (emphasis in the original).

In 1990 and early 1991, Solzhenitsyn moved closer to the position adopted by the Communist press. This condemned the activities of Rukh as posing a great danger to 'Russian national survival' and attacked advocates of Ukraine's independence for 'playing into the hands of the enemies' of the Soviet/Russian state in the West.[39] In that period, Democratic Russia and the liberal Russian media were still looking favourably at what was happening in Ukraine. But their attitude changed as well following the August 1991 coup and the adoption by the Ukrainian parliament of the declaration of independence (subject to a referendum) on 24 August. Then not only the Communist but also the pro-reform media (for instance, the newspaper *Izvestia*) began to depict the situation in Ukraine as a cause for concern. *Izvestia*'s reports on the republic particularly focused on the Ukrainian leader Leonid Kravchuk's decision in the autumn of 1991 to create the republic's own security and military forces. This development was presented as a threat to Russia.[40] The question of the Russians in Ukraine (22 per cent of the population) became central to the coverage of developments in the republic by periodicals of all political orientations. Solzhenitsyn's suggestion that the results of the Ukrainian referendum on independence should be counted on a region by region basis so each region could decide for itself 'where to belong' (to Ukraine or to Russia) was given considerable publicity.[41]

As in the early twentieth century, Ukrainian points of view were to some extent reflected in the Russian press. In the late *perestroika* period, the Moscow journal *Druzhba narodov* published works by such Ukrainian figures as the writer and politician, Volodymyr Vynnychenko, and the writer, Mykola Khvylovy, from which Russian readers could learn about Ukrainian national aspirations in the 1920s and about Stalin's crackdown on Ukrainization. Interviews with Rukh leaders were also published.[42] Their impact on public opinion in Russia seemed negligible, however.

The overwhelming majority of Russians remained unaware of the Ukrainian national point of view on the history of Kiev Rus and on various key events in the modern history of the Russian state. A few examples will suffice to emphasize the difference between Russian and Ukrainian

---

[38] Solzhenytsin, *The Gulag Archipelago*,' p. 44.

[39] *Pravda*, 30 November 1991, p. 2.

[40] A.I. Miller, 'Obraz Ukrainy i ukraintsev v rossiiskoi presse posle raspada SSSR,' *Polis*, no. 2 (1996), p. 131.

[41] *Trud*, 8 October 1991.

[42] *Druzhba narodov*, no. 7 (1989) (M. Khvylevyi, *Ukraina ili Malorossiia*); no. 2 (1990) (V. Vynnychenko, *Iz dnevnikov*); no. 6 (1990) (an interview with the Rukh leader, Ivan Drach).

interpretations of historical events. For the Russians, victory in the battle of Poltava against the Swedish army signified the elevation of Russia to the status of an important European power. For the Ukrainians, the Russian victory signalled Hetman Mazepa's failure to secure the autonomy of the Cossack Hetmanate. To the Russians Mazepa is known through Aleksandr Pushkin's poem *Poltava* (1828–29), where the two main epithets used to describe him are 'Judah' and 'snake.' Pushkin's Mazepa 'spills blood, as if it were water, he despises freedom and the fatherland does not exist for him,' whereas those Cossacks who sided with him 'have forgotten the enslavement of the past ... and the glory of the times of their ancestors' (i.e. common Kiev Rus heritage). The appearance of Mazepa on the currency of independent Ukraine (*hryvna*) comes as a surprise to today's Russians. Few Russians know why the reign of Catherine the Great, whose policies gave a great boost to the development of Russian culture, was assessed so negatively by Kostomarov and the other founding fathers of modern Ukrainian nationalism. The majority of Russians would be amazed to learn about the draconian restrictions against Ukrainian language and culture introduced under the most liberal of all Russian tsars, Aleksandr II. Although many Russians now know about the famine of 1932–33, few would share the Ukrainian nationalist point of view that it was deliberately aimed at the Ukrainians as a nation. Finally, the positive treatment in the contemporary Ukrainian press of the Ukrainian Insurgent Army (UPA), which during World War II fought against both the Germans and the Soviet Army, provokes strong condemnation in Russia.

Between 1990 and 1991, the position of the Russian government towards Ukraine had changed considerably. In November 1990, Yeltsin came to Kiev to sign a Russian–Ukrainian agreement, which stipulated that the two republics recognized each other's sovereignty and the inviolability of borders. Speaking at the Ukrainian parliament, Yeltsin emphasized that the agreement marked a new stage in Russian–Ukrainian relations. For the first time in history, the two people would deal with each other on equal terms, the Russian president argued. He categorically rejected the accusation, expressed by some politicians in non-Russian Union republics, that Russia was trying to claim a special role in the Union.[43] Yeltsin's position changed following the August 1991 coup and the adoption of the Ukrainian declaration of independence. The news of the declaration was received with great alarm by the Russian political elites. The Russian government began to warn Ukrainian leaders that the implementation of its provisions might have dire consequences for Ukraine. In response to the declaration, Yeltsin's press office issued a statement to the effect that the RSFSR reserved the right to raise the question of borders with any republics, apart from the Baltic states, which declared independence. In making the announcement, the

---

[43] TASS, 19 November 1990.

Russian leadership was backtracking on the provisions of the November 1990 Russian–Ukrainian agreement. Other Russian politicians with democratic credentials also responded negatively to developments in Ukraine. Delegations of Russian and Soviet parliamentarians were sent there to discuss with their Ukrainian colleagues 'an emergency situation' and 'a crisis' that had developed in the republic. Negotiations brought little results. In turn, the Moscow mayor Gavriil Popov argued that Ukraine's declaration of independence was illegal and that he fully supported Yeltsin on the question of border revisions.

Popov especially questioned Ukraine's jurisdiction over the Crimea.[44] It was predictable that the Crimean issue would be raised. The Crimea has indeed played a special role in Russian national mythology. Since its incorporation into the Russian empire in the 1780s, it had been presented in tsarist government propaganda, Russian literature and historiography as the cradle of 'Russian Christianity.' (According to medieval sources, the Grand Prince of Kiev Vladimir was baptized there in 988.)[45] From the mid-nineteenth century, the city of Sevastopol – the base of the Black Sea Fleet – has also been particularly important in the Russian national consciousness. The Crimean war of the 1850s was the first war to be regularly covered in the Russian press by correspondents on the front line, and to be photographed by professional photographers. The defence of Sevastopol and the city's eventual surrender to the British and the French troops were the war's most famous episode. Therefore it had a tremendous impact on Russian public opinion. The historical mythology surrounding the defence of Sevastopol is well known to all Russians from Lev Tolstoi's *Sevastopol Sketches*, which are still studied in Russian secondary schools. Tolstoi emphasized the importance of the defence of Sevastopol in Russian nation-building:

> The feeling of ardent patriotism that has arisen and issued forth from Russia's misfortunes will long leave its trace on her. These people who are now sacrificing their lives will be citizens of Russia and will not forget their sacrifice.[46]

Crimea was not incorporated into the Ukrainian Soviet Socialist Republic until 1954. Even after the incorporation, Sevastopol remained under all-

---

[44] Central Soviet Television, 27 August 1991.
[45] In the Soviet period, Russian historians began to argue that Ukrainians and Belorussians also should trace their Christian roots to Prince Vladimir's baptism. Therefore the image of the Crimea as the cradle of 'Russian Christianity' was rarely evoked in the 1990s by those Russian politicians who wanted to claim the Crimea as a Russian territory.
[46] *Leo Tolstoy's Diaries* (edited and translated by R.F. Christian) (London, Flamingo, 1984). The fact that not only Russians, but other peoples of the empire, include Ukrainians, left their mark in the defence of Sevastopol, does not seem relevant to the majority of Russians. Ukrainians keep reminding Russians about the role of the sailor Peter Koshka in Sevastopol's defence. In response, the Russian press argues that the Ukrainians want to reduce the entire defence of Sevastopol to Koshka's activities.

Union rather than Ukrainian jurisdiction. Moreover, Ukrainians have always constituted a minority in the region. These facts have made it especially hard for Russians to give up that particular piece of territory. In the 1990s, the Crimea and Sevastopol proved to be one of the main stumbling blocks in Russian–Ukrainian relations.

In the autumn of 1991, the Russian government joined Gorbachev in trying to persuade Ukrainian leaders not to take the provisions of their independence declaration literally and not to withdraw from negotiations on a new Union treaty. Following the August coup, which seriously weakened, if not altogether destroyed, the power-base of the Soviet president, Yeltsin's hitherto lukewarm interest in the Union treaty became much stronger. The Russian president began to believe that in this Union he himself, as well as other Russian politicians, could and would dominate. However, Yeltsin's attempts to ensure that representatives of Russia would occupy all key positions in the political structures of the new Union only served further to undermine the attractiveness of the Union to those leaders of the non-Russian Union republics, who earlier had had some interest in it. Kravchuk openly protested against Yeltsin's manoeuvring. Yet it seems that neither the leadership of the Russian Federation nor Gorbachev saw the futility of their efforts to reverse the course of events in Ukraine. They clearly did not anticipate the results of the Ukrainian referendum.

On 1 December 1991 it was announced in Kiev that 90.32 per cent of those who came to the polls voted for Ukraine's independence. The Soviet President and Russian politicians tried both to downplay the referendum's significance and to warn Ukrainian leaders and the world of the alleged dangers of the republic's independence. Commenting on the results of the referendum, Gorbachev stated that 'We will not view a decision of the citizens of Ukraine in favour of independence as a break from the Union. To push matters in this direction would mean heading for disaster – for the Union, for Ukraine itself, for Russia, for Europe and the world.'[47]

On 8 December, appealing to the people of Ukraine on Soviet television, Gorbachev tried to convince them that his plans to preserve the Union were 'not completely exhausted'. He also warned that Russia would lay claims to the Crimea and other predominantly Russian-populated regions of the republic. Gorbachev's insistence that the Ukrainian referendum did not mean the republic's unequivocal break with the Union was a blatant denial of reality. During the autumn of 1991, Kiev boycotted all the meetings at which details of a new Union treaty were being negotiated, as well as sessions of the USSR parliament. On several occasions in October and November, the Ukrainian leader Kravchuk unequivocally stated that Ukraine was not interested in the treaty. On the eve of the referendum,

---

[47]   *TASS*, 1 December 1991.

Kravchuk announced that his republic was not going to enter into confederal, let alone any closer, arrangements with Russia.[48]

Some Russian politicians with democratic credentials sided completely with Gorbachev on the question of Ukrainian independence. The St. Petersburg mayor, Anatolii Sobchak, among others, further elaborated on Gorbachev's vision of Ukraine's independence as a disaster, arguing that it posed numerous dangers. These included the forced Ukrainization of Russians in the republic and a probability of a Russian–Ukrainian border conflict that could result in a nuclear clash.[49] Meanwhile, upon his arrival in Belorussia on 7 December in order to discuss the future of the USSR with Ukrainian and Belorussian leaders, Yeltsin reportedly still hoped to 'get Ukraine interested' in the Union treaty.[50] It is only after the Russian President and his Belorussian counterpart Stanislav Shushkevich recognized the futility of such efforts that the demise of the USSR and the creation of the Commonwealth of Independent States were announced.

The often highly dramatized and generally negative reaction of Russian political elites towards Ukrainian independence was accompanied by a similar reaction in the Russian media. Following the Ukrainian referendum, even those media outlets generally regarded as liberal or democratic began to show much greater hostility towards Ukrainian independence than they had done in 1990–1991 when Ukrainian independence was a possibility rather than a reality. Even 'liberal' newspapers began to depict Ukrainian independence as a ploy of the Ukrainian political elites, acting against the interests of the majority of the people of Ukraine. In 1991 this position was to be found only in Communist or nationalist periodicals. Newspapers of all political orientations started to pay particular attention to Ukraine's relations with the United States and Western Europe, as they were seen as the key to understanding the West's intentions towards Russia.[51] The political symbols of independent Ukraine were treated with derision and featured prominently in political cartoons in Russian periodicals.[52] Even moderate intellectuals tended to present the situation of Russians and Russian speakers in Ukraine in a highly alarmist way. The director of the Russian Institute for Strategic Studies, Evgenii Kozhokin, opined that no other newly independent state of the former USSR conducted such 'a

---

[48]   Solchanyk, 'Ukraine, The (Former) Center, Russia, and "Russia", p. 40.

[49]   *Le Figaro*, 4 December 1991.

[50]   Roman Solchanyk, 'Ukraine,' in Vera Tolz and Iain Elliot, eds, *The Demise of the USSR: From Communism to Independence* (London, Macmillan, 1995), p. 127–8.

[51]   See Miller, 'Obraz Ukrainy i ukraintsev v rossiiskoi presse posle raspada SSSR,' pp. 132 and 134.

[52]   *Nezavisimaia gazeta*, 28 January 1994 on Ukrainian independence as a ploy of political elites; Mikhail Leontev in *Segodnia*, 30 April 1994, using the Ukrainian words *samostiinost* and *nezalezhnost* with sarcasm.

well-targeted, tough state policy' against the Russian language and the people who spoke it as the government of Ukraine.[53]

All in all, the proclamation of Ukrainian independence provoked a more hostile reaction in Moscow than similar declarations of independence by other Union republics. This was not only because Ukraine's independence sealed the fate of the Union, given that it was the second most populous and economically powerful republic. The Russians' belief that they and the Ukrainians were ethnically, historically and culturally so close that the two peoples, in effect, belonged to one pan-Russian nation, was no less important. Summing up the mood of Russians in the aftermath of Ukrainian independence, Moscow journalist Gleb Pavlovskii observed that though some viewed the events that followed the 1991 August coup as the beginning of Russia's revival, many, however, thought that with the creation of independent Ukraine 'Russian history came to an end.'[54]

Conclusions

Ukraine has been an integral part of the Russian national identity from the turn of the nineteenth century onwards. Some key Russian national myths are 'located' in Ukraine. Kiev, is seen as the capital of 'the first Russian state'. In Poltava, a military battle took place which helped to determine Russia's status as a European power. The Crimea is imagined to be the cradle of 'Russian Christianity'. These have all become important points in mapping Russian 'national space.'

From the mid-nineteenth century growing Ukrainian nationalism had begun to challenge traditional Russian views of Little Russia. Tsarist and Soviet governments used repression to suppress Ukrainian culture and traditions. Despite all this, the majority of Russians continued to take it for granted that Ukrainians and Russians had common origins in Kiev Rus and that their relationship had been largely unproblematic. Soviet nationalities policies, in effect, helped to strengthen Ukrainian nationalism. However, as far as most Russians were concerned, official Soviet historiography and propaganda reinforced many nineteenth century stereotypes. Therefore, in 1991, as at the beginning of the century, Ukraine's pursuit of independence caught the Russian elites and the public by surprise and was perceived as a major blow to the very existence of the Russians as a national community. The way the Russians have imagined their national history has made it more difficult to disentangle what is national and what is imperial in Russian-Ukrainian relations than in Russia's relations with any other nationality of the tsarist empire/the USSR.

---

[53] *Sodruzhestvo*, no. 3 (1999), p. 5 (13).
[54] *Moskovskie novosti*, 3 November 1991.

The unpreparedness of the Russians for Ukraine's independence can also serve as a prime example of how unhelpful the Russians' preoccupation with the West has been for their understanding of the empire's non-Russian nationalities. In the 1840s, Belinksii's view of Ukraine was constructed from the Westernizers' standpoint, with its aim of integrating Russia into the European mainstream. From the late eighteenth century to the 1840s Ukraine had often been depicted in Russian literary journals as the crucible of indigenous East Slavic traditions. Consequently, Belinskii could imagine it to be backward, non-European and therefore not worthy of being taken seriously. Moreover, Russians tended to view the empire's nationality problems through the prism of Russia's relations with the West. This too often encouraged them to interpret manifestations of separatism on the part of the Ukrainians as the result of intrigues by European powers and/or the United States (i.e. the West). Such an interpretation dismissed the arguments of the Ukrainian nationalists out of hand. As a result, the Russians have never given themselves a chance to listen to the Ukrainians' point of view.

PART

4

RUSSIA AND THE RUSSIANS TODAY

8

National identity and nation-building after the USSR

As a Eurasian historical and geopolitical subject, our country
was defined and is still defined in space by the boundaries of the
Soviet Union. In this sense, the present Russian Federation is not
the historical Russia. It is, if you please, a defective 'little
Russia.'

Shamil Sultanov (*The Spirit of a Eurasian*,
Nash sovremennik, July 1992)

[Russian nation-builders should] regard [post-1991 situation]
not as the disintegration of the former big Russia but as the
emergence of a new Russian state ... [They should] find a new
image for Russia and a new role that Russia can play in the
future development of mankind.

Grigorii Pomerants (a roundtable
discussion in *Polis*, no. 3, 1992)

After the downfall of the USSR, Russians in effect were confronted with the
fact that their previous attempts at nation- and state-building had failed.
Whereas the break-up of overseas empires had had only a limited political
effect on the metropolis, in the Russian/Soviet case, the end of empire
disrupted the basic state structure. In December 1991 Russia's borders
shrunk almost to those of Muscovy in the early seventeenth century. The
answer to the question: 'who are we, the Russian people?' suddenly became
more unclear than it had seemed to be for Russian nation-builders when it
was first posed in the eighteenth century. The related question of state-
building has also proved to be very complicated. For centuries, Russia was
the centre of an empire which was conceptualized as a Russian nation-state.
This explains the confusion over what constitute the 'just borders' of the

post-communist Russian state, and over the membership of the Russian nation. It also explains why this confusion is greater among politicians, intellectuals and even ordinary people in Russia than in the non-Russian newly independent states, which also embarked on the road of state- and nation-building in the 1990s. A greater variety of ideas about what the Russian nation is, and what the geography of the new Russian state should be, can be found in the Russian Federation (RF) at present than in any of the other fourteen former Soviet republics. These ideas are formulated in the course of on-going intellectual debates. The intellectuals' attempts to define what is the Russian nation to a considerable degree reflect pre-revolutionary thinking, Soviet theories and practices, and Western theories of nationalism, all of which have been discussed in this book.

This chapter argues that the very structure of the post-communist nationalist discourse, shaped through these intellectual debates, has an impact on policy-making in the Russian Federation. In other words, the way in which the concept of a nation (as an ethnosocial, ethnocultural, biological, or political and territorial category), nationalism (civic or ethnic) and national identity (as a 'given' or open to change) are defined and understood has practical implications. This is reflected in politics, as these concepts become a basis for collective actions.

By analysing the content as well as the conceptual and terminological framework of the post-communist debates on Russian nation-building, this chapter addresses the following questions: What cultural and historical heritage is used by Russian intellectuals and politicians today in their attempts to construct anew or reconstruct the Russian nation? Does this heritage have any impact on the shaping of government policies? How successful are intellectuals and politicians in their attempts to form the Russian nation after the break-up of the empire, i.e. what resonance do their ideas have among the population at large? In conclusion, the chapter deals with a central issue for the country's future development: can civic nationalism take root in Russia?

Intellectual debates

In defining what the Russian nation is, contemporary intellectuals both analyse Russia's current situation and apply, sometimes uncritically, pre-revolutionary, Russian émigré and Soviet concepts of nation and nationalism. The pre-revolutionary and émigré authors who exercise the greatest influence on today's discussion about Russian nation-building and to whom current intellectuals refer are the Slavophiles of the 1840s, the Pan-Slavist Nikolai Danilevskii and the historian Vasilii Kliuchevskii, the philosophers Nikolai Berdiaev, Georgii Fedotov, Ivan Ilin, Vladimir Solovev, and the 1920s Eurasianists. Works by these thinkers are widely available in Russia today. They appear in special collections and even regularly in mass-circulation newspapers, such as *Rossiiskaia gazeta*. These thinkers of the past are now viewed 'as if they were contemporaries' and as 'teachers, to whom [today's intellectuals] should turn in their search for spiritual and ideological inspiration.'[1] As one of today's intellectuals has admitted, from the late 1980s interest in pre-revolutionary and émigré thinkers 'acquired an unprecedented (and even worrisome) mass character.'[2] This is a remarkable phenomenon, given that the Russian state has disintegrated twice in same century – a fact that would seem to cast doubts on many of the views of old Russian intellectuals about what is Russia. In addition, the Soviet view of a nation as a primordial community is still fashionable. Finally, the influence of Western scholars, including Ernest Gellner, Eric Hobsbawm and Benedict Anderson, whose works began to appear in Russia in the late 1980s, have made Russian intellectuals think for the first time about a civic definition of a nation, which can be formed through their conscious efforts.

Like their pre-revolutionary predecessors, contemporary Russian intellectuals agree that the existence of an empire (or the multi-ethnic composition of the USSR) has had a formative influence on the national consciousness of Russians. Some argue that the empire stultified nation-building. In the words of the Moscow philosopher, Aleksei Kara-Murza 'the [Russian] empire prevailed over the nation.'[3] In the pre-revolutionary period, this was the view of Kliuchevskii. Others think that as a result of intermingling with other ethnic groups, the Russians managed to create a new type of community on the territory of the Russian empire/USSR, different from that of European-type nations. This view was widespread in the pre-revolutionary period. Contemporary ideologists are divided in their interpretations of the peculiarity of the Russian situation. Some see it as a virtue, whereas others see it as a handicap to be rectified. Some think that the inevitable result of this peculiarity will be the recreation of a union on the territory of the USSR; others argue that, at this stage of their development, the Russians finally have a chance to form their own modern nation-state.

Five main definitions of the Russian nation are currently put forward in intellectual debates:

1. *The union identity: the Russians defined as an imperial people or as a people with a mission to create a supranational state.* The decades and sometimes centuries of coexistence within one state (a common history) is regarded as the basis for continuing a multi-ethnic state within the

---

[1]   L.V. Poliakov, *Kak Rossiia nas obustraivaet* (Moscow, Institut Filosofii RAN, 1996), p. 147.

[2]   Ibid, p. 148.

[3]   A. Kara-Murza, *Mezhdu 'imperiei' i 'smutoi'* (Moscow, Institut Filosofii RAN, 1996), p. 128.

borders of the former USSR. (The influence of Danilevskii, Ilin, Solovev, Fedotov, the Eurasianists and the Soviet concept of the *Sovetskii narod* is evident.)

2. *The Russians as a nation of all eastern Slavs, united by a common origin and culture*. Ethnic and cultural similarities and a common past are viewed as the main markers of national identity. (The influence of nineteenth century Russian historiography is evident.)

3. *The Russians as a community of Russian-speakers, regardless of their ethnic origin*. Language is the main marker of national identity. (The pre-revolutionary and Soviet views of the role of the Russian language as a unifying force in the empire/USSR are evident.) Those viewing the Russians as a community of eastern Slavs or Russian-speakers also place a particular emphasis on Orthodoxy as a marker of Russian national identity. (References to the Slavophiles, Solovev and Berdiaev are often made.)

4. *The Russians defined racially, where blood ties constitute the basis of a common identity*. (The influence of the heritage of the 'Black Hundred' and of Lev Gumilev's definition of nations as a biological phenomenon is evident.)

5. *A civic Russian* (rossiiskaia) *nation*, comprised of all the citizens of the RF, regardless of their ethnic and cultural background, united by loyalty to the newly emerging political institutions and to the constitution. (The influence of Western theories of nationalism is evident.)

Union identity

The most outspoken advocates of the definition of Russian national identity by the imperial mission are communists and one of many groups of Russian nationalists, whose alliance with the communists was visible in the early 1920s (national Bolsheviks and *Smenovekhovists*) and re-emerged again in the RF in connection with the republican parliamentary elections in 1990.

Following the downfall of the USSR, the Communist and nationalist press (especially the newspaper *Den/Zavtra*, set up by neo-Eurasianists in 1990) was dominated by the belief that either the Union would eventually be recreated, or the Russians would completely disappear as a distinct community. Thus, the journalist, Aleksandr Kazintsev, stated in August 1992: 'Look at the great Russian people. In the past the mere mention of their name used to destroy the walls of impregnable fortresses. Now they are defeated by Lilliputians ... We have lost our identity: 'the Russians' – this word has become an empty sound without any meaning.'[4]

---

4 *Den*, 9–15 August 1992.

According to those who support the re-establishment of the Union, the Russian empire and the USSR were 'a unique civilization.' All its peoples had one compound identity. Not only the Russians, but all the other nation-alities would be unable to survive outside the structure of the USSR, which was 'a supranational force that reflected the interests of a multiethnic Eurasian community.'[5]

While being very critical of Russia's post-communist situation, most Unionists were, at least in 1992–93, optimistic about its future. They firmly believed that Russia would be able to regain its lost territories and become 'a model civilization of the twenty-first century.' It would show the world that the peaceful co-existence of different ethnic groups within one, huge state was possible. In order to substantiate their argument, Unionists frequently refer to the works of Danilevskii, the Eurasianists and Ilin. Contemporary Unionists follow Danilevskii in arguing that all the nationalities of the former USSR are united by a common Russian culture. Following the Eurasianists, they talk about a distinct civilization of 'Russia–Eurasia,' the inhabitants of which had in effect been fused into one unique multi-ethnic nation. Quoting Ilin, they speak about the 'three-fold mission' of the Russians: 'to create... the fatherland' for all the nationalities inhabiting the Russian state, to make them live in peace with each other and to involve the best of them into running the state.[6] According to today's Unionists, the Russians have succeeded in fulfilling their 'three-fold mission,' as manifested in the creation of the *edinyi Sovetskii narod*. In 1992, *Pravda* argued that the peoples of the USSR had 'a single genetic code, discovered by scientists at the Institute of General Genetics of the Russian Academy of Sciences.'[7]

Some Eurasianists went so far as to claim that all the peoples of 'Russia–Eurasia' had already merged into one anthropological entity. Ilin hoped that a supranational state led by Russians would be viable in the long-term. It is noteworthy, however, that they did not try to define the commu-nity of peoples of the Russian empire in terms of common citizenship and unifying political loyalties, but only in terms of cultural and religious fusion or harmonious co-existence. The same is true of their post-communist followers. They deny that membership of a nation is voluntary, and believe that a common past is enough reason for continuing co-existence within one state in the present. As *Pravda* put it, 'State formations like Russia (in its pre-revolutionary and not in its present truncated form) and the USSR do not appear by chance and do not disappear without trace.'[8]

The view that the Russians should preserve their Union identity is

---

5   *Den*, 12–18 April 1992.
6   I. Ilin, *O Rossii* (Sofia, 1934) quoted in *Russkii vestnik*, no. 1 (1990), pp. 48–9.
7   *Pravda*, 9 September 1992.
8   Ibid.

expressed not just by extreme right-wingers and communists, but also by some who regard themselves as liberals. The author of one of the first scholarly articles explaining to Russians the Western notion of a civic nation, Vadim Mezhuev, argues that the creation of a nation-state should not be the goal of the Russian people today.[9] As the peoples of the RF are not ready to form a civic nation, attempts to create a nation-state would either lead to the Russification of the non-Russians in the RF by force and/or to the disintegration of the country. Instead, the Russians should continue in their attempts to fulfil their mission of maintaining a unique supranational state. Citing Solovev and Fedotov to support his argument, Mezhuev states: 'The idea of a supranational state ... which provides all its peoples with equal rights for national development ... giving them equal access to the fruits of civilization, probably constitutes the main difference between Russia and Europe and is Russia's main contribution to world history.'[10]

Reminding his readers that the disintegration of the USSR has led to bloody inter-ethnic conflicts, Mezhuev warns that 'the collapse of the idea [of a supranational state] will turn [or has already turned] into a historical tragedy for all [former Soviet people].'[11] In turn, Kara-Murza, thinks that the break-up of the USSR was 'the destruction of the space ... within which a Russian (*rossiiskaia*) nation could have been formed eventually.'[12]

Several political alliances emerged during 1992–1994 that united Communists, nationalists and even moderate intellectuals and politicians in their desire to recreate the USSR. The National Salvation Front was formed in 1992 by Ilia Konstantinov, who in 1990 and early 1991 was a member of the main reformist movement in the RSFSR, Democratic Russia. The majority of the others in the movement had been members of Communist factions in the USSR Congress of People's Deputies. They continued to meet after the demise of the USSR, claiming to continue the work of the Congress.[13] Another example was the 'People's Alliance,' which, of all the unionist organizations, had the greatest proportion of moderates, such as the philosopher Aleksandr Tsipko and the leader of the Civic Union, Arkadii Volskii. Gorbachev reportedly strongly supported the alliance. In an interview with *Nezavisimaia gazeta*, Tsipko said that their group was united by the idea that 'historical Russia had been formed as a multi-national state community, in which all members were equal.'[14]

---

[9]   On Mezhuev's definition of a nation as a political rather than an ethnosocial phenomenon, see his article 'Natsionalnoe gosudarstvo: teoriia, istoriia, politicheskaia praktika,' *Polis*, no. 5 (1992).

[10] V.M. Mezhuev, *Mezhdu proshlym i budushchem* (Moscow, Institut Filosofii RAN, 1996), p. 103.

[11] Ibid, p. 103.

[12] Kara-Murza, *Mezhdu 'imperiei' i 'smutoi,'* p. 138.

[13] *ITAR-TASS*, 20 October 1992.

[14] *Nezavisimaia gazeta*, 13 March 1994.

The Russians as a community of Eastern Slavs

Some intellectuals argue that now, after the disintegration of the USSR, there can be no going back to the empire. At last, the Russians have the opportunity to create a nation-state by completing their formation as a modern nation. One way to define the Russian nation is to see it as a community of eastern Slavs, including Ukrainians and Belorussians.

It has been demonstrated earlier in this book that, given the way in which Russians interpret their history, many Russians take it as read that the Ukrainians are part of the Russian nation. The same applies to the Belorussians. Their territories were incorporated into the Russian state during the partitions of Poland in the late eighteenth century and as a result of the USSR's occupation of eastern Poland in 1939. This incorporation was presented in Russian/Soviet historiography as the gathering of indigenous Russian lands. Soviet historiography argued that the Belorussian people were formed in the thirteenth to sixteenth centuries out of 'the common [east Slavic] root – the old Russian nationality' of Kiev Rus. This view was reiterated in the book *Belorussians*, jointly published by the Russian and Belorussian Academies of Sciences in 1998. Pointedly, the book did not include any discussion of Belorussian national identity, whereas a volume on the Russians in the same series, had a whole chapter on Russian national consciousness and popular memory (*natsionalnoe samosoznanie i narodnaia pamiat*).[15]

By late 1993, the majority of nationalist intellectuals had abandoned their view that Russian national identity had any meaning only within a community of all the citizens of the former USSR (Union identity). Instead, they started to speak about the 'triune orthodox Russian nation' (*triedinaia pravoslavnaia russkaia narodnost*) of Russians, Ukrainians and Belorussians.[16] This signified a return to the pre-revolutionary terminology. The Soviet formulation – the 'three brotherly Slavic peoples' (*tri bratskikh slavianskikh naroda*) – had acknowledged a greater degree of separateness between Ukrainians, Belorussians and Russians.

Aleksandr Solzhenitsyn's *How Can We Reconstruct Russia?*, his major articles in *Pravda* and *Novyi mir* and his essay *Russia in the Abyss*, which passionately argued in favour of the preservation of the east Slavic union, had a major impact on the views of many Russian intellectuals in the post-communist period. Following Ukraine's independence, Solzhenitsyn's hostility towards Ukrainian separatism further increased. In the late 1990s, he began to argue that Ukrainian nationalism was full of 'wild extremist slogans' and alleged that Ukrainian politicians were striving to recreate

---

[15]   V.K. Bonarchik, P.A. Grigoreva and M.F. Pilipenko, eds, *Belorusy* (Moscow, Nauka, 'Narody i kultury' series, 1998).

[16]   A. Andreev, 'Kto est kto v rossiiskoi politike,' *Moskva*, no. 7 (1995), pp. 145–56.

'Kiev Rus', which would include all of European Russia 'to the Urals.' Like many other opposition politicians and intellectuals, Solzhenitsyn condemned President Boris Yeltsin's government for 'betraying' the Russians and Russian speakers in Ukraine and for 'surrendering without a fight' what he saw as traditional Russian territories which had been ceded to Ukraine on the whim of Lenin and Khrushchev.[17]

By late 1993–early 1994, some had concluded that the Russian national identity could crystallize in a union with Ukraine and Belorussia rather than on the entire territory of the former USSR. These included the leader of the Russian Public Union, Sergei Baburin, and the majority of leaders of the National Salvation front, such as Igor Nikolaev, Iurii Beliaev and Nikolai Pavlov. Referring to all eastern Slavs, they now speak about 'one history, one nation, one Russia.'[18]

One can argue therefore that in this instance, as with the Unionists, a vision of a common past is regarded as an important marker of national identity. As the former speaker of the Russian State Duma, Ivan Rybkin, observed in 1994 in connection with Russia's attitude towards Ukrainian and Belorussian independence: 'The countries which have a common origin *must* (emphasis added) not only have a common past but also a common present and future.'[19] Those who define the Russians as a community of eastern Slavs therefore see primordial qualities in a nation and reject the idea that membership of it can be voluntary. Thus, it does not matter to them whether Ukrainians also believe that they share a common national identity with Russians.

The Russians as a community of Russian-speakers

Another way to define the Russian nation is through language as the main marker of national identity. In the nineteenth century, many Russian intellectuals, especially writers and literary critics, as well as the Russian government, attributed great importance to the Russian language as a force unifying the different ethnic and social groups in the empire. In the Soviet period, Russification forced many non-Russians, especially Ukrainians and Belorussians, to start viewing themselves as Russian and therefore to identify themselves as Russians in internal passports and censuses. Moreover, millions of Russians were encouraged to settle outside the borders of the RSFSR. Therefore, when the USSR broke up and approximately 25 million

---

[17] A. Solzhenitsyn, *Rossiia v obvale* (Moscow, Russkii put, 1998), pp. 75–82.
[18] On Baburin, see Andreev, 'Kto est kto v rossiiskoi politike;' see also *Segodnia*, 29 March 1995, p. 2.
[19] *Reuters*, 27 July 1994.

Russians and another 5 million Russian speakers[20] found themselves outside the borders of the RF, some intellectuals asserted that they were a part of a now divided (*razdelennaia*) Russian nation. For instance, journalist V. Galenko suggested in *Nezavisimaia gazeta* that the Russian government should issue a declaration on the protection of the Russian-speaking settlers, which would clearly state that they were 'an inseparable part of the Russian nation.'[21]

Other advocates of this definition of the Russian nation, such as literary critic Ksenia Mialo and journalist and parliamentarian Dmitrii Rogozin, are aware of the weak horizontal ties between the various Russian-speaking communities in the newly independent states, and the low level of their identification with the RF. However, they do not see this as a reason to look for other definitions of the Russian nation. Instead, they believe the Russian government should try to regain those areas where Russians and Russian speakers live in compact settlements in the 'near abroad'.[22] The national consciousness of Russians and Russian speakers in the 'near abroad' should be revived and strengthened by nationalist propaganda, stressing the role of Orthodoxy and common history.[23]

Those advocating a new Russian nation-state which does not include Ukraine and Belorussia feel obliged to present Russia's historical past as separate from the Kiev Rus heritage. The same phenomenon could be seen in Russia in 1918–1919, during the existence of the independent Ukrainian republic. Fedotov condemned attempts made at that time to look for alternative historical myths for Russia: 'We ourselves … with such easiness have renounced our share in Kiev's glory and defeat, claiming that our people should trace their origin to Oka and Volga' (the Moscow and Vladimir Suzdal principalities).[24] At the same time, Fedotov himself emphasized the importance for Russia's self-image of the Novgorod Republic, which had existed from the twelfth to the fifteenth century, with its tradition of *Veche* (a popular assembly which decided upon the most important issues of Novgorod's political life). Fedotov argued that Novgorod's vibrant trade with Europe indicated that 'The West … should always have its fair share in the development of our national culture.'[25]

---

[20] Russians are those who were described as such in the 'nationality entry' in Soviet passports. Russian speakers are people of other (non-Russian) nationalities, according to their passports, whose main and often only spoken language is Russian. However, the vocabulary used by politicians and journalists to describe Russians and Russophone minorities in the 'near abroad' is often ambiguous. At least five different words (*russkie*, *rossiiane*, *russkoiazychnye*, *sootechestvenniki* and *sograzhdane*) are used to describe people over whom the Russian government and intellectuals express concern, thus making it difficult to identify precisely the group in question.

[21] *Nezavisimaia gazeta*, 11 November 1995.

[22] *Rossiia-XXI*, nos. 7–8 (1995), pp. 7–8.

[23] Dmitrii Rogozin, *Russkii otvet* (St. Petersburg, Glagol, 1996), pp. 212–14 and 250.

[24] G. Fedotov, 'Tri stolitsy,' in *Litso Rossii* (Paris, YMCA-Press, 1988), p. 64.

[25] Ibid, p. 56.

Some contemporary Russian authors agree with Fedotov about the role of Novgorod, and go even further, renouncing Russia's claims on the Kiev heritage. Mialo, for instance, traces the origins of the Russian nation to medieval Novgorod.[26] Others argue that 'the formation of the Russian people took place in the process of the creation of the Moscow state.' It was formed as the Moscow principality took over Vladimir, Suzdal, Novgorod, Smolensk and Riazan in the fourteenth to sixteenth centuries. Loyalty to a strong Russian state, which, it is maintained, needed protection from outside invaders, was an important formative experience in consolidating the identity of the Russians. The ethnographer M. Shmeleva argues that 'In the process of the formation of the Moscow state a Russian nationality (*narodnost*) emerged, connected by a stable self-identity, which was first of all reflected in the idea of ... a strong community within one state, and, in addition, in a certain degree of cultural unity.'[27]

In 1999 the mass-circulation magazine *Ogonek* popularized the discoveries of the St. Petersburg archeologist, Evgenii Riabinin, who argued that his excavations proved that Kiev was only the third 'capital' of Rus.[28] According to Riabinin, the first 'capital' of Rus had been Ladoga in North Russia, and the second had been Novgorod. Riabinin contended that a key source on the medieval history of the eastern Slavs, the *Primary Chronicle*, included deliberate falsifications by the chronicler Nestor, who, as a resident of Kiev, had exaggerated the historical importance of that city. Riabinin had first advanced his theory back in the 1970s. However, because it questioned officially accepted orthodoxies, it did not receive any publicity. Today, this theory could potentially have great political implications and boost the nation-building process within the borders of the Russian Federation. Emphasizing the significance of Riabinin's discoveries, the liberal journalist Andrei Chernov has concluded that 'Ladoga and Novgorod constituted an alternative path for Russia's development, its European path.'[29]

Identification with a certain territory is viewed, by those who argue that the Russian nation should be seen as a community of Russian speakers, as an important marker of common identity. They argue that the RF cannot even be regarded as a surrogate Russian state, because of the artificial nature of its borders with many ethnic Russians and Russian speakers living outside them. The result is that Russians are a stateless people (*razgosudarstvlennyi narod*).[30] For instance, a specialist in nationalities relations

---

[26] *Literaturnaia Rossiia*, 7 August 1992 and 14 February 1992.

[27] M.N. Shmeleva, 'Russkie,' issue no. IV, vol. 2, Series 'Narody i kultury' (Moscow, Nauka, 1992), pp. 20–1.

[28] In 1998, a film about the archeologist was broadcast on the 'Culture' channel of Russian Television.

[29] *Ogonek*, no. 8, 22 February 1999, p. 26; see also *Ogonek*, no. 9, 1 March 1999.

[30] K. Mialo, *Rus derzhavnaia*, no. 10 (1994), p. 5.

from the Institute of Ethnology and Anthropology of the Russian Academy of Sciences, Viktor Kozlov, has argued that

> The unequal position of the Russian ethnic community in the Soviet period was manifested, first and foremost, in the fact that, in the evolving process of nation-state building, no Russian republic was created in which the Russians, like the other major ethnic communities of the country, would have had the status of privileged 'titular' nation with corresponding institutions to support their ethnic existence. Moreover, when republics, oblasts, and okrugs of other nationalities were created, the Russians lost considerable territory, since almost all these structures ... incorporated relatively large areas where the Russians predominated numerically.[31]

Various proposals have been advanced concerning the possible borders of a Russian nation-state with which Russians and Russian speakers could identify, thereby strengthening their common identity. Some propose to unite Russian oblasts and krais with those territories of the RF's non-Russian ethnic autonomous areas where Russian speakers live in compact settlements and constitute an overwhelming majority. Others would also want to add those areas in the newly independent states where Russian speakers live. In 1996, the leading Russian demographer Vladimir Kabuzan of the Institute of History of the Russian Academy of Sciences published a detailed study of settlements of Russian and Russian speakers throughout the USSR. It gave policy recommendations on where the 'just borders' of a new Russian nation-state should be.[32]

Kabuzan identifies the 'ethnic Russian territories' as follows: the Crimea, Donetsk, Lugansk, Kharkov and Zaporozhe areas in Ukraine; the eastern and northern regions of Kazakhstan as well as the Karaganda oblast; the Daugavpils, Zilup, and Malt regions in Latvia; and Narva, Silimae, and Kohtla-Jarve in Estonia. He believes that rather than leaving 'ethnic Russian territories' in the newly independent states, Russians should either demand their incorporation into the Russian Federation or press for extensive political and cultural autonomy, with the recognition of the Russian language as the second state language in these countries. By contrast, Russians living in 'Central Asia, the Transcaucasus, southern Kazakhstan, western Ukraine, Lithuania and most parts of Estonia and Latvia, should leave these areas and withdraw any claims to them, since these have not become "ethnic Russian lands."'

It is noteworthy that Kabuzan's list of areas from which Russians should withdraw does not include Moldova, even though he does not classify any part of it, even the Dniester republic, as 'ethnic Russian lands.' Other

---

[31] V.I. Kozlov, 'Nationalism, National Separatism, and the Russian Question,' *Russian Politics and Law*, January–February, 1995, p. 29.
[32] V. Kabuzan, *Russkie v mire* (St. Petersburg, BLITS, 1996).

advocates of Russia as a republic of Russian speakers, such as Mialo, who
would include the Crimea, the Donbass, and northern Kazakhstan in their
new Russia, also extend their claim to the Dniester republic. This is because
although ethnic Russians are only the third-largest group in the area, when
taken together with Ukrainians, most of whom are fully Russified, they
constitute 53 per cent.

Finally, Kabuzan turns his attention to the Russian Federation's ethnic
autonomous areas, in which the Russians currently constitute 46 per cent of
the population, a figure which rises to 52.4 per cent if one includes all
Russian speakers. He proposes the creation of separate states for the non-
Russian minorities of the Russian Federation, but only within those areas
where they form compact settlements. The predominantly Russian areas
should be merged with the Russian nation-state.

The idea that non-Russians should be allowed to secede from the Russian
Federation and create states of their own in areas where they form a
compact settlement has been applied by some people to Chechnia. Russian
intellectuals and politicians, from Solzhenitsyn to General Aleksandr Lebed,
have argued that Chechnia should be granted independence, so long as it
relinquishes the predominantly Russian Upper-Terek region, ceded to
Chechnia in 1956. This position won fairly broad support among the
population during the first Russian military campaign against Chechnia of
1994–1996, which was not popular with most Russians. Public attitudes
were largely shaped by the way influential liberal periodicals and the independent television channel (NTV) depicted Chechen fighters and Russia's
policies in North Caucasus. In creating an image of a Chechen as a brave
mountain-dweller fighting for his freedom, the liberal media followed the
tradition of Lev Tolstoi's *Hadji Murat*. In their analysis of Russia's policies
in the Caucasus they presented Russia as a victim of its own imperialism, an
imperialism which had once more been claiming numerous Russian lives.
Sergei Kovalev, a leading Russian human rights activist, spent a long time in
Chechnia during the early stage of the war. He sharply condemned the
actions of the Russian government, and kept making dramatic statements to
the effect that in the capital of Chechnia, Grozny, it was the Russian people
who were the prime victims of the Russian army bombing. Russian army
soldiers were also victims: 'The ruins of Grozny are filled with corpses of the
Russian (*russkikh* rather than *rossiiskikh*) soldiers. Wandering dogs bite
pieces off their dead bodies.'[33] Works of art of this period, such as Vladimir
Makanin's *The Prisoner of the Caucasus* and Sergei Bobrov's film of the
same name, present Russia itself as 'a prisoner of the Caucasus,' a victim of
its own colonial policies. Despite their references to Pushkin and
Lermontov, these works were different from those of the nineteenth
century. Contemporary authors no longer manifested any belief in Russia's

---

[33] Quoted in *Novoe literaturnoe obozrenie*, no. 34 (1998), p. 94.

civilizing mission or its legitimate interests in the Caucasus. However, this position on Chechnia did not last and was significantly modified in 1999.

Racial definitions of the nation

One can argue that, to some extent, the multi-ethnic nature of the land-based Russian empire and of the USSR, which encouraged a high degree of ethnic assimilation, acted as a safeguard against racial prejudices. In the pre-revolutionary period, elements of nationalism based on racism were expressed only in the theories of the extreme right-wing anti-Semitic ideologists of the Black Hundreds. These ideas were revived in the late 1960s and early 1970s, when some Russian intellectuals began to see the RSFSR as the most exploited among the Union republics and to call on the Russians to shake off the burden of empire. At that period, Lev Gumilev and other scholars began to argue that nations were biological rather than social phenomena. Initially such views were confined to a very limited number of fairly obscure journals, but in the period of *glasnost* they started to receive wide publicity.

In the post-communist period, racist propaganda has increased. Those advocating a racial definition of Russianness argue that in order to survive Russians should safeguard themselves from the harmful influences of other 'ethnoses.' For instance, the journalist Igor Shishkin has argued in *Zavtra*, extensively quoting Gumilev, that there are three different forms of contact between ethnoses living in close proximity with each other. When two ethnoses with a 'negative mutual complementarity' live together and inter-mingle, this inevitably leads to the death of one or both ethnoses. Russians have had 'positive complementarity' with most ethnoses with whom they have been living side by side, but there are some with whom 'complemen-tarity' is negative. The latter are 'ethnoses with different life style and incompatible system of values, which refuse to assimilate, yet their repre-sentatives study in the same schools and work in the same institutions with the Russians.'[34] According to Shishkin, one example of such an ethnos is the Jews, whom he identifies ethnically rather than religiously.

As far as the political sphere is concerned, members of racist groups argue that only those who have 'Russian blood' should be represented in the government. In the words of the leader of the Russian Party, Nikolai Bondarik:

In Russia, the Russians must rule. In Russia, there must be only a Russian government, a Russian parliament consisting of ethnic Russians belonging to the Great Nation by blood and spirit ... 'Everything for the nation and nothing

---

[34] *Zavtra*, no. 4 (1995).

against the nation' – this slogan should be in the head, in the soul, and in the blood of every Russian, because we all are only cells in one great organism called the Nation.[35]

Similar arguments were advanced in the early twentieth century by the ideologists of the Black Hundreds. Most members of racist groups in the post-communist period also continue a trend which first emerged in the 1970s, as they see the Central Asians and the Muslim peoples of the North Caucasus, rather than the Jews, as posing the greatest danger to the survival of the Russians. This is true of the two main racist groups in post-Communist Russia – Nikolai Lysenko's National Republican Party of Russia and Aleksandr Barkashov's Russian National Unity. According to Lysenko, the main threat to the survival of the Russians as a nation comes from the Muslims of Central Asia and the North Caucasus, who should be deported from the Russian state. He also argues that the Russians should be compensated for 'their economic genocide by the southern mafia.' According to Barkashov, nations, which have a biological basis, are supreme values.[36] The survival of the Russian nation is possible only if strict laws forbidding mixed marriages that damage racial purity are imposed.

In the course of the war against Chechnia Russian government officials, the government-controlled media and the Russian nationalist press began to construct an image of Asians, particularly Muslims, as enemies of Russia. In 1994–1996, the government-controlled TV channels and particularly the government newspaper *Rossiiskaia gazeta* revived the pre-revolutionary stereotypes of Chechens as 'bandits,' 'savage' and 'treacherous.'[37] However, at that time, the criticism of the war in the liberal media mentioned above seemed to have a greater impact on public opinion. The situation changed dramatically in 1999 after the series of bomb explosions in apartment blocks in Moscow and other Russian cities, which the government blamed on the Chechens. The abduction, rape and murder of a Moscow journalist in Chechnia also seemed to contribute to the change of attitude towards the war in the liberal media. Moreover, the new military operation, which began in 1999, was closely associated with Vladimir Putin, whose election as President was supported by most liberal media organs. Consequently, since 1999 public and media support for the war has been growing. With the notable exception of NTV, in the overwhelming majority of the media, Tolstoi's image of the mountain-dweller as a tragic victim of Russian imperialism as presented in *Hadji Murat* was substituted by Lermontov's

[35] *Gazeta Russkoi partii*, no. 1 (1993), p. 4.
[36] Vladimir Pribylovsky, 'A Survey of Radical Right-Wing Groups in Russia,' *RFE/RL Research Report*, 22 April 1994, pp. 28–37; *Russkii poriadok*, December 1993–January 1994, p. 25.
[37] Aleksandr Iskandarian, *Chechenskii krizis: proval rossiiskoi politiki na Kavkaze* (Moscow, Carnegie Endowment for International Peace, 1995), p. 30.

'evil Chechen' (*zloi chechen*), a 'treacherous' and 'savage' enemy of the Russians.[38]

Forging a civic national identity

The very idea of defining a nation in civic terms is relatively new to the Russians. As mentioned above, the leading ethnographer Valerii Tishkov has been the main advocate of this civic definition of a nation, which he first put forward publicly in 1989. Since the demise of the USSR, he has been arguing that politicians and intellectuals should be working to form a civic Russian (*rossiiskaia*) nation, as a community of all citizens of the RF regardless of their cultural and religious differences . The use of the word *rossiiskaia* in itself implies a civic identity, based on citizenship of the RF (or *Rossiia*), rather than on any form of ethnic Russian (*russkii*) characteristics.[39]

Arguing against viewing nations in ethnic terms, Tishkov strongly objects to the continuing use in post-communist Russian legislation, including the new constitution, of the Soviet-era expression 'a multi-national people' (*mnogonatsionalnyi narod*), which he regards as a contradiction in terms. This terminology emphasizes 'the absence, in a legal sense, of the Russian nation (*rossiiskaia natsiia*) as a single subject of political self-determination and the source of state sovereignty ... The admission in the constitution that many nations exist among "the people (*narod*) of the RF" should lead to their [these nations'] recognition as subjects of [international] law, which have a separate right of self-determination.'[40] Nationalism, according to Tishkov, should be understood as the solidarity of citizens regardless of their ethnicity, and should therefore be encouraged. During the short period when he worked in the Russian government, and afterwards as a scholar, Tishkov has put forward various proposals aimed at constructing a civic nation of all citizens of the RF (*rossiiane*).[41] They are:

1. The dissemination of common civic values and symbols among citizens of the RF is crucial. The category of 'nationality', meaning ethnicity, in Russian passports should be abolished. From now on nationality should be understood as citizenship. The government should encourage the widespread use of new state symbols – the flag, herald and anthem,

---

[38] RFE/RL NewsLine, 3 May 2000.

[39] V. Tishkov, *Ethnicity, Nationalism and Conflict in and after the Soviet Union. The Mind Aflame* (London, Sage, 1997), p. IX.

[40] G. Burbulis, ed., *Stanovlenie novoi rossiiskoi gosudarstvennosti: realnost i perspectivy* (Moscow, RF Politika, 1996), pp. 71–2 (Part III of this report on the federal structure of the RF was written by Tishkov).

[41] *Nezavisimaia gazeta*, 26 January 1994, p. 1.

which should be meaningful for all citizens of the RF regardless of their ethnicity. It is therefore inadvisable to continue to use symbols from the tsarist period, such as the herald with the double-headed eagle, the anthem from Glinka's opera 'A Life for the Tsar', and the Russian Orthodox Church as the main state-supported church. Tishkov thinks that the only new symbol of post-communist Russia was the parliament building, 'the White House'. Consequently, its destruction in 1993 harmed the development of a civic Russian (*rossiiskaia*) nation.

2. In multi-ethnic Russia, federalism should not be ethnically based as in the Soviet Union, where constituent republics provided embryonic home-lands for non-Russians. Instead extra-territorial ethnic and cultural autonomy should be introduced, especially as the majority (18 million out of a total 27 million) of the non-Russians in the RF live outside their nominal ethnic autonomous areas. Tishkov emphasizes that local ethnic and cultural loyalties could exist without being in conflict with a broader Russian (*rossiiskaia*) civic identity. At the same time, the definition of the RF's ethnic republics contained in the constitution leads to dangerous terminological confusion, which could trigger the disintegration of the RF.

3. Laws on national minorities should not repeat past mistakes and assume that collective rights have priority over individual rights. These laws should not talk about the rights of the people (*narod*), but should follow the December 1992 UN Declaration on the rights of individuals (sic!), belonging to national, ethnic, religious and language minorities. Strict regulations should be introduced, forbidding social differentiation along ethnic lines, unequal access to power, legal and cultural discrimination, the propagation of xenophobia and negative stereotypes. Parties based on ethnic principles should be banned. At the same time the federal organs of power should not be dominated by Russians. The representa-tion of members of ethnic minorities within them should be legally safeguarded.

Views of non-Russian intellectuals

Tishkov regards the elites of the non-Russian ethnic autonomous areas as a major obstacle to the creation of a civic nation in the RF. Like national minorities elsewhere, they feel that the concept of a nation as a community of citizens is aimed at limiting the rights of minorities and encouraging assimilation with the main ethnic group. Tishkov's model explicitly calls for extra-territorial cultural autonomy for the non-Russians in the RF, which would eventually mean the abolition of autonomous ethnic administrative units in the country. At present, according to the Federal Treaty of 1992 and other pieces of legislation, these autonomous areas have the broadest political and economic rights of all the administrative formations of the RF. Tishkov's opponents argue that the abolition of these autonomous areas would mean that the range of political and economic rights of non-Russians would decrease. In their writings and public speeches, representatives of the non-Russian intellectual elites often repeat the Soviet definition of a nation as a primordial ethnos, which can trace its origins back to a common ancestor. Socio-biological definitions of a nation as a 'given,' based on pre-existing cultural and blood ties, and arguments against mixed marriages are also popular among non-Russian intellectuals. For instance, the Tatar journalist Aidar Khalim argues that 'Mixed families, encouraged by the state policy of nation-merging, serve now to deprive the people of their national features, to impose impersonality and to cause genetic decline.'[42]

The late *perestroika* and post-communist periods have witnessed a proliferation of ethnographic and historical literature tracing the origins of the 'titular nationalities' of the non-Russian republics of the RF to various medieval and ancient heroes. These texts often aim to legitimize a 'titular ethnos' as primordial and strengthen its exclusive claim on a particular territory. In fact, in many cases these titular nationalities acquired their common identities and received their names in the 1920s and 1930s, as a result of the Soviet project to classify the various peoples of the USSR and allot them their own administrative units. As a result, culturally and linguistically different groups were sometimes merged together. The argument that many ethnic groups in the RF with autonomous territories were in fact politically and intellectually constructed in the twentieth century is fiercely rejected by ethnic intellectual elites.

Most non-Russian intellectuals would prefer that a Russian republic be created out of the predominantly ethincally Russian economic regions (*oblasts* and *krais*), and that this republic then establish confederal (i.e. rather loose) ties with the non-Russian areas. However, most of these intellectuals do not consider the point that in only six of the 21 ethnic republics do the 'titular nationalities' constitute a majority.[43]

Positions of politicians

This section explores the views of Russia's politicians on what constitutes the Russian nation. It looks at the position of Russia's first popularly elected President, Boris Yeltsin, his successor, Putin, and members of their presidential apparatuses. It also considers the views of the communist and

---

[42] *Argamak* (Russian-speaking journal published in Kazan), no. 2 (1993), pp. 4–5, quoted in Tishkov, *Ethnicity, Nationalism and Conflict*, p. 9.

[43] For instance, professor of history at the Bashkir University in Ufa, D. Valeev, put forward this proposal in an interview in *Megapolis-express*, 9 June 1993, p. 15.

nationalist opposition, heavily represented in the Russian Congress of People's Deputies and the subsequent Dumas. Finally, it discusses the views of the political elites of the ethnic autonomous territories of the RF.

The Executive branch

As far as the presidents and the executive branch are concerned, we can identify three approaches to nation-building. Firstly, there are attempts to define a nation in civic terms – as a nation of *rossiiane*, i.e. a community of citizens of the RF regardless of their ethnicity. Secondly, there is a definition of the Russian nation as RF citizens plus ethnic Russians and Russian speakers residing in the 'near abroad'. Finally, there are beliefs in a common eastern Slavic identity and in the continuing strength of the Union identity. These are exactly the same notions of a nation which are put forward in intellectual debates. All these visions have had an impact on Russia's policies towards the newly independent states, with one or the other vision prevailing at different times.

Between the autumn of 1991 and late 1992, Yeltsin's government demonstrated an unequivocal commitment to de-ethnicized state-building and to strengthening the civic identities of all citizens of the RF regardless of their ethnicity. This distinguished Russia from the other newly independent states, where governmental nation- and state-building policies reflected a simultaneous reliance on both civic and ethnic identities. Most declarations of independence and most of the new laws of the non-Russian former Union republics have described these states as territorial entities created on behalf of all the people residing there. But at the same time, the same legislation defined these new states as a form of self-determination for the dominant ethnic communities.

In contrast, no ethnic national doctrine was officially promoted in the RF in 1991–1992. At the same time, there was a stronger adherence to a common Union identity among politicians in Russia than among their counterparts in the non-Russian newly independent states. Both trends were reflected in the Russian citizenship law, adopted on 28 November 1991, which calls a citizen of the RF not *russkii* (ethnic Russian), but *rossiianin* (defined in civic terms regardless of ethnicity). The law recognized all those living on the territory of the RF at the time of its adoption as its citizens.[44] All other former union republics, with the exceptions of Estonia and Latvia, also adopted a territorial definition of citizenship. However, the naturalization process is more complicated in the non-Russian newly independent

---

[44] For the text of the law see *Vedomosti Rossiiskoi Federatsii*, no. 6 (1992), pp. 308–20. See also 'Polozhenie o poriadke rassmotreniia voprosov grazhdanstva RF,' *Rossiiskie vesti*, 23 February 1994, p. 4.

states than it is in the RF. The citizenship laws of the non-Russian states make reference to what can be defined as an ethnic attribute – i.e. they state that to become a citizen by naturalization one must have a knowledge of the state language. The RF citizenship law does not include this requirement. Instead, the only requirement for foreigners or stateless people who themselves or whose parents have never had Soviet or RF citizenship is to live in the territory of the RF for three years sequentially or for five years altogether, if the period of residence was interrupted. Moreover, reflecting a belief in a common Union identity, the Russian citizenship law allowed all citizens of the USSR living outside the RF as of 1 September 1991, to obtain RF citizenship by a simple process of registration, if they did not already posses citizenship of another newly independent state. This provision did not require former USSR citizens to move to Russia. Its termination in June 1994 was a response to protests from Estonia and Ukraine. According to the law, until the year 2000, all former citizens of the USSR were free to move to Russia and get automatic registration as RF citizens.

Overall, the RF citizenship law explicitly lacked any ethnic criteria of nationality, unlike the laws of all the other newly independent states. Nor did it give any preferential treatment to either ethnic Russians or Russian speakers as compared to other citizens of the former USSR. The law indicated a mixture of RF civic and Union identities in defining the people whom the RF leadership believed it was governing. Russia's former foreign minister Andrei Kozyrev emphatically argued until the autumn of 1992 that Russians and Russian speakers in the newly independent states did not constitute a specific problem for the Russian government.[45] At the time, as far as the majority in the executive branch of the government was concerned, Russian-speaking settlers in the 'near abroad' were not part of the Russian (*rossiiskaia*) nation, which was defined in territorial and political terms.

However, in 1993–1994, largely under the influence of opposition forces in the Congress of People's Deputies and some people within the executive branch, the attitude of Yeltsin and members of his government towards Russians and Russian speakers in the 'near abroad' changed. In the discourse of Russian politicians, Russian speakers in the newly independent states started to be presented as an integral part of the Russian nation. In official speeches and various government resolutions they began to be described as the *rossiiskaia diaspora*, for whom the RF was the homeland (*rodina*). This definition of the Russian nation as all citizens of the RF plus the communities of Russian speakers abroad seems to have had the greatest impact on the policies and official pronouncements of the Russian government in 1994. In

---

[45] Neil Melvin, *Russians Beyond Russia. The Politics of National Identity* (London, Royal Institute of International Affairs, 1995), pp. 18–24 and Igor Zevelev, 'Russia and the Russian Diaspora,' *Post-Soviet Affairs*, vol. 12, no. 3 (1996), pp. 272–4.

his New Year Address to the nation that year Yeltsin specifically appealed to Russian-speakers in the near abroad by saying 'Dear compatriots [*sootechestvenniki*]! You are inseparable from us and we are inseparable from you. We were and we will be together.' A similar statement was repeated by Yeltsin later that year in his annual address to the parliament.[46] This twist in Yeltsin's position was understandable. The notion of a civic nation was still very novel in Russia, whereas the definition of Russianness by language and culture had a long tradition.

It is sometimes assumed that all Russian politicians, including those who call themselves democrats, consider ethnic and cultural, particularly linguistic, characteristics as more important than citizenship in determining national identity. They thereby disregard the fact that among the 30 million Russians and Russian speakers in the 'near abroad', only 800,000 are RF citizens.[47] This is not true, however. Yeltsin's government never fully abandoned its attempts to define Russian national identity in civic terms. In fact, even this broad definition of the Russian nation as a community of Russian speakers had an element of civic identity. That is why from 1993 to late 1994 the Yeltsin government's policy towards the 'diaspora' focused on persuading the governments of non-Russian newly independent states to grant dual citizenship to members of the 'diaspora.'

Moreover, Yeltsin's address to the parliament in 1994 also referred to a different (civic–territorial) definition of the Russian (*rossiiskaia*) nation as a co-citizenship (*sograzhdanstvo*) of people of the RF regardless of their ethnicity, culture, language or religion. Similarly, the Russian constitution adopted in December 1993 also defines the Russian people (*rossiiskii narod*) as a community of citizens.

All the newly independent states, with the exceptions of Turkmenistan and Tajikistan (which have the smallest Russian-speaking communities), refused to agree to the Russian proposal for dual citizenship. This, meant that in 1995 the Russian policy towards the 'near abroad' which took Russian speakers as the main focus of its attention virtually collapsed. The subsequent revision of Russian government policy had the following consequences: firstly, there was a partial return to the idea of a common Union identity; secondly, it tried to strengthen a common eastern Slavic identity; and finally (and simultaneously), it sought to reinforce a new civic identity by searching for a unifying national idea, to create a bond between all citizens of the RF and increase their loyalty to the new state.

Following the failure of the Russian government's policy of making newly independent states introduce dual citizenship for their Russian

---

[46] *Rossiiskaia gazeta*, 25 February 1994.
[47] Paul Goble, 'Three Faces of Nationalism in the Former Soviet Union,' Charles Kupchan, ed., *Nationalism and Nationalities in the New Europe* (Ithaca N.Y., Cornell University Press, 1995), p. 131.

speakers, the Yeltsin leadership drastically increased its efforts to facilitate the reintegration of Russia and the other newly independent states within the Commonwealth of Independent States (CIS). Instead of dual citizenship for Russians and Russian speakers, the Russian government began advocating CIS citizenship, which could strengthen the Union identity of the Russians and the other peoples of the former USSR. Even liberal members of the government began to refer cautiously to the possibility of reviving some form of union. On 23 May 1996, *Nezavisimaia gazeta* published a working paper of the Council for Foreign and Defence Policy, a body staffed by moderate reformers, which claimed that the revival of the Union was feasible. Two members of the Council, Sergei Karaganov and Oleg Kiselev, were also members of the Presidential Council. The authors of the paper believed that a Russian national statehood could not be formed without the re-establishment of a fully-fledged economic, political and military union on the territory of the former USSR. The working paper also divided the former Soviet republics into categories, according to their importance for Russia. Ukraine and Belorussia were seen as having the greatest importance.

The view of the Council on the importance of Ukraine and Belorussia for the formation of Russian national identity was shared by the majority in Yeltsin's government, although the president never claimed that Ukrainians and Belorussians belong to the Russian nation. In May 1997, the presidents of Russia and Belorussia signed a Charter on the Union between the two countries. The Charter stipulated, among other things, that the two countries should introduce common citizenship.[48] In December 1999, a new step was made in Russian–Belorussian integration, as a treaty on creating a Union state was signed. Although the treaty lays down that Russia and Belorussia are to retain sovereignty and independence within the framework of this state, a traditionally underdeveloped Belorussian national identity, separate from the Russian, will be further weakened. This, in turn, will have serious implications for determining the boundaries of the Russian nation. On numerous occasions, members of the Russian government have indicated their desire for a similar arrangement with Ukraine. They have expressed their deep dissatisfaction that such an option is rejected by the majority of the Ukrainian political elite. It was only in May 1997 that Russia and Ukraine finally signed a treaty on friendship and cooperation. The main stumbling block to signing this document was the question of Russian-Ukrainian borders and especially the status of the Crimea, with the base of the Black Sea Fleet in Sevastopol. The ratification of this treaty by the upper chamber of the Russian parliament in February 1999 provoked criticism on the part of some top political figures, including the Moscow

---

[48] *Moskovskie novosti*, 18–26 May 1997, p. 7.

mayor Iurii Luzhkov. Critics argued that with the ratification of the treaty, 'Russia has forever lost the Crimea and Sevastopol.'[49]

It is noteworthy that the efforts to facilitate CIS integration and secure a union with Belorussia were most intensive during Yeltsin's presidential election campaign of 1996. He apparently believed that most of his electorate had either Union or Slavic identities.

After the presidential elections were over, the government returned to policies aimed at strengthening the civic identity of various peoples of the RF. Members of the government suggested that this sort of compound civic identity could facilitate social mobilization in support of government reforms. Following the Soviet and pre-revolutionary Russian traditions of a strong role for the state in forging national unity, the post-communist Russian government believes in the supreme role of the state in the nation-building project. This approach has always been justified by reference to the underdevelopment of civil society. The question is: how can such a compound identity be formed? According to the main advocate of civic nationalism in Russia, Tishkov, Yeltsin's government paid insufficient attention to the need to cultivate new symbols and values which would be meaningful to all citizens of the RF, whatever their ethnicity. It seems that partly in response to this criticism, in his address to the nation after his re-election as president in July 1996, Yeltsin urged society to search for a new 'Russian national idea.' This proposal provoked a fear on the part of liberals that the government was yet again trying to invent a new political ideology for Russia. For many liberals, the 'Russian idea' revived memories of a messianic vision of Russia as 'the Third Rome' spreading either Orthodoxy or Communism beyond its borders.[50] In fact, it seems Yeltsin's goal was far more modest – it was a desperate attempt to unify a highly divided society within the borders of the Russian Federation.

Rossiiskaia gazeta was chosen as the vehicle to publicize the results of the search.[51] Most of the suggestions published in the newspaper spoke of encouraging state patriotism. This approach is not new. From the time of Peter the Great and Catherine the Great, Russian rulers have felt that it was up to them to unite society by promoting state patriotism. This tended to mean people's unity around the tsar (or the Communist Party leadership) based on pride in belonging to and serving a strong state. However, in 1917 and 1991, state patriotism proved unable to prevent the disintegration of the country when it was in deep crisis. Consequently, Yeltsin's critics immediately pointed out that with the state being so weak, attempts to unify society by instilling state patriotism were doomed. However, Yeltsin's successor Putin seems to be thinking that the revival of a strong state and

---

[49] *Nezavisimaia gazeta*, 17 March 1999, p. 5.
[50] See, for instance, D. Likhachev in *Novaia gazeta*, 9 December 1996, p. 1.
[51] *Rossiiskaia gazeta* began publishing various views on a new 'Russian idea' on 30 July 1996.

the unification of society through pride in belonging to it is the only way forward for Russia.[52]

The parliamentary opposition

The communist and nationalist oppositions do not share this commitment towards encouraging a civic identity among citizens of the RF. Among the majority of opposition members, strongly represented in the legislative branch of government, three main visions of the Russian identity coexist. The first is that Russian identity has a meaning only within the framework of a broader Union identity; the second is that the Russian identity is a Slavic one, and the third is a definition of Russianness by the linguistic marker. The leader of the Communist Party of the RF (CPRF), Gennadii Ziuganov, argues that the Russian empire and the USSR constituted a unique Russian civilization, all of whose members shared a common identity. To support his views he refers primarily to works by Danilevskii, Ilin and the Eurasianists. This position is, however, combined with his simultaneous belief that the Russian identity is actually Slavic.

From 1992 onwards, the Russian parliament adopted a very hostile position towards Ukrainian independence. As early as January 1992, it issued the first in a series of resolutions to make territorial claims on Ukraine. In his books *Derzhava* and *Za gorizontom*, Ziuganov unequivocally included the Ukrainians and Belorussiaians in the Russian nation, referring to nineteenth-century Russian historians to prove his point. He also unequivocally regarded all the Russians and Russian speakers abroad, regardless of their citizenship, as an integral part of the Russian nation and argued that 'without the reunification of the divided Russian people our state would never rise from its knees.'[53] Therefore in its use of symbols and its appeal to common values to unite the people, the CPRF mixes those of the Soviet period (particularly the red flag) with those of the Russian empire, which have an appeal only to ethnic Russians. For instance, nowadays many Communists promote Orthodoxy as a key element of the Russian national identity and favour state support for the Russian Orthodox Church. The position of the ultra-nationalists, represented in the 1993, 1995 and 1999 Dumas by Vladimir Zhirinovskii's Liberal Democratic Party of Russia, is similar to that of Ziuganov, i.e. it is a mixture of the three main above-mentioned identities. Overall, to members of the radical Communist–nationalist opposition, civic identity has no appeal. A common Union identity is overwhelmingly preferred. However, definitions of the Russian nation as a community of eastern Slavs or as a

---

[52] See Putin's address to the nation of 8 July 2000.
[53] Quoted in *Nezavisimaia gazeta*, 15 December 1995, p. 2.

community of all the Russian speakers of the former USSR are regarded as alternative possibilities, if the Union cannot be re-established.

More moderate nationalists, such as Stanislav Govorukhin who led a bloc bearing his name in the 1995 Duma, have viewed the Russian nation as a community of eastern Slavs plus all the Russian speakers in the non-Slavic newly independent states. In March 1996 this bloc voted in favour of the Duma resolution, put forward by the Communists and the LDPR, which proclaimed the Belovezhe Accord null and void. Nonetheless, Govorukhin was not in favour of restoring the USSR, as he did not consider that all former Soviet citizens belonged to the Russian nation.[54]

Finally, from early 1992 onwards, there have been moderate centrists in the Congress of People's Deputies and the Duma who argue that the Russian and Soviet identities have always been separate. They do not include Ukrainians and Belorussians in the Russian nation. Nevertheless these centrists forcefully argue that all the Russians and Russian speakers in the 'near abroad' do belong to the Russian nation, view Russia as their homeland, and that therefore their defence should be the main priority of the Russian government. The question of the formal citizenship of members of the diaspora is of little importance to those politicians. Back in 1992–94, this position was represented by such otherwise moderate politicians as the chairmen of the parliamentary Committees for Foreign Affairs Evgenii Ambartsumov and Vladimir Lukin.

Since 1992, most members of the federal and regional governments and legislatures have relied on the Russian Orthodox Church to increase their public support. Although the president, parliamentary deputies and regional leaders are popularly elected, they are aware that society is split almost down the middle between those who favour the course of reforms and those who support the communist–nationalist opposition, and that each side enjoys only limited popular support. Consequently, both sides look for alternative sources of legitimacy, and they think that an alliance with the Church could provide it. From 1992 onwards, the ROC has been using this situation to enhance its position. In violation of the liberal 1990 law on freedom of conscience, which stipulated a clear separation between church and state, the ROC has been allowed to establish representation in the army and in a growing number of schools and higher educational institutions. Representatives of the ROC, particularly the Patriarch, regularly give their blessing at important political occasions.

In 1997, under strong pressure from the ROC, the parliament adopted a new law on freedom of conscience, reflecting the Church's desire to suppress other religions on the territory of the RF, particularly Catholicism and

---

[54] Ibid.
[55] S.B. Filatov, 'Novoe rozhdenie staroi ideii: pravoslavie kak natsionalnyi simvol,' *Polis*, no. 3 (1999), p. 146.

Protestantism. The hierarchs of the Church, including the Patriarch, claim that the presence of Catholics and Protestants 'divides Russian society' and 'destroys Russian cultural and national traditions.'[55]

The law banned proselytizing activities by foreign missionaries and religious organizations and communities which had been in existence for less than fifteen years. Although the law does not impose any restrictions on religions, 'historically present in Russia,' such as Buddhism and Islam, it clearly promotes religious intolerance. It could therefore potentially contribute to the division of society along religious lines.[56] Moreover, the war in Chechnia caused politicians to play the anti-Islamic card. Putin justified his decision to resume his brutal military operations against Chechnia by arguing that the Chechens 'would not be content with remaining inside' the borders of their republic and, if Chechen 'extremists' were not stopped, 'we will have Islamization of Russia.'[57]

Opposition leaders have devoted much more space in their writings and public speeches to the question of what is the Russian nation than president Yeltsin and his supporters in the executive branch of government have done. For instance, Ziuganov's books dwell at length on the formation of the Russians as a nation. So did the articles and speeches of Yeltsin's main critic in the executive branch in 1992–93, Vice-President Alexander Rutskoi. He published a series of articles on Russian nation-building, largely based on Ilin's notion of the Russian nation.[58] In contrast, Yeltsin's books focus mainly on his rise to power and on the struggle against his political opponents. The CPRF has even set up analytical centres, such as the RAU corporation and Spiritual Heritage, with a brief to produce 'general theories' about Russia's post-communist nation-building. These institutes are staffed by former employees of the Academy of Sciences and former instructors of Marxism–Leninism. Their main sources of inspiration are conservative pre-revolutionary thinkers and Soviet theories of nationalities relations. Parliamentary deputies from the Communist and nationalist factions also organize joint conferences with intellectuals on issues related to Russia's nation-building.[59] It is these intellectuals who shape the views of the political opposition on what is the Russian nation. Finally, a number of intellectuals, among them Ambartsumov, Lukin and Rogozin, mentioned above, were elected to the parliament. This enabled them directly to integrate intellectual discourse into political debates.

The opposition also exercises a strong influence upon the positions on nation-building taken by members of the executive branch. Indeed, the shifts in Yeltsin's perception of the Russian nation usually came as a

---

[56]   Ibid, p. 143.
[57]   *The Times*, 21 March 2000, p. 8.
[58]   See, for instance, *Pravda*, 30 January 1992.
[59]   *Megapolis-express*, 7 April 1993, p. 15.

reaction to pressure from the opposition. This was at least partly the case with Yeltsin's policies towards Russian speakers in the 'near abroad.' Moreover, Yeltsin's decision in 1996 to increase his efforts to achieve CIS and Slavic integration came in response to the Communist-sponsored resolution revoking the Belovezhe Accords.

There has also been a noticeable direct influence by intellectuals on shifts in the government's views on the definition of the Russian nation. A number of intellectuals, who have actively participated in the debates on nation-building, have also served as Yeltsin's aides, advisors and members of the Presidential Council. On rare occasions, they have even occupied ministerial positions. The most well known of them are the acting prime minister in 1992 Egor Gaidar; the ethnographer and Yeltsin's advisor on inter-ethnic relations in 1992 Galina Starovoitova; Tishkov; the historian and presidential counsellor in 1992–1993 Sergei Stankevich; Karaganov; the ethnographer Emil Pain; and the political scientist Georgii Satarov. These last two both became aides to Yeltsin in 1994. Gaidar, Starovoitova and Tishkov were instrumental in promoting the idea of de-ethnicized nation- and state-building in the RF in early 1992. In late 1992–1993, Stankevich's influence was probably as important as pressure from the opposition in convincing Yeltsin that Russian settlers in the 'near abroad' should be seen as an integral part of the Russian nation. Stankevich was the author of the first major Russian government policy document 'On urgent measures for socio-cultural cooperation between citizens of the RF with their compatriots abroad,' which he presented to Yeltsin in January 1993.[60] Intellectuals like Karaganov and the political scientist Andranik Migranian also helped shape the government's attitude towards Russian-speaking settlers through their close ties to Stankevich and other members of the presidential apparatus. In 1996, Karaganov, as a member of the Presidential Council, was instrumental in Yeltsin's decision to promote CIS integration during his election campaign.

The concept of a civic Russian nation, which Yeltsin, to some extent, promoted, also emerged through the efforts of intellectuals. This concept has been advocated by Tishkov – a scholar who maintains close ties with the presidential apparatus following his short period of tenure in the government in 1992. It was largely through his efforts that the definition of the Russian (*rossiiskaia*) nation as a community of citizens of the RF was introduced in the Russian constitution and appeared in the presidential New Year and parliamentary addresses. These addresses were written by Yeltsin's advisors Pain and Satarov, both liberal intellectuals, with Tishkov's help.[61]

---

[60] Melvin, *Russians Beyond Russia*, p. 15.
[61] Ibid, p. 260.

Leaders of the ethnic autonomous territories

It is not only members of the national–communist opposition in Moscow that oppose the idea of creating a civic Russian (*rossiiskaia*) nation of citizens of the RF, united by loyalty to the new political institutions and the constitution. The idea is challenged also by the political elites of the non-Russian autonomous areas within the RF. The fact that 18 per cent of RF citizens are non-Russians, most of whom are also non-Slavs and even non-Christians, and the challenge that this situation presents to the unity of the RF has been well recognized by Yeltsin, Putin and their advisors. Moscow's inability to find a solution to its problems in Chechnia has emphasized the magnitude of the challenge. The optimists in the Russian government think that the problem can be overcome. They argue that, although many non-Russians identify primarily with their autonomous areas rather than with the RF as a whole, regional/local and national identities do not have to be exclusive. Regional or local identities could co-exist peacefully with an all-embracing all-national one. The optimists reject parallels between the Union republics of the USSR and the ethnic autonomous areas within the RF. Firstly, they emphasize that in the RF only a minority (33.4 per cent) of non-Russians actually live in their titular autonomous territories. Moreover, the non-Russians in the RF are far more Russified and versed in Russian culture than most of the non-Russians who were allotted Union republics in the USSR and who lived in those republics. However, Yeltsin, Putin, and most of the advocates of civic nation-building in their governments nevertheless have felt that it is undesirable to have administrative units in the RF with borders drawn along ethnic lines. The war in Chechnia has intensified debates in the government about redividing Russia into regions, the boundaries of which would have no relationship to the historical settlements of the non-Russians. Members of the opposition (Zhirinovskii is a prime example) fully support this plan. Whereas Yeltsin refrained from taking any measures in this direction, Putin has not. In May 2000, he put forward a plan to create seven federal districts in the Russian Federation. They would have administrations with broad powers to intervene in the work of the leaders of Russia's 89 constituent regions/republics. At the early stage of his presidency, Putin did not feel strong enough to dissolve the non-Russian ethnic autonomous areas altogether. However, he instructed their leaders to remove any provisions which contradicted federal laws from their local legislation.

Like the non-Russian intellectual elites, the members of which often serve as advisors to the political leaders of ethnic autonomous regions, these ethnic leaders argue that the notion of a civic nation amounts to imperialist Russification in disguise. The deputy prime minister for ethnic relations, the Dagestani Ramazan Abdulatipov, argued in an open letter to Yeltsin against the view of the Russian (*rossiiskaia*) nation as a community of citizens, which Yeltsin had put forward in his parliamentary addresses in 1994 and 1995. Citing the views of the ethnic political leaders, Abdulatipov claimed that this view was similar to 'the Bolshevik idea of the fusion of people.'[62] He also identified 'Western influences' in this concept and stated in this connection:

> We should not copy a Western path of state-building. It is based on assimilation, which has always been carried out by force. We are unique, because 150 different nationalities live in our country, and they preserve their ethnicity, culture and languages ... For the people of the RF collective rights have priority over individual human rights. It is only in the distant future that the latter could take priority. In the West, the supremacy [of individual rights] is achieved through the destruction of entire populations. Thank God, the Russian nation has never been historically that cynical.[63]

Popular attitudes

To what extent do the post-communist debates of intellectuals and politicians about what Russia is and who the Russians are affect the broader public? Although one can argue that the question of national identity is not something ordinary people regularly ponder over, numerous opinion polls have been conducted on the subject. They indicate that the intensive discussion of the question of national identity by the elites, prominently covered in the media, affects the thinking of the public. In evaluating the views of ordinary citizens of the RF about their national identity, this section relies largely on relevant opinion polls conducted between 1992 and 1997 by the Moscow-based Public Opinion Foundation (in 1997 renamed the Institute of Sociological Analysis), and by the Institute of Ethnology and Anthropology of the Russian Academy of Sciences. These polls cast light on a number of questions. What characteristics and values do citizens of the RF identify as being specifically Russian (i.e. how do they define Russianness)? To what extent do ordinary Russians accept that Ukrainians and Belorussians are members of separate nations? How relevant still is a Union identity for the citizens of the RF as well as for ethnic Russians and Russian speakers in the non-Russian newly independent states? What are the identities of non-Russians in the RF and to what extent do they accept a civic Russian (*rossiiskaia*) identity?

In an opinion poll conducted in February 1995 by the Public Opinion Foundation under the leadership of Igor Kliamkin, Russians throughout the entire RF were asked to name characteristics which, they thought, were 'necessary for a Russian.'

---

[62] In fact, the Bolsheviks never consistently promoted the idea of 'the fusion of people.'
[63] *Nezavisimaia gazeta*, 14 March 1995, p. 3.

Table 8.1 Characteristics which are necessary for a Russian (per cent)

To love Russia and view it as a homeland	87
To know and love Russian culture	84
To have Russian as native language	80
To regard oneself as a Russian	79
To have Russian citizenship	59
To be identified as Russian in an internal passport	24
To have Russian parents	24
To have a Russian physical appearance	22

(Source: I.M. Kliamkin and V.V. Lapkin, 'Russkii vopros v Rossii,' *Polis*, no. 5 (29) (1995), p. 87).

This evidence suggests that as far as the broad public in the RF is concerned, Russian identity is largely subjective. Identification with Russia as a homeland and self-identification as a Russian are seen as key characteristics. It is also linguistic and cultural. The question of citizenship is far less significant, whereas the 'nationality entry' in internal passports or racial characteristics (Russian parents and appearance) are peripheral. Overall, most Russians define the Russian nation as a community of Russian speakers created on a voluntary basis. The same poll also asked the respondents about the values (traditional Russian, Soviet, Western, or mixtures of two or three) 'to which Russia (*Rossiia*) should orient itself.' A very large proportion (46 per cent) singled out traditional Russian values.[64] One such value is Orthodoxy. If in the late 1970s and the early 1980s between 6 and 10 per cent identified themselves as Orthodox believers when surveyed,[65] by late 1996 their number had risen to over 50 per cent. Among those who identified themselves as non-believers, 61 per cent nevertheless identified Orthodoxy as an essential element of the Russian national identity.[66] At the same time, even in the late 1990s, opinion polls indicated high levels of religious tolerance among the Russians, who often combined self-identification as Orthodox believers with an additional interest in other, particularly Eastern non-Christian, religions.[67] But lately, as a result of the anti-Chechen propaganda conducted by politicians and the media, anti-Muslim feelings have started to rise dramatically among the Russians. Opinion polls conducted in early 2000 indicated that up to 80 per cent of those polled regarded Islam as 'a

[64]   *Polis*, no. 5 (1995), p. 82.
[65]   These figures are probably too low, as in the Communist period many people kept their religious beliefs secret.
[66]   K. Kariainen and D. Furman, 'Veruiushchie, ateisty i prochie (evoliutsiia rossiskoi religioznosti),' *Voprosy filosofii*, no. 6 (1997), pp. 35–52.
[67]   Ibid and Filatov, 'Novoe rozhdenie staroi idei,' p. 142.

bad thing.' In contrast, in 1992, only 17 per cent of Russians had subscribed to that view.[68]

As mentioned above, an identification with Russia (to love Russia and view it as a homeland) was a key characteristic of Russianness for most respondents. The organizers of the poll defined Russia as the existing RF. However, the poll indicated that a substantial number of respondents had problems with such a definition. The largest group of those polled (43 per cent) favoured giving Russians the legally recognized status of the dominant nation in the country (*ofitsialno priznanaia glavnaia natsia*), as opposed to 38 per cent who were against it. The remaining 19 per cent did not care or could not decide one way or the other.[69] According to this poll, a significant minority (33 per cent) also thought Russia should incorporate areas of other newly independent states where Russian speakers live in a compact majority. Forty-six per cent of respondents opposed this option.[70] In other words, this poll indicated public support for nation-building in the RF around the language and culture of the core ethnic group (Russians).

At the same time, an opinion poll conducted in May 1996 by the Institute of Sociological Analysis, involving 1516 people from the majority of Russian regions, found that only 7 per cent of respondents still identified themselves as Soviet.[71] The polls also indicated that only between 2 and 8 per cent of respondents were in favour of Russia reuniting with the newly independent states of the Transcaucasus, Central Asia and the Baltics.[72] The attitude towards Ukraine and Belorussia, as compared to the non-Slavic states of the former USSR, is different, however. In 1992–1995, the Public Opinion Foundation regularly conducted surveys of the Russian and Ukrainian public on their attitudes towards each other. All the polls indicated that most Russians thought Russians and Ukrainians belonged to the same nation.[73] In turn, a poll conducted by the Institute of Sociological Analysis in the spring of 1997 revealed that 64 per cent of respondents thought that Russia and Ukraine should be united into one state.[74] In March 1999, 45 per cent of those polled objected to the ratification of the Russian–Ukrainian treaty on friendship and cooperation, which stipulated the mutual acceptance by both states of their current borders. Seventy-eight

[68] Quoted in Paul Goble, 'Idel-Ural and the Future of Russia,' *RFE/RL NewsLine*, 17 May (2000).
[69] *Polis*, no. 5 (1995), p. 94.
[70] Ibid, pp. 94 and 96.
[71] T. Kutkovets and I. Kliamkin, 'Postsovetskii chelovek,' *Informatsionno-analiticheskii biulleten*, nos. 1–2 (Moscow, 1997).
[72] *Argumenty i fakty*, no. 27, July (1997).
[73] I. Kliamkin, 'Russian Statehood, the CIS, and the Problem of Security,' in Leon Aron and Kenneth M. Jensen eds, *The Emergence of Russian Foreign Policy* (Washington DC, The US Institute of Peace Press, 1994), pp. 111–12.
[74] *Argumenty i fakty*, no. 27, July (1997).

per cent of the respondents thought that Sevastopol should be under Russian jurisdiction.[75] Surveys conducted in April and June 1997 by the institute indicated 66 per cent and 75 per cent support respectively for a Russia–Belorussia unification.[76]

In order to evaluate the potential significance of civic versus ethnic national identities in the RF, it is important to look at the identities of Russians and Russian speakers in the 'near abroad' and of the non-Russians in the RF. Opinion polls continue to show that the main identity of the overwhelming majority of Russians and Russian speakers in the non-Russian newly independent states is still a Soviet one, which is usually followed by a regional identity. Identification with the RF as a homeland is extremely low (usually less than 10 per cent).[77] This low level of identification with Russia made it difficult for the Russian government to achieve any significant political mobilization among Russians and Russian speakers in the 'near abroad' in favour of the government's claim to be the main defender of their interests.

Since 1993, the Institute of Ethnography and Anthropology of the Russian Academy of Sciences has been conducting sociological surveys in all republics of the RF. The aim of these surveys, among other things, is to measure civic (*rossiiskaia*) identity versus other (most notably local ethnic and regional) identities of non-Russians in the RF. The polls indicate that the majority of non-Russians who reside in their own ethnic republics feel loyalty to both their republic and Russia. However, when asked 'citizens of what state (the USSR, the Russian Federation or ethnic republic of residence within the RF) do you consider yourself to be?', most representatives of a titular ethnic group in all the republics except Chuvashia and Mordovia considered themselves first of all to be citizens of the republic of residence and only then citizens of the RF.[78] At the same time, as mentioned earlier, only 33.4 per cent of non-Russians in the RF live in their respective ethnic republics. For the majority of non-Russians living outside their autonomous areas, Russian (*rossiiskaia*) identity is predominant, whereas identification with the respective ethnic republic is weak.[79]

---

[75] *Nezavisiamaia gazeta*, 17 March 1999, p. 5.

[76] *Moskovskie novosti*, 18–26 May 1997, p. 7 and *Argumenty i fakty*, no. 27, July (1997).

[77] *Russkie v novom zarubezhe. Programma etnosotsiologicheskikh issledovanii* (Moscow, Institut Etnologii i Antropologii RAN, 1994), p. 125. The situation is slightly different in the Crimea, where a poll conducted in early 1996 by the Crimean Liberal Arts Research Centre found that 32 per cent of the respondents considered the USSR as their homeland, 28 per cent identified it as the Crimea, 16 per cent as the RF and 11 per cent as Ukraine. The rest were undecided. The poll is quoted in T. Kuzio, 'National Identity in Independent Ukraine: An Identity in Transition,' *Nationalism and Ethnic Politics*, vol. 2, no. 4 (1996), p. 603.

[78] V.A. Tishkov, 'What Is Russia? Prospects of Nation Building,' *Russian Politics and Law*, March–April 1996, p. 18 and Tishkov, *Ethnicity, Nationalism and Conflict*, p. 253.

[79] Tishkov, 'What Is Russia?,' p. 18.

Conclusions

Russian intellectuals are actively creating a new nationalist discourse as they attempt to forge a Russian nation after the break-up of the empire. They are re-deploying old concepts, which had originally developed under circumstances markedly different from those of today, more frequently than inventing new traditions. Only the advocates of civic nationalism, who are a minority, are real innovators in the Russian context. Voluntary membership of a nation, so central to civic nationalism, is still alien to the majority of intellectuals.

Intellectuals are now represented in the political structures to an unprecedented extent, serving as advisors, parliamentary deputies and even, at times, government ministers. Nonetheless, it is tempting to dismiss intellectual debates on Russian nation-building as of secondary importance in setting the agendas of the political elites. One can say that by evoking various definitions of a nation politicians only pursue their immediate political and economic interests.[80] These interests are defined first and then, in some instances, an appropriate definition of a nation is found and used as an instrument in political struggles. Indeed, the leaders of the ethnic autonomous territories use ethnic definitions of nationhood and oppose the concept of a civic nation for purely pragmatic reasons. It helps them in their struggle to prevent ethnic autonomous areas – their main power bases – from being abolished. In turn, when a member of the opposition is co-opted into the executive branch of government he is forced to abandon his political ideology and to act purely pragmatically. Those who do not, like Rutskoi and Lebed, lose their jobs.

However, in some other instances the situation is not so simple. Politicians sometimes use various definitions of a nation in their attempts to strengthen their political legitimacy (i.e. broaden popular support). Where a politician is seeking to achieve a clearly defined political or economic gain, it is usually easy to identify an appropriate concept of a nation which he can use to strengthen his bargaining powers. In instances when political legitimacy is at stake, there are various definitions of a nation from which politicians can choose and the choice is usually not immediately apparent. In such cases nationalist discourse matters. The intellectuals put forward different competing definitions of a nation, and at different times one or another definition becomes more fashionable. Where a definition is adopted by politicians for the purpose of strengthening their political legitimacy, that definition itself will shape part of their political agenda.

---

[80] For instance, Rogers Brubaker, *Nationalism Reframed. Nationhood and the National Question in the New Europe* (Cambridge, Cambridge University Press, 1996) views a nation purely as a category of political practice rather than as a result of an interaction of cultural heritage and politics.

The Russian government's policy towards the other newly independent states is a case in point. One can regard the government's claim to represent Russian speakers abroad merely as a pragmatic instrument for regaining control over Russia's former colonies. But this claim was made and the policy of defending Russian-speaking communities from alleged discrimination was introduced in a specific domestic context – during the president's bitter struggle with the Congress of People's Deputies over the division of power. In this struggle both sides tried to strengthen their legitimacy by claims to represent the Russian nation better. There were various definitions of the Russian nation available at the time and the choice was open. In late 1992, the Russian government decided to abandon its adherence to de-ethnicized nation- and state-building. It felt that the idea of a civic nation, so new in the Russian context, would not appeal to the population. Therefore, the government appropriated the opposition's definition of the nation in linguistic terms, as this definition had a long tradition behind it. The way the Russian government formulated its foreign policy in 1992–1994 was a by-product of the way it had chosen to define the Russian nation in a domestic struggle for political legitimacy. This definition of the Russian nation, as the community of Russian speakers in the entire former USSR for whom the RF was a homeland, was an 'artificial construct' of intellectuals. It had little resonance among Russian speakers in the 'near abroad,' and therefore the Russian government had eventually to abandon it.

On other occasions when the government's political legitimacy has been at stake and broader popular support needed, traditional definitions of the Russian nation have also been chosen. During the presidential election campaign in 1996, Yeltsin intensified his efforts to strengthen both the CIS and Slavic integration, as he believed that the common Union and Slavic identities were still stronger among RF citizens than the civic identity. His efforts at integration subsided following his victory. If during crucial political battles the government appeals to traditional forms of Russian nationalism, is the formation of a civic nation within the borders of the RF still possible?

There are some grounds for optimism. Despite all the confusion which the empire brought to the self-perception of the Russians, it also had some effects which could be conducive to nation-building along civic lines. It helped to create a de-ethnicized Russian identity. Even if the claims of Russian intellectuals about the 'openness' and 'adaptability' of Russians to other ethnic groups and nations are an exaggeration, they contain an element of truth. According to opinion polls, as far as the majority is concerned it is often enough to regard Russia as a homeland to qualify as a Russian. Moreover, it seems that ordinary Russians more than the intellectual elite are inclined to see a nation as a community formed on a voluntary basis.

The multi-ethnic composition of the RF makes nation-building along civic lines the most viable option to secure the stability of the state. Many members of the Russian political elite understand that. Therefore the definition of the new Russian (*rossiiskaia*) nation as a community of citizens of the RF is reflected in the Russian constitution. It is also regularly repeated in official documents and speeches. This indicates that the line of civic nation-building is still pursued by the government, however inconsistently. Although it is true that the political and intellectual elites of Russia's ethnic autonomous territories oppose the notion of a civic nation, it is a mistake to see all non-Russians as an obstacle to forging a civic Russian nation. Non-Russians in the RF are versed in the Russian language and culture to a far greater degree than ethnic minorities in many other countries. The majority of them live outside their ethnic autonomous territories and among these a compound civic Russian identity prevails.

Finally, civic nations are only ideal types, which rarely exist in pure forms. As most countries are multi-ethnic, the ethnic elements which are necessarily present even in predominantly civic nationalisms, are usually those of the largest (core) ethnic group. Thus, the route from state to nation might well lead to the formation of a civic nation in the RF, as has usually been the case elsewhere. Potential border changes – the separation of parts of the North Caucasus and the reintegration of Russia and Belorussia – could hardly be detrimental to nation-building in Russia along civic lines. On the contrary, if Chechnia ever gets independence, Russia will lose an area which was among the last to be incorporated into their state and remained among the least integrated. In contrast, Belorussians are among the most Russified people of the former empire.

Yet the obstacles to the creation of a civic Russian nation are formidable. The notion of a civic nation is still alien to most of Russia's 'social engineers.' Even some of the supporters of this concept of a nation find it safer to rely on more traditional approaches when the stakes in political battles are being raised too high. The underdevelopment of civil society, and the major rift between political and business élites, on the one hand, and the majority of the population, on the other, are not conducive to civic nationalism. Indeed, rich and poor in today's Russia are still 'two nations,' divided by mutual suspicion and resentment. A Russian state which can command the respect of most of the population – a condition necessary for the formation of a civic nation – is also absent. Putin's measures for beginning to strengthen the state are supported by some, but strongly opposed by others. In particular, they are likely to increase the divide between the centre and the periphery, and between the ethnic Russians and the non-Russian, particularly Muslim, citizens of Russia.

If attempts to forge a civic nation of all citizens of the Russian Federation fail, what are the alternatives? A revival of a strong Russian imperial identity does not seem to be a serious prospect at the moment. Russia has neither the economic nor the military power to attempt to recreate the union. Moreover, such an enterprise is unlikely to receive popular support. A much greater danger could come from the rise of an exclusive, xenophobic Russian nationalism, which regards the non-Russians, particularly the Muslims, of the Russian Federation as 'others.' Such nationalism leads to brutal violations of the rights of ethnic minorities, yet does not allow them to secede from the state because that will mean the loss of 'national' territory. Charles Fairbanks has described this phenomenon in relation to Serbia:

> There is something new and alarming going on. There is a kind of nationalism very different from nineteenth-century nationalism in that it is not imperialistic … Even in the case of Serbia what the Serbs want is not at all that Serbs should rule Croatia or Slovenia. They simply want to have a greater Serbia which is their own – a kind of isolated, autarkic community. In order to do that they think they must kill or drive out people who don't fit into that vision.[81]

Russians are still far away from such a vision, but the war in Chechnia, and the ways in which the elites are trying to solicit popular support for that war, bring it closer.

---

[81] Quoted in Anatol Lieven, *Chechnya. Tombstone of Russian Power* (New Haven CT, Yale University Press, 1999), p. 382.

Conclusions: Russian tradition and the post-communist concept of nationhood

In concluding this book, I would like briefly to focus on the main peculiarities of Russian nation- and state-building over the past two hundred years. These peculiarities are still highly significant, and will have to be dealt with if a concept of a nation conducive to the stability of the state and compatible with democracy is to prevail in the Russian Federation.

The first main feature of Russian historical development with direct relevance to Russian nation-building is the Russian empire. Its creation and maintenance prevented the tsarist and Soviet governments from implementing policies which could have facilitated Russian nation-building along both civic and ethnic lines. The imperial legacy had a profound impact on the thinking of Russia's most active nation-builders, its intellectuals, about the state and the nation. Their attempts to compare and contrast Russia with the West were contradictory. Russian intellectuals simultaneously, and therefore somewhat inconsistently, imagined the empire as a Russian nation-state similar to Great Britain, France or Germany, while emphasizing its uniqueness, that is, its difference from those same countries. In their view, this difference stemmed from Russia's multi-ethnic character. In discussing Russia's multi-culturalism, some intellectuals drew parallels with the United States. But comparisons with the United States, on the one hand, and with Western Europe, on the other, proved deceptive. On the one hand, the way in which Russia became a multi-ethnic state was very different from the way the United States came into being. On the other hand, in the Romanov state and the Soviet Union Russians were simply not numerous enough to Russify the empire's non-Russian subjects in the same way as the English made their culture dominant in Great Britain and the Paris government turned Bretons, Corsicans, Provençals and other non-French speaking subjects into French-speaking citizens. Moreover, neither the tsarist nor the Soviet government conducted Russification policies consistently. When and where they were pursued, these policies were largely aimed at maintaining the political stability of the state, rather than being an act of Russian nation-building. The majority of intellectuals, in turn, did not think that any Russification policy was necessary. In a somewhat contradictory manner, they simultaneously argued both that multi-culturalism was Russia's strength and that the supremacy of Russian culture was anyway recognized by most non-Russians who would be voluntarily Russified at their own pace.

The disintegration of the empire in 1917 clearly proved that the Russian intellectuals' perception of the tsarist empire as a Russian nation-state was erroneous. However, in the aftermath of the revolution Russia's imperial legacy was questioned and revised only to a limited extent, as the state was relatively quickly recreated by the Bolsheviks. By the 1960s, an anti-imperial Russian nationalism had begun to emerge. This was a product of the nationalities policies of the Bolshevik government, along with its other initiatives conducive to the construction of modern nationalist ideas, such as industrialization, urbanization and the mass spread of literacy. Yet, the tendency to see the entire Soviet Union as a Russian nation-state continued to prevail among the Russians up until the demise of the USSR in 1991. Today, however, the situation has changed considerably. The latest opinion polls indicate that the overwhelming majority of Russians no longer want most of the former Union republics to merge into one state with the Russian Federation. Moreover, the Russian government is too weak to conduct consistent policies to restore Moscow's control over the non-Russian newly independent states. Yet, so far there is one part of the Russian imperial legacy where very little rethinking and change of attitude has taken place. This concerns Russia's relations with the two other east Slavic states – Ukraine and Belorussia. Most Russians continue to regard the citizens of these states as, in effect, belonging, together with the Russians, to one pan-Russian nation. It remains to be seen whether the view of the Russians about the nature and the significance of their 'east Slavic roots,' especially in relation to Ukraine, will persist or be revised. Either way, this question will have a profound impact on the eventual outcome of the current phase of Russian nation-building.

At the same time, the Russian Federation itself is a legacy of the imperial past and of the absence of a genuine Russian nation-state. It was created in the 1920s from the territories left over once the borders of the non-Russian Union republics had been determined. It is no wonder that its current borders are contested by both the Russian elites, who are particularly concerned that territories with Russian-speaking majorities are now part of foreign countries, and the public, which, to some extent, shares the same sentiments. Some non-Russians, particularly the Chechens, whose administrative units are part of the RF, also contest the state's integrity by demanding the right to secede. As long as the Russian state is in flux, no consensus over the membership of the Russian nation can be forged.

The second important legacy of the past is the socialist concept of the Russian nation. It was first articulated by Aleksandr Herzen in the 1840s and 1850s, who adopted certain Slavophile ideas. It was subsequently modified by his successors from the 1860s onwards. Of all the various definitions of the nation, it was the socialist concept which eventually acted as the force that transformed Russia's social and political structures. Scholars have noted that when the idea of a nation as a sovereign people first appeared, it was a profoundly democratic idea. All members of a nation were supposed to be in some sense equal, and any government, claiming to represent the nation, had to have a popular mandate to rule. These main elements of the modern concept of a nation are 'at the same time the basic tenets of democracy.'[1] In the Russian case, however, the absence of any tradition of democratic government led to the revision of the definitions both of the nation and of democracy as they were first formulated in England and France. Despite customary references to the tradition of the French revolution among Russian socialists from the mid-nineteenth century on, their definition of a nation was different from the inclusive French definition, which emphasized the fundamental equality among various strata of the French society. Following the Slavophiles, Russian socialists excluded the 'exploiting classes,' who by 1917, began to be described as *burzhui*, from membership of the Russian nation. Additionally, from the 1860s onwards the word 'democracy' was also interpreted to mean 'the common people – and its opposite was not "dictatorship" but the "bourgeoisie" or indeed the whole of privileged society.'[2] Moreover, within the socialist definition of a national community, the symbolic elevation of the 'masses' to the level of the sole representative of the nation went hand in hand with the view that the Russian people were so backward that they were neither able to recognize their own interests nor act upon them. (This view of the 'masses' was not unique to Russian socialists. It was prevalent among broader circles of Russian educated society from the early nineteenth century onwards.) This combination of egalitarian and elitist approaches led to the emergence in the mid-nineteenth century of the idea that it was up to a group of the Russian educated elite to articulate on behalf of the masses what their interests were, and to act upon those interests. In the twentieth century, this profoundly undemocratic view of a

---

[1]   Liah Greenfeld, *Nationalism: Five Roads to Modernity* (Cambridge MA, Harvard University Press, 1992), p. 10.

[2]   Orlando Figes and Boris Kolonitskii, *Interpreting the Russian Revolution. The Language and Symbols of 1917* (New Haven CT, Yale University Press, 1999), p. 122 argued this on the basis of the material for 1917. James Billington, *The Icon and the Axe* (London, Weidenfeld and Nicolson, 1966), p. 378 showed the emergence of such definition of democracy back in the 1860s.

national community provided a justification for the dictatorial policies of a government, which, unlike its tsarist predecessors, claimed to rule by popular mandate.

All the other definitions of Russianness, from religious to linguistic, stressed the idea of Russian uniqueness rather than popular sovereignty and in effect, denied that membership of a nation could be voluntary. Consequently, they were not conducive to democratization either. In the early twentieth century, even the liberals of the Constitutional Democratic Party, in effect, denied the non-Russians of the empire the right to decide how to define their national identity. It was only in the late 1980s that a democratic concept of a civic nation of equal citizens, with voluntary membership, entered the discourse of Russian political elites. So far, the application of this concept to the realities of the post-communist Russian Federation has proven difficult. This is a result of various factors. The current political and social situation in Russia is unpropitious. Russia does not have a state with uncontested borders, able to gain the respect and loyalty of most citizens. There remains a persistent gap and distrust between the privileged few and 'the masses'. Additionally, there is the continuing effect of the historical legacy. The eventual outcome of this crucial period of Russian nation-building is still far from clear, as, indeed, is the very destination of Russia's post-communist transition.

Selected bibliography

Russian and Ukrainian literary, historical and philosophical works

Aksakov, K.S., *Polnoe sobranie sochinenii* (Moscow, Universitetskaia tipografiia, 1861)

Annenkov, P.V., *Literaturnye vospominaniia* (Moscow, Khudozhestvennaia literatura, 1960)

Averintsev, S.S., 'Zapadno-vostochnye razmyshleniia, ili o neskhodstve skhodnogo' in *Vostok-Zapad. Issledovaniia, perevody, publikatsii* (Moscow, Nauka, 1988)

Belinskii, V.G., *Polnoe Sobranie sochinenii* (Moscow, Izdatelstvo Akademii Nauk SSSR, 1953–1959)

Berdiaev, N.A., *Sudba Rossii* (Moscow, Izdanie G.A. Lemana i S.I. Sakharova, 1918)

Berdiaev, N.A., *Russkaia ideia* (Paris, YMCA Press, 1971)

Berdiaev, N.A., 'Filosofiia neravenstva' in *Russkoe zarubezhe* (Leningrad, Lenizdat, 1991)

Blok, A.A., *Sobranie sochinenii* (Moscow-Leningrad, Khudozhestvennaia literatura, 1960–1963)

Brodskii, N.L., compiler, *Rannie slavianofily* (Moscow, Tipografiia Sytina, 1910)

Brodsky, J., *Less Than One. Selected Essays* (New York N.Y., Farrar, Straus, Giroux, 1986)

Bunin, I.A., *Pod serpom i molotom* (London, Zaria, 1982)

Burbulis, G., eds, *Stanovlenie novoi rossiiskoi gosudarstvennosti: realnost i perspectivy* (Moscow, RF Politika, 1996)

Butler, W.E., A *Discourse Concerning the Just Causes of the War between Sweden and Russia: 1700–1721* (Dobbs Ferry, N.Y. Oceana Publications, 1973)

Byliny, vols I and II (Moscow, Khudozhestvennaia literatura, 1958)

Chaadaev, P.Ia., *Sochineniia i pisma pod redaktsiei M.O. Gershenzona* (Moscow, Tipografiia A.I. Mamontova, 1914)

Chastushka (Moscow-Leningrad, Sovetskii pisatel, 1966)

Danilevskii, N.Ia., *Rossiia i Evropa*, 5th ed. (St. Petersburg, Tipografiia brat. Panteleevykh, 1895)

Dostoevskii, F.M., *Polnoe sobranie sochinenii v tridtsati tomakh* (Leningrad, Nauka, 1974–1984)

Fedotov, G.P., *Polnoe sobranie statei v shesti tomakh* (Paris, YMCA-Press, 1998)

Gaidar, Egor, *Gosudarstvo i evolutsiia* (Moscow, Evraziia, 1995)

Gerzen, A.I., *Byloe i dumy* (Moscow, Pravda, 1983)

Gogol, N.V., *Polnoe sobranie sochinenii* (Moscow, Izdatelstvo Akademii Nauk SSSR, 1940–1952)

Gorbachev, Mikhail, *Perestroika: New Thinking for Our Country and the World* (London, Fontana, 1988)

Gumilev, L.N., *V poiskakh vymyshlennogo tsarstva* (Moscow, Nauka, 1970)

Gumilev, L.N., *Ot Rusi do Rossii* (St. Petersburg, UNA, 1992)

Gumilev, L.N., *Ritmy Evrazii* (Moscow, Ekopros, 1993)

Ilin, Ivan, 'O Rossii' (1934) reprinted in *Russkii vestnik. Izdanie Leningradskogo otdeleniia Vserossiiskogo Fonda Kultury* (Leningrad, Molodaia gvardiia, 1990)

Inoe. Khrestomatiia novogo rossiiskogo samosoznaniia (Moscow, Argus, 1995)

Istoricheskaia pesnia XIX veka (Leningrad, Nauka, 1973)

Ishimova, A.O., *Istoriia Rossii v rasskazakh dlia detei* (St. Petersburg, Alfa, 1993)

Kara-Murza, A., *Mezhdu 'imperiei' i 'smutoi'* (Moscow, Institut Filosofii RAN, 1996)

Karamzin, N.M., *Pisma russkogo puteshestvennika* (Moscow, Sovetskaia Rossiia, 1983)

Karamzin, N.M., *Istoriia gosudarstva rossiiskogo* (Moscow, Nauka, 1989)

Karamzin, N.M., *Zapiska o drevnei i novoi Rossii v ee politicheskom i grazhdanskom otnoshenii* (Moscow, Prosveshchenie, 1991)

Kasianova, K., *O russkom natsionalnom kharaktere* (Moscow, Institut Nationalnoi Modeli Ekonomiki, 1994)

Kelly, Catriona, ed., *An Anthology of Russian Women's Writers (1777–1992)* (Oxford, Oxford University Press, 1994)

Khomiakov, A.S., *Polnoe sobranie sochinenii*, 3rd ed. (Moscow, Universitetskaia tipografiia, 1900)

Kliuchevskii, V.O., *Sochineniia v deviati tomakh* (Moscow, Mysl, 1987–1990)

Koialovich, M.I., *Istoriia russkogo samosoznaniia* (Minsk, Luchi Sofii, 1997)

Kostomarov, N.I., *Russkaia istoriia* (Moscow, Mysl, 1991)

Lebed, A., *Za derzhavu obidno* (Kirov, Viatskoe slovo, 1995)

Leontev, Konstantin, 'Vostok, Rossiia i slavianstvo,' in *Sobranie sochinenii*, vols V–VII (Moscow, Tipografiia V.M. Sablina, 1912–1913)

Lermontov, M.Iu., *Sochineniia v shesti tomakh* (Moscow-Leningrad, Izdatelstvo Akademii Nauk SSSR, 1957)

Leskov, N.S., *Levsha. Povesti i rasskazy* (Moscow, Khudozhestvennaia literatura, 1981)

Likhachev, Dmitrii S., *Reflections on Russia* (Boulder CO, Westview Press, 1991)

Lindheim, Ralph, and George S.N. Luckyj, eds, *Towards an Intellectual History of Ukraine* (Toronto, Toronto University Press, 1996)

Makagoneko, G.P., compiler, *Russkaia literatura XVIII veka* (Leningrad, Prosveshchenie, 1970)

Maslin, M.A., compiler, *Russkaia ideia* (Moscow, Respublika, 1992)

Mendeleev, D., *Zametki o narodnom prosveshchenii* (St. Peterburg, Tipografiia V. Demakova, 1901)

Mendeleev, D., *K poznaniiu Rossii*, 7th ed., (St. Petersburg, Izdanie A.S. Suvorina, 1912)

Mezhuev, V.M., *Mezhdu proshlym i budushchim* (Moscow, Institut Filosofii RAN, 1996)

Miliukov, P.N., *Ocherki po istorii russkoi kultury* (Moscow, Kultura, 1993)

Nolde, Boris, 'Natsionalnyi vopros v Rossii' (1917) reprinted in *Druzhba narodov*, 8 (1992), pp. 169–72

Pobyedonostseff, K.P., *Reflections of a Russian Statesman* (London, Grant Richards, 1898)

Poliakov, L.V., *Kak Rossiia nas obustraivaet* (Moscow, Institut Filosofii RAN, 1996)

Prokopovich, Feofan, *Sochineniia* (Moscow-Leningrad, Nauka, 1961)

Pushkin, A.S., *Polnoe sobranie sochinenii* (Moscow, Izdatelstvo Akademii Nauk SSSR, 1937–1959)

'Puteshestvie na Vostok, Pisma Andreiia Belogo' in *Vostok-Zapad. Issledovaniia, perevody, publikatsii* (Moscow, Nauka, 1988)

Raeff, Marc, *Russian Intellectual History. An Anthology* (New York N.Y., Brace and World, 1966)

Rogozin, D., *Russkii put* (St. Petersburg, Glogol, 1996)

Rossiia mezhdu Evropoi i Aziei. Evraziiskii soblazn (Moscow, Nauka, 1993)

Rovinskii, D., *Russkie narodnyia kartinki* (St. Petersburg, Tipografiia

Imperatorskoi Akademii Nauk, 1881) (reprint Munich, Otto Sagner Verlag, 1989)

Russkie pesni i romansy (Moscow, Khudozhestvennaia literatura, 1989)

Shafarevich, Igor, *Est li u Rossii budushchee?* (Moscow, Sovetskii pisatel, 1991)

Solzhenitsyn, Alexander, *Letter to Soviet Leaders* (Glasgow, Collins/Harvill, 1974)

Solzhenitsyn, Alexander, *et al.*, *From Under the Rubble* (Glasgow, Collins/Harvill, 1975)

Solzhenitsyn, Alexander, *Kak nam obustroit Rossiiu* (Leningrad, Sovetskii pisatel, 1990)

Solzhenitsyn, Alexander, *Rossiia v obvale* (Moscow, Russkii put, 1998)

Solzhenitsyn, Alexander, *The Gulag Archipelago* (New York N.Y., Harper and Row, 1976)

Solovev, Vladimir, *Nationalnyi vopros v Rossii* (St. Peterburg, Tipografiia M.M. Stasiulevicha, 1888)

Solovev, Vladimir, *Russkaia ideia* (Moscow, Put, 1911)

Solovev, S., *Istoriia Rossii s drevneishikh vremen* (Moscow, Nauka, 1959)

Struve, P.B., 'Chto takoe Rossiia,' *Russkaia musl*, no. 1, January 1911, pp. 175–8

Sumarokov, A.P., *Izbrannye proizvedeniia* (Moscow-Leningrad, Sovetskii pisatel, 1957)

Tolstoi, L.N., *Sobranie sochinenii v dvenadtsati tomakh* (Moscow, Khudozhestvennaia literatura, 1972–76)

Trubetskoi, N.S., *The Legacy of Genghis Khan and Other Essays on Russia's Identity* (Ann Arbor MI, Michigan Slavic Publications, 1991)

Vekhi-Landmarks: a Collection about the Russian Intelligentsia, trans. by Marshall S. Shatz and Judith E. Zimmerman (Armonk N.Y., M.E. Sharpe, 1994)

Ziuganov, G.A., *Za gorizontom* (Moscow, Informpechat, 1995)

Russian newspapers and periodicals

Beseduiushchii grazhdanin
Den/Zavtra
Druzhba narodov
Gazeta Russkoi partii
Izvestiia
Komsomolskaia pravda
Kuranty
Literaturnaia Rossiia
Molodaia gvardiia
Moskovskie novosti (*Moscow News*)

Moskva
Nash sovremennik
Nezavisimaia gazeta
Novoe literaturnoe obozrenie
Novyi mir
Ogonek
Paradigmy
Polis
Pravda
Priroda
Prozhektor
Rossiiskie vesti
Rossiiskaia gazeta
Rus derzhavnaia
Russkaia mysl
Russkii poriadok
Segodnia
Sodruzhestvo
Sovetskaia kultura
Svobodnaia mysl
Voprosy Istorii
Voprosy Filosofii
Zvezda

Secondary sources

Agurskii, M., *Ideologiia natsional-bolshevizma* (Paris, YMCA-Press, 1980)

Alston, Patrick L., *Education and the State in Tsarist Russia* (Stanford CA, Stanford University Press, 1969)

Anderson, Benedict, *Imagined Communities: Reflections on the Origins and Spread of Nationalism* (London, Verso, 1991)

Anisimov, Evgenii V., *Rossiia v seredine XVIII veka* (Moscow, Mysl, 1986)

Anisimov, Evgenii V., *The Reforms of Peter the Great. Progress through Coercion in Russia* (Armonk N.Y., M.E. Sharpe, 1993)

Azadovskii, K., and B. Egorov, 'Kosmopolity,' *Novoe literaturnoe obozrenie*, 36 (2/1999), pp. 83–135

Azrael, Jeremy R., *Soviet Nationality Policies and Practices* (New York N.Y., Praeger, 1978)

Balakrishnan, Gopal, *Mapping the Nation* (London, Verso, 1996)

Bassin, Mark, 'Inventing Siberia: Visions of the Russian East in the Early Nineteenth Century,' *The American Historical Review*, 96 (1991), pp. 763–94

Bassin, Mark, 'Russia Between Europe and Asia: The Ideological

Construction of Geographical Space,' *Slavic Review* 50, Spring (1991), pp. 1–17

Bassin, Mark, 'Turner, Solov'ev, and the "Frontier Hypothesis": The Nationalist Signification of Open Spaces,' *The Journal of Modern History*, 65, 3 (1993), pp. 473–511

Bassin, Mark, *Imperial Vision. Nationalism and Geographical Imagination in the Russian Far East, 1840–1865* (Cambridge, Cambridge University Press, 1999)

Barghoorn, Frederick C., *The Soviet Image of the United States* (New York N.Y., Harcourt, Brace and Co, 1950)

Barghoorn, Frederick C., *Soviet Russian Nationalism* (New York, Oxford University Press, 1956)

Barkey, Karen, and Mark von Hagen, eds, *After Empire. Multiethnic Societies and Nation-Building* (Boulder Co, Westview Press, 1997)

Barlett, R., and K.M. Hartley, eds., *Russia in the Age of the Enlightenment* (London, Macmillan, 1990)

Batalden, Stephen K., *et al.*, eds, *Seeking God: The Recovering of Religious Identity in Orthodox Russia, Ukraine and Georgia* (DeKalb IL, Northern Illinois University Press, 1983)

Becker, Seymour, 'The Muslim East in Nineteenth Century Russian Popular Historiography,' *Central Asian Survey*, 5, 3/4 (1986), pp. 25–47

Becker, Seymour, 'Russia Between East and West: the Intelligentsia, Russian National Identity and Asian Borderlands,' *Central Asian Survey*, 10, 4 (1991), pp. 47–64

Beissinger, Mark R., 'The Persisting Ambiguity of Empire,' *Post-Soviet Affairs*, 11, 2 (1995), pp. 167–80

Bendix, Reinhard, *Kings or People. Power and the Mandate to Rule* (Berkeley CA, University of California Press, 1978)

Berlin, Isaiah, *Russian Thinkers* (New York N.Y., The Viking Press, 1978)

Bespiatykh, Iu, ed., *Peterburg Petra I v inostrannykh opisaniiakh* (Leningrad, Blitz, 1991)

Billington, James H., *The Icon and the Axe* (London, Weidenfeld and Nicolson, 1966)

Billington, James H., *The Face of Russia* (New York N.Y., TV Books, 1998)

Bonarchik, V.K., P.A. Grigoreva and M.F. Pilipenko, eds., *Belorusy* (Moscow, Nauka, 1998)

Bonnell, V., ed., *Identities in Transition: Eastern Europe and Russia after the Collapse of Communism* (Berkeley CA, University of California, International and Areas Studies, 1996)

Borison, Iu.S., et at. eds., *Rossiia i zapad. Formirovanie vneshnepoliticheskikh stereotipov v soznanii rossiiskogo obshchestva pervoi poloviny XX veka* (Moscow, Institut Rossiiskoi Istorii RAN and Lampeter, The Edwin Mellen Press, 1999)

Breuilly, John, *Nationalism and the State* (Manchester, Manchester University Press, 1985)

Brooks, Jeoffrey, *When Russian Learned to Read. Literacy and Popular Literature, 1861–1917* (Princeton N.J., Princeton University Press, 1985)

Brower, Daniel R., and Edward J. Lazzerini, *Russia's Orient. Imperial Borderlands and Peoples, 1700–1917* (Bloomington IN, Indiana University Press, 1997)

Brubaker, Rogers, 'Nationhood and the National Question in the Soviet Union and Post-Soviet Eurasia: An Institutionalist Account,' *Theory and Society*, 23 (1994), pp. 47–78

Brubaker, Rogers, *Nationalism Reframed: Nationhood and the National Question in the New Europe* (Cambridge, Cambridge University Press, 1996)

Brudny, Yitzhak M., *Reinventing Russia. Russian Nationalism and the Soviet State, 1953–1991* (Cambridge MA, Harvard University Press, 1998)

Bushkovitch, Paul, 'The Ukraine in Russian Culture 1790–1860: The Evidence of the Journals,' *Jahrbücher für Geshchichte Osteuropas*, 39, 3 (1991), pp. 339–63

Carr, E.H., '"Russia and Europe" as a Theme of Russian History,' in Richard Pares and A.J.P. Taylor, eds., *Essays presented to Sir Lewis Namier* (London, Macmillan, 1956)

Cherniavsky, Michael, 'Holy Russia,' *The American Historical Review*, LXIII, 3 (1958), pp. 517–37

Cherniavsky, Michael, *Tsar and People: Studies in Russian Myths* (New York N.Y., Random House, 1969)

Clarke, Katerina, *Petersburg. Crucible of Cultural Revolution* (Cambridge MA, Harvard University Press, 1995)

Colley, Linda, *Britons. Forging the Nation 1707–1837* (New Haven CT, Yale University Press, 1992)

Connor, Walker, *The National Question in Marxist–Leninist Theory and Strategy* (Princeton N.J., Princeton University Press, 1984)

Cracraft, James, 'Empire versus Nation: Russian Political Theory under Peter I,' *Harvard Ukrainian Studies*, 10 (December 1986), pp. 524–41

Cracraft, James, *The Petrine Revolution in Russian Imagery* (Chicago IL, the University of Chicago Press, 1997)

Crummey, Robert O., *The Old Believers and the World of Antichrist: the Vyg Community and the Russian State, 1694–1855* (Madison MO, University of Wisconsin Press, 1970)

Drobizheva, L.M., ed., *Sotsialnaia i kulturnaia distantsiia: opyt mnogonatsionalnoi Rossii* (Moscow, Izdatelstvo Instituta Sotsiologii RAN, 1998)

Drobizheva, L.M., and M.S. Kashuba, eds., *Traditskii v sovremennom obshchestve: issledovaniia etnokulturnykh protsessov* (Moscow, Nauka, 1990)

Dukes, Paul, *World Order in History. Russia and the West* (London, Routledge, 1996)

Dunlop, John B., *The Faces of Contemporary Russian Nationalism* (Princeton N.J., Princeton University Press, 1983)

Dunlop, John B., *The Rise of Russia and the Fall of the Soviet Empire* (Princeton N.J., Princeton University Press, 1993)

Dunlop, John B., *Russia Confronts Chechnya: Roots of a Separatist Conflict* (Cambridge, Cambridge University Press, 1998)

Ellis, J., *The Orthodox Church: A Contemporary History* (Bloomington, IN, Indiana University Press, 1986)

Engel, B., *Mothers and Daughters. Women of the Intelligentsia in Nineteenth Century Russia* (Cambridge, Cambridge University Press, 1983)

Farnsworth, B., and V. Lynne, eds., *Russian Peasant Women* (Oxford, Oxford University Press, 1992)

Fedoseev, I.A., ed., *Istoriia SSSR* (Moscow, Prosveshchenie, 1973)

Figes, Orlando, and Boris Kolonitskii, *Interpreting the Russian Revolution, The Language and Symbols of 1917* (New Haven CT and London, Yale University Press, 1999)

Figes, Orlando, *A People's Tragedy. The Russian Revolution, 1891–1924* (London, Pimlico, 1996)

Filatov, S.B., 'Novoe rozhdenie staroi idei: pravoslavie kak natsionalnyi simvol,' *Polis*, 3 (1999), pp. 138–49

Frierson, Cathy A., *Peasant Icons. Representations of Rural People in Late Nineteenth Century Russia* (Oxford, Oxford University Press, 1993)

Furman, Dmitrii, 'Ukraina i my,' *Svobodnaia mysl*, 1 (1995), pp. 69–83

Geertz, C., *The Interpretation of Cultures* (New York N.Y., Basic Books, 1973)

Gellner, Ernest, *Nations and Nationalism* (Oxford, Basil Blackwell, 1983)

Georgi, I.G., *Opisanie rossiisko-imperatorskogo stolichnogo goroda Sankt-Peterburga i dostopamiatnostei v okrestnostiakh onogo, 1794–1796* (St. Petersburg, Liga, 1996)

Gerschenkron, Alexander, *Europe in the Russian Mirror* (Cambridge, Cambridge University Press, 1970)

Gleason, A., *European and Muscovite: Ivan Kireevsky and the Origins of Slavophilism* (Cambridge MA, Harvard University Press, 1972)

Goble, Paul A., 'Three Faces of Nationalism in the Former Soviet Union,' in Charles A. Kupchan, ed., *Nationalism and Nationalities in the New Europe* (Ithaca N.Y., Cornell University Press, 1995)

Gordin, Ia., *Kavkaz: zemlia i krov* (St. Petersburg, Zvezda, 2000)

Goscilo, H., and B. Holmgren, eds., *Russia. Women. Culture* (Bloomington, IN, Indiana University Press, 1995)

Greenfeld, Liah, *Nationalism: Five Roads to Modernity* (Cambridge MA, Harvard University Press, 1992)

Gromyko, M.M., *Mir russkoi derevni* (Moscow, Molodaia gvardiia, 1991)

Guroff, Gregory, and Alexander Guroff, 'The paradox of Russian National Identity,' in Roman Szporluk, ed., *National Identity and Ethnicity in Russia and the New States of Eurasia* (Armonk N.Y., M.E. Sharpe, 1994)

Hastings, Adrian, *The Construction of Nationhood. Ethnicity, Religion and Nationalism* (Cambridge, Cambridge University Press, 1997)

Hauner, Millan, *What Is Asia to Us? Russia's Asian Heartland Yesterday and Today* (London, Routledge, 1992)

Hellberg-Hirn, Elena, *Soil and Soul. The Symbolic World of Russianness* (Aldershot, Ashgate, 1998)

Heuman, Susan, *Kistiakovsky: The Struggle for National and Constitutional Rights in the Last Years of Tsarism* (Cambridge MA, Harvard University Press, 1998)

Hilton, A., *Russian Folk Art* (Bloomington IN, Indiana University Press, 1995)

Hirsch, Francine, 'The Soviet Union as a Work-in-Progress: Ethnographers and the Category of *Nationality* in the 1926, 1937, and 1939 Censuses,' *Slavic Review*, 56, 2 (1997), pp. 251–78

Hobsbawm, Eric, *Nations and Nationalism since 1780* (Cambridge, Cambridge University Press, 1990)

Hobsbawm, Eric, and Terence Ranger, eds., *The Invention of Tradition* (Cambridge, Cambridge University Press, 1995)

Hokanson, Katya, 'Literary Imperialism, *Narodnost*' and Pushkin's Invention of the Caucasus,' *The Russian Review*, 53, 3 (1994), pp. 336–52

Hosking, Geoffrey, *Russia: People and Empire, 1552–1917* (London, HarperCollins, 1997)

Hosking, Geoffrey, and Robert Service, eds., *Russian Nationalism Past and Present* (London, Macmillan, 1998)

Hosking, Geoffrey, and George Shopflin, eds., *Myths and Nationhood* (London, Hurst and Company, 1997)

Hosking, Geoffrey, 'Can Russia Become a Nation-State?' *Nations and Nationalism*, 4, 4 (1998), pp. 449–62

Hroch, Miroslav, *Social Preconditions of National Revival in Europe: A Comparative Analysis of the Social Composition of Patriotic Groups among the Smaller European Nations* (Cambridge, Cambridge University Press, 1985)

Hubbs, J., *Mother Russia. The Feminine Myth in Russian Culture* (Bloomington IN, Indiana University Press, 1988)

Hughes, Lindsey, *Russia in the Age of Peter the Great* (New Haven CT and London, Yale University Press, 1998)

Hunczak, Taras, ed., *Russian Imperialism from Ivan the Great to the Revolution* (New Brunswick, N.J., Rutgers University Press, 1974)

Ikonnikov, V.S., *Opyt Russkoi istoriografii* (Kiev, Tipografiia Imperatorskogo Universiteta Sv. Vladimira, 1891)

Iskandarian, Aleksandr, *Chechenskii krisis: proval rossiiskoi politiki na Kavkaze* (Moscow, Carnegie Endowment for International Peace, 1995)

Jahn, Hubertus F., *Patriotic Culture in Russia during World War I* (Ithaca N.Y., Cornell University Press, 1995)

Kabuzan, V., *Russkie v mire* (St. Petersburg, Blits, 1996)

Kaiser, Robert, *The Geography of Nationalism in Russia and the USSR* (Princeton N.J., Princeton University Press, 1994)

Kamenskii, Aleksandr B., *The Russian Empire in the Eighteenth Century. Searching for a Place in the World* (Armonk N.Y., M.E. Sharpe, 1997)

Karianen, K., and D. Furman, 'Veruiushchie, ateisty i prochie (evolutsiia rossiiskoi religioznosti), *Voprosy filosofii*, 6 (1997), pp. 35–52

Kartashev, A.V., *Ocherki po istorii Russkoi Tserkvi* (Moscow, Terra, 1993)

Keenan, Edward L., 'Muscovite Political Folkways,' *The Russian Review*, 45 (1986), pp. 115–181

Keenan, Edward L., 'On Certain Mythical Beliefs and Russian Behavior,' in Starr, S. Frederick, *The Legacy of History in Russia and the New States of Eurasia* (Armonk, N.Y., M.E. Sharpe, 1994)

Kelly, Aileen M., *Toward Another Shore* (New Haven CT, Yale University Press, 1998)

Kim, Maxim, *The Soviet People – A New Historical Community* (Moscow, Progress, 1974)

Kingston-Mann, Esther, *In Search of the True West* (Princeton N.J., Princeton University Press, 1999)

Kliamkin, I.M., and V.V. Lapkin, 'Russkii vopros v Rossii', part 1, *Polis*, 5 (1995), pp. 78–96

Kliamkin, I.M., 'Russkii vopros v Rossii,' part 2, *Polis*, 1 (1996), pp.78–90

Knight, Nathaniel, 'Grigor'ev in Orenburg, 1851–1862: Russian Orientalism in the Service of Empire?' *Slavic Review*, 59, 1 (2000), pp. 74–100

Kolstoe, P., *Russians in the Former Soviet Republics* (Bloomington IN, Indiana University Press, 1995)

Khoroshkevich, A. L., *Simboly russkoi gosudarstvennosti* (Moscow, MGU, 1993)

Kotkin, Stephen, and David Wolff, *Rediscovering Russia in Asia. Siberia and the Russian Far East* (Armonk N.Y., M.E. Sharpe, 1995)

Laitin, David D., *Identity in Formation: The Russian-speaking populations in the Near Abroad* (Ithaca, N.Y., Cornell University Press, 1998)

Lapidus, Gail W. and Victor Zaslavsky, eds., *From Union to Commonwealth: nationalism and Separatism in the Soviet Republics* (Cambridge, Cambridge University Press, 1992)

Laqueur, Walter, *Black Hundred. The Rise of the Extreme Right in Russia* (New York N.Y., HarperCollins, 1993)

Layton, Susan, *Russian Literature and Empire. Conquest of the Caucasus from Pushkin to Tolstoy* (Cambridge, Cambridge University Press, 1994)

LeDonne, John P., *Absolutism and Ruling Class. The Formation of the Russian Political Order 1700–1825* (Oxford, Oxford University Press, 1991)

Lehning, James R., *Peasant and French. Cultural Contact in Rural France During the Nineteenth Century* (Cambridge, Cambridge University Press, 1995)

Lieven, Anatol, *Chechnya. Tombstone of Russian Power* (New Haven CT, Yale University Press, 1998)

Lieven, Dominic, 'Dilemmas of Empires 1850–1918. Power, Territory, Identity,' *Journal of Contemporary History*, 34, 2 (1999), pp. 163–200

Likhachev, Dmitrii S., *Nationalnoe samosoznanie drevnei Rusi* (Moscow, Leningrad, Izdatelstvo Akademii Nauk SSSR, 1945)

Likhachev, Dmitrii S., 'Religion: Russian Orthodoxy' in Nicholas Rzhevsky, ed., *Modern Russian Culture* (Cambridge, Cambridge University Press, 1998)

Lotman, Iu. M., *Izbrannye stati* (Tallin, Aleksandra, 1993)

Lotman, Iu. M., *Besedy o russkoi kulture: byt i traditsii russkogo dvorianstva, XVIII–nachalo XIX vv.* (St. Peteresburg, Iskustvo, 1994)

MacFarlane, Neil S., 'Russian Conceptions of Europe,' *Post-Soviet Affairs*, 10, 3 (1994), pp. 234–69

MacMaster, R.E., *Danilevsky. A Russian Totalitarian Philosopher* (Cambridge MA, Harvard University Press, 1967)

de Madariaga, Isabel, *Politics and Culture in Eighteenth Century Russia* (Harlow, Longman, 1998)

Malia, Martin, *Alexander Herzen and the Birth of Russian Socialism* (New York N.Y., Glosset and Dunlap, 1965)

Malia, Martin, *Russia under Western Eyes. From the Bronze Horseman to the Lenin Masoleum* (Cambridge, MA, The Belknap Press of Harvard University Press, 1999)

Martin, Terry, 'The Russification of the RSFSR,' *Cahiers du Monde russe*, 39, 1–2 (1998), pp. 99–118

Martin, Terry, 'Modernization or Neo-traditionalism? Ascribed Nationality and Soviet Primordialism,' in Sheila Fitzpatrick, ed., *Stalinism. New Directions* (London, Routledge, 2000)

McDaniel, Tim, *The Agony of the Russian Idea* (Princeton N.J., Princeton University Press, 1996)

Melvin, Neil, *Russians Beyond Russia. The Politics of National Identity* (London, Royal Institute of International Affairs, 1995)

Miller, A.I., 'Obraz Ukrainy i ukraintsev v rossiiskoi presse posle raspada SSSR,' *Polis* 2, 1996, pp. 130–5

Milner-Gulland, Robin, *The Russians* (London, Blackwell, 1999)

Mirovospriiatie i samosoznanie russkogo obshchestva (XI–XX vv.) (Moscow, Institut Rossiiskoi Istorii, RAN, 1994)

Molchanov, Mikhail, 'Borders of Identity: Ukraine's Political and Cultural

Significance for Russia.' *Canadian Slavonic Papers*, 28, 1–2 (1996), pp. 177–93

Nechkina, M.V., and P.S. Leibengrub, eds., *Istoriia SSSR* (Moscow, Prosveshchenie, 1972)

Neumann, Iver B., *Russia and the Idea of Europe* (London, Routledge, 1996)

Novikova, A.M., 'Narodnye tiuremnye pesni vtoroi poloviny XIX-nachala XX vv.,' *Russkii folklor*, XV (Leningrad, Nauka, 1975)

Panchenko, A.M., 'Nachalo petrovskoi reformy: ideinaia podopleka,' in *Itogi i problemy izucheniia russkoi literatury XVIII veka* (Leningrad, Nauka, 1989)

Petrov, P.N., *Istoriia Sankt-Peterburga s osnovaniia goroda do vvedeniia v deistvie vybornogo gorodskogo upravleniia po Uchrezhdeniian o guberniiakh, 1703–1782* (St. Petersburg, Izdanie Glazunova, 1885)

Pilkington, Hilary, *Migration, Displacement and Identity in Post-Soviet Russia* (London, Routledge, 1998)

Pipes, Richard, ed., *The Russian Intelligentsia* (New York N.Y., Columbia University Press, 1961)

Pipes, Richard, *Russia under the Old Regime* (New York N.Y., Charles Scribner's Sons, 1974)

Pipes, Richard, *Struve. Liberal on the Right, 1905–1944* (Cambridge MA, Harvard University Press, 1980)

Pipes, Richard, *The Russian Revolution* (New York N.Y., Alfred A. Knopf, 199)

Potichnyj, Peter J., Marc Raeff, Jaroslaw Pelenski and Gleb N. Zekulin, eds., *Ukraine and Russia in Their Historical Encouter* (Edmonton, Canadian Institute of Ukrainian Studies Press, 1992)

Prizel, Ilya, *National Identity and Foreign Policy. Nationalism and Leadership in Poland, Russia and Ukraine* (Cambridge, Cambridge University Press, 1999)

Procyk, Anna, *Russian Nationalism and Ukraine. The Nationality Policy of the Volunteer Army during the Civil War* (Toronto, Canadian Institute of Ukrainian Studies Press, 1995)

Raeff, Marc, *Origins of the Russian Intelligentsia* (New York N.Y., Harcourt Brace & Co, 1966)

Raeff, Marc, 'Patterns of Russian Imperial policy Toward the Nationalities,' in Edward Allworth, *Soviet Nationality Problems* (New York N.Y., Columbia University Press, 1971)

Raeff, Marc, *Understanding Imperial Russia* (New York N.Y., Columbia University Press, 1984)

Rakowska-Harmstone, Teresa, 'The Dialectics of Nationalism in the USSR,' *Problems of Communism*, 23, 3 (1974), pp. 1–22

Rakowska-Harmstone, Teresa, 'Chickens Coming Home to Roost: A Perspective on Soviet Ethnic Relations,' Journal of International Affairs, 45, 2 (1992), pp. 519–48

Ranum, Orest, ed., *National Consciousness, History, and Political Culture in Early-Modern Europe* (Baltimore Md, Johns Hopkins University Press, 1975)

Rashin, A.G. 'Gramotnost i narodnoe obrazovanie v Rossii v XIX i nachale XX vekov,' *Istoricheskie zapiski*, 37 (1951), pp. 45–9

Riasanovsky, Nicholas V., *Russia and the West in the Teachings of the Slavophiles* (Cambridge MA, Harvard University Press, 1952)

Riasanovsky, Nicholas V., *Nicholas I and Official Nationality in Russia, 1825–1855* (Berkeley CA, University of California Press, 1959)

Riasanovsky, Nicholas V., *The Image of Peter the Great in Russian History and Thought* (New York N.Y. and Oxford, Oxford University Press, 1985)

Robson, Roy R., *Old Believers in Modern Russia* (DeKalb IL, Northern Illinois University Press, 1995)

Rogger, Hans, 'Nationalism and the State: A Russian Dilemma,' *Comparative Studies in Society and History*, IV (1961–1962), pp. 253–64

Rogger, Hans, *National Consciousness in Eighteenth Century Russia* (Cambridge MA, Harvard University Press, 1960)

Rossiia i vneshnii mir: dialog kulur (Moscow, Institut Rossiiskoi Istorii RAN, 1997)

Rubakin, N.A., *Sredi knig*, 2nd ed., vol. 3, part 1 (Moscow, Knigoizdatelstvo Nauka, 1915)

Russkie v novom zarubezhe (Moscow, Institut Etnologii i Antropologii RAN, 1994)

Rutherford, Andrea, 'Vissarion Belinskii and the Ukrainian National Question,' *The Russian Review*, 54, 4 (1995), pp. 500–15

Said, Edward W., *Orientalism* (London, Penguin Books, 1995)

Sanders, Thomas, ed., *Historiography of Imperial Russia. Profession and Writing of History in a Multinational State* (Armonk N.Y., M.E. Sharpe, 1999)

Sarabianov, D.V., *Istoriia russkogo iskusstva vtoroi poloviny XIX v.* (Moscow, Izdatelstvo MGU, 1989)

Saunders, David, *The Ukrainian Impact on Russian Culture, 1750–1859* (Edmonton, Canadian Institute of Ukrainian Studies Press, 1985)

Saunders, David, 'Russia's Ukrainian Policy (1847–1905): a Demographic Approach,' *European History Quarterly*, 25 (1995), pp. 181–208

Shmeleva, M.N., *Russkie* (Moscow, Nauka, 1992)

Shalin, Dmitrii N., *Russian Culture at the Crossroads. Paradoxes of Postcommunist Consciousness* (Boulder CO, Westview Press, 1996)

Sindalovskii, N.A., *Mifologiia Peterburga* (St. Petersburg, Norint, 2000)

Slezkine, Yuri, 'The Soviet Union as a Communal Apartment, or How a Socialist State Promoted Ethnic Particularism,' *Slavic Review*, 53, 2 (1994), pp. 415–52

Smith, Anthony D., *The Ethnic Origins of Nations* (Oxford, Basil Blackwell, 1986)

Smith, Graham, Vivien Law, Andrew Wilson, Annette Bohr and Edward Allworth, *Nation-Building in Post-Soviet Borderlands. The Politics of National Identities* (Cambridge, Cambridge University Press, 1998)

Shmurlo, E., *Petr Velikii v otsenke sovremennikov i potomstva* (St. Petersburg, V.S. Balashev, 1912)

Shternberg, L., 'Inorodtsy. Obschii obzor' in A.I. Kastelianskii, ed., *Formy nationalnogo dvizheniia v sovremennykh gosudarstvakh. Avstro-Vengriia, Rossiia, Germaniia* (St. Petersburg, Obshchestvennaia polza, 1910)

Solchanyk, Roman, 'Ukraine, The (Former) Center, Russia and "Russia,"' *Studies in Comparative Communism*, 1 (March 1992), pp. 26–45

Solchanyk, Roman, 'Russia, Ukraine, and the Imperial Legacy,' *Post-Soviet Affairs*, 9, 4 (1993), pp. 337–65

Sobolev, N.A., and Artamonov, V.A., *Simvoly Rossii* (Moscow, Panorama, 1993)

Stites, R., *Russian Popular Culture. Entertainment and Society since 1900* (Cambridge, Cambridge University Press, 1992)

Summer, B.H., 'Russia and Europe,' *Oxford Slavonic Papers*, 2 (1951), pp. 1–16

Suny, Ronald G., *The Revenge of the Past. Nationalism, Revolution and the Collapse of the Soviet Union* (Stanford CA, Stanford University Press, 1993)

Szporluk, Roman, *Communism and Nationalism. Karl Marx versus Friedrich List* (Oxford, Oxford University Press, 1988)

Szporluk, Roman, 'Dilemmas of Russian Nationalism,' *Problems of Communism*, 39 (July–August, 1989), pp. 15–35

Szporluk, Roman, 'After the Empire: What?' *Daedalus*, 123, 3 (1994), pp. 21–39

Szporluk, Roman, 'The Fall of the Tsarist Empire and the USSR: The Russian Question and Imperial Overextension' in Karen Dawisha and Bruce Parrott, eds., *The End of Empire? The Transformation of the USSR in Comparative Perspective* (Armonk N.Y., M.E. Sharpe, 1997)

Szporluk, Roman, 'Ukraine: From an Imperial Periphery to a Sovereign State,' *Daedalus*, 126, 3 (1997), pp. 85–119

Tillett, Lowell, *The Great Friendship. Soviet Historians on Non-Russian Nationalities* (Chapel Hill N.C., The University of North Carolina Press, 1969)

Tishkov, Valery, *Ethnicity, Nationalism and Conflict in and after the Soviet Union* (London, Sage, 1997)

Tolz, Vera, 'The Radical Right in Post-Communist Russian Politics,' in Peter H. Merkl and Leonard Weinberg, eds., *The Revival of Right-Wing Extremism in the Nineties* (London, Frank Cass, 1997)

Tolz, Vera, '"Conflicting Homeland Myths" and Nation-State Building in Postcommunist Russia,' *Slavic Review*, 57, 2 (1998), pp. 267–94

Tolz, Vera, 'Forging the Nation: National Identity and Nation Building in Post-Communist Russia,' *Europe–Asia Studies*, 50, 6 (1998), pp. 993–1022

Torukalo, V., *Natsiia: istoriia i sovremennost* (Moscow, Institut Etnografii i Antropologii RAN, 1996)

Urban, Michael, 'Remythologising the Russian State,' *Europe–Asia Studies*, 50, 6 (1998), pp. 969–92

Ushakov, Iu. S., and T. A. *Slavina, Istoriia russkoi arkhitektury* (St. Petersburg, Stroiizdat, 1994)

Velychenko, Stephen, *Shaping Identity in Eastern Europe and Russia. Soviet-Russian and Polish Accounts of Ukrainian History, 1914–1991* (New York N.Y., St. Martin's Press, 1993)

Venturi, Franco, *Roots of Revolution* (New York N.Y., Glosset and Dunlap, 1966)

von Laue, Theodore, 'Imperial Russia at the Turn of the Century: The Cultural Slope and the Revolution from Without,' in Reinhard Bendix, ed., *State and Society. A Reader in Comparative Political Sociology* (Berkeley CA, University of California Press, 1968)

Volkov, Solomon, *St. Petersburg. A Cultural History* (London, Sinclair-Stevenson, 1996)

Vucinich, Wayne S., ed., *Russia and Asia: Essays on the Influence of Russia on the Asian People* (Stanford CA, Hoover Institute Press, 1972)

Vzdornov, G.I., *Istoriia otkrytiia i izucheniia russkoi srednevekovoi zhivopisi, XIX v.* (Moscow, Iskustvo, 1986)

Walicki, Andrzej, *The Controversy over Capitalism: Studies in the Social Philosophy of the Russian Populists* (Oxford, Oxford University Press, 1966)

Walicki, Andrzej, 'Russia' in Ghita Ionescu and Ernest Gellner, eds., *Populism. Its Meaning and National Characteristics* (London, Weidenfeld and Nicolson, 1969)

Weber, Eugen, *Peasants into Frenchmen: The Modernization of Rural France, 1870–1914* (Stanford CA, Stanford University Press, 1976)

Weeks, Theodore R., *Nation and State in Late Imperial Russia. Nationalism and Russification on the Western Frontier, 1863–1914* (DeKalb IL, Northern Illinois University Press, 1996)

Weiner, Amir, 'The Making of a Dominant Myth: The Second World War and the Construction of Political Identities within the Soviet Polity,' *The Russian Review*, 55 (October 1996), pp. 638–60

Wortman, Richard S., *Scenarios of Power. Myth and Ceremony in Russian Monarchy* (Princeton N.J., Princeton University Press, 1995)

Yanov, Alexander, *The Russian New Right: Right-Wing Ideologies in the Contemporary USSR* (Berkeley CA, Institute of International Studies, University of California, 1978)

Zaslavsky, Victor, *The Neo-Stalinist State: Class, Ethnicity, and Consensus in Soviet Society* (Armonk N.Y., M.E.Sharpe, 1982)

Zaslavsky, Victor, 'Nationalism and Democratic Transition in Postcommunist Societies,' *Daedalus*, 12, 2 (1992), pp. 97–121

Zorin, A., 'Krym v istorii russkogo samosoznaniia,' *Novoe literaturnoe obozreniie*, 31, 3 (1998), pp. 123–43

Index

Russian–Japanese war, 140
Russian language, 45, 46–7, 56, 58, 59,
    173, 176, 202, 204, 205, 208,
    218, 231, 238, 242–7, 258, 263,
    267
Russian National Unity, 248
Russian Orthodox Church (ROC), 9,
    24–5, 32, 41, 78, 79, 102, 117,
    135, 187, 194, 197, 250, 257
  anti–foreign propaganda, 49
  contemporary influence, 258–9
  power reduced by Peter the Great,
    37, 43, 192
  reinstatement of Patriarch, 187
  seventeenth century reform and
    schism, 25, 71
  Ukrainian influence, 24–5, 43, 211
Russian Party, 247
Russian People and Socialism (Herzen),
    95
Russian Public Union, 242
Russian revolution (1905), 101, 107
Russian revolution (1917), 12, 15, 131,
    147, 177, 210, 219–20
Russian Social Democratic Workers'
    Party, 97, 217
Russian Soviet Federated Republic
    (RSFR), 183–4, 205, 208, 227,
    240, 247
  declaration of sovereignty, 206–7
Russian–Steppe civilization, 150
Russian–Turkish war (1787–1791), 84,
    102, 163, 167
Russian–Ukrainian agreement, 227,
    164–5
Russification, 6–7, 8, 13, 17, 100, 172,
    174, 175, 177, 195–6, 201, 219,
    220, 242, 271
Russkaia mysl, 173, 201, 217, 219
Russkoe znamia, 202
Rutskoi, Alexander, 259, 266
Rybkin, Ivan, 242

Said, Edward, 132, 141, 144
Sakharov, Andrei, 119, 120–1, 223
Saltykov-Shchedrin, Mikhail, 215
Salutskii, Anatolii, 123
Samarin, Iurii, 82
samizdat, 118, 119, 148, 205, 206
Sammlung Russischer Geschichte, 50
Satarov, Georgii, 260
Saunders, David, 200, 212, 213
Savistskii, Peter, 149, 202

Scandinavians, 51
Schelling, Friedrich, 82
Schloezer, A. L., 51–2
Scythian people, 145–6
'Scythians' (Blok), 132
Scythians (literary group), 145, 147
Searching for the Imaginary Kingdom
    (Gumilev), 149
Sechenov, Dmitrii, 49
secularization, 24, 29–32, 37
Sejm, 76
self-immolation, 25
Semenov, Peter, 143
Serbia, 130, 269
serfdom, 58
  ambiguous contribution of Catherine
    the Great, 54–5, 57
  emancipation, Baltic region
    (1816–1819), 76
  emancipation, Russia (1861), 1, 13,
    89–90, 99, 176
  entrenchment and expansion under
    Peter the Great, 24, 34–5, 43, 73
  intellectual debate on, 45, 60, 61, 62,
    63, 76, 77, 93
Serov, Valentin, 91
Sevastopol, 228–9, 255–6, 265
Sevastopol Sketches (Tolstoi), 228
Shafarevich, Igor, 123, 187, 206
Shafirov, Peter, 29–30, 49, 160
Shchekotikhina-Boturskaia, 109
Shcherbatov, Prince Mikhail, 55, 84
Shevchenko, Taras, 213, 215
Shevyrev, Stepan, 39
Shishkin, Igor, 247
Shmeleva, M., 244
Shternberg, Lev, 200–1
Shushkevich, Stanislav, 230
Shuvalov, Ivan, 52
Shuvalov, P. A., 102
Shvart, Viacheslav, 89
Siberia, 25, 35, 61, 77, 135, 157, 159,
    163–4, 171, 179, 180, 192
  idealization, 163–4
Signposts, 14
Skobelev, Mikhail, 138
Slavic-Greek-Latin Academy, Moscow,
    46
Slavophiles, 15–16, 81–5, 85–6, 93–4,
    98, 99, 103, 107, 109, 110, 111,
    131, 133, 141, 162, 171, 195,
    196, 213–14, 215, 236, 238, 272
  neo-Slavophiles, 119, 121, 122–4

Index